The Unemployed

The Unemployed

Eli Ginzberg

With an introduction by Ben B. Seligman

Transaction Publishers
New Brunswick (U.S.A.) and London (U.K.)

Published in 2004 by Transaction Publishers, New Brunswick, New Jersey. Originally published in 1943 by Harper & Brothers Publishers. Introduction published by arrangement with the estate of Ben B. Seligman.

This book is printed on acid-free paper that meets the American National Standard for Permanence of Paper for Printed Library Materials.

Library of Congress Catalog Number: 2003061645
ISBN: 0-7658-0574-X
Printed in the United States of America

Library of Congress Cataloging-in-Publication Data

Ginzberg, Eli, 1911-
The unemployed / Eli Ginzberg ; with an introduction by Ben B. Seligman.
p. cm.
Originally published: New York : Harper, c1943.
Includes index.
ISBN 0-7658-0574-X (pbk. : alk. paper)
1. Unemployment—New York (State)—New York—Psychological aspects. 2. Unemployment—New York (State)—New York—Sociological aspects. 3. Unemployment—New York (State)—New York—Psychological aspects—Case studies. 4. Unemployment—New York (State)—New York—Sociological aspects—Case studies. 5. Depressions—1929—New York (State)—New York. 6. Charities—New York (State)—New York—History—20th century. 7. Unemployed—United States—Psychological aspects. 8. Unemployed—United States—Sociological aspects. 9. Depressions—1929—United States. 10. Charities—United States—History—20th century. I. Title.

HD5808.2.U62N74 2004
331.13'77'09747109043—dc22

2003061645

To

WESLEY CLAIR MITCHELL

CONTENTS

BOOK TWO — CASE STUDIES

TRANSACTION INTRODUCTION: THE SCOURGE OF UNEMPLOYMENT

We have conquered unemployment by creating weapons of war. That is the great irony of our industrial civilization. While men are fighting for that civilization we are preparing presumably to give them jobs in peacetime. It has been suggested that an incentive tax scheme be adopted to induce a high level of consumption, that we eliminate monopolistic restrictions on production. These ideas are undoubtedly worthwhile and undoubtedly will be torn apart in legislative chambers when the time comes to make them real. But then, there is always the WPA and Home Relief.

Yet the unemployed have asked and will ask again, "When shall we find real productive work?" How ineffectual an answer the WPA and Home Relief really are may be seen in this amply documented and warmly written study of what unemployment does to people. It is a vivid reminder of things that were and a depressing portent of things to come. Dr. Ginzberg and his associates (statisticians, psychiatrists, and social workers) interviewed in 1940 some two hundred families that were caught in the bitter maelstrom of unemployment. Over a hundred were still struggling pitifully to extricate themselves; they were either Home Relief "clients" or on the WPA. Dr. Ginzberg analyzed their reactions and attitudes toward such varied matters as trade unions, marriage, politics, religion, and relief with the meticulous care and scientific detachment of the anthropologist. He shows, by a recital of case histories and by statistical description, their background, their educational attainments and home life, and their amazing domestic management with the niggardly allowance granted by the welfare authorities. He shows, moreover, how the increasing annoyance of home trivia, the weakening of parental control, and the overpowering sense of frustration contributed to the destructive emotional shock brought on by a depressed economic status.

This volume is not so broad in scope, perhaps, as Professor E. W. Bakke's *The Unemployed Worker*, yet it is more incisive. The study was limited to the economically dependent of New York City, and for analytic reasons included only Irish-Catholic, Jewish, and Anglo-Saxon Protestant families. The story it tells, however, is not atypical; the effects of unemployment are quite the same in Oklahoma, Boston, and New York.

After waiting too long for prosperity to peek out from behind its corner, the government resorted to the age-old expedient of make-work as monetary relief. Ginzberg does not evaluate only the economic aspects of the WPA (Works Projects Administration) and Home Relief. He is concerned primarily with psychological impacts. The WPA, he points out, unquestionably was the better part of Depression policy; at least it helped to develop some new skills. All that can be said for Home Relief is that "it kept people alive." Relief policies in the thirties suffered from a curmudgeonly desire to reduce the cost per case. A more liberal approach should have been adopted, it is argued, to help clients return to private employment. "In the last analysis," says Ginzberg, "the wealth of a nation is the quality of its human resources. Only if every individual has the right to work can the United States be true to its heritage and fulfill its promise."

The methods used by public agencies only forced a sharp wedge between the employed and the unemployed. Close personal supervision did not always uncover the malingerers. It did, however, discourage the search for outside private work. People on relief and on the WPA were not inherently lazy; that notion is shown to be nothing more than a cruel and brutal canard. The unemployed were not less efficient than the rest of the working population. Yet private employers discriminated against anyone who came from the public-assistance rosters. And the lack of cooperation between public employment offices and welfare agencies did not ease the situation. It took a war to put people back to work.

Dr. Ginzberg has told us, in no uncertain terms, what we failed to do for the unemployed. His book is an eloquent plea to recast our thinking. We may not be able to eradicate completely the scourge of unemployment, but we can try to mitigate its ravages.

BEN B. SELIGMAN

PREFACE

THIS study on What Unemployment Does to People was conducted under the auspices of the Columbia University Council for Research in the Social Sciences, which subventioned three exploratory investigations in the field of Economics and Group Behavior. Grateful acknowledgment is made to the Council for its liberal support of these exploratory studies in the borderline between economics and psychology. *The Unemployed* represents our major effort.

In planning and carrying through the investigations, the Director of Research sought and received the co-operation of many experts; he owes a particular debt to Dr. Karen Horney. The specific plans for this study matured after lengthy discussions between Dr. Sol W. Ginsburg, associate psychiatrist, Mt. Sinai Hospital, New York City, and the director. Dr. Ginsburg also acted in a volunteer capacity as psychological consultant to the project.

In outlining the study and in establishing basic statistical controls, the staff was greatly aided by the generous assistance of Mr. Milton Friedman of the National Bureau of Economic Research. At a later stage of the investigation, Major C. Ashley Wright, formerly of Columbia University, advised on statistical procedures.

Acknowledgment is due the National Youth Administration for providing the funds for Irwin Fine, John Francis, and Seymour Kwerel to work on various statistical computations.

Three social workers carried the burden of assembling and charting the case studies. Mrs. Ethel L. Ginsburg had the largest responsibility. Not only did she interview 90 families, but the basic categories which guided our interviewing procedures, as well as the methods used in scaling the data, were largely her work. She also supervised the other members of the staff and acted as assistant to the director. Miss Dorothy L. Lynn, collected about 60 cases, and Miss L. Mildred Vickers, who worked with us during the summer and early fall of 1940, was responsible for the collection of 30 cases.

Mrs. Ruth J. Mayer, secretary to the director from 1939 to 1942, was in charge of all office work connected with the project. Her efficient handling of the multiple details contributed materially to the success of the investigation.

This study could never have been undertaken nor completed were it not for the wholehearted co-operation of the late Commissioner William Hodson of the Department of Welfare, New York City, and Lieutenant General Brehon Somervell, formerly United States Works Progress Administrator for the City of New York. Commissioner Hodson and General Somervell made available to us, without reservation, all information we needed. Moreover, we had the opportunity to discuss with them various phases of our work and to benefit from their counsel.

Their staffs, from district administrators to file clerks, were co-operative and helpful. If all were singled out for specific acknowledgment, the list would run to several pages. Note must be taken, however, of the constant help we received from Mrs. Louise T. R. Spero, assistant to the director of Finance and Statistics, Department of Welfare, and from Lieutenant Colonel John D. Witten, formerly State Statistician, Works Progress Administration.

Dr. Meredith B. Givens facilitated our access to the inactive files of the New York State Employment Service, from which we drew one part of our sample.

Former Commissioner John L. Rice of the Department of Health, New York City, granted us permission to interview men at the Mott Haven and the 168th Street Health Centers.

Mr. Graenum Berger made it possible for us to hold a large number of our interviews at Bronx House.

A subcommittee of the Columbia University Council for Research in the Social Sciences—Professor Robert S. Woodworth, chairman; Dean Roswell Cheney McCrea; Professor Robert M. MacIver; and Professor Albert T. Poffenberger—

not only assumed responsibility for sponsoring the project on Economics and Group Behavior, but also gave generously of their time to consult with the director and the staff about the work in process.

Professor Albert Abrahamson of Bowdoin College, formerly Works Progress Administrator for the state of Maine, contributed many helpful suggestions, on procedure and interpretation.

Professor Frederick G. Fassett, Jr., of the Massachusetts Institute of Technology, advised on style and presentation.

The Unemployed is divided into two books: "Interpretation" and "Case Studies." "Book One—Interpretation" follows a chronological order: Part I sketches the background of the families and their circumstances when the men were still in private employment; Part II deals with the interim period between the man's loss of a job and the acceptance of the family on Relief; Part III is a detailed account of the experiences of families on Home Relief and WPA; Part IV sketches the obstacles to re-employment; Part V deals with the significance of the findings for Relief and for the broader problem of social and economic amelioration.

The Epilogue summarizes the impact of the war on the re-employability of the men on Home Relief and Work Relief. The Appendix contains a detailed statement of our method as well as a tabular presentation of our basic data.

"Book Two—Case Studies" presents twelve cases. The selection includes representative families from our subsamples: Home Relief, Work Relief, Closed to Private Employment, and Private Employment. Moreover, the selection has provided for the inclusion of an equal number of Irish Catholic, Jewish, and Anglo-Saxon Protestant families. These case studies are printed in full.

All proper names of persons and places have been altered to ensure maximum protection to the families who were kind enough to co-operate. Since this study deals with only three racial-religious groups—Irish Catholics, Jews, and Anglo-Saxon Protestants—a simple system of disguised nomenclature has been followed. In telling the stories of these families, we have identified each family by using a name typical of the group to which it belongs.

Statements in quotation marks are taken from the case records in our files. Statements in single quotation marks are the exact words used by the interviewee.

BOOK ONE

INTERPRETATION

INTRODUCTION

In the fourth year of World War II, democratic and fascist countries are both preoccupied with labor shortages. There is more than an even chance that manpower reserves will yet decide the issue! War has brought many changes in its wake, not the least startling of which has been the momentary elimination of widespread unemployment.

The overwhelming present makes it difficult to recall the recent past. Today industries reduce output, farms go unplowed or unharvested, services are eliminated, because of labor shortages. Yet it was only a few years ago that industries ran below capacity, farms were neglected, services were discontinued because of surpluses of unemployed laborers.

However, it is doubtful whether all that went before will be completely forgotten, especially by soldiers at the front who are themselves children of the depression. These men, fighting in the South Pacific, North Africa, or the Arctic Circle—these men, training in Georgia, Texas, or North Ireland—these men, wherever they are and whatever they are doing, have only one preoccupation—the defeat of the enemy. To this end they willingly make every sacrifice.

There are days and weeks and months, however, when time hangs heavy on their hands. Waiting is difficult for these men, for they do not want to be cheated of an opportunity to contribute to victory. It is clear that during these quiescent periods the men have a sublime faith in the outcome of the struggle. As far as the war is concerned, they have no doubt, they have no fear.

But when they think of peace, they are uneasy. These soldiers recall that the country fumbled badly in coming to grips with that scourge of peace—unemployment. They remember that pregnant women were dispossessed from their homes, that farmers were thrown off their land, that husky men became soft from idleness. They remember all this and more and they wonder what will happen when they have won the victory on the battlefield. They wonder whether the country will also win the peace.

They are uneasy, but they are not pessimistic. They have seen much these last years. They have seen their country suffer the consequences of an unpreparedness born of ignorance, and they have seen this failing remedied with speed and efficiency. They know there is nothing within reason that the United States cannot do, if it will. But to act intelligently and effectively, a people must understand.

When peace comes, unemployment will return. Of that we can be sure: little else is certain. We may master it or we may be victimized by it, depending on whether we understand what we are up against, and having understood, whether we will act. The tragedy of the 1930's was twofold: we lacked knowledge and we lacked courage. We will not again lack courage, but we may lack knowledge.

The unemployment of the 1930's has been studied extensively, but no one will contend that the literature has exhausted the subject. Conspicuously lacking are studies of the unemployed themselves. Yet this is the nub of the matter, one which must be investigated if we are to act intelligently and efficiently.

This book deals with what unemployment does to people. It seeks answers to questions which beset and agitate every citizen, questions which must be answered before we can act.

Who were the unemployed? Did they fail to earn a living even in prosperous times? What precipitated their unemployment? When business declined, were they the first to be dismissed because they had been the least efficient? How did they adjust to unemployment? Was it true that they preferred Relief with its regular allowance to work at slightly higher wages? What was the influence of the Relief system on the unemployed? Did the clients resent the monthly visits of the Relief investigators as intrusions upon their privacy? Did their acceptance of Relief break their morale and make them more dependent persons?

Was it true that unemployment brought about changes in their thinking and feeling? Did the unemployed break with the church? Did they become radicals and join the Communists? Did they indulge in sexual excesses or take up drinking?

What stood in the way of their re-employment? Why did they remain on the Relief rolls while others succeeded in getting off? What was desirable public policy: Was it dangerous to raise Relief allowances? Should earnings from odd jobs be deducted from Relief allowances? Was retraining worth while or should the unemployed be written off and the cost of their support kept at a minimum?

The search for answers to these questions was a co-operative undertaking, one participated in by an economist, psychiatrist, social workers, and statistician. But co-operation went further. The unemployed themselves, Irish Catholic, Jew, and Anglo-Saxon Protestant, on Home Relief, on WPA, and those lucky enough to have escaped from the rolls co-operated to the fullest. If the knowledge of their misfortune could help in the discovery of a cure, they felt they had not suffered in vain.*

* As detailed in the Appendix, *Method*, pp. 173 ff., this study was limited to families living in New York City and the findings must be interpreted in light of this fact.

PART I. BEFORE RELIEF

Chapter I

THE BACKGROUND OF THE FAMILIES

To UNDERSTAND what unemployment does to people one must trace not only their experiences on Relief but have some knowledge of their lives prior to their coming to Relief. Unemployment and Relief will probably have a different effect on a man of middle-class circumstances from that which it has on a laborer who has always lived on the borderline of poverty.

How did the men and women whom we interviewed start life? Were they brought up in the United States or abroad? Was theirs a normal family or did they lose one or both parents in early childhood? Did they suffer serious deprivations during their early years and did their pinched childhoods make it easier for them to accept misfortune later? Or were their early years secure, both physically and emotionally? Did this security stand them in good stead later or was the shock of adult misfortune greater because of the contrast?

Only Irish Catholics, Jews, and Anglo-Saxon Protestants are included in the study. By definition, foreign-born Irish Catholics were those born in the British Isles, usually in Eire. Foreign-born Anglo-Saxon Protestants were defined as immigrants who came to the United States from an English-speaking country—i.e., England or the Empire. Without deliberate selection, it was found that most Jewish immigrants came from Central and Eastern Europe, primarily from Poland and Russia.

The basic contours of these people's lives prior to their coming to Relief are easy to trace. Men and women were about equally divided between native-born and immigrants; the Home Relief sample had a slight majority of immigrants, the WPA sample a majority of native-born. The most striking contrast among the three racial-religious groups as to place of birth was found between Protestant men on Relief (Home Relief and WPA combined), three-quarters of whom were native-born, and Jewish women, three-quarters of whom were foreign-born.

Originally it had been planned to pick only families in which the male head of the household was between the ages of 25 and 45, but this proved impracticable. Instead, 59 years was established as a maximum age for the man but no minimum was set.

The age distribution of men on Relief is shown in the following table:

Age	Number of Men
20-24	3
25-29	7
30-34	18
35-39	21
40-44	26
45-49	18
50-54	19
55-59	8

Just under 70 per cent of the men were between 30 and 50 years of age, which meant that they had been in the labor market long enough to have acquired some experience and skill, yet were not old enough to be definitely handicapped for re-employment. The sample also included a few youngsters who had never really had a chance to find a place for themselves in the labor market. About 20 per cent were over 50 years old and therefore definitely handicapped in their search for private employment. The men on WPA were, on the average, slightly older than the men on Home Relief; and the Catholics had more men in the youngest age group and somewhat fewer men in the highest age group than either Protestants or Jews.

A considerable number of men and women on Relief had been born into large families. About one-third of the men came from families of seven or more children and another third came from families of four to six children. Five men were "only" children. There were more large families among the foreign-born; and the Catholic families ran somewhat larger than either the Jewish or the Protestant families. Infant mortality was very high in the large families; some mothers lost five or more of their youngsters.

The men and women who had been brought up in large families did not think their childhoods exceptional, for they recalled that in the old days large families had been typical. Occasionally an interviewee was resentful of having been one of many children. "Mr. Martin is very bitter and resentful toward his parents. He has frequently said that they had no right to have six children when his father was unable to support any of them." Mrs. Epstein also spoke "rather bitterly of her large family, feeling that it was wrong for her parents to have more children than they could care for adequately; that her mother's health was ruined through constant childbearing and that none of them had much of a chance in life. Most of the children had died in early infancy and the others had survived only a few years. She and her brother were the two youngest and she felt that they lived only because her father died shortly after their birth."

In many families, especially in those with a large number of children, economic conditions had been strained. The parents of these Relief clients had struggled hard to earn a living. Mr. Brown tells this story: "His father was an ironworker who earned about $9 a week and his mother, in order to help support the family, took in washing. He said he remembered his childhood as being very poor and he had to leave school at the completion of the sixth grade to go to work." Few, if any, Relief clients complained about shortage of food, and some had really enjoyed secure childhoods. There was Mr. McCabe, whose father had a small shoe business in Ireland which provided the family with a comfortable living, and Mr. Epstein's father had been a well-to-do cattle dealer in Poland.

The sample was heavily urban: Most native-born men and women had been born and brought up in New York and a considerable number of the foreign-born were city people. Only a few of the foreign-born Irish Catholics and a few of the native-born Protestants came from farms.

A noticeable number of men and women on Relief had lost

one or both parents in childhood and had been brought up in foster homes or orphanages. Several women commented on the fact that their mothers had been sent to their graves prematurely by excessive childbearing. Several women, in discussing their present plight, recalled their youth—a father struggling to make a living, an overworked mother, and a home full of sprawling children—and added "there were hard times then, too."

The facts already presented suggest that most men and women were unable to climb far up the educational ladder, for then, as now, the education of children depended largely on the economic position of parents. Most fortunate were New Yorkers who had considerable free educational resources at their disposal and most handicapped were those born on Irish farms or in the ghettos of Poland and Russia.

The educational achievements of the men in the Relief sample follow:

Did not graduate from elementary school	40
Elementary school graduates	36
Some high school education	29
High school graduates	4
College education	9
College graduates	2
Total	120

The men had slightly more education than the women; men on WPA had slightly more education than those on Home Relief, probably a reflection of the higher percentage of native-born on WPA; Jews and Protestants had a little more book learning than Catholics.

A considerable number of foreign-born Catholics and Jews received their basic education in poverty-stricken parochial schools, and many never progressed beyond learning to read their prayers and write their names. Foreign-born Jews, unlike foreign-born Catholics or Protestants, had a specific language handicap—they had to learn English.

Because of the economic plight of their families many children had to leave school and go to work before they had completed grammar school, not to mention high school. However, few persons recalled the early termination of their education with resentment. Apparently they did not consider themselves possessed of aptitudes or skills that could have been developed by further instruction. They had remained in school as long as most boys and girls in their communities and therefore did not feel especially deprived.

The immigration data are interesting. Of the 117 men and women who migrated to the United States, only a few were more than 30 years old at the time of their arrival. Except for the Jews, there was little "family" migration. The Catholic and Protestant immigrants came to this country in late adolescence or early adulthood; the modal age for male immigrants was 22. Because of the larger amount of "family" migration among the Jews, the modal age for Jewish immigrants was 15.

Many factors conspired to uproot people from their birthplace and send them on their way to the United States. Broadly defined, the economic factor played an important role. Several Catholic and Jewish foreign-born commented on the fact that from earliest childhood they had realized that their only hope lay in eventual migration to the United States. This was especially true of children born into large families, whose fathers eked out a living on a small Irish farm or in a ghetto shop. When starvation in Europe was not the spur, gold in America was the lure. Every European knew that in the New World riches were to be had for the taking.

Several Jewish families left Europe because they feared for their lives even more than for their pocketbooks. "Mrs. Brill was born in Kiev, Russia. . . . Her father had a small business which brought in a comfortable income . . . but repeated pogroms and the difficulties which the Jews had to face in Czarist Russia made it impossible for him to keep an adequate part of his earnings." War caught Mr. Epstein traveling in Western Europe and rather than venture a return to his home in Poland, he set out for the United States.

Among the Irish, familial bonds played an important part in stimulating migration. Mrs. McCabe, one of eleven children, left Ireland to join her aunt who had come to the United States some years previously and had established herself here.

Many Irish men and women, after gaining a toehold in the New World, helped out the folks back home by finding openings in this country for adolescent children.

Several Protestant immigrants came to this country because it promised more rapid advancement. Oftentimes marriage was the spur; a man contemplating matrimony frequently takes stock of the future. Mr. Knight, a Scotsman, who had learned shipbuilding and shippainting in Glasgow, followed his sister to this country "to see whether he could get a job and make a home for his wife. Five months later he sent for his wife and his mother, who came to the United States together."

Many girls were brought to this country by men who had returned home to marry them or who sent for them to come over to be married in the United States. Brothers occasionally set out together. Familial lines cross in all directions.

Some boys left home because they were unhappy; usually because they were at odds with their fathers. Mrs. Reid related that her father-in-law "was a very strict man . . . a strict disciplinarian and on the whole a rather unpleasant person." Although he earned a comfortable income from his work in an old printing establishment, "Mrs. Reid thinks that it is a fine commentary on his personality that not one of his sons followed his trade. Mr. Reid left home at an early age after completing only the third grade. He left England at the age of 12 and came to Canada to be with an older sister who had preceded him there."

Nor must one forget the restless and the adventurous. "Mr. Eisner left home (Austria) at the age of 12 and wandered about for several years, slowly working his way toward America, where he finally arrived when he was 18." Occasionally the United States was not the migrant's objective. Several Protestant lads were headed for Australia, but found things to their liking in the United States and remained.

Several Catholics traveled back and forth before taking up permanent residence in this country. Mrs. McCarthy told that "she came to the United States in 1902 and remained here until she completed public school. At about that time her father died and her mother took her back to Ireland to live with her grandmother. Her mother remarried there. When her mother died, in 1921, Mrs. McCarthy came to the United States. Her stepfather, of whom she was very fond, came here somewhat later."

With few exceptions, Protestant and Jewish immigrants were glad to have shaken themselves free of Europe. This was particularly true of Jewish immigrants who had little reason, especially in recent years, for nostalgia. Time and again these Jewish immigrants expressed heartfelt thanks that they had been spared the horrors and persecution that were being visited upon their relatives and friends by Hitler and his murderers.

The foreign-born Irish were less certain of the wisdom of having emigrated. "Her parents are still living on their farm in Ireland and Mrs. Shannahan secretly wishes that she could go home again and live with them because they are much better off than people in New York. Whereas they never had any money, they always had enough to eat and there was plenty of sunshine and fresh air. She has often talked to her husband about her home and he, too, would like to go there with her, although he has lived most of his life in New York City. They feel that New York has a great many advantages, but only for those who have money enough to live comfortably. If one must be poor, it is easier to be poor in Ireland."

Although most of the native-born were New Yorkers by birth, a few had been lured to the city by prospects of better working conditions and higher wages. Mr. Martin said that he came to New York "because the depression had caused most of the Fall River factories to close down. They tried their luck in Fall River again in 1933, remained there ten weeks and then came back because there was no work." Mrs. Hewitt came to New York from Gadsden, Alabama, where her father is a Baptist preacher. "For a number of years, Mrs. Hewitt explained, her father worked in a Coca-Cola plant, but when the work slackened he secured a preaching job in Gadsden and has been preaching there for the past ten years. She said that she came here because she did not find much chance to work as a nurse in Gadsden. Her brother Charles suggested that she come to New York. She did so and stayed with him for some time."

The problem of citizenship dovetails into immigration. Although most foreign-born men and women were eligible for citizenship, many remained aliens. A considerable number had not even taken out their first papers. Since Congress legislated, in 1937, that aliens could not be employed on WPA, all the 22 foreign-born men in our WPA sample were citizens. However, there were 10 aliens among the 25 foreign-born women whose husbands were on WPA. Of the 33 foreign-born men on Home Relief, 17 were aliens; and of the 37 foreign-born women, 25 had failed to obtain citizenship.

These figures suggest that many men and women failed to become American citizens and that women were even more remiss than men in regularizing their status. Of the 21 foreign-born men and women in the Catholic Home Relief sample, 19 were aliens, a higher percentage than among foreign-born Protestants or Jews. This can be explained, at least in part, by the doubts which many Irish immigrants entertained about settling permanently in this country. As long as they thought seriously of returning home, they had good reason to hold on to their Irish citizenship.

Several foreign-born were ashamed of their alien status and explained at length that they were really 100 per cent Americans, ready to die for the United States if need be. Recently, it has become more difficult for aliens to acquire citizenship. They must pass an examination that is not always easy. Although the fee has not been raised, $5 is a considerable sum for people on Relief. Mr. Ahearn "is not a citizen because he has not been able to save the money for it, but recently was helped by one of his friends to take out his first papers." Mr. Eisner "had his first papers some years ago, but lost them, and has been unable to afford to get them again."

Mr. Kennedy "explained that he did not take out his first citizenship papers earlier because he had expected to move on to Australia, but now 'I guess I'm planted here'." Mr. O'Hara "was never quite sure about staying in America during the years before his marriage and since then the family has been in very poor straits. When he was broke he said he did not want to get citizenship just to go on the dole."

Several men had entered the country illegally and were therefore unable to apply for citizenship, and several others had difficulty producing the necessary credentials. Most aliens had no legitimate excuse. They had been eligible for citizenship during the years when the examination was easy and the fee was no burden. One is forced to conclude that the schools, the churches, and other communal organizations have been remiss in furthering an Americanization program.

Most foreign-born arrived on these shores with some work experience. Only the very young were without training. Mr. Kennedy told how he "had worked very hard first as a farmer, then as an apprentice mechanic, then at various jobs having to do with car repair. He had attended school only until the age of 12, at which time he was placed on a neighbor's farm and his small wage was sent to his parents." A considerable number of foreign-born Jews had been taught the trade of butcher, harnessmaker, tailor, or shoe repairer, and some were able to utilize their training in this country.

Formal apprenticeship was found mostly among foreign-born Protestants. Upon completing high school, Mr. Dixon "became apprenticed to learn the woolen fabric trade. He became quite proficient in this and always held good jobs." Mr. Knight, a native of Scotland, completed the sixth grade and then "was apprenticed to a painter with whom he served a four-year term, during which time he earned six shillings a week. At the completion of this period, he was considered an experienced painter and was issued a union card." Mr. Lewis was graduated "from the English equivalent of grammar school and was then apprenticed to a cloth examiner. He became a cloth examiner himself and, in 1913, came to the United States with his wife and child."

Several native-born men also acquired a trade early in life. Mr. Meade had to leave school in 7A "to contribute to the family. He was never ambitious, did not like school, and so did not mind leaving at that time. His father was a painter, and through him Mr. Meade learned the trade." Mr. Elliott recalled that as soon as he was old enough "he went to the woods of Maine and found work in the lumber camps and for many years made his living as a chef."

The majority were not so fortunate. With little specific preparation for mechanical or commercial work, they had to take what they could find. This meant work as messenger boys, stock clerks, soda fountain attendants, and garage helpers. Mr. Mitchell sketched his early years in the labor market: He was graduated from elementary school in 1924 and immediately looked for work. "His first job was errand boy. He then worked for a year or so for a large utility company, connecting meters, at $22.50 a week. Following this, he went to work for an uncle who owned several apartment houses. He received free rent and $75 a month and continued in this job for five years. This was not too satisfactory, he stated, since it is difficult to work for relatives and his uncle expected a great deal of him."

Most men found little difficulty in landing a first job or in changing jobs whenever they wished. Employment conditions remained good in New York City right up to the Great Depression of 1930. Mr. Barnes gives this picture of New York in 1908, the year he came north from Norfolk, Virginia. "The best explanation that he could give for migrating north was the fact that several friends thought that they would like to come here and he went along. He told how he secured four jobs within a single day. He checked in at a hotel on 38th Street and Broadway and started to walk up and down the avenue, leaving his name in three places and in the fourth being offered a job that started that very evening at seven o'clock. He accepted the night job. When he returned to his hotel the following morning, the three postcards which he had left with prospective employers were waiting for him. He gave these cards to his buddies, who had been less successful in their job hunting, and they were taken on in his place."

Few boys entered the labor market well prepared for work and among these few were several who refused to make use of their specialized training. They were willing to work at anything except the job for which they had been trained. Some explained their distaste as a reaction to parental pressure; others to a conviction that they were unsuited to the work.

The work history of the women tells an interesting story. About 80 per cent of the entire sample had held down jobs before their marriage and the majority had been employed steadily, a minority intermittently. There was a marked occupational concentration in domestic work, factory employment, and office positions. These three fields accounted for 70 per cent of the total. Catholic girls accounted for the largest number of domestics; Jewish girls were heavily represented in factory employment. The job history for women in the WPA sample showed more diversification than for women in the Home Relief sample, especially in the skilled jobs, such as nursing and teaching. This fact is probably correlated with the higher educational achievement of the women in the WPA sample.

The women were even more poorly prepared for the labor market than the men. Mrs. Corcoran was an exception, for after she had completed the eighth grade, her father sent her to business college for a year. At college she learned "to operate bookkeeping machines, printing machines, and the typewriter. At 15 she began to work and continued until she was married, at which time she was earning $24 a week plus frequent overtime."

Many foreign-born Catholic women, in order to supplement their families' meager incomes, were placed in service in early adolescence. Upon arriving in this country, they usually continued in their old line of work and found jobs as domestics. Since wages were higher and the work was easier in the United States, many women recalled this period in their lives with pleasure. "Mrs. Brennan came to the United States in 1924 to live with her aunt, who ran a rooming house. She helped a bit there, then found work as a nursemaid with a family which lived on Fifth Avenue. She spoke animatedly of this period of her life. She had liked the work and the pay had been excellent.

Her only duties had been the care of the child, and in return she received maintenance and $60 a month."

Most women apparently considered their employment as an interim adjustment between school and marriage, although there were some, like Mrs. Mitchell, who had worked for the Telephone Company for $22 weekly and "had enjoyed her work." There were a few high earners in the group who recalled with pleasure not their jobs but their wages. Mrs. Casey left school in the sixth grade, to go to work. "She was employed as a sorter of soiled wash on a piecework basis and managed to earn about $26 a week. Later she worked as an egg candler in the A & P, also on a piecework basis, and earned about $30 a week."

The impression is inescapable that few women found their work satisfying. They surely did not think of their jobs in terms of a career. This helps to explain why they gave up their jobs at marriage or during their first pregnancy and why they failed to return.

If the early lives of the men and women in the Private sample—those who avoided coming to Relief—be compared with the Relief group, the similarity is more striking than the difference. True, the percentage of native-born men and women is greater in the Private sample and the contrast is most marked in the Jewish group.

More important is the suggestion that the men and women in the Private sample, although born into large families, nevertheless had economically secure childhoods. This is borne out in part by their higher educational achievements. At both ends of the scale the Private sample had the advantage over the Relief group: A smaller percentage of men and women in the Private families terminated their education with the completion of grammar school and a greater percentage received their high school diplomas or went beyond.

The Private group entered the labor market not only with more general education, but with better vocational training than was typical of the Relief families. This superior preparation was reflected in less shifting around from job to job, although Mr. Duncan, a Private case, had the most diversified work experience of any person in the entire study. The following is a résumé of his employment history:

1924, steamship company, $47.50 and maintenance, monthly.
1925-32 intermittently, boilermaker's helper, shipyards, $18-$20 weekly.
1928-29, U. S. Engineers, $80 a month and maintenance.
1929, private engineering firm, $80 monthly.
1929-30, fireman, American Telephone Company, $22.50 and maintenance.
1930, insurance company, $18 a week (three weeks).
1930, pan greaser, bakery, $18-$20 (six months).
1930, selling, Electrolux, $15 commission (two months).
1931-32, dredging company, $80 a month and maintenance.
1932 fireman, hotel, $18 (eight months).
1932, painting contractor.
1933-34, blood donor, Board of Health, $35 a pint.
1934, operator, wood-finishing mill, $45-$50 a month (three months).
1934-35, boilermaker, shipyard, $20 a week.
1935, City Service Transportation, $65 and maintenance (three months).
1935, boiler fireman, hotel, $18 a week.
1936-38, electrician, apartment house, $90 a month plus maintenance.
1938, to present, fireman, hospital, $95 a month plus meals.

The explanation for the relatively low wages which Mr. Duncan earned is found in the fact that he worked mostly below the Mason and Dixon line.

The only important contrast between the work history of the women in the Relief and Private samples is the small percentage of Private women who had been employed as domestics or factory workers. Reflecting their superior education, a larger percentage of Private women were found in commercial and professional work. Moreover, many remained at work after they married.

Statistical manipulations would probably enable one to uncover many differences between the Relief and Private samples, but it is doubtful whether these differences would be revealing. If the data are not forced, one contrast emerges. The men and women in the Private sample had the advantage of more academic and vocational education and came to the labor market better prepared than the Relief group.

Chapter II

MARRIED AND SELF-SUPPORTING

Ours is a culture in which most men and women marry in their late teens or early twenties. This is true for the majority, although small groups, such as college-trained women, do not conform to the pattern. The average age at marriage does not vary greatly throughout Western Europe and the United States. Eire, however, has a high average, and a considerable number of foreign-born Catholic women stated that their emigration was greatly influenced by the belief that they could find a husband more easily in New York than in Cobh.

The following table shows the distribution of ages at marriage for the men and women in the Home Relief and WPA samples:

AGE AT MARRIAGE OF MEN AND WOMEN

	Below 20	20-23	24-26	27-29	30-32	32 Plus
Men	5	39	22	27	11	16
Women	28	44	23	9	9	7

The modal age at marriage for both men and women was between 20 and 23. A close inspection of the figures shows, however, that almost 25 per cent of the girls married before they reached their twentieth birthday and only 20 per cent married after 26, while the corresponding figures for men are only 4 per cent before 20 and almost 50 per cent after 26. Most men were slightly older than the women they married, although the disparity in ages was usually not more than three years. Only a few women were older than their husbands.

There was nothing in the figures to support the belief that some men married before they had achieved reasonable economic security, while others delayed until such time as they had.

Worthy of note is the fact that in 9 Catholic, 3 Protestant, and 1 Jewish family the first-born arrived in 7 or less months after nuptials. A consideration of these cases did not disclose that they were really "shotgun" marriages. A more reasonable interpretation suggests that the couple were having sex relations, and when pregnancy unexpectedly occurred the man was willing to marry the girl. However, in only one case was marriage the goal prior to the unexpected pregnancy.

In other families, the first child was usually born during the first or second year of marriage. In only 25 per cent of the cases was the first child born after the couple had been married for two or more years. Apparently, most people looked forward to having children, and this explains why so many women gave up their jobs at marriage. At the time when these families first came to Relief, there were 23 childless couples—the recently married, and the sterile unions. In the remaining 97 families with children, just under half had 2 or more children; a third had three or more children. Many families had children after their first application for Relief, and many women were still in their child-bearing years at the time of the interviews, so that these figures are indicative of a trend rather than of any final tabulation.

When a woman gave up her job at the time of marriage or early in her first pregnancy, the entire economic support of the family fell upon the man. The men met their responsibilities. They provided for their wives and children without seeking private or public assistance. The unemployed were not the proverbial misfits, the bums, the ne'er-do-wells, the economically incompetent; not that the sample was completely free of marginal families.

One is reminded of Mr. Kades's record, which disclosed that

from the time of his marriage in 1928 until his acceptance on Relief in 1932, he and his family lived with his in-laws and were largely supported by them. Then there was Mr. Waldman, who was stricken with tuberculosis early in his working life. After an enforced rest in the Rockies, he returned to New York but was never able to gain a real foothold. Two of the foreign-born, Mr. O'Hara and Mr. Ryan, had the misfortune to arrive in New York in 1929. This is Mr. Ryan's story: "He and his wife came 'out here' at the worst possible time, September, 1929. He was out of work nearly a year after arriving in the United States, and they used up their entire savings. Finally, they moved in with his sister because they would have been unable to exist otherwise. Then he got a job as a painter, but it lasted only a few months; later, he found work as an elevator operator and porter; still later as a laborer. In his opinion, he has not had a real job in all the time he has been in this country, and he went on to say that he actually never had enough spare money to apply for citizenship." Three younger men, born in 1913, 1914, and 1916, had the same hard luck as Mr. Ryan, for they too entered the labor market at the onset of the severe depression and found that they could not compete successfully with more experienced people who were looking for work.

Mr. Meade, a painter by trade, had also run into difficulties. Since his marriage in 1927, he had supported his family only one year. Mrs. Meade said "there was no reason for this other than his 'lack of gumption.' He simply would not go out and look for work and risk hearing the word 'No.' He was a good worker and willing to work when a definite job was handed him, but he would wait for one to fall into his lap rather than go out to look for one." According to his wife, Mr. Meade is neurotic, but Mrs. Meade on her own testimony is far from stable. "From the time she was 12 she was physically very mature and attractive to men—even after marriage, men pursued her. Once, the iceman to whom her husband owed 50 cents suggested that she might pay him by being nice and giving him what he wanted. Another time, her husband's employer made advances to her. She had been too young and inexperienced, even though she had had a child, to realize that she could have created a scene and sued him for everything he owned, for there were witnesses in the next room. She was sorry she had not known that, for she could have made him pay plenty."

Mr. Shannahan had also had a hard time of it. He started work as a hall boy for one of the large utility companies, and then served as office boy for the same concern. In 1927 he enlisted in the United States Army, from which he was dishonorably discharged for insubordination in 1930. He had worked as a truck helper for about six months, when he became involved in a robbery and was sentenced to a reformatory for one year. After serving his time, he found work as a substitute elevator boy, but managed to keep the job for only one month. "He found it very difficult to get work during the parole period because employers were wary of hiring men with a prison background."

At the time of their marriages, Mr. Aiken and Mr. Lish did not earn more than $20 weekly, but they found that "although this was not a large salary, it was sufficient to meet one's needs." This exhausts the marginal group except for a few additional families that were in and out of difficulty because the husband was a drunkard. Prior to 1929 drunkards were able, however, to lose a job one day and find another the next.

The job history of men in the low income group is well illustrated by the employment record of Mr. McCormack. "From 1922 to 1924, Mr. McCormack was a messenger boy for Western Union earning about $15 a week. From 1924 to 1926 he worked for a biscuit company as a machine helper at $22 a week. He was a relief man for the Interborough Rapid Transit from 1926 to 1927 at $4 a day. From October, 1930, to March, 1932, he earned $18 weekly as a driver for a taxi company. From 1932 to 1934 he worked part time as a clerk in the A & P, averaging about $12 a week. During the same period he worked as a utility man for $18 weekly. From 1934 to 1936 he was employed as a roofer, at which he averaged $15 a week. He also worked as a counterman during 1936, supplementing his work as roofer."

Most men had a less variegated experience than Mr. McCormack, although there were only a few who did not change jobs now and again. The following tabulation summarizes, roughly, the skills which the men possessed and the occupations which they pursued:

Unskilled manual	33
Semiskilled manual	51
Skilled manual	7
Commercial, white-collar	24
Skilled non-manual	5

Just under 30 per cent were unskilled laborers—elevator operators, porters, bellboys, superintendents' helpers. Slightly more than 40 per cent were semiskilled manual workers—plumbers, cement masons, refrigerator repairmen, electricians. Twenty per cent can be grouped together as white-collar and mercantile workers—salesmen, independent businessmen, bookkeepers. The remaining 10 per cent were skilled workers in manual and nonmanual occupations.

The industrial pattern of New York was strongly reflected in this occupational distribution. Many men had found employment in the service and construction industries, while few had held factory jobs. There were only 8 independent businessmen included in the sample.

This summary is based upon the last major occupation of the man prior to his acceptance on Relief. Most men had worked in at least one other trade: superintendents had been meter readers or carpenters; a grocery clerk had owned his own restaurant; a factory worker had once been employed as a radio repair man; an insurance agent had spent several years as a bookkeeper. Occasionally, the shift was more striking: a man who owned a dry goods store during the 10 years prior to his coming to Relief had previously supported himself as a cornettist; a compositor had been a milkman; a grocery clerk had once been a cataloguer.

Catholics, Jews, and Protestants had similar work histories, except that a larger percentage of Jews were found in commercial activities. However, the only three factory workers were Jews. Including the very young who were new to the labor market and the few older men with choppy employment records, just under 40 per cent of the entire group had worked in their major occupation for less than 4 years. About 25 per cent had a working span of from 4 to 8 years, and the remaining 35 per cent had a record of 8 or more years. In this last group were men like Mr. Solomon, a shoe laster, who emigrated to the United States in 1918. "When he arrived in the U.S.A., he went to live with a cousin who got him a job in a shoe factory where he remained until 1937 . . . working steadily as a laster on the same job for the same employer for 20 years."

Mr. Atkinson never changed his line of work from the time of his first job in 1905 until his unemployment in the 1930's. "Mr. Atkinson's first job was with the Stevens Packing Company, where he learned wooden box-making. After completing his apprenticeship, he earned $3.50 a week. He slowly advanced himself until he was earning $30 weekly. The owner died in 1921, his widow remarried, and her husband ran the business to the ground within the year. Atkinson found employment with another box-making firm, earning about $27 weekly, but after 10 years this firm went out of business. He realized that with cartons being used for local shipments, the box-making trade was on the slide. However, he found another job as boxmaker and kept it until November, 1931. Early in 1930 it became clear that this firm would be forced out of business because there were less and less calls for wooden boxes, but Atkinson said that the boss was fond of him and kept him on after all other employees had been dismissed."

Mr. O'Donnell "had worked for one firm of contractors throughout his 16 years as a plumber. According to his wife, he was a skilled man who could do all the difficult jobs. Moreover, he knew how to install oil burners. When work was slow, he would pick up other jobs, but in the busy seasons he went back to his old boss, who always rehired him."

What wages did these men earn during the years when they were regularly employed? About 5 per cent had not been self-maintaining prior to their acceptance on Relief and another 15 per cent averaged less than $25 weekly. The largest group, more than 60 per cent, averaged between $25 and $40 weekly. Just under 15 per cent were in the $41 to $60 class, and three had weekly incomes between $61 and $100.

On an annual basis, these families earned between $1,600 and $1,700, which gave them a larger income than most laboring families in urban communities.

Since most men were employed in manual trades, the fact that only 25 per cent belonged to unions is surprising. The lack of a union card was a serious handicap to many who sought to improve themselves. Mr. O'Donnell stated: "He was never a member of the union because in the early days the union was not very important. Later, when it became necessary to be a union member, the entrance fee in the plumbers' union was $300. Mrs. O'Donnell said that by saving and scraping as best they could, they managed to get together $200 which Mr. O'Donnell took down to union headquarters, requesting that it be accepted as down payment and that he be allowed to make further payment out of his wages. He was turned down and was told that nothing under $300 was acceptable. They were poor people and it was impossible for them to get the additional $100. They did not try very hard because Mr. O'Donnell always felt fairly sure of a job with his old boss."

Unions proved an obstacle, but by no means an insurmountable one, in the path of some men who sought to improve themselves. Actually, one-third of the sample voluntarily relinquished their jobs during the prosperous 1920's in order to take better ones. Of course, many men who remained with their old employers also improved themselves, but it is doubtful whether they did as well as those who changed bosses. The fact that only one-third of the group shifted might be interpreted to mean that many men failed to make the most of their opportunities, but in the absence of reliable data about the general New York laboring population, this question cannot be answered.

Men who establish their own businesses are usually pointed

to as the go-getters, but our cases suggest the opposite. Mr. Lish, who arrived in the United States in 1923, first worked as a clothing operator, later as a salesman, and early in 1928 opened his own dry goods store. During the succeeding 8 years, his earnings averaged only $20 weekly. "Mrs. Lish said that her husband was never a good businessman." Mr. Brill set himself up in business, but, according to his wife, "she was the businesswoman and her husband her assistant. She had to work very hard, but she loved the business world and enjoyed every minute of it. She could never expect any real help from Mr. Brill because he had no initiative or ambition. If she bought the stuff and planned the display, he could sell whatever the customer wanted, but as far as doing anything on his own, Mrs. Brill said she had never known him to be able to do much." Mr. Berman did not think about setting himself up in business until his eyesight began to fail and he could no longer continue to work as a bookkeeper. He invested his savings in a trucking concern, but within 6 months it failed. With much difficulty, he scraped together enough money to start a private school to teach English to immigrants.

Prior to the Great Depression of 1929 these men had, with few exceptions, been regularly employed at wages which enabled them to maintain their families at reasonable standards. What were these standards? In 1940 many families were still living in the same neighborhood, many even in the same house or apartment, in which they had lived during the years when their menfolk were in private employment. These neighborhoods were not slum areas, although by 1940 many houses were in a state of disrepair. These families looked back with satisfaction at their old standards. This was true even of families where the man had earned only $20 or $25 weekly. Mr. Aiken had earned only $20 a week at the time of his marriage. "Although this was not a large salary, it was sufficient to meet their needs. The woman had come from a family accustomed only to low income, and she was a good manager. The salary was not sufficient for them to save anything or even to permit them to take out insurance, but they were adequately housed, clothed, and fed, and even had a little left over for recreation. They had saved sufficient during her pregnancy to pay for her delivery, and thus avoided going into debt."

The Higginses, with two children, found that "they got along well on $30 a week. This was more than ample for their needs." Mrs. McCormack stated that "they were able to manage nicely on Mr. McCormack's average earnings of $25 a week. They were able to take the children to the beaches and often went away for weekends. They entertained a great deal. They also carried insurance and had a bank account of $100."

When weekly earnings ran to $40 and during holiday seasons even to $75, as was the case with the Brennans, a family could be very comfortable. "They were able to set up housekeeping with nice furniture immediately after their marriage. The woman was a good manager and they always had a good savings account. They had not worried about the cost of having children, had never gone into debt, had lived in nice neighborhoods. They felt so secure that as late as 1929 they had drawn on their savings in order to take a three months' vacation in Ireland. When Mr. Brennan lost his job in 1931, they still had $1,000 in the bank."

Some families lived frugally, even though their income would have permitted them some latitude. Mrs. Levin stated "that she used to think that if they were careful and saved what they could, things would be better later on. They planned that when the girls got older they would move to a better neighborhood and buy new furniture so that the girls could bring their boy friends to visit. They never had a car and Mrs. Levin went to the country only twice in her life, both times to seek relief from her arthritic pains."

Mrs. Klein said "she had never been to the country in her life and does not know what she would do if she had the opportunity." However, she went on to add "that they had had many friends who visited frequently and they had always been able to make their visitors comfortable by giving them enough to eat. The children had been given everything that the parents felt they needed, and they were content."

Food, housing, and clothing took most of one's income, but not all. Some people spent their surplus on better living quarters; others on furniture. A few found their greatest pleasure in entertaining. Some saved during the winter months in order to leave town for a few weeks during the hot summer.

Most families made provision for the future. Almost 75 per cent carried insurance—many had several policies—and more than 30 per cent had savings accounts. Only 15 per cent had neither. Insurance really served a double purpose: it offered protection against the death of the principal wage earner and provided a convenient method for regular saving.

When illness struck, savings evaporated. Excluded from the sample were the chronically ill, but included were several families that had been drained dry by sudden illness. The elaborate hospital and clinic service maintained by the municipal authorities proved a poor bulwark against the financial ravages that illness brought in its wake.

The pattern of these people's lives prior to the unemployment of the man begins to emerge. They married in their early or middle twenties. Because their jobs did not interest them and they looked forward to raising a family the women quit work at time of marriage or shortly thereafter, and the sole responsibility for the support of the family devolved on the man. For the most part, the men discharged their responsibilities satisfactorily. They earned sufficient to provide their families with all essentials and even a few luxuries.

Social activity centered around their own immediate family, especially their children. Visiting one's relatives was an important week-end institution. Intimate friends were few, but most women spent some time gossiping with neighbors. Usually, family ties were close, but not always. Several early marriages had been precipitated by unpleasant conditions at home. Mrs. Rattner said that she was quick to marry "after her father's death, in order to get away from her mother." Mr. Martin had an unhappy time at home. Although he made $30 a week as a painter, "his mother took all his money and gave him carfare and a small sum for spending purposes. They resented his marriage because it meant that he would cease to be their chief support. His mother has frequently told him that he owes them everything because they are his parents and they raised him."

Neither the men nor the women were joiners. A few men belonged to unions, more for economic than for social reasons. A few were lodge members and a few others, about 10 per cent in all, belonged to the local political club. The women had even less contact with organizational life. Brought up in religious homes, most Catholic and Jewish men and women continued to follow tradition. Many Protestants, however, had lost contact with the church.

In the case of Catholics, orthodoxy was defined in terms of regular attendance at mass, communion, and confession; sending one's children to parochial school was further evidence of close ties to the church. The Jews were less easy to categorize. If orthodoxy were strictly defined, it would have to include observance of the Sabbath. Hence, only those Jews could be considered orthodox who refrained from working on Saturday. But economic pressure, not to search for other explanations, had led most Jews in the United States to break with this tradition. Orthodoxy is here defined as observance of the dietary laws in the home, attendance at the synagogue on the High Holy Days, religious instruction for boys.

Religious behavior changed more slowly than religious belief or feeling. Mrs. Silverman "says that she keeps a strictly kosher home and that she and her husband attend synagogue on holidays. . . . She could not stand the look in her mother's eyes if she failed to observe the dietary laws and rituals." At an office interview, Mr. Silverman stated that they keep a strictly kosher house because "the house was his wife's."

The Kleins have more positive feelings. Mrs. Klein stated that her children used to speak Hebrew very well, but now "refuse to speak anything but English although they understand what is being said to them." One of her sons attends Hebrew school and her husband, who is very orthodox, is much interested in his son's religious education. Typical of devout Catholics is Mrs. Ryan. "She said that faith and belief in God are very important to her because she believes that faith is the greatest thing in the world."

The religiosity of the Protestants is difficult to assess. About 40 per cent were deeply interested in religion and were church members; another 40 per cent attended services periodically or at least sent their youngsters to Sunday school; the remaining 20 per cent were completely cut off from religious thought and practice.

Since five Catholic families deviated from the teachings of the church on birth control, it is not correct to say that all Catholic families were orthodox. Among the Jews and Protestants, birth control presented no theological difficulties and only 8 per cent of the families in these two groups failed to use contraceptives.

Aliens aside, the political affiliations of these families disclose an overwhelming concentration. With the exception of a few Republicans and two Communists, all were Democrats.

In reconstructing the pattern of these families prior to the unemployment of their menfolk, one negative finding should be stressed. Criminality was almost completely absent. The only antisocial characteristic was excessive drinking, typical of only a small group. Mrs. Casey stated that her husband lost every job he ever had because of drinking. "He is a good man except when he drinks. At such times he gets fighting mad, but she knows how to handle him." Then there were the McCanns: "The family has never managed well. Although Mr. McCann had many periods of steady, well-paid employment, he drank and gambled away most of the money he earned, deserted the family frequently, and lost every position because of his drinking."

If the adequacy of these families be assessed in terms of the following three criteria

1. The man's attitude toward self-maintenance.
2. Personal relations within the family.
3. Social responsibility of the family.

one is impressed with the finding that 90 per cent were clearly adequate and only 10 per cent inadequate. The small minority of inadequate families includes all drunkards, criminals, and economic incompetents.

There are many points of similarity and only a few of contrast between the families who came to Relief and those who managed to keep clear of it. The age at marriage of men and women in the Private sample did not differ from that in the Relief group. There were, however, no "forced" marriages. Children came along shortly after marriage, but there was a higher percentage of childless and one-child families.

The Private group had a smaller percentage of unskilled manual workers and a much higher percentage of commercial and white-collar workers. A higher proportion of semiskilled and skilled men belonged to unions. These facts were reflected in higher earnings: $50 weekly was the average income, while $30 had been the average in the Relief cases.

A typical work history was Mr. Monahan's. He served a 4-year apprenticeship as a plumber and received his union card at 18. He worked at his trade for several years, using his spare time to learn steamfitting. Mrs. Monahan said that "she had considerable savings when she married and thought it wise to invest them in better training for her husband. She did not remember the name of the school, but said there was a 'Captain Somebody-or-other' who gave evening courses in steamfitting. When he was sufficiently skilled, Mr. Monahan joined the Steamfitters' Union at a cost of $300. He used his wife's savings to meet the entrance fee. Several years later he received a license as a stationary engineer. He had steady employment until 1930, working last as maintenance engineer for a large chain of restaurants. During the middle 1920's he earned $100 a week, but in 1929 his salary was reduced to $80."

The standard of living of the Private group had been superior to that of the Relief families. Many had had telephones in their homes and had kept a car. Moreover, they had had more money in the bank and carried larger insurance policies.

Despite these differences, there was also much in common between the two groups. In reviewing her experiences during the 1920's, Mrs. Monahan said "that she and her husband have always had simple tastes and at no time was recreation, for which one paid, important to them. She explained that movies and theater had very little interest for them; that seeing their relatives and having family get-togethers were much more enjoyable. They always saved a good part of their income, chiefly in the form of insurance. It was no hardship for her to live on a budget smaller than her husband's income because she had always been accustomed to manage carefully and was used to doing all her own work. In fact, once the children were of school age, housework was no trouble at all."

A significant difference between the two groups was the fact that more than 50 per cent of the Private women who had been employed prior to their marriage continued to work after marriage.

As regards religion and politics, there is little to distinguish the Private from the Relief group. Once again, Catholics and Jews were observant, while the Protestants had at best tenuous contacts with their church. Most Catholics failed to practice birth control. The Democratic party was again the favorite, although not so overwhelmingly.

Only 10 per cent of the Relief families were judged inadequate. The record of the Private families is even better. There were no pathological cases, neither drunkards, criminals, nor other deviates. But 10 per cent is a small difference!

PART II. THE INTERIM PERIOD

Chapter III

FROM WORK TO RELIEF

DURING the unprecedented expansion of the United States in the late nineteenth and the early twentieth century, a man, if willing to work, had little reason to be unemployed. Hence the public came to look upon the unemployed in much the same light as the hobo, the alcoholic, the criminal.

After the stock market collapse in the fall of 1929, the ranks of the unemployed were swelled, not by thousands but by millions. Even the most hidebound conservative began to realize that there was more to unemployment than the economic or moral failings of an individual. But old attitudes give way slowly. People were willing to admit that the unemployed were the innocent victims of industrial decline, but they suspected that many victims, especially those on Relief, found their new state to their liking. Ordinary folk have to work hard for room and board, while the unemployed got both for the asking. They wouldn't have been normal if they hadn't liked the handout.

The Relief programs of the 1930's were greatly influenced by this widespread conviction that the unemployed were glad to give up the struggle and were quick to accept help. What was the experience of our families between the time that the man lost his job and his first application for Relief?

It is frequently overlooked that even in the depth of a depression, most workers are still employed. Surely three out of every four members of the working population were employed on the day that President Roosevelt was inaugurated for the first time. What precipitated the unemployment of the unlucky 25 per cent? Were they really unlucky or were they incompetent, untrustworthy, or otherwise deficient?

Seventy-five per cent lost their jobs because of "lack of work." In 10 per cent of the cases, illness was the precipitating factor. About 7 per cent lost their jobs because of inefficiency, i.e., drinking. The remainder were the victims of political machinations, racial prejudice, and the like. Since the Department of Welfare, prior to accepting a family for Relief, undertakes a careful investigation of the circumstances influencing a man's loss of employment, the information about job severance is highly reliable.

Many men lost out gradually. Mr. O'Brien, a construction worker earning about $50 weekly, saw his employer go out of business in 1928. He then found work as a porter in a cordial shop at one-third his former wage. He lost this position in 1931. Construction workers like Mr. O'Brien were among the first to know of the depression. Mr. Shubow's unemployment was really brought about by a combination of circumstances—the general decline in business and the specific decline in his own trade. He was a skilled workman employed by one of the largest silk firms in the industry. Although this firm was able to meet the initial competition of rayon, it was finally forced out of business. When Mr. Finkelstein found his earnings as a taxi driver falling off, he gladly accepted the offer of a job in his brother-in-law's furniture factory. Finkelstein showed great aptitude, but after two years the factory closed its doors.

Despite the severity of the depression, many business establishments would have pulled through had it not been for the death or retirement of their owners. Mr. Burke tells this story: "After steady employment in the stock department of a large firm for more than 8 years, unemployment came suddenly. The company failed after the death of the owner. Unemployment was a great shock to the family, but they had not anticipated that he would have much difficulty in finding another job. It was some time before they realized that they were definitely in the ranks of the unemployed. He took any kind of work he could find, and for about a year succeeded in making a living by picking up odd jobs. He went around to laundries, moving concerns, and would help load and unload trucks. For one short period he worked as an elevator operator and for another as a chauffeur. However, as the depression deepened, odd jobs became more and more difficult to find."

The white-collar workers had a particularly bad time of it. Mr. Dixon had been salesman and assistant buyer for 15 years for a large New York department store. He related that "he had some uneasy years before he was laid off because people in the department were being dismissed. The buyer was the first to go, then a girl who had been there for 10 years, and finally a floorwalker who had been with the firm for 45 years. When it was Mr. Dixon's turn, he was given two months' salary and a good reference. But he lost the money that he had paid into the retirement fund because the Insurance Company had failed and his employer was not responsible." Mr. Gilbert, a bank clerk, had an even worse experience: "Long before his dismissal, he saw other men being laid off. They were always older men with long service, and gradually he understood that when one reaches 40 and has been with the company 10 years or more, one is certain to be let out. One day, about ten minutes before quitting time, his turn came. He was called into the office and told the news. The manager explained that his work had been excellent, but he could keep him no longer and was forced to dismiss him."

In the company for which Mr. McCarthy worked, employees were let out in accordance with their years of service; the last on the payroll was the first to go. Since Mr. McCarthy had been with the company for only 2 years, he was dismissed early in the depression. Mr. O'Connell was the victim of a change in ownership. After 20 years' service as a bakery driver for the same company, new owners took over. The new group "brought their own men in and kept only the young employees who were willing to take a wage cut. The older men, though willing to take wage cuts, were not retained. No attention was paid to the length of time a man had been on the job."

A man's efficiency had little to do with his continued employment or dismissal. Sometimes the last man on the payroll went first, at other times the oldest employee was the first to be dismissed. A change in ownership frequently resulted in the dismissal of many old employees, and when a business was liquidated, everybody was let out. Fate decided who would continue in employment and who would become unemployed.

Occasionally, dismissals were based on more objective grounds. Several men lost their jobs because of their fondness for the bottle. Breach of the rules, such as the insurance salesman who failed to register a new policy, cost several men their jobs.

Illness claimed its victims. Mr. Brown had worked for a large paper company for 17 years. "For some time before he was actually laid off, he suffered from stomach trouble, diagnosed as ulcers. For 2 months prior to the time he was actually dismissed, he had been out because of his condition. When he came back, he was told that at the moment there was no work for him. It was some time before he realized that the company planned not to take him back." Mr. Higgins "was forced to give up his job with a roofing company because the work was too hard for him. In moving the heavy barrels of tar from the shop to the truck he strained himself and found that he had a bilateral hernia. It was difficult for Mr. Higgins to accept the fact that he could not find an easier job." After 11 years of employment as sorter and marker in a laundry, Mr. Polikoff suddenly became ill and was unable to continue at his work.

Upon losing their jobs, most men set about seeking new ones in the same field in which they had previously been employed. When Mr. O'Donnell lost his job in the construction trade "he went about looking for work but quickly realized that other firms were as bad off as his own firm. He was told repeatedly that people were firing, not hiring, in 1930." Mr. Shubow began to worry even before he lost his job, for he knew that his company contemplated liquidating. "Before he was actually out of a job, he tried a number of other firms but soon discovered that they were all suffering. He realized that his chances for re-employment in his own field were small." Mr. Solomon watched the mechanization of the shoe plant in which he was employed without doing anything about it. When he was finally discharged, he felt sure that there was a place for him in the shoe trade. He canvassed all the shops in Brooklyn, only to find that they were all thoroughly mechanized. He tried without success to get his old employer to let him learn to operate the new machines. Men like Mr. Solomon, who had only one skill, did not limit themselves in their search for employment. When Mr. Solomon realized "that the shoe trade had nothing to offer him, he started going to trucking companies to get work as a helper."

One man, who lost his job as elevator operator in 1932, managed to get along for a while by working in restaurants for $3 a day. Mr. Wallace earned as much as $250 a month as superintendent of a large building. Early in the depression his wages were cut in half, and in 1931 he lost his job. "For a while he was able to make enough at odd jobs to keep the family in food, but there were other pressing needs, odd jobs became more difficult to find, and within a few months they had to ask the Charity Organization Society for help." "Mr. Marshall, landscape gardener and florist, managed to keep going for 18 months after the loss of his job. He found work during the busy seasons. There was scarcely enough money for food and the landlord seldom got his rent."

Men who became unemployed early in the depression were completely at sea. Mr. Boyle said "that he had not anticipated that it would be difficult to get another job, for he had worked steadily for many years." Mr. Hollingsworth was shocked to lose his job but expected to find another within a week or two.

White-collar workers had particular difficulties in finding odd jobs. Several shopkeepers and salesmen scraped together what they could find to start again in their old line. Few men sought retraining. Mr. Reid was an exception: "When his work as a waiter began to drop off, Mr. Reid learned painting in order to fill out the slow seasons." When Mr. Finkelstein realized that his lack of skill made his re-employment uncertain, he sought assistance from his brother-in-law to study welding at a Y.M.C.A. school. Mr. Silver, who came to the attention of the Jewish Social Service Association, also retrained as a welder, his fee being paid by the agency.

Most men, prior to losing their jobs, suffered severe reductions in income, either from a revision of wage rates or from short time or from both. When they finally lost their regular employment they were worse off, for the odd jobs which they picked up paid poorly. As their income declined they reduced their living standards, but frequently they failed to push the reductions to the extreme. The Jaffes said "they did not retract in their standards but used their money to go on living as they had been accustomed to because they believed that Mr. Jaffe would get a job. It did not seem possible that this marvelous salesman whom everybody admired could really go on being unemployed." The Israels used to earn about $50 a week from their grocery business. When things turned bad "they were unable to realize at first that this was the end of a long and prosperous situation. They kept expecting and hoping that something would turn up momentarily which would reestablish them. It was some time, therefore, before they began to readjust to a greatly reduced income and to realize that they were dependent on friends and relatives."

However, some became panicky as soon as the man lost his job, a few even before. These people took care to make their resources stretch as far as possible. The Solomons began to retrench as soon as they recognized the threat of unemployment. "They moved to the Bronx because they could find nothing cheaper in Brooklyn; they wanted to pay less than their customary $35 rental." The Maguires "lived very carefully on their savings as long as they lasted, then cashed their insurance policies, put the money in the bank and drew it out as slowly as possible."

For families intent on retrenchment, the largest saving was in rent, but leases and moving costs made the savings potential rather than immediate. A few families disregarded possible savings in rent because they feared to move into what they considered "bad neighborhoods," not on their own account but because of their children.

Income from odd jobs and reductions in living standards helped prolong the independence of these families, but their savings accounts and insurance policies were more important in delaying their applications for Relief. Savings accounts seldom exceeded $500, and the cash surrender value of the average insurance policy was less than $500. To prove the truth of the old dictum that misfortune strikes more than once when it strikes, several families had accounts in banks which closed their doors. The Kaufmans had as much as $1,500 in a bank that failed. Mrs. Kaufman stated that "they had been particularly concerned when they lost their resources in the bank, which occurred during a very hard period for them, for they were depending heavily on their savings. This seemed to them actually worse than unemployment."

During the years when their menfolk earned good wages, several women bought expensive jewelry. When conditions became strained, these women pawned their jewelry; some went so far as to pawn their wedding rings. It was difficult to part with jewelry, but more serious conflicts arose when insurance policies had to be cashed, especially under pressure of the Department of Welfare. Many families looked upon their small policies as their only anchor. However, in the early days of the depression, they were not accepted for Relief until they had cashed in their policies. Later they were permitted to retain one small policy. Mr. Levin tried hard to avoid coming to Relief. He used up his savings, accepted help from Mrs. Levin's sister, but at no time did he think of cashing his insurance policies "which were the only protection for his family if anything were to happen to him. He expressed a great deal of feeling as he told about his struggles against the insurance adjustment."

Most families borrowed from relatives, and even from friends and tradespeople, in the hope of staving off the evil day when they would have to seek public assistance. Less than 15 per cent of the sample were clear of debts when they first applied for Relief. Fifty per cent of the debtors owed less than $100; 30 per cent owed between $100 and $250; and the remainder had debts in excess of $250. More families were in debt to tradespeople than to relatives or friends. This does not mean that the unemployed ran up large bills at the corner grocery. They fell behind in the payment of their rent and utility bills. Because of the large number of vacancies, landlords would have gained little by dispossessing these families. Moreover, many owners were personally acquainted with their tenants and sympathized with their plight. The utility companies made it a practice to wait several months before discontinuing service for nonpayment of bills.

The Grosses had considerable borrowing capacity: "Mr. Gross borrowed $300 from his sister, $150 from one of his brothers, and two friends lent the family $75 and $50, respectively. When his borrowing power was exhausted and he could no longer maintain his family, Mr. Gross applied to the Emergency Works Bureau for a job." The Mittlemans borrowed $120 from Mrs. Mittleman's father, $150 from her sister, and $55 from Mr. Mittleman's brother. "When they could borrow no more, Mrs. Mittleman pawned her watch and her ring, and only then did they apply for Relief." Some families, realizing that their borrowing power was very limited and that the men had little chance of returning to work in the near future, made application for Relief as soon as their savings were exhausted.

Few families turned to private agencies, such as the Charity Organization Society, the Jewish Social Service Association, or the Society of St. Vincent de Paul, before applying to the government. They were unacquainted with these agencies or else believed themselves ineligible for support. In the early days of the depression, the Catholic Protective Association and the Catholic Charities found odd jobs for the Boyles and the O'Donnells, but as conditions deteriorated private organizations became increasingly hard-pressed. Catholic families in particular were quick to recognize that there was little the church could do because the needs of the people were so much greater than its own resources. Some Catholics were ashamed to make their plight known to their priest, for they had always been supporters of the church and now found themselves in need of support.

A few Protestant families sought and received help from the Charity Organization Society. When Relief became firmly established, their cases were transferred to the public rolls.

Most women were busy running their households and looking after their children when their husbands became unemployed. In a desperate attempt to stave off economic collapse, many women thought about getting a job, but few ventured the attempt and no one succeeded. There was good reason why their plans were stillborn. The decline in employment was not limited to men, but also affected women workers. With little or no skill, with no recent work experience, frequently handicapped by age and health, most women had little chance of competing successfully for the few jobs that were available. However, several aided the economic readjustment of their families by encouraging their husbands to find jobs as superintendents and janitors, and promising to share the work with them. These were not self-maintaining jobs, but they usually covered the rent and a little more. Mrs. Maguire said "that she did not mind doing the janitor work because her health was good and it took very little time to keep the building in condition." The Hewitts "are superintendents of the building and receive free rent for their services, but do not receive a salary. Utilities must be paid for by the family."

Most children were below working age and therefore unable to help. The Coles were one of the few families who "for a number of years prior to their application for Relief were able to manage on the earnings of their children and Mr. Cole's odd jobs."

One would think that after a family had used up all its savings, cashed in all insurance policies, borrowed to the hilt, it would no longer hesitate to apply for Relief. But such was not the case. Mrs. Berman said "that they were pretty desperate, but neither she nor her husband would swallow their pride and go and make application for Relief. When he sprained his ankle, she decided to apply because he could not even look for work with this additional handicap. Both cried as they spoke of this period. They were without food or money, the children were crying from hunger, and they were quarreling with each other about what they should do, but each was too nervous to take action until Mr. Berman was injured. When her application was turned down, Mrs. Berman went home feeling licked and decided that suicide for the entire family was the only answer. They felt as if the end of the world had come and they almost lost their desire to live."

The Mittlemans and the Margolises both said that had it not been for the children, who were innocent victims, they would somehow have struggled along rather than apply for Relief. The Boyles told the same story. They were forced to apply for Home Relief in 1932 "because the children were beginning to show the result of inadequate food and clothing, and the family was frequently dispossessed because of its inability to pay rent."

The Epsteins also had a bad time. "As they saw the period drawing nearer when they would have to accept Relief, they became panicky. They were more upset by their son Harry's reaction than by their own feeling of shame. They had been afraid that Harry would lose his mind. He had offered to go without food and, if he found a small job, to walk to work and go without luncheons. He sat staring into space, moving his lips, and they realized that he was trying to figure things out for himself."

In extreme instances, the family went hungry for several days before approaching the Department of Welfare. Several women fainted on their way to the Relief office. Occasionally, the plight of a family was called to the attention of the Relief authorities by neighbors or the policeman on the beat.

Despite the desperate efforts that most families made to avoid Relief, many were forced to seek assistance shortly after the man lost his job. The following table illustrates the waiting time between loss of employment and first application for Relief:

	Per Cent
Less than 1 month	20
1-3 months	20
4-6 months	10
7-12 months	20
More than 12 months	30

These calculations are based on the time that elapsed between the man's last job and his first application for Relief. If an estimate had been made of the time spread between the man's loss of his regular employment and his first application, years rather than months would have been the measuring rod. Only one family received public assistance prior to 1931 and only seven were accepted in 1931. The distribution follows:

	Before 1934	*1934-1938*	*1939-1940*
Home Relief	24	29	7
WPA	24	35	1
Total	48	64	8

These figures are self-explanatory. The Great Depression was largely responsible for the unemployment of these families, although many were able to shift for themselves for several years before applying for Relief. Illness of the major wage earner was largely responsible for the unemployment of the families that applied for the first time in 1939 and 1940.

The Private families avoided Relief but they too, with few exceptions, suffered from unemployment and underemployment. During the 1930's half the Private families earned only 50 per cent of their previous maximum. Several high earners who in the good days had a weekly income of between $75 and $100 were forced to get along on $40 or $30, and sometimes even on $20. A few were able to count on nothing more than an occasional day's wages. At the time of our interviews, four men were not in regular employment, and their intermittent earnings were very small. Yet these families avoided Relief. How did they do it?

They were able to tide themselves over short periods of unemployment and underemployment by drawing on savings accounts and insurance policies, and by borrowing from friends and relatives. However, these resources did not suffice for long spells. Working wives and working children played important roles in keeping the families independent.

The role of the wife as supplementary wage earner in prosperity and depression is well illustrated by the Sheehans. "Mr. Sheehan came to this country from Ireland in 1928 and secured work with one of the large oil companies. After a little while, Mr. Sheehan was forced to buy the station which he had previously managed, and his earnings dropped from $30 weekly to $30 monthly. He was finally forced to let the station go. Mrs. Sheehan, however, had been working first as saleslady, later as office manager of a large export and import company. She has been regularly employed by this concern for 10 years, except for a 2-year period which she took off when her child was born."

Mr. Bates held a responsible position in a Carolina bank from the end of World War I until the depth of the depression in 1932. Although he had earned as much as $6,000, his salary had been considerably reduced prior to his dismissal. When he lost his job he came to New York "because the prospect of getting into something in a large city seemed better than trying to fit oneself into a small town. He found, however, that the New York banks refused to hire executives of closed banks. They would not even offer them minor posts because they feared that such people would be discontented with the work and salary. By a stroke of good luck, Mr. Bates secured a supervisory post in a large educational institution, a position which he held until a retrenchment program led to his dismissal in 1939. The family was never under great pressure, because Mrs. Bates developed a flair for buying clothes. She became a specialty buyer for thirty out-of-town stores. Although her books during the past year showed a profit of almost $3,000, collections were slow and her net earnings probably were nearer $1,500."

Mr. Steele was earning $85 weekly as a construction worker

in the middle 1920's when a girder fell on his foot and he was hospitalized for a long spell. He fell in love with his nurse and married her. For several years he supported himself in radio repair work, sometimes earning as much as $75 weekly, and seldom less than $40. Conditions took a turn for the worse in 1935, and by 1938 he was no longer able to make a living. However, the family has managed quite well since Mrs. Steele, even after her marriage, continued to work. The Steeles have no children.

The Private women, because of their superior training and lighter household duties, were able to hold down relatively good positions, but the independence of their families is found largely in the continued employment of the men. Many men lost their jobs but they had luck and found others. Relatives and friends were frequently helpful.

Mr. Kalish left his post as a bank teller when he saw his dismissal looming and joined his father in the real estate business. After losing his job with one of the large milk companies, Mr. Herman lost his savings in the optical business. With the small amount that he could salvage from this venture he set himself up in the cake business. "This work was suggested to him by Mrs. Herman's brothers who were in the restaurant business and were able to help him get started by giving him their cake orders. The Hermans were able to live modestly on these profits, and when they secured additional customers, through the help of their relatives and their own initiative, they could count on drawing $40 weekly from the business." Mr. Salzman worked himself up from a runner to a department manager in a large brokerage firm, but when his salary was substantially reduced he realized that his dismissal was approaching. He tried to get into the insurance business but found that he needed fifty signatures and felt discouraged by the work involved in securing them. Through Mrs. Salzman's brother-in-law he secured a job with a large brush company, and, after a two weeks' training course, was assigned a route. Mrs. Salzman states that "her husband is making out much better than on Wall Street. Moreover, the work has made a new person of him. He was formerly a very quiet unassuming person but now is an excellent salesman who is able to converse with anybody. Although his work is very hard—he leaves the house at eight and frequently doesn't get home until nine in the evening—he likes it and is very successful."

Mr. Quinn was helped by friends. Although he had worked himself up from fireman to marine engineer, he disliked the sea. "Through friends he was able to get up-to-date experience as a stationary engineer and obtained his license." Mr. Donnelly fell out of work in 1930. "Through his friends in the Longshoremen's and Checkers' Union, he secured a job with a coastwise steamship company and has been employed there ever since."

Mr. Haggerty had been apprenticed in the printing trade, but when business became slow in the middle 1930's he was dismissed just as he was ready to join the union. "It was a practice in printing establishments to discharge men just before the end of their apprenticeship, and thereby avoid raising their wages. The union was party to this scheme. When Mr. Haggerty was let out, he found a job through friends in an electrical manufacturing plant. Once at work, his friends taught him the more difficult phases of the work, and he was soon able to get a better position at higher wages."

Clearly, relatives and friends contributed materially to the continued economic independence of the Private families by helping the men who lost jobs to find new ones. But it must also be remembered that these men were more skilled than the Relief group.

PART III. RELIEF

Chapter IV

HOME RELIEF

THE unemployed were able to adjust to the loss of their jobs, the exhaustion of their savings accounts, even to the cashing-in of their insurance policies, but they broke down on the day they asked for Relief. That was the dividing line. Yet, many families were better off after being accepted on Relief than they had been during the preceding weeks. At least they could be sure of a roof over their heads and something to eat, which had not always been the case when they were struggling alone. Why did they struggle so hard and delay so long in making application? Was it solely a question of their tenacious belief in an outmoded doctrine which held that every person was responsible for his own economic well-being and that public Relief was a disgrace?

Not entirely. These people knew from the experience of relatives and friends that Relief was not solely a matter of asking. Once a person applied, his past, present, and even his future were subject to the scrutiny and control of officials in the Department of Welfare. Being subject to such control was not easy to contemplate and things were not made any easier when they had to fill out detailed blanks, go to the office for lengthy interviews, and permit investigators to enter their home. After all, they had always been self-supporting and, though their incomes had never been large, they had been masters of their own fate. They decided where to live, what to eat, what clothes to buy. Now others would make these decisions for them.

They became still more uneasy when, on making application, they were forced to answer many intimate questions which they had never discussed with relatives, and certainly not with strangers. However, most persons realized that the public authorities could not hand out money until they were in possession of these facts. Upsetting as was the procedure, most clients felt that the inquiries were justified. This particular procedure was reasonable, but many others were not.

Basic to the administration of Home Relief was the home visit by the Department of Welfare investigator. Each family was to be visited once a month, and the typical investigator had a case-load of approximately 60 families. His was difficult work: visiting, dictating, consulting.

The home visit was predicated on the theory that periodic checks had to be made on the living standards of the family and the man's efforts to secure employment. The investigator did not announce his visit ahead of time. If he found the woman wearing a new dress, or if he noticed some new furniture, he might submit the family to a grueling cross-examination. Of course, not all investigators were alike. Mrs. Solomon said that she understood there was a time when investigators "used to snoop into pots and pans and look in iceboxes to check up on clients." But her investigators have been pleasant people who do not make her feel any worse than necessary under the circumstances.

Mr. Higgins had been less fortunate. "His investigator is a detective whose attitude is always suspicious and faultfinding. If he is out when the investigator calls, on the next visit the investigator will ask where he was. If he says he was visiting, the investigator wants to know the name and address of the person visited and 'everything you say goes down in the book.' " Mrs. Wolf also had had unfortunate experiences with her investigators. Once, after a long, hard winter, during which she had to nurse a sick son, her brother-in-law had sent in a cleaning woman who worked for a dollar a day. "While this woman was cleaning the windows, the investigator came in. The first thing she said was that she saw Mrs. Wolf was able to afford household help. This made Mrs. Wolf feel so guilty and uncomfortable that she was unable to explain the situation adequately.

She felt miserably guilty, flushed, began to stammer, and in her anxiety to explain the situation had said more than she wanted to in some respects, and not enough in others. She dreaded telling the investigator that she would no longer receive money from Mr. Wolf's brother because such a statement would lead to more investigation, more suspicion, more discomfort. It is the investigators' attitude, their constant air of suspicion that makes one feel guilty."

Many men resented the fact that the investigators failed to announce their visits. The men had to stay close to home, for if they were out when the investigator called, they would be suspected of working. If the investigator missed them on two or three consecutive visits their Relief could be automatically suspended. Yet the men had to follow up job leads or attend clinic. And some preferred to watch the corner baseball game to sitting at home.

Mrs. O'Connor was particularly resentful of the many questions asked by investigators. "She said that this country is becoming Communistic. Because they give you money they think they own you—like in Russia." That some investigators overreached themselves is borne out by the experience of Mr. Gross who related that "their first investigator had asked his wife why she had married him. Had he been at home at that time he would have thrown the investigator out of the house. He was incensed by the incident and has never forgotten it." Despite orders to the contrary, several investigators took it upon themselves to reprimand Catholic women for becoming pregnant while on Relief. Such criticism always aroused the deepest hostility.

"Mrs. Robinson expressed a great deal of discouragement over the attitude of Home Relief workers. Her worker had tried to make things more difficult for them. She was very spiteful and threatened them so much that it seemed as if she got pleasure out of making them uncomfortable. The worker often came into the building calling out 'Relief' so loudly that every person could hear her. Once, when the family was not at home, she left a note with a neighbor. This made things more difficult since the neighbor had not known that they were on Relief."

Clients did not blame investigators for conditions outside their control. Mrs. Jones stated that "she objects not to the fact that the budget is low, since she knows that the investigator has no jurisdiction over that, but to his attitude. He is a distrustful person who assumes that everybody is trying to take advantage of him and he thinks it is his job to be hard and strict so that everybody will be afraid of him."

Several people sought to excuse investigators who made them suffer. Some thought that the investigators were themselves strictly supervised. Others suspected that the worker's promotion depended on tight budgeting. In Mr. Levin's words, "The girl wanted to impress her superiors and make a name for herself and was therefore particularly hard on him and others."

Certain clients had other grounds for complaint: Mr. Mittleman did not see how young investigators "could possibly understand the problem of adults. He stated that his last worker was probably no more than twenty-one." Older women who had been running their households for years without benefit of advice or supervision from others were particularly sensitive about young women workers.

Harsh investigators had their counterpart in others who tried their level best to minimize the unpleasant aspects of Relief. The Epsteins feel "that they have been well-treated, that the workers have been very kind in not embarrassing them by interrogating the neighbors or the landlord and they appreciate this very much." Even Mr. McCarthy, who knows that certain investigators play favorites and have little sympathy with their clients, "believes that investigators do the best they can." The Cavanaughs were particularly fortunate in regard to their worker. They were very much ashamed of applying for Relief and for several months even kept the fact from Mrs. Cavanaugh's mother. "It was through the Home Relief worker that they gradually began to feel better about it. She convinced them that there was nothing to be ashamed of; that the depression was not their fault. They felt better about Home Relief after the worker talked it over with them. They found workers helpful and did not mind the investigation too much."

Less than 25 per cent of the Home Relief families objected to their investigator, and only slightly more than 25 per cent complained about Relief investigators in general. However, more than 50 per cent had serious objections to particular administrative procedures.

Many clients failed to appreciate the administrative necessity for cross-examining former employers and relatives when such steps could actually handicap a man's chances for re-employment. Objection also was voiced to the exact verification of minors' earnings. Mrs. Leventhal was sufficiently wrought up about this to burst out with the statement "Hitler kills the Jews in Europe and you kill them here." Her son, Joseph, had the good luck to be apprenticed as an auto mechanic and to earn $5 weekly during his training period. The investigator did not believe that he received so little and insisted upon learning the name of his employer. Joseph, fearing dismissal, refused to co-operate, but the worker discovered it nonetheless. When she asked to see the books, the employer, fearing prosecution for violation of the wages and hours law, took the simple step of dismissing Joseph.

When the Israels applied for Relief, their daughter was earning $12 a week as a stenographer. "The family requested that no contact be made with her employer. They feared her humiliation even more than her possible loss of the job." Her father volunteered to bring her pay check to the office but the department insisted upon a statement from her employer.

Many families complained about the rules and regulations governing the definition of a "household." Under the Public Welfare Law, "a husband, wife, parent, grandparent, or child of a person in need of public relief is responsible for the support of such person provided the relative is financially able to support or contribute towards support." In a desperate effort to stay off Relief, families had "doubled up" with relatives not legally responsible for them. The Kleins could not understand why a new investigator removed them from the Relief rolls when she discovered that Mr. Klein's sister and her newly-wed husband were both working. Mr. Klein felt "that his brother-in-law was under no obligation whatever to support him or his family and the only logical step was for his sister to move out."

The Polikoffs had an even worse experience. Mrs. Polikoff, an arrested T.B. case, was under orders of her physician to lighten her household duties. To help her out, her sister, who had four children, took a large apartment suitable for both families. Because the sister's husband earned $40 weekly, Relief was denied the Polikoffs until they moved out and established their own home.

When the Flynns first applied for Relief they were living with Mrs. Flynn's sister. Their application was denied because the Department of Welfare insisted upon including the nephew's earnings in the budget. Mr. Flynn protested "that his wife's nephew could not be expected to support the Flynn family. The investigator, refusing to deviate from the policy of the Emergency Relief Bureau, noted that 'man is disgusted at this policy.' Shortly thereafter, the Flynns moved out and were accepted for Relief."

The families on Relief had many complaints but they realized that it was not easy to administer properly a system of public assistance. It was difficult to recruit good investigators. Moreover, it was not easy to establish rules governing eligibility for Relief. Administration aside, the allowances were good cause for complaint.

During the years when the men were regularly employed, their monthly income averaged $140. On Relief, a typical budget for a family of two adults and two children was $27.50 semimonthly. This figure might vary a few dollars in either direction, depending largely on the rental. A large family, with six or seven children, would receive about $42 or $44 semimonthly. Two-thirds of the families on Home Relief considered their allowances inadequate. Large families found it a little easier to manage. In cases where the women were strong enough to do their own washing and walk substantial distances to shop more cheaply, the pressure was somewhat reduced.

Even large families had their difficulties. "Mrs. Jaffe finds it very difficult to feed her husband and three adolescent sons adequately. Their total budget is $36.10 semimonthly, which includes a special diet for Mr. Jaffe, Murray and Robert. Their rental is $34 and, since their rent allowance is only $27.50, the deficit of $6.50 must be filled from the food allowance. Mrs. Jaffe, because of severe pains in the back and pelvis, cannot bend and must therefore send out part of her laundry. The family seldom eats meat because it is too expensive. The children need carfare for school and Mr. Jaffe needs it to look for work. The children are not deprived of the movies because Mrs. Jaffe feels that they are deprived of enough as it is. She thinks that the entire family is slowly starving to death under present conditions but she feels that they must continue to live in a decent neighborhood for the sake of the children."

About 25 per cent of the Home Relief families complained specifically about high rentals and 35 per cent complained about food stringency. The two are interrelated. Small families found it almost impossible to secure adequate living quarters without taking money from their food budget to cover their rent deficit.

The Catholic group, living in a low rent area, alone escaped this dilemma. However, they were not well off. Not one Catholic family lived in "good" quarters; some had "adequate" housing, but many lived in "poor" surroundings. The buildings were in a run-down condition; the lighting and ventilation were poor; the families suffered from overcrowding. A few families had to get along without central heating or without a toilet in their apartment. The standard of housing was noticeably higher among the Jewish and Protestant groups, but they, too, knew substandard conditions. Crowding was the most common complaint.

The Department of Welfare had no interest in the debts which the families had accumulated prior to their acceptance on Relief, but it sought to prevent them from accumulating new debts. Families were under pressure to pay their rent and utilities as promptly as possible. Hence, they were frequently short of cash. Many women were forced to buy food on credit.

Mrs. Wolf says that "when she has cash she goes to Bathgate Avenue and shops inexpensively, but when she has little ready money she has to go to neighborhood stores where the prices are higher, but where she can get credit." Several families never catch up with themselves. "The Eisners, who have three adolescent children, find it almost impossible to manage on the $34.80 which they receive semimonthly. Their rent is $30, but their rent allowance is only $28. They pay half of their rent out of each check. During the latter part of each semimonthly period they buy food on credit and they then pay what they owe when their next check arrives. Thirty-five cents a week goes for insurance policies. These have no cash value, but they provide for a decent burial. The children insist on going to the movies at least once a week, which means an additional 30 cents." The Maddens, who have four children, are in the same predicament. "They buy on credit because they are not able to catch up with their expenses. It is more expensive this way, but it is the only way they can manage."

Few people complained of actually going hungry. However, there is more to the food problem. There can be little doubt that the food budget was insufficient for a balanced diet. "Mrs. Cavanaugh budgeted as carefully as possible but they were always having difficulty in purchasing sufficient food. As a result, she and the children were frequently ill." Mr. Madden "laughed when he told of the doctor at the hospital advising him to eat plenty of nourishing foods—steaks, eggs, etc." Mrs. Perlstein, who has only one child, allows herself 80 cents a day for food. "With this small food allowance, she purchases mostly starches because they are cheaper. However, she does buy other things for Sandra, for she believes that fresh vegetables, fruits, and milk are necessary for her growth. Mrs. Perlstein plans one good meal a day for her husband."

The children come first—that is the usual pattern in these families. Mr. Davidowitz says that in his family "the baby is considered first. Money is taken out for her milk, and plans are made in terms of her need for tomato and orange juices, occasional meat, and fresh vegetables. Although his wife is an excellent manager, she has real difficulty in covering their needs. Both adults have lost considerable weight." The Morans tell that "at no time have the children suffered because of the financial situation, for they get what they need and then the parents consider themselves." Mrs. Grogan related that "in comparison to what they had been used to, they are barely existing at present. They came from adequately furnished, steam-heated apartments to cold-water flats with a few sticks of furniture. There is a great difference in their food. They have only two meals daily because by rising late they manage better on two good meals than on three poor ones. They depend largely on starchy foods with a little stewing meat and a few fresh fruits and vegetables. They are aware of the difficulties they both face but they feel that the situation is harder on the man because it is his responsibility to provide for the family. They see to it that the children get what they need and they come second. Food money is often spent to keep the children adequately clothed."

"Surplus commodities" have eased the food situation. Through the cooperation of the United States Department of Agriculture and New York City, Home Relief families can secure certain "surplus" foods free of charge. All the Catholic families and most of the Protestant and Jewish families avail themselves of this opportunity. The Epsteins state that "the surplus foods add quite a bit to their food allowance and the fruit that they get this way is the only fresh fruit they have. Other than cabbage and potatoes, they cannot even afford fresh vegetables." The Morans find the surplus commodities helpful "because they are frequently staples which can be kept for a long period." Some families feel that many commodities which are declared "in surplus" have little value. Jews will not use lard and do not know what to do with corn meal.

There were further difficulties: Mr. Higgins said that he seldom goes to the depot because people, fearing that the supply would be exhausted before their turn came, "pushed and shoved more like animals than human beings." The Jacobowitzes, the Bermans, and several other families "do not use the surplus food because they cannot face the danger of being recognized as Relief clients when they call for it." Mrs. Silverman refuses to go to the depot but she gets around it by sending her husband.

A further effort was made in recent years to ease the food problem of families with children of school age. The children were provided with a hot lunch at school. However, certain children refused to eat in school. Mrs. Wolf said that her son Alvin "does not have lunch at school because he knows that only Relief children have lunch there and he does not want to be classed with them. He knows that his family is on Relief, but he prefers not to have others know about it." "Maxine used to have lunch at school but does not any longer because at Passover the Jewish children were asked to sit apart and were given matzoth instead of bread. The Christian children made fun of her. She comes home for her meals now." In several other families the children refused to eat at school because they were fussy about their food and preferred to eat at home.

Surplus commodities and school luncheons did not solve the food problem. Many families suffered not only physically, but socially. The Robinsons relate that they "often saved money in order to entertain their friends. Since their own needs were few, they thought it worth while to go without a few meals in order to have the pleasure of entertaining their friends."

The most frequent complaint, voiced by 50 per cent of the families, related to clothing. Adults and children alike had insufficient attire. "Mr. Jaffe pointed out that not so long ago his son was unable to attend school because of lack of shoes. Not until this happened was the family given an adequate clothing allowance." The Relief record of the Shea family contains the following notation dated November, 1937: "The man said that they have no warm clothing and that the neighbors threatened to report the family to the Society for the Prevention of Cruelty to Children because of the children's lack of clothing." Several months later there is a further notation: "The man pawned his WPA overcoat for liquor."

Handed-down clothing was a real boon. Mrs. Lewis "could

never return to professional dressmaking, but, except for her husband's suits and coats, she was able to keep her family well-dressed with the warm clothing and materials given her by friends."

The Horowitzes stated that "they have some difficulty keeping their children adequately clothed and keeping decent household linens on hand." The Silvers recall that when on Home Relief "it was practically impossible for them to get clothing." The Clarks complain "that there is no allowance in their budget for clothing or household replacements. They are both getting very shabby." Recently the Higginses had a lucky break: "They got a $15 clothing check and did not know what to do with it at first. They usually get a clothing allowance of $3 to $5 (for their family of eight) and almost always buy shoes for the school children because this is the most important item."

During the early 1930's clothing needs were neglected. Fortunately, most clients had reserves, but as their spell of unemployment lengthened, they had need for replacements. Later on, clothing allowances took the form of an allotment in kind or a special cash allowance. However, these did not suffice. It became the practice, therefore, to permit clients who had the good fortune to find odd jobs to apply their earnings against clothing needs. Mrs. Jones hated her investigator because he "had not let them have anything out of the $40, which Mr. Jones had earned during the Christmas season, for clothing or other replacements. She said that she told him so clearly what she thought of him that he has not been back since."

The following descriptions noted at the time when the men were interviewed throw additional light on the clothing problem: "Mr. Clark was decidedly poorly dressed, his trousers did not match his jacket and his coat was of poor quality." Mr. Solomon "ragged-looking, pale man, poorly dressed." Mr. Levin "poorly-dressed, sunken cheeks." Mr. Eisner "short, stocky, rough attire." Mr. Elliott "tall, toothless—has been waiting two years for a set of teeth despite intercession of Medical Center. He is suffering from an intestinal obstruction which is made worse because of his inability to chew his food. More than a year has passed since he first requested eyeglasses. The ones he is using were given him by a friend, but they are no good for close range. His suit, mended in several places, was neat." Only Mr. Cole came for his interview "with a new hat, good shoes, and a well-pressed suit. He stated that he had three suits which had been handed down to him by friends." Poor clothing intensified the impression that these men were "down and out."

Mr. Elliott was not the only person who had difficulty in obtaining dentures or eyeglasses. Mrs. Mittleman waited almost half a year for glasses, and others waited even longer. Men without teeth appear older than they really are and this increases their difficulties in finding a job.

In case of illness, families on Home Relief were entitled to medical attention. Pregnant women received special allowances, and housekeeper service was available for the bedridden.

The tight budget forced most men to withdraw from their unions, lodges, and sometimes even from their churches. Because they did not have a dime for a glass of beer, many men stopped seeing their friends and acquaintances. Not without serious consequences, however, for the isolated man does not hear of job openings.

Short of food and clothing, few people saw fit to complain about the lack of amusements. Most parents had a hard time finding 10 cents which their youngsters needed for the movies. Mr. Higgins related "with considerable pleasure that he had been to a movie last week for the first time in many years, and that he had enjoyed it very much." Several women said that "they had not been to the movies in years and would be too tired to go anyway." The only recreation available to these families was "to pack a lunch, take the children, and walk across the bridge to Randall's Island and spend the day there." Or one could visit Riverside Drive.

The women, bound to the house for the greater part of each day, found escape in the radio. However, fear of a big utility bill forced them to ration the playing. In many families, differences in taste led to friction, for the man wanted to listen to a sports program, the woman to a symphony, and the children to a serial.

On the average, families on Home Relief suffered a decline of 60 per cent in their monthly cash income. Prices were somewhat lower in the middle 1930's than at the peak of 1929, so that the reduction, measured in real goods and services, was somewhat less than 60 per cent; but not much less.

A few families actually improved their condition while on Relief. The authorities forced the Kennedys out of their cellar room into a decent apartment, and the same was true of the Robinsons. Mrs. Kennedy said that she is glad "that her husband is not working because when he has a job she is never sure of the money. Now she has an identification card and the Home Relief checks can be cashed only by herself, not by her husband."

However, there were only a handful of basement dwellers and drunkards. Because of inadequate allowances, most people on Relief, adults and children alike, suffered physically and emotionally. All that can be said for Home Relief is that it kept people alive.

Chapter V

WORK RELIEF

A COMPARISON of WPA with Home Relief must differentiate between "income" and "work." Otherwise, one might ascribe to Work Relief advantages which reflected nothing more than higher income. But such comparisons are complicated by the fact that Work Relief underwent multiple changes during the 1930's.

In the early days of the depression Work Relief payments were made from private, city, and state funds. The men who were employed on these jobs did not consider them "Relief." Mr. Eisner said: "This was definitely not Relief because it was real work and paid $16.50, a sum sufficient for a man to support his family." It was not until the middle 1930's that the Works Progress Administration, operating primarily with federal funds, became responsible for the bulk of the Work Relief program. During its short life, WPA underwent important administrative changes; three have particular bearing on this study. In 1937 Congress prohibited the employment of aliens on WPA. Somewhat later, the "18 months ruling," providing for the dismissal of most employees after eighteen months of consecutive work, was put into effect. Occupational classifications and wage rates also were frequently revised.

Unlike families on Home Relief, whose incomes were determined by need, those on WPA were better or worse off depending on the work assignment of the man. When men on WPA earned less than they would have received on Home Relief, their families were eligible for supplementation from the Department of Welfare. At the time of our interviews in 1940, the basic wage of an unskilled man on WPA was $52.80 monthly; the semiskilled received $60.50; the skilled, $82.80. Most men were worse off in 1940 than previously, because classifications and wage scales had been revised. The extent of this revision is illustrated by the fact that half the group had at one time or another earned in excess of $82.80, and only 10 per cent had ever failed to earn more than $60. At the time of our interviews only 40 per cent had earnings in the $80 bracket, 33 per cent received about $60, and the remainder earned only $52.80.

A skilled mechanic, father of two children, would be definitely better off on WPA than on Home Relief. On WPA he would earn $82.80 monthly, while his cash income on Home Relief would be between $55 and $60. On the other hand, a laborer with five children could not live on his WPA earnings, but would need supplementation from Home Relief. Comparisons should not be limited only to cash incomes, because families on Home Relief received valuable services. The cash value of these services may be difficult to estimate, but they must not be disregarded. One family prolonged its stay on Home Relief because the woman had been promised dentures; if her husband returned to WPA, she could never afford to buy them.

However, all advantages were not with the Home Relief client. Once a family was certified for WPA and the man placed on the rolls, the Department of Welfare faded out of the picture until the next certification examination. If a family preferred to live in substandard housing in order to have more income available for food, clothing, or recreation, no one interfered. More important, it could keep for its own use whatever supplemental income was earned by any member. Mr. Israel, assigned as a laborer on WPA at $52.80 a month, "found the work extremely fatiguing since he had never done heavy labor, but he is much more content to do it than to accept Home Relief and have his daughter's income budgeted so closely that she gets practically no benefit from it."

Several WPA families increased their real incomes by finding jobs as superintendents. Usually they received no money for their work, but their apartment was rent-free. With no rent to pay, a man who earned as little as $52.80 could frequently make ends meet. About 10 per cent of the WPA group held jobs as janitors. In another 10 per cent of the families, the women had part-time employment as domestic workers. Since most men worked only three weeks out of every four, they had a chance to pick up an occasional job. Mrs. Casey emphasized that "she doesn't like the Home Relief situation with the investigator always snooping around and asking questions. On WPA there was no one to question you; and if you could get a part-time job on the side, that was all right."

A true comparison between Home Relief and WPA would consider not only income but also expenditures. Men on Work Relief had to allow almost $2 monthly for carfare and in extreme cases almost 40 cents daily. "A man doing hard laboring must eat more than a man doing nothing." Men working in sewers wore out their clothing more quickly than men sitting in rocking chairs. When allowance is made for expenses incidental to working, one can appreciate Mrs. Wharton's comment that "management is almost as difficult as it was on Home Relief, since her husband's income is only $52.80 and his carfare amounts to 20 cents a day. In addition, he buys his lunches. The rent is still $30, which leaves very little for clothing and food. On his previous assignment he earned $71.50 a month, and on that amount they were able to manage comfortably."

Many families complained about the difficulties they were up against because of fluctuations in their income, brought about through reclassifications or loss of work because of inclement weather. Mrs. McManus said that "there was no possibility of definite planning or budgeting because of frequent reratings and losses in income due to bad weather. They never knew how much they had to spend. Their average income was perhaps $56 monthly, which was little better than the $50 they had received on Home Relief when one considered carfare and daily lunches."

During the winter, men on construction and laboring jobs lost many days' work because of bad weather. Although the administration tried its best to permit the men to make up lost time, this was not always possible. Mr. Elliott decided that with things as they were he could not afford to accept a WPA job.

"When assigned to an outside project, too many days may be lost because of bad weather. On his last assignment, Mr. Elliott had to spend 50 cents daily to get to and from work. The hour's pay which men receive for reporting on days when they cannot work does not even cover carfare. Since earnings are so irregular, one cannot plan or budget with any degree of success."

Frequent reclassifications, usually resulting in reduced income, also made budgeting difficult. Moreover, the "18 months ruling" created additional problems. Many families were hard-pressed to find something to use for money in the period between dismissal from WPA and acceptance on Home Relief. Mr. McCormack used to receive $70 on WPA, then $60, and currently $56. "He does not look for work in private industry at this time because he is afraid to make a change. It takes so long to get back on Home Relief. It would take about a month, and they are unable to save anything at all on Mr. McCormack's WPA earnings." Many families told about the difficulties they had in getting back on Home Relief after dismissal from WPA or private industry.

About 50 per cent of the WPA families complained specifically about low earnings. In the Home Relief sample, 66 per cent stated that their allowances were inadequate. Interestingly enough, the WPA group complained about the same shortages: Their greatest need was clothing, next food, then rent.

The relative advantages of Home Relief and WPA were not solely a question of differentials in income. For instance, most Home Relief families were critical of WPA not because they opposed Work Relief, but because they objected to how it operated. In particular, they complained about faulty assignments of men to jobs. These criticisms were not spun out of thin air, since 50 per cent of the Home Relief group had had a spell on work relief. Moreover, the attitudes of the WPA group to Home Relief were also grounded in personal experience, since every WPA family had spent at least one month on Home Relief and many had spent a much longer period.

The best-informed group, those currently on WPA, were friendly to Work Relief. Only 25 per cent disapproved. Paralleling their favorable attitude toward Work Relief was their negative feeling toward Home Relief. Only 15 per cent had anything good to say about Home Relief, and this group was primarily impressed with the opportunity of Home Relief clients to hunt for a job in private industry. Mr. O'Keefe told this story: "His wife does not want him on WPA. She prefers him to remain on Home Relief until he gets a private job. He said that while the WPA allowance is O.K., there is much more opportunity to look for work while on Home Relief."

The Home Relief group felt antagonistic to WPA. Mrs. Jacobowitz recalled her husband's assignment as a nightmare. "It was a shame to expect a white-collar person of 50 to dig sewers. She moved 'heaven and earth,' kept getting letters from doctors until he was permitted to resign. His continuing on WPA would have meant that he would have lost his only chance to make a comeback. He was so stunned by it that he lost hope. But she forced the issue." Similarly, Mrs. Jaffe said that white-collar workers are poor laborers because they "are ashamed and miserable. The man so assigned feels buried emotionally, and his health is usually not equal to it anyway." Interestingly, Mr. Eisner, who had worked for several decades as a truck helper, took the same point of view. He stated that "WPA is no good. He believes that pick and shovel work is not acceptable to most men, especially to most Jewish men." Mr. Gallagher, who had worked as a file clerk for many years, was even more belligerent. "He stated he was willing to do clerical work but not laboring. 'Not me—just let them try.' "

However, men assigned to clerical work were frequently dissatisfied. Mr. Berman "told how he and a number of others had been put to filing slips of paper, had put them away with no effort to sort them alphabetically, and had no interest in the number they sorted. He was highly indignant that a man of his caliber was asked to do what any high school boy could have done adequately and that he was paid a salary adequate for a boy but certainly not for the head of a family."

Sometimes the men felt that they had been properly assigned but the project made little sense. Mr. Weiss, a former bookkeeper, had the good luck to get a clerical assignment on WPA but "realized that the project was 'made work.' " Mr. Levin was unhappy for the same reason. "On his first Work Relief job with the Emergency Works Bureau, he was satisfied and happy. He worked and was proud of what he did. WPA in his opinion is not work—it is just 'made work.' Formerly, when one made something, it was finished and you felt a sense of accomplishment, but on his first job on WPA they built something, then someone else came along and tore it down and did it over again. It had no purpose and no importance. It definitely made him feel that he was getting charity. This feeling of receiving charity is a 'bitter pill and makes one feel as if he were dead.' " Mr. Higgins thought that WPA was noticeably better than Home Relief, especially when New York City gets something for its money in the way of a public improvement. He believed, however, that "the work should be something the men know how to do and want to do; otherwise they are discontented, the work is poor, and nobody benefits from it." Mrs. Higgins chimed in to say that she has known "men accustomed to working in a trade who became very bad-tempered when they were on WPA and took out their discontent on their families." Both Mr. and Mrs. Higgins felt that WPA should make more of an effort to fit the man to the job.

Good assignment was more than the establishment of useful projects and the utilization of men's specialized skills. Health played a role. Of the 30 men on Home Relief who had had one or more spells on WPA, 15 had been taken off for reasons of health. This helps explain why so large a percentage of the Home Relief group was opposed to WPA. In several cases illness had been the ostensible rather than the real reason for dismissal, but there was evidence to prove that many men were physically incapable of fulfilling their assignments. Mr. Moran had first been put to work as a marble polisher, his regular trade, but later had been reassigned to a laboring job. "He was a willing laborer, although frail and undersized. After a spell in the ditches during February, he took severely ill with rheumatism and other complications, and was finally forced to leave WPA on orders of his physician."

Mr. O'Keefe "was unable to do anything but rest when he came home from work. In his undernourished condition, his assignment to park work was too strenuous." According to his wife, Mr. Brill "is too old and too sick to work in sewers, where he is currently assigned." He is 50 years old, suffers from rheumatism, and prior to coming to WPA had supported himself in business. Several other men complained that their jobs on WPA were too strenuous. They were willing to work, but not as laborers, since they feared injuring their health. This was true of 10 per cent of the WPA group. Another 15 per cent had definite physical disabilities, such as hypertension, arthritis, hernia, but this group did not complain because their assignments were scaled to their capacities. The men on Home Relief were in poorer health. Not more than 33 per cent were fit for laboring jobs on WPA.

Certain Home Relief clients had great difficulty in convincing their investigators that they were really unfit for work on WPA. Mr. Horowitz felt very bitter about the treatment he received. In the face of supporting letters from his physician to the effect that he should remain on Home Relief, his investigator suspected him of malingering. "Instead of telling him of her suspicions, the investigator had him assigned to laboring work on WPA so that he would have to go to the WPA doctor to prove that he couldn't work."

Congress may have had good reason for prohibiting the employment of aliens on WPA and for severing all workers from the rolls after 18 months' continuous employment. Many Relief clients disapproved. Mr. Mitchell criticized "the government plan of permitting noncitizens to remain on Home Relief and making citizens work on the WPA program. Not that most people mind working, in fact they want to be working, but he fears this will create laziness among the noncitizens."

Mr. Weiss believes that the "18 months ruling" was established "to make them more uncomfortable. The only result was to force them to go through another period of investigation before reinstating them." Mrs. O'Donnell considered WPA better in every way than Home Relief but objected to the job insecurity on WPA. "Dismissal frequently has no relation to ability, need, or any other factor except the finances of the government, and it makes the men feel that, no matter how good they are, they can be dropped at a moment's notice or even without a moment's notice." If the project on which they were working was completed or discontinued, men could be dropped before the end of their eighteen months.

Mr. McCabe found a serious shortcoming in WPA because of "its lack of incentive for advancement and lack of reward for extra or harder work." Of course, men could improve their position on WPA, but usually advancement depended on "knowing the right person." The Wilsons felt "that WPA was an excellent idea. There were abuses which they realized were certain to arise in so unwieldy a structure as WPA. A person who knew the right people on WPA had a better chance for rerating, reclassification or getting a good position than one without connections. Apart from this, they felt that WPA was a good and honest organization."

Mr. Elliott said that "he could quote chapter and verse about the importance of 'pull' on WPA. The organization was so unwieldy that there was much opportunity for abuse. He told of an offer by a foreman, who had a friend in the main office, to get him a better assignment if he were willing to pay a certain amount from each check. The friend in the office placed the name of the worker who was ready to pay for the service near the top of the pile, so that when a requisition came in, this particular worker would be chosen. The foreman was the contact man who split the pay with his friend in the office. They did not ask much from each man, but since it was a regular split and many men participated, it was a good racket."

Personalities rather than politics stood in the path of some workers who sought promotion. Mr. Levy related that "he had difficulty in being assigned to a higher category on WPA because the chief inspector at headquarters was a dyspeptic man." Mr. Levy also complained that on one project, he ran into considerable anti-Semitism.

Marked differences in wages for the same work led to trouble. Mr. McManus objected "to working in a sewer for practically a subsistence wage while other men doing the same work, standing right next to him, were civil service employees earning adequate salaries. Since the work had to be done he felt that, if there had been no WPA labor available, more men would have been employed at adequate salaries." Among the other things that Mr. Levy found wrong with WPA was the fact that he received only $20 a week as a surveyor, while the city civil service surveyors earned $40 weekly. As far as he could see, his work was as good as, if not better than, theirs. Mr. McCarthy was so upset about this wage problem that he felt WPA was "definitely not the answer to the unemployment problem. WPA at cutthroat wages is doing enough public work to last 50 years. By making all these improvements at such low wages, the government is hamstringing the contractors with the exception, of course, of 'Farley's boys who get all the fat contracts.' "

Many people found the alien regulations foolish; others felt that the "18 months ruling" was aimed to make them uncomfortable; there was ample evidence to prove that many men were poorly assigned; one could find projects that had little or no social value; occasionally, WPA undermined the health of the men; hard work frequently went unrewarded; WPA was not free of politics. These complaints must not obscure one fact: most men, even those who felt particularly aggrieved by one or another administrative regulation, much preferred WPA to Home Relief.

The Kleins put the matter thus: "Relief means charity. It means that one is taking something for nothing. On WPA you work for what you get. When Mr. Klein was on a mosquito control project, he came home covered with mud and oil, wearing heavy boots and looking like a laborer. At first, Mrs. Klein was ashamed that the neighbors should see him looking like this. But he was happier working and so was she. There were times when his rheumatism bothered him so much that he did not see how he could continue. Despite this, he went on because it meant that he had a job." The Leventhals felt the same. "They both think that WPA is much better than Home Relief since it gives a man a chance to work for the money he receives." Even the Rattners, who had a very hard time managing on WPA, "felt better about being on WPA since Mr. Rattner was at least earning his way."

The great achievement of WPA was to offer work to men who otherwise would have deteriorated from idleness. But WPA did more: in many instances it gave them the right kind of work. "One of the finest things that WPA has done was to permit men not to forget their skills; this was not true of Home Relief." Occasionally, WPA improved on the assignments which men had received in private industry. Mr. Leibowitz spoke with the warmest feelings about what WPA had done for him. He had always wanted to paint, but had been forced to eke out a living clerking until his inner conflict resulted in his having a nervous breakdown. "Mr. Leibowitz speaks most favorably of WPA and what it has contributed, not only to him but to other people on the art projects. It has enabled him to do what he really wants to do. The wages have not been high, but he is very appreciative of the fact that he has been able to express himself. He says that many coworkers have literally blossomed under the kind guidance of WPA and they are most appreciative."

Artists were exceptions; the WPA force was composed of run-of-the-mill workmen. Seventy-five per cent of semiskilled and skilled mechanical and construction trades workers were given the opportunity to use their skills. More striking is the fact that work was found for a photographer in his own line; a lawyer was put to work on briefs; an accountant was given a set of books to supervise.

Difficult to place were men who had earned their living as storekeepers, salesmen, grocery clerks, soda fountain attendants. An exact counterpart to their old job was impossible. WPA did the next best thing. It put them in allied occupations: salesmen became clerks; storekeepers were turned into watchmen. The excess—and it was considerable—had to be assigned to laboring.

A few men, seeking to improve their classification and increase their earnings, attended classes, but this schooling was highly specialized, since instruction was limited primarily to administrative procedures unique to WPA. However, a few men added to their skills by learning from coworkers on the job.

The break with the past was hard on all Relief clients although it was easier for families on WPA. Fifty per cent of the WPA families had a monthly income of $80 or more—in some cases based solely on the man's earnings, occasionally supplemented from other sources. This group had a clear financial advantage over Home Relief families. But most people preferred WPA aside from any monetary gain. The O'Connells consider "WPA a lifesaver. It is the most wonderful thing the government could have done for the people. Of course, there are shirkers on WPA as there are everywhere, but the principle of it is right. Mrs. O'Connell says that she shudders to think what would have happened to her husband if he had had to sit and get the dole. She thinks that he would have been older, sicker, and perhaps dead from worry."

Mrs. Atkinson summed the matter up by saying that Home Relief "is an un-American thing. It is a dole. No real person with a sense of responsibility wants Home Relief, and those who seem to want it and are not ill should be forced on to WPA. She fails to understand how people are satisfied to be told by an investigator what they are to do with their daily lives. She thinks, too, that the effect on the man when he sits around all day and does nothing is particularly devastating." Mrs. O'Connell added that Home Relief not only takes the backbone out of a man but "a woman cannot look up to him any longer. The most terrible thing is to force children to see this happen to their parents." These opinions were based on experience.

Chapter VI

LIVING ON RELIEF

WE LEARN from contrast. We learn from unemployment the true significance of work. Only when a man is thrown out of employment does he perceive how much of his life is under the dictatorship of the job.

Work establishes the basic routine of modern living. Men must get out of bed, whether they like to or not, to get to work at a stipulated hour. This they must do day after day. Even when they work only a 40-hour week, men see relatively little of their wives and children, for they are away from home at least 10 hours daily. This explains why Mr. Israel "always helped his wife with the dishes, not because he liked housework, but he wanted to have her free in the evenings so they could talk or listen to the radio. While she is preparing supper, he will come out and set the table for her, just to be near her so that they can talk."

What is pleasure to the employed man—to be at home with his family—is a burden to the unemployed. With no job to report to, and no place in particular to go, the man who had previously been at home only evenings and weekends was now constantly underfoot. He could not always be looking for work, for among other things carfare and lunches cost money. Nor could he listen to more than a limited number of refusals per week. Every "no" was a stab.

The fact that the men hung around the house led to friction. Mrs. Silverman said: "There is constant bickering and quarreling in the household. Her husband is nervous. He yells at the children and at her and she nags at him because she can't stand this poverty. Maybe it is not his fault that he's unemployed, but it's a man's business to support his family. Sometimes she feels sorry for him, but her children's needs are more important." Mrs. Berkowitz exploded: " 'He hangs around most of the day and drives me crazy.' She cannot stand it when he is at home because they quarrel and it seems to her that usually they do not even know the reason for the quarrel. They are both nervous and pick on each other. She is glad when he goes out and leaves her alone. But he has less and less to do in the repair shop, and therefore finds it more comfortable, especially when it is cold, to sit at home. He does not help her with the housework because she does not want him to. She has always managed her own affairs in the home and prefers to continue to do so."

Mr. Berman, who is forced to stay at home a large part of the time because of his hernia, reacts badly to his confinement. "He cannot listen to the radio during the day because it makes him too aware of the fact that he is not working. It is unnatural for him to have time to listen. Evenings, he enjoys it." The tension in the Wolf household is so great "that Mr. Wolf clears out of the house every morning. He feels that he is going 'nuts.' He just keeps walking around town all day long. Mrs. Wolf described the situation as one in which 'nerves are worn thin.' She yells at him and he yells back, 'Do you think I don't try?' She is sorry after she has yelled at him, but sometimes, when she is sufficiently miserable, she isn't even sorry. Then she feels malicious enough to want to hurt him, for this is the only outlet she has for her pent-up emotions."

One might think men would welcome the opportunity of getting out of the house, if only to visit museums, attend lectures, or read in the library. Such was not the case. Mr. Levin related that he went to libraries "from time to time but has little patience to read the books or papers that he finds there." Some men felt that they were not making the best use of their time, but they doubted whether they could really profit from lectures since "one could not learn from words, one only learned from trouble."

These men were not used to reading for relaxation and they

did not acquire the habit during their unemployment. Some tried to acquire a taste for books but found that their diffuse restlessness and nervousness made it difficult for them to concentrate on anything other than their own plight. Apparently, they could not shake free of their unemployment; cosmic problems—such as wars, revolutions, presidential elections—had little meaning for them.

The loss of a job also deprived a man of friends and acquaintances, who play such a large role in the life of the average citizen. Men travel together; they work together; they play together. Most unemployed men were deprived of companionship.

Depressed by his failure to provide for his family, the unemployed man suffers additional frustration. He cannot spend his energies in work. He is deprived of the pleasure that a farmer has when he sees the wheat which he has sowed blowing in the wind. And the butcher, the baker, and the candlestick maker also experience satisfaction at the end of a day's work. Even the man on the assembly line or the clerk behind a counter feels that he has contributed something useful. The unemployed man goes to sleep with his strength unspent, or worse still, dissipated in frustration. He has seen the clock go round but he has nothing to show for the hours that have passed.

This is not altogether true, for many unemployed, in a desperate effort to do something, lend a hand at home. They take care of the shopping, the heavy cleaning, the laundering, and even act as nursemaid. If his wife is in poor health, the man can be extremely helpful. Mr. Levin said that he "keeps fairly busy helping his wife, who is frequently incapacitated by arthritic pains. He does her shopping, helps her with the washing, and even with the cooking. All in all, this takes considerable time each day." Even Mr. Shea, who drinks and beats his wife when she nags him, helps a little around the house when he feels well enough. He does most of the shopping because Mrs. Shea is unable to climb stairs.

In the McCarthy household, Mrs. McCarthy "goes for surplus commodities and their daughter, Nora, does most of the shopping. Mr. McCarthy is at home most of the time and does all the cooking. Mr. McCarthy stated that he is very proud of his ability to cook and bake, that the men in his family have always been interested in cooking. His father liked to cook and taught his children, just as he is teaching his son. His wife laughed and said that, while it was to her advantage to say that he is a good cook, even if he were not, in order to encourage him to continue, she has to admit that he cooks and bakes a lot better than she."

The Kennedys always work together. "Mr. Kennedy does the washing, cleaning, and anything else that needs doing. 'It's my home as well as my wife's, so why shouldn't I help?' " Mr. Eisner felt differently, however, for he refused to help with the housework and especially with the washing. " 'Washing is women's work' and under no circumstances would he do such a thing."

Sometimes, even men on WPA helped out. Mrs. McCabe said that her husband "does her work for her at night after working all day on the job. Despite her illness, she tries very hard to get some of her work done in order not to put too much pressure on him." In the Wharton family, one finds much the same situation. "The woman is not at all well and is unable to do her housework most of the time, which places a great burden on her husband."

The work which men do around the house helps their morale and also eases their wives' burden. Some women, able to handle their own work, deliberately encouraged their husbands to help them, because they thought the men would be better off for having something to do. But working around the house was not all profit to the unemployed man. By taking on feminine duties he widened the breach between his old life and the new. His failure was underlined by this transgression of sex boundaries. Some men took so easily to their new work that one must suspect that it fulfilled an inner need. The better adjusted the unemployed man became, the more difficulties he had fighting his way back into private employment.

Many women were distressed by their husbands' failure to

provide for the family. They had taken it for granted even prior to marriage that a husband would provide for his wife and children. When a man failed to carry out his obligations, his wife frequently lost her balance.

The most telling evidence is found in the changed attitude of many women toward intercourse. Mrs. Berkowitz said "that she had always hated 'it' but never felt that she could do anything about it. But now, 'thank God,' it was possible for her to sleep apart from her husband." Mrs. Wolf, a much younger woman, was even more outspoken. "She said that she had always been a cold person, little interested in sexual matters. When her husband was working and supporting her, she supposed it was his right to have sexual relations and she therefore acquiesced. Now she avoids it. She has limited sexual relations to once a week, and even tries to get out of this. She has not gone to the birth control clinic because she saw no reason for going through an examination and using contraceptives just to give her husband pleasure."

The excessive demands of Mr. Cohen had long been cause for friction, but Mrs. Cohen said that "as long as he made a living, they went along from day to day. Now it was impossible." In his office interview, Mr. Cohen plaintively remarked "that his wife is now 'wearing the pants' and this makes for disturbance in the family. He said that not even in Italy or Germany, where all sorts of queer things are happening, did the man fail to remain the head of the household. He realized that his wife had reason for complaint, now that he was no longer earning money. She keeps repeating 'F.D.R. is the head of the household since he gives me the money.' "

Even in families free of marital tension, the failure of the man to continue as breadwinner led to a shifting in authority, usually to his wife, occasionally to an older child. Mr. Jacobowitz knows "that his wife has lost all respect for him. She keeps nagging and annoying him for not being able to do better, but makes no helpful suggestions." Mrs. Jacobowitz is aware that when she is very much discouraged she scolds and nags him, but she tries to make up for it afterward. However, she feels sure that "the mother must be the backbone of the family." Conditions have changed in the Jaffe family. "Mr. Jaffe is no longer the man he once was. He was proud, confident, and admired. His wife looked up to him and was happy with him. She did her job in the home, and he out of it. They had many friends. Now they seem to be crawling around in a hole which seems to be closing over them. She is cross, scolds, and nags. She tries to stop, but cannot."

No family on Relief escaped without some heightening in tension, but most men and women tried hard to keep the tension within bounds. The Davidowitzes said "that they know how each suffers, and they do all that is possible to understand and help each other." Mrs. Finkelstein believes that not only "have family ties not suffered during unemployment, but, if anything, they have been strengthened 'since they all recognized that there was a need to work together and make a go of a very difficult situation.' "

When women understood that the men were not personally responsible for the family's plight, but were victims of circumstance, they had little reason to nag and scold. But they did not always understand, at least not at first. Mrs. Finnan remarked that "she had not realized that her husband had been caught in a widespread economic disaster, and at first had believed that he failed to put forth the effort necessary to support the family. She had even gone so far as to leave him temporarily. She quickly realized, however, that she had been very unjust and came back, and spent the remainder of the time trying to encourage him and helping him to keep up his spirits." Few wives went so far as Mrs. Finnan, but many went through the same cycle of accusation and understanding.

Despite the genuine efforts of many wives to support their husbands emotionally, the man's status deteriorated, especially in households with adolescent children. The fact that their fathers were not working, the fact that they were around the house all day, the fact that their mothers had to budget every penny—all these things proved their fathers were failures.

Many men were particularly sensitive about their failure to

provide adequately for their children. Mrs. Atkinson said that her husband is most concerned about his inability to give his young daughter the things she really needs and wants. Her daughter, however, is very understanding and has never alluded to her deprivations. The Brills have a less understanding daughter. She wants things that other girls have and does not understand why she cannot have them. She does not see why her father cannot get a job like other men, and she tells him so. Mr. Brown related "that it makes him feel badly that his children have so little. It hurts him particularly because his daughter lets him know how little she has in comparison with other children." In the Gallagher family, things have reached an even worse impasse. "According to both parents, the older children are unhappy because they want things they cannot have, and refuse to listen to reason when their father tries to explain why they cannot have certain things. They point to other fathers. This leads to much quarreling, for Mr. Gallagher has no patience with them because they are so unreasonable. When they make noise or annoy him, he flies off the handle."

Younger children were frequently unaware of being deprived, and many older children, sympathizing with their father's plight, spared him. Occasionally, as in the Solomon family, the father was able to give the children something other than money. "He has always taken an interest in the children and allowed them to monopolize as much of his time as they wished. Although he has had no schooling in this country, he is able to help them with their homework, and they are particularly proud of his mathematical ability."

Although few children went to the extreme of Mr. O'Brien's daughter, who said "that she does not believe her father is the person to criticize her because he doesn't have a real job himself," they observed that unemployment had deposed their father as head of the household and turned him into just another member of the family.

While the unemployed man was hard-pressed to find something to do for the sixteen hours that he had to wait until he could again escape into sleep, his wife was under pressure for the opposite reason. Although used to hard work, most women found running a household more difficult as they grew older. When family income was cut in half or even one-third, the pressure became great. Yet many continued to keep their homes in good condition. Mrs. O'Connell related "that the landlord tells her that if he paints he will have to raise the rent and this, of course, would be impossible." Although her rooms are small and dark, her home was spotlessly clean and attractive. "While the furniture is obviously old and somewhat shabby, it has been extremely well taken care of. Mrs. O'Connell showed the worker a crocheted bedspread which she now uses as a cover for the dining room table. She said that it was at least thirty-five years old and yet is as good as new. She washes it very carefully, as she does all the other crocheted pieces on the bureaus, tables, chairs."

Despite the many hardships under which they labored, few women gave up the struggle. Only 12 per cent could be called "poor" housekeepers; 20 per cent were "passable"; and almost 70 per cent were "good." The key to this good housekeeping record is found in Mrs. Horowitz's statement. "She had always taken a good deal of pleasure in her home, and now it was almost her only pleasure. Her furnishings were lovely and looked like new, although Mrs. Horowitz said that she had had them for nineteen years."

To keep a home looking nice with no money available for replacements meant extra hours of labor. Many women did all their laundry and spent their few free minutes repairing and otherwise lengthening the life of their aging possessions.

The women were constantly harassed—they walked long distances to save a penny or two on purchases; they washed and ironed everything, even the heavy sheets; they tried to cheer up their husbands; they helped their children to get along on very little. However, they found time to worry. Mrs. Shannahan said "that she worries and worries about her troubles and does not see any way out. She worries a great deal about the children because she wants them to have what they need, but it is very hard to manage. It is extremely important for her to keep her home scrupulously clean and to follow a prescribed routine for her children as to their food and exercise. In her attempt to do all this, she sometimes has trouble keeping her courage up. Although she is not yet 31, she sometimes feels that she has been working for centuries and cannot remember when she last had a rest."

Although most women, especially those who had been on Relief for a considerable time, had a minimum wardrobe, we heard few complaints. Only when they had nothing warm to wear did they call attention to the inadequate clothing allowances. Style was no problem. Apparently these women were so overburdened with household duties that they did not need clothing for social purposes. Except for an occasional movie in the afternoon—and one could slip into the local movie house in a work dress—these women seldom went out.

The most serious strain was their gnawing fear that they would never escape from their present predicament. Many women cried during the interviews. They excused themselves by saying that they were depressed, not only by what they had been through, but what they feared they would still have to go through. Mrs. Ryan is an extreme example. She was so rundown that one of the social agencies sent her to a nursing home to recuperate. "They were very good to her at the home and she tried to do as they told her in order to show her appreciation, but it was almost impossible for her to pull herself together. She said that when other patients would talk about their husbands' jobs, she would feel so sick 'inside' that she almost fainted. She felt sure that if her husband were working and she had enough money to run her home adequately, her health would be all right and she would be a real person again."

The influence of unemployment on the children is of the utmost importance. There were few childless families in the Home Relief and WPA group—9 in all, of which 8 were in the WPA group. However, at the time of the interview, 26 families, or more than 20 per cent, had no child living at home. There was evidence to suggest that in 66 of the 94 families with children living at home unemployment of the father had adversely affected the physical, emotional, or occupational condition of the children. In larger families, sometimes only one child showed ill effects, sometimes all had been harmed.

However, there were only a few cases in which unemployment and its associated stresses appeared to have aggravated a medical condition. The Corcorans believe that they lost their little girl because she contracted pneumonia while they were on Relief. Mrs. Corcoran said "she had been unable to afford medical care and had not known they could get a doctor through Relief. Her children had been sick before, and her investigator had not suggested medical care. For this reason, she failed to realize that it was available." The Brennans feel certain that their daughter suffered an aggravation in her condition because they were on Relief. "After two attacks of scarlet fever within one year, the child developed a serious cardiac condition. The parents know that if they could have given her better care, she would not have become so ill, and this has been one of their bitterest associations with unemployment." Mrs. McCarthy had the misfortune to lose her twins, John and Joseph, from pneumonia. "The mother wept as she talked about the cruelty of Lincoln Hospital which refused to admit John until a few hours before his death. She firmly believes that had they not been on Home Relief and had they been able to afford a private physician, John would be alive today."

Even if the Corcorans, Brennans, and McCarthys were correct in their appraisal, the fact remains that in only 5 of the 66 families did children suffer a marked physical deterioration because of the Relief status of their parents.

One reservation is in order. This low percentage relates only to marked deterioration, not to minor handicaps. For instance, malnutrition was widespread, although in the absence of a physical examination no definite proof can be adduced. The records and interviews are replete, however, with indirect evidence: "Judy was a slight, fragile child; Jean also was a slight child with poor coloring, yet looked stronger than Judy; Frances had better coloring, yet looked small for her age and is undernourished; Catherine seemed small and undernourished; John, the exception, was a sturdy, healthy-looking boy." This is the social worker's impression of the McCann children. In the Gallagher family, James and Daniel were not at home when the social worker called, but she met Catherine, "a tall, thin, pretty child with good coloring, and Leroy, who is a thin child with deep circles under his eyes." Mrs. Gallagher says she does not know why Leroy looks so sickly. She thinks he gets adequate food, although he does not get enough milk and she cannot afford cod-liver oil. The Callahans have two children, John "who is big for his age but seems slow in developing. He is not very strong, has poor coloring, and talks very little." His younger brother, Hughie, is "a thin, bright, very active baby, but his color also seems very poor. His mother has not taken him to the baby clinic for some time, since she is afraid that they will put him on whole milk and she does not see how she will be able to provide it for him." Home Relief provided extra allowances for undernourished children, but not all families knew their rights.

Tooth decay, like malnutrition, took a steady if silent toll. Home Relief provided dental service, but only extraction work. Many youngsters, especially girls, refused to avail themselves of this service, for they saw no reason to mar their looks by needless extractions. One boy, recently returned from a CCC camp, complained about inadequate dental care at the camp. He related that "he had suffered a great deal from toothache but refused to allow his teeth to be removed." No matter how low dentists kept their fees, the unemployed could not afford to pay them, even on the installment plan.

Children probably suffered from other conditions associated in whole or in part with the fact that their families were on Relief. Poverty, however, stood in the way of periodic medical examinations and thereby conspired to keep such conditions from being recognized and treated. Examinations in school helped a little, especially in picking up youngsters with defective eyesight.

If the effects of malnutrition or dental neglect can remain hidden for a score of years, emotional disturbances can escape detection for even longer periods. Great care must be taken, however, not to ascribe to unemployment emotional difficulties predating the family's acceptance on Relief. This is well illustrated by the case of Miriam Cohen, who was nine at the time when the family first came to Relief. According to her mother, "she had been a 'problem child' since birth. In infancy, she had colic, slept poorly, and was a feeding problem. Even now, at the age of nine, she asks her mother to feed her. Her mother answers 'that even if she were to look at her food until she was old and gray, she would not lift a spoon.' Since infancy, Miriam has had nocturnal enuresis. She does very poorly in school and has been tardy almost daily. She is in the slow class, but fails to do satisfactory work. Her I.Q. is normal, hence her failure in school points to emotional difficulties. Miriam verbalizes intense jealousy toward her younger brother, whom she says she hates and with whom she fights whenever they are together. She tells her mother that she knows her mother hates her and prefers her brother. Miriam also expresses self-hatred. She says that she does not know why she is living and that if she is careless and allows a car to run her down, everyone would be satisfied since there is no point in her going on."

Clearly, Miriam was disturbed long before the family came to Relief, but her father's unemployment probably intensified her difficulties. One illustration will suffice. Following Mr. Cohen's unemployment, Mrs. Cohen, seeking to limit intercourse, had Miriam sleep with her and banished Mr. Cohen to a couch in the living room. Frequently, Mr. Cohen is unable to control himself long enough to get Miriam out of her mother's bed, and the parents have intercourse with the child present.

Mrs. Solomon does not believe that her two younger children are affected by the Relief situation, but she knows that Robert "worries about the family and about the future. He is nervous and bites his nails continuously." During the office interview, Robert stuttered badly.

"Because his carfare and necessary shoe repairs used up the money which he might otherwise have had for spending purposes," John Duffy dropped out of high school before completing his course. He did not feel that additional education was sufficient job insurance to warrant the sacrifice. He has been unable to find anything to do and just hangs around all day. Only nineteen, he is already disgusted with life. John does not like the people in the neighborhood and when he can afford it he goes back to University Avenue to visit his friends. But when he sees that they have good clothing and other nice things he gets embarrassed and is cross. He quarrels with his parents all the time.

The Browns have three children, Evelyn, Charles, and Wallace. "Both parents say that Charles is backward. From his appearance, the social worker would judge that he is borderline. He is a quiet child, gives no trouble, and apparently the parents ignore him. Evelyn gets her own way quietly but surely. Her father complained that she has little respect for him. When she is listening to a radio program and he wants to tune in on another station, he cannot do so because she always has her own way. Wallace also manages to get his own way all the time. He gave evidence during the interview of having the upper hand and flaunting his parents' authority. Mrs. Brown said that she did not mean to have Wallace—he was an accident—and she certainly will not have any more children."

If relatively few children deteriorated physically because of the unemployment of their fathers, the opposite was true of their emotional state. In 80 per cent of the families, one or more children showed evidence that their psyches had been damaged. True, the damage frequently predated the family's acceptance on Relief, but Relief usually intensified it.

Most children were too young to be faced with occupational problems or even with educational decisions related to occupational choices. However, several older children showed occupational frustration. Mrs. Gallagher said that her daughter, Alice, "left high school six months before she was to graduate because the family could not afford the carfare and clothing that she needed. The only thing that Alice was fit for was domestic work, but she considered this beneath her. However, to get better jobs, children needed a college degree. Mrs. Gallagher is certain that Alice married very young because she was jobless and feeling unhappy."

Mrs. Horowitz's boy, Daniel, had always been a good student but had never been fond of school, for he was taller than most boys of his age and strangers thought him retarded. "When he became aware of the financial problem the family was up against, he decided to leave school. He completed the sixth term and then found work as an errand boy." The Brills' eldest son dropped out of college at the end of his second year because he was assigned by the National Youth Administration to a laboring job. "He thought it silly for a laborer to be going to college." Robert Solomon was confronted by a real dilemma: "He does exceptionally well in his studies and is now completing the first year of high school. His principal believes that if he continues to do good work, he will obtain free tuition at the College of the City of New York, and therefore advises him against taking the commercial course. He and his mother are both confused because if he takes the commercial course, he will have a better chance of getting a job when he finishes high school; but such a course would spoil his chance of going to college."

The economic pressure under which these Relief families lived was responsible for much waste of personal and communal resources. As was true of most poor children, talents remained undeveloped and skills could not be acquired, for immediate rather than prospective earning power was a prime consideration. These unemployed families were very poor and their children were therefore under extreme pressure. The $5 or $6 a month that a student needed for carfare, lunches, and incidentals presented such a huge sum that many left school prematurely. The $5 bill which the employment agency demanded for a registration fee also was hard to find.

Adolescent children had almost as difficult a time out of

school as in. Finding a job was no easy matter, and deriving any benefit from one was even more difficult. Children living at home could retain only a part of their earnings; the remainder was deducted from the family's Relief allowance. The rough formula was 60-40: 60 per cent was considered available for the family, 40 per cent could be retained by the worker. At first glance, this might appear liberal, but if one makes allowance for carfare, extra cost of meals, additional clothing, expenses for tools and other accessories, a person could frequently be working for nothing.

Many young adults resented what they believed to be the excessive harshness of the partial-earnings formula. Ruth Levin found a Christmas job which paid her $11 a week. Home Relief budgeted $6.50 and the girl was allowed $4.50 for herself. "She resented this very much, constantly scolded and nagged at her mother because she thought a sacrifice was being demanded of her. She felt that other girls were permitted to keep their earnings, and saw no reason why she should contribute to the household budget. Both parents felt that, although Ruth's attitude was affected by their Relief status, it was only one further manifestation of her usual lack of consideration."

Daniel was different. When he found work, he looked forward to paying his parents for room and board, and thus help the family to become independent. "He was very much upset when he found that his earnings were so closely budgeted that there would be almost nothing for himself. His discontent grew, and finally he threatened to move out of the house. His mother, seeking to have the investigator reduce the amount that was budgeted, mentioned Daniel's threat. The investigator pointed out that the family could be removed from Relief, and Daniel sent to jail, if the threat were carried out. This threw Daniel's mother into a panic, for she remembered that Daniel had recently said that it might be better to be in jail, since one could be as free there as on Relief."

The strict budgeting of minors' earnings not only created familial conflicts but also helped keep many young people out of the labor market. The following notation in the Hollingsworth record illustrates this: "Although the investigator has been urging her to look for employment, Bertha, the eighteen-year-old daughter, said that she was not interested in work outside the home. Her earnings would be deducted from the Home Relief allowance, and neither she nor her family would be better off. Her energy could better be spent in her own home, where her mother can use her assistance in taking care of the three youngest children." Ralph Brill is another case in point. He was called into the office for failing to report to the occupational division. "He said that he saw little point in reporting, since his father was already on WPA and he knew that two members of the family could not be employed at one time. He did not go to the New York State Employment Service because he was too discouraged." Later in the record, Mrs. Brill reported that Ralph was making between $10 and $11 a week. Since this covered the deficit supplemented by Home Relief, the case was closed over the protests of Mrs. Brill, who pointed out "that her son needs this money for clothes and expenses."

Some boys, like Charles Adams and Harry Epstein, were willing to turn over all their wages to their parents. Mrs. Adams said that Charles had "recently been placed on an NYA job that paid him $22 monthly, all of which he turned over to her without any question. He occasionally asked for a few cents for cigarettes or a show, but he did not think that he had any more claim to the money than any of the other children." The Epsteins' poverty made it impossible for Harry to go to college. For a while he set his heart on attending the Delehanty Institute with the intention of studying to become a policeman or fireman, but he found even this beyond him. His mother said "that he took the application for Relief harder than any other member of the family. He threatened to kill himself if anyone found out that they were on Relief. His parents did not consider this an idle threat and they were terrified that they could not keep the secret. Harry is a little happier now but still is very restless. He gives every cent that he makes to the family and is constantly asking whether it is enough to get them off Relief."

Home Relief insisted on the 60-40 formula because the administration believed that employed children should contribute an amount equal to the cost of room and board. As long as children lived in their parents' homes they were unable to have the psychological gratification which comes from true independence. The fact that the deductions were compulsory deprived them of any pleasure which they might have had in making voluntary contributions. In the Israel and O'Brien families, both on WPA, the older children were glad to contribute a share of their earnings because they could see how their action helped the other members. Thomas O'Brien gives his younger brothers and sisters "their spending money and, from time to time, buys things for them." James Knight was lucky. Although his family was on Home Relief, the investigator shut his eyes to his earnings. "From his $15 weekly wages, James buys his clothing, takes care of his lunches and carfare, and gives his younger brothers and sisters their spending money."

Children growing up in homes where their fathers were unemployed missed the subtle discipline that work and wages bring. It was shortsighted policy, therefore, to reduce whatever incentives these adolescents might have to find employment in private industry.

When unemployment struck, life became much more difficult for the man, his wife, his children. The fact that tension seldom reached the boiling point should not obscure the finding that almost every member of an unemployed family, young, middle-aged, and old, had increasing difficulties in adjusting to each other.

Unemployment also left its mark on the external relations of these families. In an effort to reduce expenses, many families "doubled up." They usually achieved their primary objective of reducing living expenses, but frequently at high emotional cost. Mrs. Klein had her parents living with her. "The present situation is rapidly becoming unbearable. She hopes for the day when she can again have her own home as had been the case when she was first married. Her mother is not so difficult, but her father, who has had two strokes, causes considerable disturbance. His nose runs because he has no control over it, and he is unaware that it runs. When eating, he makes a sighing, gasping noise which proves very disturbing. The children become upset when they see him at the table. If the children are noisy, their grandfather yells at them. The old folks, simply by sitting around and looking so sad, make Mr. Klein uncomfortable."

Mrs. Jaffe's father was such an irritant that the Jewish Social Service Association agreed to move him out of the home and supplement the Home Relief allowance by $10 or $12 monthly. They thought this a necessary step to safeguard the family. Shortly after he became unemployed, Mr. Silverman moved his entire family back to his mother's home, which she shared with two unmarried sons. Mr. Silverman's brothers were so resentful that there was nothing left for the Silverman family to do but move out again. Occasionally, "doubling up" did not lead to emotional friction but the anticipated gains seldom materialized because of Home Relief's strict regulations which forced a pooling of all available resources.

About 80 per cent of the families incurred debts prior to coming to Relief. Much of their borowing was from relatives and friends. Once on Relief, such borrowings declined but they did not cease completely. The Mittlemans "had always been helped and protected by Mrs. Mittleman's sister. When the Relief investigator visited this sister, she said that 'she cannot continue to help any longer because her husband quarrels with her for giving the Mittlemans money.' " The same thing was true of the Finkelstein family, which had received considerable assistance from Mrs. Finkelstein's brother. "A conflict was started when Mrs. Finkelstein's sister-in-law wanted her husband to help her family rather than his." The Silvermans had some well-to-do relatives, but they refused to help because of an earlier experience with unemployed relatives.

Many relatives were in no position to extend more than a little help. One woman was able to invite her daughter and grandchildren for meals several times weekly. In another case, a priest took care of the extras in his brother's family, such as medicine, toys at Christmas, and the like. Clothes were frequently handed down.

Some families, like the Atkinsons, felt badly about the treatment they received from their relatives. "Mrs. Atkinson has very little to do with her relatives. She says that when people are down and out, strangers are frequently kinder than one's own people. She is glad that she has been able to get along without help from her brothers, and added that she has little desire to see them." Mr. Gilbert was even more morose. "In the situation in which they find themselves, they can expect no help from anyone. Relatives tell you, before you ask, that they are unable to help."

If relatives frequently failed one in time of need, many unemployed seeking to hide their Relief status broke all social ties with friends. Sometimes the breach was not of their own making. Mr. Davidowitz summed up the matter in these terms: "Their friends know their circumstances and fear to visit because they know they will be offered refreshments, which can only come out of the limited budget which the Davidowitzes have at their disposal. Hence, rather than deprive the Davidowitzes of much-needed food, they stay away and deprive them of much-needed company." Mrs. Horowitz said that one of the most difficult problems in management is "to be able to furnish light refreshments when friends call, especially the children's friends." Mrs. Burke, however, did not find refreshments a stumbling block. "They had always had a wide circle of friends and visited back and forth a great deal. Since Mr. Burke lost his job, this was almost their only source of recreation. One could always serve a cup of tea. Usually, friends would bring a cake with them. This did not hurt the family's pride because it was done in friendship."

Unemployment was more than a question of shortages in food, clothing, and amusements. Unemployment transformed the life of the man, changed the position of the woman, and left its imprint on the physical, emotional, and occupational life of the children. But it did even more. Unemployment left its mark on the thinking of people.

Chapter VII

THINKING ON RELIEF

Two of Karl Marx's many prophecies have particular bearing on unemployment. Marx believed that industrial capitalism would be afflicted with recurring and deepening economic crises, each one of which would throw additional workers on the scrap heap of unemployment. Convinced that people would not stand idly by while they were ground down into nothingness, Marx prophesied that these disfranchised workers would organize to hasten the demise of the capitalistic system.

Until 1930, there was in American experience little to confirm, and much to deny, Marx's prophecy of a cumulative growth in the numbers of unemployed. During the early 1930's, however, the scrap heap grew very large. What of the second prophecy? Did the unemployed change their ways of thinking and acting? Were they intent upon destroying capitalism?

In the field of communication much has happened, since Marx first prophesied. In the mid-nineteenth century workers read no daily newspaper; political opinion was molded largely by discussions, with occasional broadsides and pamphlets playing a part.

Every family in our study had a radio. The women listened to plays and serials; the children followed exciting Westerns; the men were interested in the sports news. Many families listened to news broadcasts, and everybody tuned in when the President spoke. But it was the newspaper, not the radio, that supplied the regular political fare.

The unemployed were newspaper readers. Almost 75 per cent read at least one newspaper daily. The others, with few exceptions, read a paper at least several times weekly. These figures really understate the facts, for many read more than one paper daily. Some took a morning and an evening paper; others, two morning papers; occasionally, the combination consisted of a morning paper and a specialty publication such as the *Bronx Home News* or a foreign-language paper.

The most popular newspaper was the *Daily News,* read by two-thirds of the families. The New York *Times* came second, but a poor second. It was purchased by only a third, largely families with adolescent children whose teachers required them to read the *Times*. The *Mirror,* the *Journal-American,* and the New York *Evening Post* each had a small following; the *Bronx Home News* and the Yiddish press were somewhat more popular. Only two men read the Communist press, and one family subscribed to an Irish paper.

The direct influence exerted by newspapers over the political thinking and acting of their readers is not easy to trace, but one fact is worthy of note: the unemployed did not speak in stereotypes; they relied on personal experiences for illustrative materials. Their most pervasive experience was unemployment.

Most Catholic and Jewish families, and some Protestant families, had had close ties with their church. What happened to these ties when unemployment struck? This much is certain: Men and women did not turn to religion for solace and comfort. On the other hand, the believers did not revolt. In general, there was a loosening, if not a severance, of religious bonds. Prior to their unemployment, 75 per cent of the families had been orthodox; 15 per cent, moderate; and the remainder had no religious bonds. Only one was antagonistic. At the time when these families were interviewed, only 40 per cent were orthodox; 33 per cent, moderate; and 17 per cent were without ties. Ten per cent were antagonistic.

Although there was a trend away from the church, many people continued in their strict adherence to dogma and tradition. "Mrs. Maguire is the most thoroughly religious, devout, unquestioning person the social worker has ever met. In her home, she is completely surrounded by religious objects which take much of her attention and thought. Nearly all her pleasures are found in religion. She has a complete altar set up in the hallway. She has embroidered rosaries and crucifixes, and has framed them. She has also cut out religious pictures from newspapers and magazines. Her conversations and activities are all tinged with religion. Her favorite radio programs are the Catholic Hour and the Ave Maria Hour. She apologized for listening to a hymn-singing program which was not Catholic, but added that they were good songs, sung by good souls, and she was certain that they could do no harm. She is a member of the League of Decency and makes sure that the moving pictures she sees are approved by the church. She talked affectionately of the priests and nuns whom she has known, and of the good work they did. Her husband and she attend church regularly and contribute as much as they can to the novenas, missions, and other worthy causes."

Mrs. Maguire was extreme, but Mrs. O'Donnell was typical of devout Catholics. "Her family attends the neighboring Catholic church regularly. Since it has few debts, it makes few demands on its parishioners. Mrs. O'Donnell has a very warm feeling toward the priest, knows many of the members, and is well-versed in the history of the church. She asked the worker if the latter had read about the policeman who had become a priest. She thought this very beautiful. There are two priests in her family in Ireland. If her daughter wants to be a nun, as seems indicated by the child's fondness for playing the part, Mrs. O'Donnell would approve heartily."

Economic adversity had no influence on the Coyles' relation to their church. "The Coyles are devout Catholics and attend mass and confession regularly. Mrs. Coyle believes that a great deal of the difficulty with the world is its lack of faith in God. Mrs. Coyle does not see how anyone can honestly claim that financial matters interfere with his religious obligations. The church does not force one to contribute. Mrs. Coyle gives ten cents when she can, and nothing when she cannot." "The McManuses agreed with Mrs. Coyle that the Catholic religion was not based on the theory of 'pay as you practice' no matter what people may think. They like to put a few pennies in the collection plate, but when they cannot, they do not feel at a loss."

Prior to their acceptance on Relief, every Catholic family on Home Relief and WPA had been orthodox. At the time of the interviews, 31 were still orthodox; 9 had loosened their bonds. The Jewish group shows a much greater shift. Before Relief, 38 out of the 40 Jewish families had been orthodox, but when interviewed only 9 were found in this category. The change in observance centered around the dietary laws.

The Levins continued "to buy kosher meat, but did not keep separate sets of dishes because they could not afford to do so. When the dishes broke, they were unable to afford replacements for two sets." The Mittlemans tell the same story. "Although reared in orthodox homes, they are unable to keep all the dietary laws. They buy only kosher food but are no longer able to afford separate sets of dishes, pots, pans."

The fact that many families continued to purchase kosher meat, which was more expensive, suggested that they continued to observe as many traditions as they could afford. Financial considerations played a role in weaning Mr. Eisner away from strict observance. "He no longer goes to synagogue because it is too expensive, and the children no longer go to Hebrew school, because Mr. Eisner understands that, in the Bronx, one must pay for instruction."

Some families held fast. They felt that religion was of paramount importance in helping them through troubled times. "Without it one might as well be dead."

Before Relief, only 14 of the 40 Protestant families were vitally interested in religion, and unemployment failed to shake this group. Typical were the Joneses, who attend church regularly. "Fred goes to Sunday school and is very much interested in the work there. Mrs. Jones thinks that it is very important to maintain one's faith in God in the face of all the things that happen on earth. Faith in religion is all that keeps her going, and people who have no faith frequently get into trouble in trying to run away from their worries. Not only is faith a source of comfort, but it is definitely a stabilizing influence."

Several Protestant families found their poverty a bar to regular church attendance. In the Brown family, "the children go to Sunday school and Bible class, but it is difficult to find the money which the children want to take to Sunday school. Sometimes they stay home when the parents are unable to give them money for contributions. The church is very poor and needs every penny, but the Browns say they cannot contribute no matter how much they would like to." The Rodgers are faced with the same problem. Mrs. Rodgers said that "her husband and she seldom go to church because they cannot contribute and they are ashamed of this fact. Recently, cards were handed them by the minister and they were asked to indicate how much they would contribute regularly. Since they could not afford more than 5 or 10 cents a week, they felt uncomfortable. When their daughter was confirmed, she too was given a card, which worried her a great deal. She is very religious and would like to attend church regularly."

Poverty can explain many but not all changes in religious observance. In several Jewish families the following opinions were advanced: "The Jewish religion is one of grief—there is no joy in it"; "there's no logic in religion"; "people who profess faith think themselves better than other people, yet are not necessarily good."

Disturbed by the treatment which they received from the Catholic Charities, several men and women questioned their relations with the church. Mrs. Gallagher "expressed considerable resentment against the Catholic Charities for refusing temporary help, even though she had frequently donated to their charities, and all her children had attended parochial school. She stated that now she planned to transfer them to public school." Mrs. McCabe was upset about the fees in parochial schools. "While she intends to send her child to parochial school, she resents the church's attitude. They tell you in church to send your children to parochial school, but if you can't pay all the fees, they say get out and go to public school. She believes that the approach is all wrong and will have to be changed, or else the people will leave the church behind."

Most Catholics realized that strong as the church was it could not care for the many thousands of parishioners in need. A few families secured work through their church affiliations. Moreover, the Society of St. Vincent de Paul assisted some families by paying moving expenses, distributing secondhand furniture, and providing dresses for the confirmation ceremony.

Striking contrasts could be found among the three religions. As far as the Jews were concerned, the synagogue was a place for religious devotion, nothing more. A weekday or Sunday school in which the young were instructed in the Hebrew language and cognate subjects was a frequent adjunct. But the synagogue did not serve as a social center.

In contrast, the Protestant churches offered their members not only religious values but also social companionship. The Knights, the Dixons, and the Gilberts reported that they were close friends of their ministers. Mrs. Dixon "sings in the choir and says she enjoys it very much." The Dixons have always "felt that the church is an important part of their spiritual and social life." Mrs. Gilbert spoke feelingly about the help which her family had received from different church groups. She was especially pleased with the fact that "the members of the church never make one feel that he is a charity case. They are all simple people, and they help each other whenever they can."

But organized religion had its strongest hold on Catholics. The faithful were punctilious about attending religious services. Moreover, through the institution of the confessional they brought the details of their personal lives within the orbit of religious supervision and sanction. Moreover, their children were educated in parochial schools. Compared to Jews or Protestants the Catholic families were much closer to their church. Conflicts over birth control grew out of this close relation.

When men had been earning a wage sufficient to support

their families, birth control presented no problem to orthodox Catholics. Not more than 5 of the 40 Catholic families had used contraceptives. At the time of our interviews, the 35 orthodox families had dwindled to 12; the users of contraceptives had increased from 5 to 18. In 10 families, illness or menopause had led to a cessation in sex relations, but in several families abstinence was practiced not for medical but for religious reasons.

Birth control presented a serious problem to many Catholics. Mrs. McCabe tells this story: "After the birth of her son, she informed the priest during confession that she was practicing birth control and would continue to do so because she could not afford to have any more children and, in addition, her health was poor. The priest, as a condition of granting her absolution, asked her to promise to desist but she refused. She visited an aunt who lived on Long Island, who advised her to go to a church across the street where the priest would not 'bother her' about birth control. The McCabes then looked around for a church nearer home where the priest would be equally liberal. They found one in an Italian neighborhood. Although she confessed to the practice of birth control, the priest granted her absolution. Mrs. McCabe added that he said so little that she is not sure whether he could understand English. It was her impression that if she told him that she had just murdered somebody, he would either misunderstand or not hear what she said. She attends her old church on Sundays, but goes to confession at the Italian church. Mrs. McCabe said that she noticed that in Jackson Heights, Catholic families have only one or two children."

Several other women shopped around for lenient priests. Mrs. McCarthy would not go to a birth control clinic "because she does not think it right for a Catholic to go to such a place, but they use their own methods of contraception. She told the priest in confessional about how she feels on the subject, and he scolded her for holding such an opinion. He tried to make her promise not to use any birth control methods, but she refused. 'It would be like promising God, and it would be a real sin to make such a promise when one knows that one will not keep it.' Mr. McCarthy added that the priest had to say what he did because it is church law; in fact, it is natural law that people should have children. It is much bigger than the priest—it is universal, except times have changed and people must take control of such matters into their own hands. He thinks that if the truth were told, perhaps even the priest would wish that things were different."

Mrs. Maguire took the point of view "that it was part of one's duties towards the church to raise children properly. She thought that large families were for wealthy Catholics." Mrs. Finnan made a distinction in her own mind "between prevention and destruction. She does not approve of the use of devices such as pessaries, condoms, and jellies. She has always relied upon a douche immediately after the act, and has never been censored by a priest or refused absolution upon confessing to its use."

Intense conflicts were not rare. Mrs. Callahan told of a recent argument in the confessional. "Both she and her husband love children and would like to have a large family if they could care for them adequately. But they have come to feel that there are two sins: birth control is one; the other is making children suffer because you cannot provide for them. When she told the priest what she was thinking, he became very angry. She replied that he could not understand the situation until he had experienced it. When she told him that she would not have another child until they were off Relief, he put her out of the confessional. She did not mind, since she knows several Catholic families that practice birth control. Moreover, she thinks that the Lord really meant what he said: 'Even as ye do unto the least of these.' "

Mrs. Burke had been using contraceptives for a long time because she thought "that the size of the family is a subject to be determined in the home, not in the church." She had a hard time caring for her three children and saw no reason to add to her family. At the bidding of a very religious friend, she went to confession before Easter. "She avoided the subject of birth control, but the priest asked her how many children she had and their ages. When she told him, he said that she must be practicing birth control. She admitted that she was, and he then read her the riot act from 'A to Z.' She refused to promise that she would stop practicing birth control, and the priest left without finishing the confession. She said that perhaps she will be damned, but, if she goes to hell, she will go with the knowledge that she has not deliberately produced children whose lives were warped because of deprivation. overburdening, and lack of attention."

Mrs. Higgins pointed out that some people "make a compromise with their religion by going to mass but not to confession. But they are fooling themselves. One cannot get absolution without confession, and if one fails to confess during a twelve-month period, one is excommunicated." The Higginses have a serious problem as far as birth control is concerned since they do not want to add to their six children but they will do nothing against their religion. They know about the church's approval of the rhythm method, but they doubt whether it works. "Mrs. Higgins says that she has a friend who has a rhythm book. This friend had four children in four years, and Mrs. Higgins advised her to take the book back to the priest. The Higginses abstain from sexual relations as much as possible, and will try to control themselves even more in the future because their family is already too large."

Many families had never heard of the rhythm method, and only Mrs. McManus spoke approvingly of it, but even she was guarded in her praise, saying "it has worked up till now." Mrs. Shannahan worries a great deal about the question of birth control. "She is weak and worn and she knows that she should not have any more children, at least for a few years, until her husband is able to support the three that she already has. She does not know what to do about it. The nurse told her to go to the birth control clinic, but she cannot make up her mind. In the meantime, they have been practicing abstinence, but she knows that this cannot go on." Mrs. Madden said that abstinence was no great trial for her: "To tell the truth, I could go all the rest of my life without 'it.' A woman who works hard all day uses up all her energy and has little need for sexual intercourse at night, but a man seems to have more need and capacity for it, especially when he isn't working. Abstinence may be a hardship for her husband, but they cannot go on having children when they can't clothe and feed the ones they already have. It makes her sick to see them going to school looking so shabby and thin."

Only families in which the women were unable to conceive were free of conflict. Mrs. O'Donnell considered interference with conception "murder," but, without an operation, she herself could not conceive. Mrs. Maguire thought that "birth control was dreadfully wrong, but she had been torn so badly during the delivery of her first child that she had never been able to conceive again."

Protestant and Jewish families had no religious scruples about practicing birth control. In the days when the men had been in private employment, only 10 out of 80 families had failed to practice birth control, and at the time of the interviews, the number had shrunk to 3. However, illness, menopause, and frigidity accounted, in 1940, for 34 cases of abstinence. The families which used contraceptives were most concerned with the efficiency of the several devices. Mrs. Mitchell "believes that abortion is 'sinful' since it destroys life, but prevention is good. The Mitchells believe in birth control, and Mr. Mitchell approves of the clinic method (pessary). Mrs. Mitchell is happy about this, since many couples do not agree and this causes marital difficulty." Mrs. Robinson tells this story: "She does not take any precaution but leaves that to Mr. Robinson. Some of her friends have gone to a birth control clinic, but she believes that the devices used often cause cancer. She knows she is a 'baby' and is afraid of being hurt, but still she doesn't want to take any chances on cancer. Mr. Robinson agrees with her. Sometimes she worries, but he tells her that everything will be all right."

Twenty-two Catholic families had children after their initial acceptance on Relief, and 10 families had more than one. Eleven Jewish and 13 Protestant families also had children after their acceptance on Relief. However, no Jewish family and only 5 Protestants had more than one child. In many cases, especially in the Jewish group, conception occurred prior to the man's loss of his job but the child was born when the family was on Relief. Conception was frequently unplanned. Mrs. Jaffe had been ill and for a long time had not realized she was pregnant. The doctor to whom she went said it was too late for an abortion. Mrs. Scott "had the symptoms of change of life, and for the first 8 months of her pregnancy, the diagnosis was tumor. When she realized that she was pregnant, she became hysterical." The Blodgetts tried to avoid having children while on Relief. Mrs. Blodgett had gone to a birth control clinic, where she was given a contraceptive pessary, but her womb was tipped and the mechanism did not work. She became pregnant. Not wishing to rely on this means of contraception, her husband used condoms, but they failed and she again conceived. She has recently talked the matter over with the doctor at the Medical Center, and he promised to fix her up so that she will not become pregnant again."

Of the 13 children in the Adams family, several had been born on Relief. As far as the worker could learn, "Mrs. Adams knew nothing about birth control and had never heard of it." Mrs. Scott, who had a large family, "never used contraceptives because of her belief that they would make a person insane."

Several families with only one child planned an addition while on Relief, because they believed that "only" children would be spoiled. Sometimes spouses disagreed about the wisdom of such action. Mrs. Jacobson said "her husband had objected to their having a second child because he felt that, on a WPA wage, they had no right to increase their family." Mrs. Silverman agreed to have another child because her mother-in-law kept after her husband, "telling him he should have more children since it is important to have sons to pray for their father when he is dead."

Many women went to great lengths while on Relief to keep their families from increasing. When Mrs. Cohen unexpectedly found herself pregnant, she borrowed money from a relative and went to a doctor "who did the abortion so inexpensively that he did not give anesthesia. She said that the pain was harrowing. Moreover, he allowed part of the foetus to remain in the uterus, and for several weeks she bled profusely, until one day she had a spontaneous abortion." Mrs. Wolf had not one but three abortions. "They were paid for by her brother William's sister-in-law. Mrs. Wolf could not face the thought of having a child while on Home Relief, and would rather die than have this happen. Under such circumstances, she could not face her investigator, let alone herself."

As practiced by these families, contraception was far from efficient. Apparently, the vaginal diaphragm—recommended by most clinics—has its limitations. These limitations are largely psychological. In many families, intercourse is not planned for ahead of time and the woman is likely to be unprepared. Moreover, many women are skeptical of the diaphragm and fail to use it regularly, because they believe conception takes place in the vagina, not in the womb. As for condoms, they are relatively expensive. Moreover, the market is flooded with poor merchandise and men seeking to save 5 or 10 cents on their purchases are likely to buy imperfect wares.

Many Relief families deeply regretted their inability to rear large families. For them, birth control was a necessity. If only they had been able to feed and clothe them adequately, these families would have welcomed having more children. They had a modest conception of adequate. "Because they both felt that children should be given a college education," Mrs. Weiss failed to have children even when her husband earned $55 and $65 weekly. But most families would have considered a steady income of $35 sufficient for rearing several children. When the Cavanaughs said "if their financial situation should change for the better, they would both like more children," they were thinking about a $35 weekly wage. Joseph Kennedy was the idol of Mrs. Higgins because he had nine children and was able to give them everything they needed. Many women shared Mrs. Higgins's feelings.

Women were more vitally concerned than men with the problems of religion and birth control. They were more closely tied to the church and its associated organizations. Among the Catholics, the woman's attitude toward birth control was crucial. Reflecting a patriarchal tradition, the Jewish men were more concerned with religion than the women; the synagogue was their preserve. Only in the home did the wife have religious responsibilities.

If religion was closely woven into the lives of these families, politics was not. If religion had its greatest hold on the women, politics interested the men most. A distinction must be made between national and local politics. These families did not follow Congressional debates and Cabinet meetings, but they were concerned with the actions of the Department of Welfare and the Works Progress Administration. The latter had a direct bearing on their daily lives.

The Workers' Alliance offered the unemployed an opportunity for political action. Open to all families on Relief upon payment of small monthly dues, this Communist-led organization acted as a pressure group to secure better treatment for the unemployed. Organized into locals, the Workers' Alliance was strong in certain sections of the city, weak in others, and practically unknown in some areas. The organization reached its peak in 1937-1938, and declined thereafter; by 1940 it was definitely on its way out.

Although most families in the study were on Relief at the time when the Workers' Alliance was at its peak, they lived in areas where the organization was weak. A substantial number of the interviewees had never heard of the Workers' Alliance.

Of the 60 Home Relief families, only 2 men were active and 3 others passive supporters of the organization. In the WPA sample, there was only one active and one passive member. Since people usually try to hide the fact that they hold membership in a Communist organization, both home and office interviews probably failed to uncover all members. After making allowance for those who hid their status, it is questionable whether as many as 10 per cent had been or were currently members of the Workers' Alliance.

Counterbalancing the few activists was an almost equal number of violent opponents. Moreover, if people had been better informed about the structure and functioning of the Workers' Alliance, the number of opponents would have been still greater.

Mr. Eisner is the prototype of an activist: "In the old days when he lived on the East Side, he was an active member of the Workers' Alliance and one of its leaders. He related with great glee the role that he had played, and he was exceedingly bitter about the lack of group consciousness among the unemployed in the Bronx. He thought that the families that lived in the Bronx were foolishly proud. They did not realize that without fighting they could get nothing; yet they refused to fight because they wanted to hide their Relief status. Mr. Eisner was also bitter about the high dues one had to pay in the Bronx; dues were much lower on the East Side, and the organization was much more tolerant of people in arrears." Mr. Eisner's Relief record reflects his associations: "A representative of the Workers' Alliance came to the office of the Emergency Relief with him." "Interviewed by insurance adjuster. Man was accompanied by representative of the Workers' Alliance." "Workers' Alliance requesting surplus book for the family." "A complaint from the Workers' Alliance demanding clothing and linen." "Urgent complaint by the Workers' Alliance stating that the family is in dire need of clothing."

Mr. Levin had difficulty in being accepted for Relief and finally sought assistance from the Workers' Alliance, which succeeded in getting him on the rolls. Mr. Levin feels "that the Workers' Alliance is a group designed to help poor people who cannot help themselves. For instance, they helped him get on Home Relief. Although he didn't belong to the Workers' Alliance, they helped anyway. He does not believe that the Workers' Alliance is a Communist organization. The capitalist papers say that it is, but they believe that anyone who wants to help the poor is a Communist."

Asked to join, several families investigated the organization. Mrs. Silverman came away approving of the "Workers' Alliance's efforts to help people by talking for them, but definitely disapproved of communism. She is against taking from one to give to another because she believes that the rich people worked for their money and have a right to it." Mr. Klein attended one meeting, where he found the members "discussing Spain and other problems which he did not think were closely connected with Relief, and he therefore refused to join up."

For many, the tie-up between the Workers' Alliance and the Communists queered the organization. The Jacobsons "disapproved of the Workers' Alliance and similar societies. They have very strong American feelings and have no use for any foreign, subsidized parties at this time." The Solomons "have never considered affiliation with the Workers' Alliance because they believe it to be Communist and therefore inimical to America's best interests." Mr. Higgins "thought that there were some Communists in the organization, but added that he knows a local on 149th Street which is all Irish and 'all those Irishmen couldn't be Communists.' He believes that too much preference is given to the Workers' Alliance and he pointed out that they even have space in the district office of the Department of Welfare. He thinks this is neither right nor proper. He believes that in this country every American has a right to ask for what he needs, and should not have to rely on a fighting group to get it for him. He was very much disturbed to find that the Workers' Alliance leads strikes and is responsible for picketing, which he thinks is not the way to deal with a government agency. He thought that the problem could be handled better if men and women who understood the clients' points of view and were also familiar with Home Relief would act as 'go-betweens.' He feels that this would be much better than 'all this fighting.' "

Mr. Clark, who had been active in his union before losing his job, "attended several meetings. As far as he could see, 'they were not much' since the rank and file were unable to speak English and seemed to be 'Bolshies.' " The most common statement was that of Mrs. Rogers', who "has no interest in the Workers' Alliance and does not even know what it is."

As for national politics, these families present a clear-cut picture. During the time when the men were in private employment they voted the straight Democratic ticket: 75 were Democrats; 5, Republicans; and 2, Communists. Despite the difficulties which beset these families during their unemployment, they failed to change their political affiliations. Neither the Republicans nor the Communists gained strength; a few changed their affiliations from the Democratic to the American Labor party.

Most families talked freely about politics. It must be recalled that the interviews took place in 1940, a presidential election year. Mr. Levin stated that politicians are frequently thieves and that he no longer voted for the Democrats, but he refused to discuss his present affiliations.

Occasionally, men had subtle reasons for voting as they did. Mr. Gross said that "he votes American Labor because he is afraid to jeopardize his Relief status by voting Communist." Mr. Mittleman is aware of the "conservative, even reactionary policies of the Republican party, but will vote for its candidate because he believes the people who have been holding on to their money because of their antipathy for Roosevelt will loosen up and bring about a boom if a Republican president is elected. He stated that, like everybody else, he will look out for himself and will vote for the man who is likely to bring prosperity, however temporary it might prove to be."

Although Mr. Gross did not vote the Communist ticket for fear of jeopardizing his Relief status, it is a striking fact that not a single family complained of political coercion—from the administration, the foreman, or the investigator.

The attitudes of these families toward President Roosevelt throw additional light on their politics. Of the 120 families on Relief, only 15 were "negative" to President Roosevelt, although at the time of the interviews another 20 were "undecided." However, most of these families finally went over to the Roosevelt camp. Mr. Willkie had few supporters: in the WPA sample, only 4 "approved," 13 were "neutral," and 11 were "hostile."

The Kleins were typical Roosevelt admirers. "They both think Roosevelt a very good man, who has the interest of the people at heart, and they hope he will run again." Even the Communistically inclined Mr. Gross thought "that Roosevelt has wanted to help people. But he is too weak. When he first became President, he had the opportunity to do a great many things, but strong capitalistic groups were able to overpower him." In Mrs. Jones's opinion, "Mr. Roosevelt is a good man who likes the people and would want to do more for them if he could. The problem of unemployment, however, is too big for any one man to solve."

The Atkinsons realized that the President had made many mistakes, but they felt that his heart was in the right place and that if he ran they would vote for him again. Despite the fact that Mr. Corcoran lost his $12 a month disability allowance during Mr. Roosevelt's term in office, the Corcorans believe the President to be doing his level best against great odds. The Wolfsons went further in their admiration: Mrs. Wolfson said "that she and her husband are both strongly pro-Roosevelt because they believe he is a wonderful man who loves the people and would do anything in his power to make their lot easier. She believes that all poor people, certainly all Jews, should vote for him because he is a real friend of the people. She said that her entire family is for Roosevelt except one brother, who is hesitating because of the third-term issue, which she feels is unimportant."

The McCarthys feel differently about the President. Although a Democrat all his life, Mr. McCarthy said that he will not vote in the next election, rather than vote for "that man Roosevelt. He believes that Roosevelt and his wife are both thinking only of their own class, by which he means the New Deal group. He is particularly resentful of Farley, whose Colonial Sand and Gravel Company has all the good contracts with WPA. He thinks that Mrs. Roosevelt is a very bad person because she is against her own people. She is against the whites and in favor of the 'niggers.' She is all for the 'niggers' in order to get their vote. There are plenty of 'niggers' instead of whites working now, and he thinks this is a great shame." Mrs. O'Connor shares many of Mr. McCarthy's feelings. "She certainly would not vote for Roosevelt because she does not believe that he has the interests of the poor at heart. A man born with a silver spoon in his mouth cannot understand how poor people feel. He makes whatever laws his advisers tell him to, and, as a result, the poor get poorer. Mrs. O'Connor is very much concerned about the influx of Negroes into the Bronx. 'Why not build a reservation for them and keep them apart from white people?' "

As for Mr. Willkie, most people felt that they were in poor position to judge; his most ardent supporters were persons like Mr. Johnson who disliked the President and "who found the spending program of the New Deal bad," or like Mrs. Siegel, who was upset by the third-term prospect. There was no pronounced feeling against Mr. Willkie. The skeptics, like Mrs. Robinson, said that "the Willkie family is making too much effort to get themselves on the map. The Robinsons do not believe that Willkie is interested in the welfare of the people as a whole."

The feelings of these families toward Mr. Roosevelt and Mr. Willkie were much influenced by their attitudes toward the war. During the first half of 1940, when the Home Relief group was visited, the war was still far distant and this was even true, though to a lesser degree, during the second half of the year. The WPA sample interviewed during the third quarter of 1940 showed that about half the families had only "slight" interest in the war; a quarter were "moderately" concerned; and only one-quarter were "greatly" interested in the European conflict. As to American policy toward the war, about half the families felt that we should avoid involvement at all costs; 4 were interventionists; 3 felt certain that we would be "dragged into the mess." The others were beset by the same confusion and uncertainty that typified the country at large—east and west, rich and poor, urbanites and farmers.

In the late spring of 1940, the President delivered a speech which the Wilsons felt "was a practical declaration of war. They objected, since they felt that the United States should keep out of war except for immediate defense." Mr. Leibowitz, a Communist sympathizer, "accused the President of selling out on the war situation, and added that he does not believe that Mr. Willkie is the person for the job." Highly personal considerations influenced the opinions of some families. Mrs. Flynn stated that, although her son "is only seventeen, she is frightened by the possibility of America's entering the war because if the war should drag on, as did the last one, Francis will eventually be called. The thought of war is horrible and frightens her when she thinks of it." Mrs. O'Donnell "finds the war news most upsetting. There is so much horror in it. She worries greatly about relatives and old friends in Ireland who would be exposed to its horrors if it spreads to Ireland." The Brennans were much interested in the war because of their relatives in Ireland. They hoped, of course, that England would win, but they also hoped that this country would not send men abroad although they approved of sending other aid.

Several families of Irish extraction felt antagonistic toward England. Mr. McCabe "is very much against American participation and believes that America should stay on her side of the water. As an Irishman, he feels strongly that we should not pull England's chestnuts out of the fire." Mrs. Coyle was even more outspoken. She thought there was no reason for us to go abroad last time. "It's too bad for England, but she took 'the cream off Ireland,' and lived off it for many years. Now she is getting a dose of her own medicine. Ireland will not fight for England. Why should she?"

Many families were pulled in several directions at the same time and had great difficulty in crystallizing their reactions. Mrs. White said that "she feels that the United States will be in the war very soon and she is afraid that conscription will even take Mr. White. She does not approve of war, but believes that it is probably necessary to keep Hitler out of the United States." Mr. Rhodes was more definite. He was an interventionist and he thought his position made good sense. "Although a Republican, he voted for Roosevelt and believes that he has been a good President. He thinks that if Roosevelt is reelected, the United States will go to war. In his opinion, it is essential that this country should not wait until Hitler comes here, but we should go after him. Both Mr. and Mrs. Rhodes were firm believers in conscription, and Mr. Rhodes felt that it might help him get a job."

Several men saw the connection between conscription and improved job opportunities for themselves. Mrs. Roberts realized that her husband might have an easier time getting a job once the country had conscription, but she was worried "because her five nephews were just the age to be called." Mr. O'Connell also had doubts about conscription "because he doesn't think it a good idea for young men to get killed just in order that he may have a job, so he would just as soon see this country stay out of war."

The question of permitting refugees to enter the United States, as well as the allied question of sending money abroad to aid the victims of Hitlerite aggression was discussed with families on WPA, but only half the group had given the matter much thought. As was to be expected, the Jewish group had a greater interest in the problem than either Catholics or Protestants. But the Jewish families were not always the most sympathetic. Mr. Silver complained that "in the old days, the Queens subway was filled with two sorts of people—Americans going to WPA jobs, and German and other refugees going to the new factory out there." The Leventhal family also was resentful, since Mr. Leventhal, a union member who had earned 70 cents an hour, was dismissed to make room for German refugees who were willing to work for 30 cents an hour. "People who are persecuted should be helped, but they have no right to take work away from others."

Mrs. Cole supposed that "refugees must have some place to go, but she did not think that they ought to come to this country, since there is not enough food here." The Mitchells were disturbed because they knew several department stores "that had employed refugees in place of citizens." Mrs. Coyle felt differently. "She knows that in her husband's field, refugees are willing to work for less money than Americans, but she does not actually blame them. It is essential that they become self-supporting. She thinks that it is very important to bring over children in as large numbers as possible, not only the children of the rich but all children." Mrs. Siegel thinks there are two sides to the question of refugees working for less money than Americans. "Many refugees have started businesses here and put Americans to work."

When in private employment, most men had little active interest in politics. Less than 10 per cent belonged to the local Democratic club; only 5 per cent were members during the period of their unemployment. Despite the pressures under which these families lived, they did not seek comfort and strength by joining esoteric movements and accepting strange ideologies. A few families, like the O'Connors, thought Father Coughlin made sense when he said that "people have a right to work, and to a living wage." But extremism in matters political was as rare as in matters religious. There was nothing revolutionary about these families.

In what ways do the Relief families differ from the Private group? Two-thirds of the Private families read at least one newspaper daily and the remaining third saw a paper several times a week. Once again the *Daily News* led the field, but by a much smaller margin, for the New York *Times* was close on its heels. Reflecting the higher percentage of native-born Jews in the Private sample, the Yiddish press had little following.

The radio was used for entertainment, and family conflicts over favorite programs were common. Because of their superior economic position, many families were able to solve these conflicts by having two radios. Mrs. Donnelly said that "she enjoys listening to the radio and has two of them—one in the living room and one in the front room, so that if the children want to hear something that does not interest her, they can go into the other room."

As to religion, there is little to distinguish the Private from the Relief families. Once again the Catholics and the Jews were found to have been orthodox, while most Protestants had only tenuous associations with their church. The Monahans were typical Catholics, raised in religious homes. Mrs. Monahan said that "neither she nor her husband had ever varied in their observance of their religion. They have attended St. Paul's Church in the neighborhood for years, and all their children went to parochial school." The Sheehans also were "devout Catholics who attended church and confession regularly." This was true of the majority.

However, birth control presented difficulties. Mrs. Haggerty told that "she confessed the practice of birth control during the early months of marriage. 'The priest gave me a terrible bawling-out just as if I were a criminal.' It was only three weeks after her marriage, and she thought the priest's attitude most unfair. She did not go to confession, and even failed to attend mass for a while. Her mother told her not to worry." Mr. Cassidy suggested "that about 90 per cent of the people use birth control methods although they do not admit it. He questioned what people did before marriage, if they didn't use birth control, since about 50 per cent have sexual relations before marriage. He does not see any difference in birth control before or after marriage. He stated that when first married, and again recently, he discussed this matter with a young priest, who suggested that he use his own judgment. Mr. Cassidy stated that he was not going to have a large family so long as he would be unable to take care of it." The Sweeneys, who have nine children "and do not believe in birth control for themselves, nevertheless feel that it may well be a matter for individual decision. Mrs. Sweeney said that one cannot be too harsh with young people who refuse to have children when they are barely able to manage themselves."

Time weakened the orthodoxy of the Private Jewish families. Mrs. Scher stated that she had remained orthodox until her mother died. She then went to live with her sister. "When her sister's children came along, the family was unable to observe the dietary laws, since the food disagreed with the children and it was too expensive. They could not afford separate dishes. They no longer observe the dietary laws although they do observe the Holy Days."

Possibly, the Jewish families in the Private sample were more emancipated than those on Home Relief. Mrs. Salzman's theory, that "there would be less persecution if there were more intermarriage between Jews and Christians, and that everyone should worship the 'American God,' " could scarcely have been voiced by a Home Relief family. Such thinking was more likely to be found among native-born Jews.

Only three Protestant families had been closely affiliated with their church in former years, and at the time of the interviews there was only one. The Davies "had been Chapel folk in Wales and have always attended church regularly. They have many social contacts in their church group." More typical of the Protestant sample were the Carters, who shifted from the Episcopal to the Methodist church because the latter "is more friendly and comfortable for poor people." However, they attend irregularly and are not very religious. Mrs. Carter said "that her family is much more important to her than formal religion. By devotion to one's children, and helping one another, it is possible to do more good than by going through the motions of attending church."

The average number of children in the Private families was smaller than in the Relief group, and one could jump to the conclusion that this reflected a more widespread and, especially, a more efficient use of contraceptives. Perhaps so, but the higher percentage of recent marriages among the Privates must also be taken into account. During the 1930's people thought twice about having a child.

As regards politics, there was only a shade of difference between the Private and the Relief groups. In former days, most Private families voted for the Democrats, and this was still true at the time of the interviews. But the percentage of

Republicans and independent voters was somewhat higher among the Privates. President Roosevelt was again the favorite, although a minority continued to oppose him even after his election for a third term. The Warrens, who had been strong Republicans for generations, "were very disappointed by the outcome of the election and they even feared that there was a danger of a dictatorship in this country." The Quinns had voted against Mr. Roosevelt "because he had spent too much money in an unproductive fashion, and, in addition, they were against the third term." Mrs. Quinn related that they had stayed up late on election night and when she learned that he had been re-elected, she told her husband, "'well, the majority must have wanted him,' and he replied with considerable anger, 'I hope they get their belly full of him.' Mrs. Quinn thinks that her husband was being 'a sore-head about this.' "

Probably reflecting the later date of their interviews, a larger percentage of the Private families were actively or fatalistically interventionist. The isolationists composed only one-third of the sample, but they had some outspoken people in their ranks, especially among the Irish Catholics. "Mrs. Quinn is emphatically against any help to England. 'England be damned.' She does not believe that Britain deserves help. 'You'd think that Britain had always been so kind to minorities.' " Mrs. Monahan not only had anti-Jewish feelings, but also liked the Germans. "England is getting what she deserves, and although she feels sorry for individual English citizens who are suffering, she thinks the English government had to reach the end of its rope sometime, and it might just as well be now. She has always found Germans to be nice people, clean, neat, industrious, kindly, and generally respectable and honest."

The Private families found difficulty in crystallizing their reactions to refugees, since few had thought about the problem. Mrs. Carter went so far as to say that "the question of refugees is academic, since there are no refugees coming over now." Mrs. Donnelly "wanted to know why we should bring over only English children. 'What about German children?' They are suffering just as much and are just as deserving of help.

She does not understand why everybody is against the Germans. They have many Germans in the neighborhood and she knows them to be good people." On the basis of their limited knowledge, the majority favored a liberal policy in sending money abroad and offering asylum in this country. This represents a more favorable attitude toward refugees than was found in Relief families.

Minor differences between the Private and Relief groups could be multiplied, but in political and religious essentials, there is little to distinguish the two. Karl Marx notwithstanding, loss of income and loss of work did not throw people into the arms of revolutionists. The unemployed changed their ideas and behavior, but very slowly; and they changed not because of their unemployment but in response to certain broad cultural forces which affected the entire community.

PART IV. RE-EMPLOYABILITY

Chapter VIII

IN SEARCH OF A JOB

THE study of these unemployed families has disclosed two important facts bearing directly upon their re-employment. In reconstructing the backgrounds of these families, one discovered that until the depression of 1930 the unemployed could not be distinguished from the basic laboring population of which they formed a part. The menfolk had been able and willing to work, and they had earned enough to support their families. Only a few found difficulty in adjusting to the demands of private industry, but the number of drunkards, petty criminals, and ne'er-do-wells was small. In all important regards, the majority was normal.

A careful review of the circumstances surrounding the men's loss of employment disclosed that fate, not inefficiency was the principal precipitant. Sometimes the older men were let out; at other times, the most recent additions were the first to lose their jobs. When a concern went out of business, the entire staff was dismissed. Those who found themselves on the street were less lucky than those who continued in employment; but, aside from luck, there was nothing to distinguish the two.

During the first months of their unemployment, these men strove hard to find jobs so as to avoid seeking public assistance. Many succeeded in finding at least part-time work. Eventually, these positions petered out, and they were forced to come to Relief. On the day that these people made application they cut themselves off from the rest of the population, and each day they stayed on Relief the gulf widened. When employed, even when unemployed but self-supporting, these families were not unique. When they settled on Relief, this was no longer true.

To appreciate what Relief did to these families, one must review the length of their stay on the public rolls. Forty per cent were first accepted for Relief before the end of 1933; slightly more than 50 per cent did not seek public assistance until the middle 1930's (1934 through 1938); and the remaining 7 per cent first came to Relief in 1939 or early in 1940.

These families did not remain on Relief continuously from the time of their first acceptance. Actually, more than 40 per cent managed to get off the Relief rolls at least once, and 20 per cent left the rolls two or more times after their initial acceptance. Unfortunately, the jobs they found were not good, and many positions folded up after a few weeks or months. That is why these people were back on the rolls in 1940.

At the time these families were interviewed, about 20 per cent were currently employed on part-time work, but they earned so little that they were forced to rely primarily on WPA or Home Relief. In most instances, this supplementary income was earned by either the man or the woman, occasionally by minor children.

That 40 per cent of the families were able to get back into private employment at least once after being accepted on Relief suggests that some hiring was going on even during the depression and the initial stages of the revival. The majority, however, failed to get off even once. During this same period, other heads of households earned sufficient to keep their families independent. In fact, some had been on Relief, but once off, stayed off. Why were our families different?

The first factor influencing re-employment is age: according to the eligibility requirements of the sample, no family was chosen in which the head of the household was more than 59 years of age. Slightly more than one-third were between 46 and 59; slightly more than half were between 31 and 45; about 20 per cent were still in their twenties. The modal age for the entire group was between 41 and 45. These figures might suggest that only men over 50—about 23 per cent of the sample—

had cause to be concerned. Actually, men in their forties, even men in their thirties, found themselves handicapped.

"Mr. Jones is particularly bitter about the fact that, when seeking employment, the question of age is thrown in his teeth. He is just 40, and he says that no one wants to hire anybody above the age of 18." Mr. Gallagher, only several years Mr. Jones's senior, stated that as soon as an employer "looks at a man and sees that he has white hair, he concludes that the man is too old to work, even though he can do much more than the young 'snips' who are hired. Of course, these youngsters work for much less than would any self-respecting adult." Mr. O'Brien, who had just turned 50, said "that he doesn't go looking for private jobs any more because he has been told too many times that he is too old and he has now accepted it as a fact." And Mr. White, a 38-year-old electrician, discovered that younger men were given preference.

Any man above 30, surely above 35, was handicapped because of age. Many concerns had routinized their hiring policies, and older men were frequently disqualified without a hearing. Several men pointed out that group insurance was to blame. Employers did not consider young men more efficient, but they preferred to hire them because of savings in premiums.

As regards health: No family was included in the study where the head of the household was severely handicapped for employment for reasons of health. Despite this eligibility requirement, many men found their search for private employment impeded because of poor health. As for the Home Relief sample, about 30 per cent were in good physical condition, sufficiently strong to be assigned to laboring jobs on WPA. An additional 20 per cent might have been able to hold down a laboring job on WPA. Fifty per cent had specific handicaps—bilateral hernias, duodenal ulcers, hypertension, and arrested tubercular conditions. Of the 27 men in the Home Relief group who at one time or another had been on WPA, 14 had been removed for reasons of illness.

The WPA group was in better health. Only 20 per cent suffered physical handicaps. Several older men could no longer hold down laboring jobs—at least, they said they could not—and several others suffered from rheumatism, hypertension, and ulcers.

Many men were blocked from returning to their major occupation. Mr. Wolf used to make a good living as a cab driver "until a childhood injury in his arm flared up in the early 1930's, at which time the doctors forbade him to drive. Although told to stop, he continued to work until the pain became so great that he could no longer stand it." Men with hernias were greatly handicapped in seeking employment, since they could accept no job involving heavy labor. Moreover, Mr. Higgins pointed out that "having his hernias repaired would still make it impossible for him to qualify for heavy work."

Many men, especially in the Home Relief group, had formerly worked on jobs that made small physical demands on them. These men had never been robust, and age, worry, and poor diet had further reduced their strength. At the time we interviewed them, many were found to be in poor condition.

As regards skill: Although no factor outranked "skill" in influencing the unemployed man's chance of returning to work, "skill" is difficult to define. Perhaps the simplest and best definition of skill is the ability to perform the required work.

The following summarizes the major occupations of the men prior to their first acceptance for Relief:

	Per Cent
Unskilled manual	27
Semiskilled manual	43
Commercial, white-collar, etc.	20
Skilled manual and nonmanual	10

This distribution relates to the late 1920's and early 1930's, but fails to take account of economic changes which destroyed the skills of several men: shoe laster, harnessmaker, marble polisher, brass bed manufacturer. The disabilities of this group are high-lighted when one realizes that employment opportunities during the middle and late 1930's were best for men with mechanical skills. Only 6 per cent were skilled manual workers. If the large group of semiskilled manual workers are combined with the skilled, one accounts for half the sample. But the semiskilled were hard put to find jobs for themselves. Mr. McManus, after losing his job in the construction trades in the late 1920's, learned bartending but found that his experience with straight drinks was not sufficient to get him work in most bars. Only good mixers were wanted.

While on Relief, Mr. Finkelstein and Mr. Levy acquired training in welding and surveying, but their experience was limited to WPA. Private employers refused to consider them trained. Although many men on WPA were well-assigned, one cannot overlook the fact that many others suffered a loss, or at least a deterioration in their skill. As for Home Relief, much specialized knowledge and training went over the dam, especially among businessmen, who lost all their contacts. Nor did mechanics improve their skills by sitting around all day doing nothing.

The few youngsters under 30 had a hard time because they had not been in the labor market long enough to acquire real skills. Mrs. Gallagher complained that "they won't hire her husband because he's too old, even though he's had experience, while they won't hire her children because they've had no experience. They want people with experience, but won't give young people a chance to get it."

Age, health, and lack of skill were some of the serious difficulties confronting the unemployed who sought to return to private industry. Implicit in their Relief status was another complex of handicaps.

Inadequate clothing was a frequent complaint of families on Home Relief and WPA; 50 per cent stated specifically that they could not clothe themselves adequately. Men came to the office for an interview wearing patched trousers, frayed collars, and shoes with holes in the soles.

Many men were further handicapped by lack of teeth. In Mr. Brown's record one reads: "Man feels that if he had teeth, he would look younger and have a better chance for a job." This notation is dated August, 1936. At the time the man was interviewed, on March 19, 1940, he still had no teeth. "His wife explained that he had recently received dentures from the Relief Bureau, but they fit so badly that he is unable to wear them." So, too, Mr. Finkelstein, who retrained as a welder, feels that his one real handicap for employment in private industry is his lack of teeth. "He needs dentures, since all his own teeth had been extracted some time ago and the family has been unable to save enough for a set of false teeth. If they knew where they could go and pay a few dollars each month they might be able to manage, but they found that the lowest down payment is $45. This was too large a sum for them to manage. Apart from his need for false teeth, Mr. Finkelstein is young looking, makes a good appearance, talks well, and would be highly employable."

Most men lived considerable distances from the center of employment and every time they looked for a job, they had to spend at least 10 cents on carfare. When one realizes that 10 cents would buy an additional quart of milk, one understands why many hesitated before starting out. If they were to make a day of job hunting, they would need another 10 cents for a bite of lunch. Many sought to cut these costs: "Mr. Kennedy goes downtown three or four times a week looking for work. He saves carfare by riding only one way. He takes the subway to Wanamaker's at Ninth Street and does his job hunting as he walks back to East 180th Street in the Bronx. The walk usually takes four to five hours. He starts by asking the employment division at Wanamaker's whether there is anything for him, then stops at the Heide Candy Company, and then works his way north. He does not go to employment agencies because he thinks that they are interested in finding short-time jobs for people so that they can earn their commissions." Mr. Mittleman walks many miles each day. He leaves the house about six o'clock in the morning and walks all the way to the Barbers' Exchange. "He knows that the agency is primarily a lead-on for business deals, but nevertheless he goes there every day in search of employment."

When Mr. McManus was on Home Relief, he spent almost every morning looking for employment. "Although carfare was a great drain on the family, they thought it sufficiently important and made sacrifices in other directions. He usually managed to come home by noon in order to save lunch money and because he realized that the afternoon was not a good time for job hunting." Men on WPA were handicapped because the morning was the best time to look for work. Although many men worked only three out of every four weeks, they actually had few mornings free. Mrs. Maguire pointed out that "her husband had little free time on WPA because he was always making up days lost through bad weather. Even on bad days he had to report for work. This cut into the morning, the best time to look for employment, and there was little point in his going out once he came home."

Families on Relief frequently broke off social relations with friends and acquaintances, a step that handicapped them greatly, for the men failed to hear of job opportunities. Mr. McManus summed up the situation in these terms: "It was during this period that he definitely learned that there were two groups of people likely to get work—those already in employment who heard about new openings while on their jobs; those with relatives and friends who had an 'in.'" Mr. Madden took a pessimistic view of his own chances to find a private job because he believed that "without powerful friends or relatives who are well situated, it is impossible to get a job. These days only 'pull' counts."

Except for 10 per cent, all the unemployed families had adult relatives in the United States, but few were in a position to help. Only 30 per cent of the families had relatives all of whom were self-supporting. In 50 per cent of the cases at least one relative was currently on Relief. The remaining 20 per cent of the families had one or more relatives not self-supporting, but free of Relief. Only an adult child out of the home, parent, brother, or sister of either the husband or the wife was considered a relative. The poor economic condition of relatives is emphasized by the finding that in about 35 per cent of the sample more than half the relatives were not self-supporting or were on Relief.

The Callahans had self-supporting relatives. Mr. Callahan is the second of four children; his older sister is married and his younger brother and sister are living at home with his parents, and are still in high school. His father is employed as a fireman and earns betwen $30 and $35 a week. Mrs. Callahan is the second of five children. Her father is employed as a baggage man at a hotel and earns about $15 weekly plus tips. Her brother, Michael, a grocery clerk, is married and lives in Pennsylvania. Another brother, John, also a grocery clerk, is married and has one child. William, a younger brother, is unemployed and living at home; and the youngest, Joseph, is still in high school.

This is the Wolf family: Mrs. Wolf's father is dead, and her tubercular mother lives with one of her sisters. Her brother William was a plumber on WPA until recently dismissed because of the "eighteen-months ruling." His wife is tubercular. He is barely able to maintain himself and his family, and Mrs. Wolf frequently has the family come to her house for meals. Another sister is married and has two children. She and her husband both work very hard peddling millinery from door to door. Another sister, Laura, is married to a substitute post-office clerk who will probably receive a permanent assignment in the near future. Mrs. Wolf says that Laura is the only member of the family who has any real security. There is an unmarried brother, who is the "black sheep" of the family. Still another sister lives in California, is married, and has three children. Her husband is barely able to support her. Mrs. Wolf said "that the members of her family would do anything for each other. Sometimes, despite her own worries, she worries about them. If any one of them were successful, all would be safe, since whatever belongs to one belongs to all."

Mr. Shannahan is the seventh of eight children. His father is a laborer, employed by the Department of Highways, and earns $33 a week, which he uses to keep himself and a defective son who lives with him. Mr. Shannahan has no contact whatever with his only sister, who lives out of town. He has several married brothers, each of whom has several children. One brother, a policeman, lives beyond his income. He is usually in debt and unable to help any other member. Another brother is a truck driver who has been on and off Relief. Still another is a laborer who has also been on Relief, although at the moment he is able to support himself. A fifth brother, formerly on Work Relief, is now employed as a track man for the Interborough Rapid Transit Company. The sixth, a printer, was on Relief until recently. Mr. Shannahan says that he expects no help from any of his relatives, since all have a pretty hard time of it.

That relatives were seldom in a position to help these unemployed families re-establish themselves is borne out by the finding that with one or two exceptions, no legally responsible relative contributed to the upkeep of these families. The Department of Welfare might have overlooked one or two people in a position to help but it is doubtful whether the Department would have overlooked many.

If an unemployed man had the good luck to find a job opening, either through his own initiative or with the help of others, it did not follow that the job was his. There was still the hurdle of the union. Mr. Kennedy, after walking the length of town several times weekly in search of employment, "was very happy last week when he was offered a job as a plumber's helper. However, when he reported to work, the union representative didn't permit him to take the job and start work. Mr. Kennedy believes in unions, but he believes it is unfair for a union to prevent him from getting work, since there is no other way for him to become a union member except by holding down a job."

Only 25 per cent of the group had been union members, but more than half had lost their cards because of a failure to pay dues. Mr. Rhodes was formerly "a member of the Carpenters' Union but lost his membership when he was unable to pay dues. At one point, Mrs. Rhodes used her rent money to pay Mr. Rhodes's dues, believing that the union would help her husband get a job. But they got nothing out of it." Mr. Hunt had a similar experience. On the other hand, Mr. Hawkins did not think that it would be difficult for him to be reinstated in the Elevator Constructors' Union from which he had been suspended 4 years ago for nonpayment of dues. He did not go back because the union was not very hopeful of placing him.

Mr. Madden, however, did not look forward to easy reinstatement in the Truck Drivers' Union. He says that his union "sold books at $50 a head to many people who had never driven in their lives. When jobs finally opened up, there was a large force available. He had fallen hopelessly behind in his dues and realized that there was no chance for re-employment in his own trade. He told the 'Relief people' a long time ago that they could make a real contribution to his re-employment if they would get him back into the union, but they said that they were unable to pay union dues."

Members forced to drop out for nonpayment of dues could not look forward to reinstatement unless they had $50, sometimes several times that amount. This was a barrier few men on Home Relief or WPA could surmount. Moreover, unions presented serious obstacles to the re-employment of men who had never been members. The middle and the latter 1930's saw many old unions grow in strength and many new ones spring up. Mr. McCarthy believes that he will never get back into the refrigerator repair busines "because there is a man downtown who has the whole electrical refrigerator industry 'sewed up.' He is the leader of a union which he organized under the C.I.O. a few years ago. As soon as he had the union organized, he closed the books and accepted no new members. He also has the manufacturers 'sewed up' and, as far as Mr. McCarthy can see, has a monopoly on the whole industry. Mr. McCarthy thinks that unions are all right in principle, but as they are currently organized they keep people out of work who have a right to work."

Mr. Levin said that "in the old days he failed to join the union for he did not see how any good could come of it since his boss treated him fairly and his wages were adequate for the work he was doing. Today, however, the unions have divided the restaurant business between them. The A. F. of L. has the large restaurants and the C.I.O. has the small restaurants. The only nonunionized places are the dumps." Mr. Barnes, who had never had any difficulty getting work during the 1920's, thinks that the growth of the C.I.O. during the 1930's was particularly unfortunate for men like himself. "One cannot get a job unless one belongs to a union and one cannot join a union unless one has a job. He said that the C.I.O. has made it very much worse than the A. F. of L. because the A. F. of L. used to concentrate on skilled trades, but the C.I.O. has tied up just those places where a man like himself would ordinarily get a job."

With unions standing in the way of their re-employment, many men felt confused about their reactions to organized labor. This confusion was verbalized by Mr. McManus. "He knew that unions were rather necessary, for if it had not been for them, the laboring man would still be working at a very low wage scale. However, in many unions, in fact in most, the whole thing had become a racket. They offered very little to the workingman, and frequently interfered with his getting and keeping a job."

Of the 47 men who discussed trade-unions, 21 were definitely in favor of unions while the remaining 26 were equally divided between the "ambivalent" and the "negative." Some men went so far as to distinguish between their reactions to trade-unions and to labor leaders. Mr. Knight and Mr. Clark, both members of the Building Service Employees' Union, had many unpleasant things to say about Mr. Scalise, for a long time the leader of their union. Mr. Clark put it this way: "Scalise and a few other top henchmen had never worked in the industry, knew nothing about it, and had very little interest in the people who were employed in the industry. Mr. Clark felt that there was little point to a union unless the rank and file was organized from the bottom up rather than forced into a union from the top down."

The primary purpose of Home Relief and WPA was to see that the unemployed man and his family had food to eat and a roof over their heads. But they were also concerned with speeding the re-employment of their clients. Hence, the Department of Welfare made it obligatory for all men to report monthly to the New York State Employment Service. Failure to report jeopardized a man's Relief status. It was believed that compulsory registration and monthly visits to the State Employment Service would provide a check on the willingness of the unemployed man to accept a job. These expectations were not fulfilled.

Many employers made little or no use of the State Employment Service, but continued to rely upon their own personnel departments or on private agencies. The State Employment Service usually had jobs to fill in fields where the work was hard, the hours long, the wages low. It received many requests for hospital orderlies, dishwashers, firemen, casual laborers, and the like. Frequently, these jobs paid less than what the men were currently receiving on Home Relief or WPA. At least, the jobs paid less in cash, for remuneration was frequently in the form of board or room, or both. Wages in kind might prove attractive to single men, but not to heads of households.

The State Employment Service also had calls for better jobs, but Relief clients seldom had a chance. With more men than jobs, the officials were in a position to pick and choose, and they tried to find the best man for the opening. Registered with the State Employment Service were not only men on Relief but also newcomers to the labor market, the recently unemployed, and persons who wished to change positions. Convinced that youngsters just out of school or men who had only recently lost their jobs were in better physical and psychological condition than men on Relief, the officials slighted the latter. Sometimes they went so far as to segregate the cards of Relief clients and place them in an inactive file.

Realizing that they had little or no chance of being referred to a good job by the State Employment Service, many men on Relief greatly resented having to report regularly. Mr. Silverman stated "that the New York State Employment Service is no good because he has never heard of anyone whom they have placed." Mr. Clark told that "he had gone to the State Employment Service on many occasions, but remarked that their work was 'just plain ridiculous.' It was a stamping bureau and nothing else. In fact, there was nobody in the office who was sufficiently interested to talk with him about his problems. He was afraid to leave his name for fear that they might really find him a job which on the surface was satisfactory, but which on closer inspection would place him in an even worse position than his present lot on Relief. If such a job were offered him and he refused to take it, his Relief could be cut off." Mr. Jones said the State Employment Service "was nothing but a farce. It made work for the clerks in the bureau. They stamp his card every two months, and that's all there is to it."

The private social service agencies—Catholic, Jewish, and Protestant—like the State Employment Service failed to find jobs for men on Relief. In the early days of the depression, when these agencies were still supporting the unemployed, they occasionally found a job for one of their clients. After they transferred the unemployed to the public rolls they lost interest in them. The important Protestant and Jewish agencies concentrated on families with emotional rather than economic problems.

Only a few families knew of the existence of these private agencies, and those who sought help did not always have fortunate experiences. When illness forced Mr. Clark to give up a good job as superintendent, he sold all his earthly possessions, including his tools, to stave off Relief. Later he approached one of the private agencies for help. "They suggested a job to him in the Rockaways, but he realized that since he would not be paid until the end of the month, and since he was without clothes and tools, he could not accept it. When he asked for clothes and tools, or for a loan of $50 with which to buy them, the agency said that it could do nothing to help him. Some time later they offered him another job, but again refused to make him a loan which would have enabled him to accept work."

Legal and racial discrimination kept some men from getting back into private industry. Although his brother had a place for him in his Miami barber shop, Mr. Mittleman could not take the job because Florida refused to license out-of-state barbers. Mr. Silverman was up against the fact that Germans controlled the photostat industry in New York and refused to hire Jews. Mr. McCarthy ran into considerable discrimination. "He said that Breyer and Horton employ only Germans and this has been true for many years. The American Express Company want only Irish, in fact, only immigrant Irish. They send their men to Ellis Island to meet the boats. He himself stood in line at the American Express Company and discovered that one had to show his passport before one could get a job. In the refrigerator division of General Motors, Germans are employed in preference to others. Mr. McCarthy, who has worked with Germans, believes that they are no better than other workers except that they will put up with more. This goes also for the foreign-born Irish."

Every man was up against the widespread prejudice of businessmen who feared to hire anybody who had been on Home Relief or WPA. Employers knew that men on Home Relief did not want to work; that men on WPA never did a full day's work; that Relief clients were radicals; that only the most inefficient workers ever sank so low as to apply for Relief. All this was common knowledge and employers acted on it.

The discrimination against hiring men on Relief was so intense that one WPA administrator established a special division, manned by public relations experts, to break down the prevailing prejudice. But the experts failed to deliver. The business community refused to see the light. Mrs. Rattner said that she "was very much disturbed over certain newspapers, like the New York *Times,* talking of WPA people as 'chiselers.' She says that it is hard enough for them to get along on WPA without having to put up with such statements. It is a 'vicious circle' and one just cannot win."

Many men went to extremes to hide their Relief status. Mr. Silver told "that when he, himself, goes looking for private employment, or even when he signs a lease, he always hides the fact that he is on WPA. 'One always lies like hell to hide the fact that one is on WPA.' He says that it is absolutely essential to do so because the discrimination, the suspicion, and the dislike which exist in the community at large are terrific."

With Relief offering them little and with their prospects for re-employment far from good, many men took a pessimistic view of the future, not only for themselves but also for their children. Some did not lose hope, and a few remained optimistic. Mr. Sullivan, who had been precipitated onto Home Relief by sudden illness but was well on the way to recovery at the time of the interview, said "Now that he is about to start work on a steady job which will pay him $30 a week, everything looks swell. He expects to pay off his debts. Since his furniture is all paid for, he can start saving passage money for Ireland. Once he is home again, he is certain that everything will be O.K." The Polikoffs also felt that their future was looking up because Mr. Polikoff was on the road to complete recovery and had many leads for employment. Mrs. O'Hara realized that it would not be easy sailing, but she feels fairly sure "that her husband will get a job in the spring. What worries her is the fact that her children will be only slightly better off on the $18 or so that their father will earn in private employment than on the family's Relief allowance. Nevertheless, she is looking forward to Mr. O'Hara's getting a job because, if he works steadily, they will be able to count on a regular income and plan accordingly. If necessary, she will go back to work later on, when the baby is a little older. It might be possible for her to live near one of her sisters who could look after the children. She feels sure that she could command a good wage as a cook."

Although Mr. Kennedy and Mr. Moran did not have definite promises of jobs, they considered their chances good. "Mr. Moran definitely expects one of his leads to come through. He does not have quite the assurance he used to have when his old employer was in business, because in those days he knew that the spring would bring a job. However, he has several people interested in him who know building superintendents, and they are trying to find a spot for him. 'There should be some work somewhere for an able-bodied man to do.' "

Mrs. Israel said that, on the whole, her family "was very optimistic about the future. They regretted that their son has no vocational training beyond a little business training which he received in high school, scarcely sufficient to get him a white-collar job at this time. They were in hopes, however, that things would pick up so that they could give him the same training their daughter had received. The boy, himself, is very optimistic. He realizes that he is up against a big problem, but here and there individuals do have luck and there is no reason why he should not share some of that luck and get employment."

Despite the fact that her husband was on WPA and that she had to care for eleven children, Mrs. Adams felt that "in time, everything would be all right for the family. Sooner or later, the boys would get work and perhaps even the girls, and their combined incomes would be sufficient to keep them comfortable. She thought that perhaps some day her husband might even get work."

Approximately one-third felt optimistic about what the future had in store for them; just under one-third was "ambivalent." This group had been through some hard years and it saw nothing on the horizon to suggest a change. Yet a change might occur. Mrs. Blodgett put the matter in these terms: "She does not know what is going to happen in the future. Mr. Blodgett has had no luck in finding a job these last years, but he has never given up hope. It is going to be more difficult for him to get a superintendent's job because, among other things, he is up against the question of union membership."

Mr. Klein could not get back into his old business of selling clothing to sailors on foreign boats, unless he secured $1,000 capital. "He emphasized that since he had once gone bankrupt on borrowed money, he was no longer a good risk to the jobbers." He thought, however, that he might approach a wealthy uncle of his wife's to see whether he could get a loan. "Mr. Klein feels 'one cannot plan for the future, one can just keep hoping that something will turn up.' "

Mrs. O'Connor, whose husband worked hard as a waiter but was unable to support her and her five children without supplementation from Home Relief, stated that "she is sick and tired of hearing how things will pick up. She is afraid that her husband will be dead before they do. 'I'll be damned if the blasted government knows any more about what to do with this bloody mess than the common people.' All the family can do is to hope that things will be better before they all crack up under the strain."

About one-third of the group had cracked under the strain. "Mr. Gallagher is beginning to lose hope, and Mrs. Gallagher has already lost hope. They both feel that there is nothing to hope for with Mr. Gallagher's age and gray hair against him. Age is against her husband, while youth is against her children." "The future looks black to Mr. and Mrs. Leventhal. Even if Mr. Leventhal gets a job on WPA again, and they expect that he will, he will work just to keep the family going. They will have no opportunity to save and build up any security for their old age. With the employment situation in his trade what it is, there is little likelihood of his finding a job in private industry. Mrs. Leventhal says that she worries a great deal about her children's future. What with the war coming closer and anti-Semitism growing, she does not see how they will have much opportunity to lead comfortable, happy lives."

People felt slightly more optimistic about their children than about themselves. Just under 50 per cent of the families thought that the promise of America would still be fulfilled for their children, if not for themselves. Only a few, less than 10 per cent, were pessimistic about their children's future.

People's attitudes toward the future were determined largely by their job prospects. Many were willing to make their peace with remaining on WPA for the rest of their lives. After a man has been rebuffed time and again when seeking private employment, he finds some comfort in protecting himself from further hurt. Older men had no reason to keep looking for private employment indefinitely. It was the better part of wisdom for them to realize that they were through. In fact, only 60 per cent of the entire group had strong drives for private employment. Thirty per cent still tried to find jobs in private industry, but their search for employment was not wholehearted. And 10 per cent had definitely ceased looking.

All calculations about the future were affected by the defense boom, although New York City received few contracts. Even prior to the outbreak of war in the late summer of 1939, a considerable number of men had succeeded in extricating themselves from Relief and returning to private industry. If escape from the rolls was possible prior to the boom, a man's prospects surely looked brighter now that the country was in the throes of a serious defense effort.

A study was undertaken of 30 Relief families who had succeeded in returning to private employment, to learn how they had managed their escape. That these families had had a hard struggle for a long time is borne out by the fact that half had been on Relief more than once. However, these families, with few exceptions, had had no contact with Relief for at least two years preceding our interviews, which suggested that they were well on the road to permanent rehabilitation.

No striking differences could be found between the average earnings of these Closed families prior to their coming to Relief and those of families on Home Relief and WPA. The Closed group contained a higher precentage of skilled men. As was true of the Relief sample, the men in the Closed group came to Relief because of "lack of work." However, when business improved many were rehired by their old employers or found employment elsewhere.

As regards relatives, these Closed cases were only slightly better off than Relief families. They, too, had many relatives who were not self-supporting or were on Relief. But the average number of indigent relatives was less in the Closed than in the Relief group.

Relatives failed the Closed families, but friends and even strangers proved helpful. "Mrs. Talmadge told how her husband had received several jobs through the help of friends, and how his present post as superintendent of a Jewish temple was obtained with the help of the former incumbent who knew Mr. Talmadge and recommended him for the post."

Mrs. Doyle's story was one for the fiction magazines. "She

had taken her children to the park and had given them, and the children with whom they were playing, some fruit. The strange children politely refused to take the fruit, and their father came over to explain that he had taught them not to accept anything from strangers. They started to talk, and in the course of the conversation Mrs. Doyle mentioned that her husband was unemployed. The man asked Mrs. Doyle what her husband's trade was, and she thought that was the end of his interest. A day or so later, this man met her husband coming out of the subway. He recognized Mr. Doyle because of his red hair and general expression, which was the same as his son's, whom he had met in the park. The stranger told Mr. Doyle that a plumber was retiring at the seminary where he worked, and suggested that Mr. Doyle apply for the job.

"Both Mr. and Mrs. Doyle were somewhat in awe of going to see a priest about work, but after thinking about it all night and discussing it again in the morning, they decided that there was nothing to be lost if Mr. Doyle made the attempt. Father Flannery told Mr. Doyle that the plumber would retire in about three weeks, that there were twelve men on the waiting list, but that he could make application and in the meantime could do some work on the grounds. Mr. Doyle said that he was glad of the chance to do anything and cheerfully took the job. Three weeks later Father Flannery called him in, said that he had received good references from Mr. Doyle's former employer, and that the job of plumber was his, although he had been thirteenth on the list."

There is more to Mr. Curley's story than luck. He had been a weaver in Ireland, a streetcar conductor in this country. The Curleys were precipitated onto Relief by the sudden and serious illness of Mrs. Curley, which made it necessary for her husband to give up his job in order to take care of the youngsters. After Mrs. Curley improved, Mr. Curley was assigned to tree surgery work on one of the city-supported projects. Later he was transferred to WPA, where he advanced himself from assistant gardener to job foreman. On the last post he earned as much as $175 a month. Despite these promotions, Mr. Curley wanted to get back into private industry. He looked for work as a landscape gardener but discovered that there were no openings. He then took the civil service examinations for the Department of Parks, passed with a high grade, and shortly thereafter received a job.

The behavior of Mr. Corrigan and Mr. Peres suggests that Congress really accomplished what it set out to do when it passed the "eighteen-months ruling." Mr. Corrigan said that "the frequent shifts in job and income with the insecurity that they brought with them were more than he could bear. He saw his future stretching ahead, full of the same kind of insecurity and inadequacy, and he knew that he must do something about it. Because he was employed as a clerk, which meant that he had to be on the job five days a week, he was unable to look for work. He decided that there was only one thing to do and that was to make a clean break of it. He knew that as long as he stuck to the semisecurity of WPA he would never do anything for himself, whereas if he quit and spent his time looking for work there was a possibility that something might happen. He therefore resigned and began following up the leads that he had long known about but had been unable to investigate because of his hours of work on WPA."

When Mr. Peres realized "that he would shortly be dismissed from WPA because of the 'eighteen-months ruling,' he decided to do his best to get a job in private industry because he was fed up with work which had no promise. He found a partner and with the little money that his mother-in-law was able to advance him, they opened a parking lot from which he currently secures about $20 to $25 weekly."

Mr. Cantor, a skilled pocketbook framer, "kept up his standing in the union even during his unemployment, and recently the union has sent him out on small jobs. The field is still slow, but he manages to average about $25 weekly. He is an expert in his line and will be one of the first to be taken on steadily when business improves." Mr. Glass, a skilled hatcutter, got back to work, not through the union, but through "persistent contacts with past employers and people in the industry. His present employer has advanced him money to pay up his union dues, and he is slowly repaying the loan from his salary."

Mr. Crandall, a union bricklayer, had a hard time during the many years the building industry was depressed. Between 1934 and 1937 he had to seek help from Home Relief on four different occasions. Since 1937 he has been able to swim alone. "On one or two occasions, the family's determination not to return to Home Relief was almost shaken by their need, but something always turned up at the last moment. Mr. Crandall, who is slight of build, found bricklaying very difficult, especially when he had to keep the pace set by 'two hundred-pound' Irishmen and Italians. He often came home with eight of his fingers, all but the two small ones, raw with flesh and bleeding." Because of the defense boom, he has recently been able to get back into shipplating, a trade he learned in his youth in Glasgow, but at which he had not worked for more than 12 years.

Mr. Fowler, a chauffeur, had worked for the Packard Exporting Company for 28 years. He had four spells on Relief, but whenever business picked up his old employer was glad to take him back. Many years ago he had worked for a short time as a gravedigger and recently he had the good luck to be taken on permanently. Mr. Goldin has had a varied career, having worked as printer, theatrical producer, and bailiff. When Roosevelt took office he lost his job as bailiff and for the next 5 years was on Relief. Somehow or other, he managed to extricate himself and he is currently peddling cosmetics and clothing, averaging between $15 and $25 weekly. Although he never knows from one week to the next what will happen, the family is able to live on his earnings.

With more men than jobs in the New York area during the late 1930's, it was inevitable that many people would remain on Relief until the job situation improved. Just who would remain and who would get off depended, among other things, on the man's skill and his luck. In these two respects the Closed families had the edge over the Relief group.

PART V. POLICY

Chapter IX

A GOOD SYSTEM OF RELIEF

A GOOD system of Relief is really a contradiction in terms. There is no substitute for the wages that a man earns by his work. True the family of a drunkard may be better off on Relief; with the woman in control of the Relief check, food for the children takes precedence over drink for the man. An old man with a cardiac condition may find a berth on a WPA project. But the number of drunkards and cardiacs in the general laboring population is relatively small and a Relief system cannot be assessed in terms of these exceptional cases. In general, Relief is always second best, usually a bad second. This is true of both Home Relief and Work Relief.

Public policy must be directed therefore toward eliminating the causes of unemployment. One need not set the eradication of all unemployment as the goal. An economy like ours, subject to seasonal fluctuations, to the growth and decline of individual industries, to trade disturbances overseas, must be allowed some latitude. To grant that it would be impossible or impracticable to do away with unemployment completely does not mean that we should tolerate unemployment on the scale of the 1930's.

Based upon our unhappy experience, theorists have restudied our contemporary economic institutions and have concluded that the following changes would contribute to the elimination of unemployment: a tax system designed to prevent the rich from saving too much and to increase the spending power of the poor; to prohibit private industry from restricting output and stabilizing prices; large-scale governmental investments for socially desirable improvements such as rehousing the urban poor and rehabilitating depressed areas. These are only a few of the suggestions found in the literature of economic reform.

We cannot address ourselves to this important area of economic research—the boundaries are really much broader than economics, since the questions raised and the solutions offered have political, legal, social, and even moral aspects—beyond recognizing that, if business fluctuations were substantially reduced, unemployment would become a minor problem. The hope that the economy of the future will be free of the extreme instabilities that have characterized its recent past should not stand in the way of our learning what we can about the administration of Relief. If the stabilization efforts do not succeed, or succeed only in part, we must improve our system of Relief.

An appraisal of Relief during the 1930's can be approached from several angles. One can study the relative money cost of supporting a man on WPA or on Home Relief. This method would apportion the planning, administrative, and material costs of WPA on a per capita basis and add this figure to the average wages of a WPA worker, before comparing the total with the average allowance received by a family on Home Relief. But this would be only the beginning, not the end of the comparison. It would be necessary to translate into money terms the immediate and long-time value of the work performed by WPA laborers. Moreover, consideration would have to be paid to the thorny problem whether a large-scale Work Relief program directly or indirectly acted as a deterrent to private investment. We cannot be concerned with these and other problems, not because they are unimportant but because our data are not relevant.

The facts and figures presented in the foregoing chapters throw light primarily on the influence of different systems of Relief on the unemployed. They illuminate many facets of planning and administrating Home Relief and WPA. Moreover, they set the framework for a study of the re-employability of persons on Relief. Finally, they are relevant to most discussions of economic and social reform.

A primary objective of this investigation into What Unemployment Does to People was to discover the relative efficiency of caring for the unemployed on Home Relief or on WPA. It was found that almost all persons on Home Relief and WPA suffered serious reductions in income. The wages men received on WPA or their budgetary allowances on Home Relief were noticeably less than what they had earned in private employment. Hence, these families had to adjust to less food, less clothing, less medical care.

Many men suffered a serious loss of status, for they fell in the estimation of their families and the community. Many persons were greatly upset because they were forced to seek and accept help from the public authorities. Such disturbance was less marked in the WPA families because the men worked for the money they received. However, few overlooked the fact that their checks were drawn in the name of the United States. There was a marked difference between working in private industry and on WPA.

The superiority of WPA over Home Relief was rooted in the fact that families on WPA suffered less of a break with their past. Men continued to work. They arose early in the morning, ate their breakfasts, left for work, from which they did not return until the late afternoon. Twice a month they brought home their wages, a smaller check than they had been accustomed to, but still a pay check.

Moreover, these families on WPA escaped the periodic visits inflicted on Home Relief clients, and their relatives and former employers were not harassed by investigators. Aside from the initial investigation to which they had to submit in order to establish their eligibility, and a periodic checkup of their financial resources, the families on WPA retained the rights and privileges of free citizens. WPA was better than Home Relief, much better, but it could have been improved.

Prior to their unemployment, the men on WPA had been employed as chauffeurs, plumbers, salesmen, tailors, and butchers. One man had taught English to foreigners, another had worked for an advertising agency, a third had been employed as an accountant. With the exception of a petty racketeer, everybody had been employed in useful work. Even the two men who had served prison sentences held down good jobs when out of jail.

To these men work meant effort contributed to making the wheels of business go round or at least adding to the social resources of the community. A considerable number were, therefore, disturbed by their assignments on WPA. To copy figures, day in and day out, from the Census of 1880 could demoralize most men, especially if they were never told to what purpose these figures were to be put. Such assignments had the hallmark of the British system of "task work," which meant that the unemployed had to do something, no matter what, for their allowances.

Most men were assigned to useful projects but this fact alone did not ensure them a maximum adjustment. During the early years of the Work Relief program, there were men who worked only a few days a month. Because they had to be paid union wages, skilled laborers frequently worked only eight or eleven days per month. Men with strong drives to return to private employment made good use of their free time, but others deteriorated from the lack of disciplined routine.

Resentful of their low wages, many men refused to work hard. They were bitter because they could not support their families on $52 or even $62 monthly. They were particularly resentful when working shoulder to shoulder with civil service employees who received twice their wages or even more. Reclassifications resulting in lower wages were further cause for dissatisfaction. Men on WPA were rated by their foremen on the following six points:

Quantity of Work
Quality of Work
Personal Characteristics
Ability to Understand New Ideas and Instructions
Knowledge of the Job
Overall Rating

and the grades which they received were reviewed by the foremen's superiors. Despite this elaborate system, few men were marked "excellent," and still fewer were graded "unsatisfactory." Industry had difficulty in checking malingering despite its use of the incentive wage and the dismissal threat; WPA was handicapped by an inability to make use of either technique.

Realizing that they were relatively safe from dismissal, most men did not strain on the job. They did as much work as the next man. A competent foreman could usually get a good day's work out of his men even though he was unable to reward good workers and penalize bad ones. But competent foremen were rare.

Poor projects, short working time, the difficulties of enforcing discipline do not exhaust the shortcomings of the WPA program. There was little point to the Congressional act which barred aliens from WPA. Many thrown off Work Relief when the bill was passed and many others who were never assigned were aliens in name only. This country was their home and their children's home. To speed the demoralization of these aliens by preventing them from working on WPA contributed to the demoralization of their children and these children were Americans.

Every Work Relief program has to rely primarily on construction projects, and a good assignment system must pay close attention to the health of the workers. Assignments, such as Mr. Elliott and many others received, were most unfortunate. Mr. Elliott, 54 years old, with an arrested T.B. condition, was put "on a hothouse project in the middle of the winter, although he warned them that this would be injurious to his health and asked for a transferral. Despite several attacks of grippe, they forced him to remain on the project and he was removed only after he had been stricken with pneumonia." Overtaxing a man's strength was one danger; undertaxing his skill was another.

WPA had a threefold objective: to provide work and income for the able-bodied unemployed; to preserve the skills of trained personnel; to offer the untrained an opportunity to acquire skills. We have seen that WPA had serious difficulty in accomplishing its primary objective of providing the unemployed with meaningful work. It had even greater difficulties in seeking to preserve and add to the skills of the unemployed. Most fortunate were men who had been employed in construction and allied trades, for they usually received assignments which enabled them to utilize their skills and occasionally even to add to them.

Worse off were men of little brawn who had previously been employed in commercial pursuits. They were up against it on several scores: Many were unfit to work with pick and shovel. Many resented laboring assignments, since they considered themselves too good for manual work. WPA fell short of its promise in still another regard. Many skilled workers complained that they could not keep up to the standards of private industry because the work on WPA was too easy and the scope for initiative too limited.

Private industry has failed to put men to work in accordance with their desires and abilities. WPA also failed. However, the improvement of Work Relief lies along lines of a closer approximation to conditions in private industry. A reform program should aim to establish a full working week; to increase the power of foremen to fire workers for inefficiency or other just causes; to make available new opportunities for advancement; to revise the wage scale upward so that even unskilled laborers can support their families without supplementation from Home Relief. Clearly, such a program has its dangers, for as Work Relief more closely approximates conditions in private industry, people may become immobilized on the public rolls. However, this difficulty could be met by a closer integration of Work Relief and the public employment exchanges. Such an integration would make it impossible for a man to remain on WPA if offered suitable employment in private industry.

Work Relief can never take care of all the unemployed, for there will always be the sick, the aged, and the maladjusted who cannot or should not be put to work. Hence, the experience of Home Relief during the 1930's should be reviewed, since direct assistance will always have a part to play, in any Relief program.

Home Relief in New York City was probably the equal, if not the superior, of any system of direct Relief and all criticisms must be read in the light of this statement. Since the depression of 1930 descended without warning, no city, large or small, was organized to cope with the large numbers who sought help. During the period when administrative personnel was being recruited and procedures established, it was inevitable that confusion, if not chaos, would prevail. But time alone did not establish a good system of Relief.

The Home Relief families we interviewed were visited during the first half of 1940. We were impressed with the fact that even at this late date many investigators and supervisors had little knowledge of these families. Apparently, recurring emergencies had led to the frequent shuffling of their case-loads. For instance, in the latter part of 1939 the enforcement of the "18-months ruling" on WPA sent tens of thousands from Work Relief to Home Relief.

Despite its short and hectic life, there is a basic core to the theory and practice of Home Relief which warrants critical assessment. Home Relief had the responsibility of determining the eligibility of a family for public assistance. Public opinion, crystallized into legislative action, would tolerate no mistakes. Only the needy were to receive public funds. Whether he approved or not, the commissioner of welfare was obliged by law to check and recheck the financial responsibility of applicants for Relief.

An interesting side light on the efficiency of the Department of Welfare is the finding that in slightly more than two-thirds of the total sample the Relief records had a high degree of factual accuracy, and in another 15 per cent the records were passable. This evaluation is based on a comparison between the Relief record and our interviews. Although families on WPA were visited only once every 18 months, while those on Home Relief were visited monthly, it is noteworthy that there was little to choose between the factual accuracy of these two sets of records.

The Department of Welfare got the facts, but the facts which it got failed to tell the whole story. There were people on Relief, and people are more than dates, ages, and wages. If one appraises the "feeling tone"—a rough indication of the adjustment of the family to Relief—the records were woefully inadequate. Only 5 per cent were accurate; the remainder were blurred or false. When one realizes that supervisors were forced to decide many issues on the basis of these records, the shortcomings were serious.

The clue to this poor "feeling tone" must be sought in the attitudes of investigators toward their clients. Only one-third of the workers were truly sympathetic with their clients' problems and difficulties. The others failed to understand their clients or were emotionally hostile to them. It is barely possible that pressure of work was at the heart of these misjudgments. Forced to sleuth, many investigators lost sight of the basic problem. One can understand the community's concern that the public treasury should not become a grab bag for the lazy and the ne'er-do-wells, but this objective could have been secured without turning Relief investigators into detectives.

If one assumes that people on Relief will try to get whatever they can from the public treasury, then multiple checks and careful supervision are in order. Our evidence lends no support to this belief. We found that most unemployed persons went to great lengths to avoid Relief, and once on the rolls, made strenuous efforts to get off. Intelligent and sensitive investigators could have made a real contribution to the rehabilitation of these families if permitted to carry 30 instead of 60 cases. It is remarkable, however, how much good work some investigators accomplished despite the handicaps under which they labored. Public policy failed because it concentrated on reducing the cost of maintaining people on Relief while neglecting the problem of facilitating their return to private employment.

Even if differentials in the cost of living are taken into consideration, Relief allowances in New York City were higher than elsewhere. Moreover, some unemployed received as much from Relief as employed workers were able to earn in private industry. If one assumes that men work only because they must, the authorities had good reason to fear any narrowing of the differentials between Relief allowances and wages. But do men prefer idleness to work? Some might, but not many. Moreover, there are serious risks in keeping Relief allowances so low that men cannot buy the clothing, the dentures, the tools which they need if they are to return to private employment.

If Relief investigators really knew their families, little danger would attach to liberal allowances, for the staff could distinguish between the few who were content to remain on Relief and the many who sought to return to private employment at the first opportunity. Wide discretion for investigators would introduce administrative difficulties, but a staff operating with little or no latitude cannot fulfill its duties.

Control over partial earnings is a related problem. Admittedly, any system of Home Relief must exercise some control over partial earnings, else the total income of unemployed families might exceed, sometimes by substantial amounts, the earnings of a full-time worker in private employment. Criteria must be established that will prevent the waste of public money without deterring the unemployed from accepting work. The Relief regulations provided that expenses specifically allocatable to a part-time job—such as carfare, lunches, tools—could be deducted from the income which the client earned, but all wages above this amount were to be considered available for living expenses and the Relief allowance could be reduced accordingly. Only when men found a few days' work—usually at holiday time—could they use their earnings for the purchase of clothing, household essentials, and the like.

These strict regulations militated against people leaving the Relief rolls. There was little point for a man to accept a part-time job if he would be no better off working than not working. Many clients reached this conclusion. The removal of all incentive contributed to the isolation of the unemployed. By neglecting to take part-time employment, they lost valuable contacts which might have led to permanent jobs.

Regulations governing the part-time earnings of members other than the head of the household also were questionable. Although the 60-40 formula appeared reasonable, it frequently gave no bonus to a family where a member was employed. Hence, many refused part-time employment. This meant that the full burden of the family's keep was on the community. Moreover the formula had a detrimental effect upon work drives, especially those of adolescents.

Children growing up in Relief families were likely to underestimate the importance of work as life's discipline, and public authorities should have taken special care to counteract such influences. Public policy was based, however, on the belief that children and other relatives would welcome an opportunity to contribute to the support of their unemployed families. This was a false assumption. Most people are willing to help relatives in distress, but they balk at being forced to do so. To make a contribution is one thing; to have one's earnings subjected to regular deductions is something else again.

Perhaps the most serious drawback to Home Relief was the subtle but potent influences that transformed independent, self-reliant people into dependent, supervised clients. The dispensing of public money could not take place without some control over the recipients, but insufficient thought was given to the importance of keeping this control at a minimum. Families on Home Relief lived in a pathological environment. True, unemployment rather than Relief was responsible for their plight, but Home Relief intensified it.

Widespread unemployment precipitates a need for both Work Relief and Home Relief, but the maintenance of people on Relief must never be the sole or even the primary objective of Relief. All efforts must be directed toward speeding the reemployment of clients. Maintenance is only an interim adjustment. Some may think this approach unrealistic for they know that wide-scale unemployment reflects a major breakdown in the economy. No Relief system, not even the best, can give the unemployed their old jobs back. Within wide limits, there is something to be said for this criticism, but only within wide limits.

There is no basis in theory, and even less basis in fact, for believing that the demand for labor is independent of the quality and location of the unemployed. If wage rates are reduced, the demand for certain types of labor will probably be increased. Even if one granted that it is impossible to affect materially the total demand for labor through improvements in the quality, changes in the location, and reductions in the wages of the laboring population, it may still be good policy to help the unemployed to compete for whatever jobs are available. When a Relief system concentrates on maintenance rather than on re-employment, the laboring population tends to be split into two groups—the employed and the unemployed. Yet it is probably preferable to have twenty men out of work for three months than to have one man unemployed for five years.

A major drawback to the efficient administration of Home Relief and WPA was the poor integration which existed between them and the New York State Employment Service. Unfortunately, the State Employment Service was still in its infancy and in a poor position to help materially in removing people from the Relief rolls. However, if the "work-shy" are to be controlled and the working population is not to be split into the regularly employed and Relief clients, a close liaison must exist between Relief and the employment service. Such an integration might also have the advantage of making Relief clients more venturesome. If people knew that they could get back on Relief whenever they had a legitimate need, they would have less fear of relinquishing their Relief status when opportunities for private employment presented themselves. Closer integration between WPA and the employment service would be a necessary preliminary to narrowing the differentials in wages between public and private employment. Otherwise, one runs the risk that the public rolls will become swollen with people who fear to give up the security of a government job.

During the early days of the depression, private agencies were largely responsible for the care of the unemployed. The rapid decline in economic activity caught everyone unawares, and private agencies, having had some experience with the care of the poor, were forced to expand. It was not long, however, before these private agencies were swamped. Government took over and the private agencies, having had a taste of large-scale Relief, fled to safer lands.

This decision to turn their backs on the Relief problem and to sow other fields was unfortunate, for our study revealed a wide "no man's land" between public and private agencies. Many unemployed were trapped on Relief because they could not lay their hands on $50, which they needed for a down payment on dentures, for a kit of tools, for clearing up union arrears. Perhaps the public authorities should have underwritten these expenditures in the form of either outright grants or loans. But they did not. Here was work that the private agencies should have undertaken but they turned their backs on mundane tasks in favor of expanding their services to the emotionally disturbed. This is no indictment, but some contributors may feel that their funds would have shown greater returns if invested in the economic rehabilitation of normal people rather than in the emotional reconstruction of neurotics. If an explanation be sought for the agencies' preoccupation with psychiatric work, one must look to the schools of social work whose graduates sought to put into practice the theories which they had been taught.

Not only the private agencies but also the churches and the unions failed to interest themselves in "no man's land." Aware of the fact that the government was providing the unemployed with room and board, most groups felt free of responsibility. The depression had greatly weakened many churches and unions so that, even with the best will in the world, they would have been hard put to contribute to the economic rehabilitation of the unemployed. Many churches and parishes were poverty-stricken; and many unions were reeling under losses of membership and dues. But the fact remains that these churches and unions could have contributed more than they did. Most unions failed to help even their own members, and their rules and regulations placed specific obstacles in the path of nonmembers who sought employment. The churches were blind. They failed to contribute to the poor, and in fact sought contributions from them. People without food in their homes were offered pledge cards on Sunday mornings.

Retraining played a minor role in the experience of our families, but the problem merits attention in any analysis dealing with the economic rehabilitation of the unemployed. The sample contained a few men who had been trained as welders, and a few others who had received instruction in special WPA schools. The majority had little or no contact with the training program.

Men in their forties or fifties are not good prospects for a training program and these age groups accounted for a large part of the total. However, many men still in their thirties, some even in their twenties, would have benefited by an opportunity to acquire a skill. One can argue that at times when there are more men than jobs there is little point to a training program. Admittedly, training could not guarantee a man a job—there could be no guarantee in the 1930's—but a clerk who received mechanical training would surely have a better chance of finding a job.

In seeking to understand the many shortcomings of Home Relief and WPA during the 1930's, one is impressed with the importance of communal attitudes. What happened to the unemployed was largely a decision of the employed. Early in the 1930's the employed were shocked out of some of their prejudices. When the unemployed totaled 15 million, it was no longer possible for the average citizen to believe that unemployment was proof of personal failings.

Although the public became more realistic in its thinking, the fact that the WPA worker ran a close second to Mrs. Roosevelt as the butt of malicious humor is indicative of how slowly we progressed. Only those citizens who had intimate personal contacts with one or more unemployed families had the perspective for a balanced judgment. But it is a tragedy of urban civilization that people from different social and economic classes have little contact with each other. At best, the relationships are formalized; frequently, they are nonexistent. Ignorance of the facts was responsible for much callousness, but it was not ignorance alone. Selfishness also played its part. Two-thirds of our Private families resented Relief because they knew that the unemployed were getting something for nothing. These workers, who had escaped with their skins, were skeptical of the integrity of the unemployed. If such was the thinking and feeling of laborers, one need not be surprised at the attitudes of stockbrokers and clubwomen.

It was the particular misfortune of the unemployed—at least, from one point of view—to have President Roosevelt for their champion. So deep-seated and unreasoning was the antagonism of the business community to the leader of the New Deal that the unemployed were condemned before they were heard. This antagonism not only manifested itself in discriminatory personnel policies, but it robbed the unemployed of the positive assistance which might have been forthcoming if the business community had been co-operative rather than antagonistic. The business community left unemployment and Relief to the government and contented itself with grumbling about taxes and bureaucratic inefficiency. It never realized its responsibility. Once again "everybody's business was nobody's business."

Despite the pressures that they were up against, most unemployed came through with flying colors. Only 10 per cent of the families were adjudged inadequate prior to coming to Relief. Even after the man's loss of his job, the precipitate decline in family income, the loss of social status, the increased difficulties of management, the besetting uncertainties about the future—even after these doleful developments, not more than 30 per cent of the families were found to be inadequate. Seventy per cent had held ranks.

This finding does not mean that we have little to fear from unemployment so long as its victims receive Relief. True, the unemployed were not seething with revolt, but only the naïve can find security in this fact. A democracy must be concerned with the future even more than with the present, and our evidence disclosed widespread deterioration in the physical, emotional, and occupational condition of the children of the unemployed.

If the plight of the present generation were not proof enough of the need for the utmost exertion of the body politic to cope with unemployment, the threat to the next generation dare not be brushed aside. In the last analysis, the wealth of a nation is the quality of its human resources. Only if every individual has the right to work can the United States be true to its heritage and fulfill its promise.

Chapter X

ONE-THIRD OF A NATION

T. E. Lawrence said of Homer that he was "married but not exclusively," and it can be said of this book that it deals with unemployment but not exclusively. The families included in this study had once been independent and self-sufficient, and there is a good chance that once the demand for labor increases many will again be self-supporting. Prior to coming to Relief, these families had an average income of between $30 and $40 weekly. This placed them considerably above the rural poverty line and even above the lowest urban group. To talk of them in terms of "one-third of a nation" is conservative, for they were more than one-third up the scale.

Unemployment tore the web of their lives; yet these people did not disintegrate. When one remembers how neurotic personalities react to minor pressures, one must conclude that most Relief families were well-endowed emotionally. A comparison can be made with the victims of war, but there is this difference: war involves the entire community; unemployment afflicts only a minority.

Insight into the stuff these people were made of is obtained from testing the hypothesis that racial-religious factors influenced their adjustment to Relief. In a "race-mad" world, suffering from the excrescences of Hitlerian thinking and action, the finding that Irish Catholics, Jews, and Anglo-Saxon Protestants reacted alike is surely important. Yet their backgrounds differed: the Irish Catholics were orthodox; most of the Anglo-Saxon Protestants were not. Many of the Irish Catholics were brought up on farms; the Protestants and Jews were not. The Jews, foreign-born and native, had language difficulties, of which the Catholics and Protestants were free. Despite these and other differences, the three groups reacted substantially alike to unemployment and Relief.

This does not mean that every family reacted like every other family; but it does mean that no important differences could be found in the reaction of the Catholic, Jewish, and Protestant groups. The explanation for this striking fact must be found in the experiences of these families before and on Relief. The "melting pot" had done its work. It was almost impossible to distinguish an immigrant Irish Catholic, born and brought up on a farm, who came to this country in his early twenties, from a native of the West Bronx. The same was true of foreign-born Jews and Protestants, most of whom, could not be distinguished from the native-born members of their respective groups. In fact, similar difficulties existed in differentiating between farm-bred lads from the South and boys brought up on the sidewalks of New York. Apparently, living and working in New York tended to erase earlier markings. Unemployment had the same result. It swept all before it.

Minor differences could be uncovered. No Catholic family on Home Relief took the trouble to hide its status. In contrast, a substantial number of Protestant and Jewish families were embarrassed to the point where they sacrificed real advantages to keep their Relief status secret. There was a neat theory at hand to fit these facts: Catholic families, because of their long dependency on the church, did not feel ashamed of becoming dependent on the state. They were willing to bow to authority. The Protestants and the Jews had no comparable experience. An interesting theory, but probably false. A less strained explanation suggests that the Catholics lived in an area with a high incidence of families on Relief. There were blocks in which every second family was on Home Relief or WPA. In contrast, most Protestant and Jewish families on Relief lived in neighborhoods where the majority was working.

In a world seduced by Hitler's "blood theories," it is impossible to emphasize too strongly the finding that racial-religious factors played a minor role in determining the behavior of these three groups. What were the important factors? Living in the same type of apartments, working at similar jobs, traveling in the same conveyances, reading the same newspapers, seeing the same movies—these forces made for uniformity.

Not every cultural difference had been obliterated. Only Irish Catholics expressed violent anti-British sentiments. Only Protestants voted the Republican ticket. The few radicals were Jews. But in politics, as in other things, the sample gave evidence of great uniformity.

Birth control alone offered some clear-cut distinctions, but even here the differences were constantly diminishing. Orthodox Catholics had to tussle with a problem which did not exist for either Protestants or Jews. But time was working to narrow the differences between Catholics and the other groups. Soon this last significant difference will have disappeared.

Our cases contain interesting sidelights on economic motivation. Professional economists have always assumed that people strive with might and main to increase their income and property. Occasionally a student of human behavior has questioned this assumption, but he has usually been hard put to present evidence in support of his criticism. These cases present such evidence.

During their years in private employment, most men earned $30 to $40 weekly. Neither their planning nor their action suggested that they placed great weight on improving their economic position. They saved a little, but they did not skimp in order to save more. Their "nest eggs" were for emergencies, not for business ventures. Nor did they turn their leisure into money. They burned no midnight oil nor did they work week ends to swell their bank accounts. They were ordinary folk willing to work and, if necessary, work hard to provide for their families, but little interested in sweating and straining to rise a rung or two on the income ladder.

At the time of the interviews, many men appeared to have less than an average amount of drive. Many had ceased to look for work and many others found satisfaction in their WPA jobs. But these facts alone do not prove that these men had always been below par. The evidence points in the opposite direction. In the years preceding the Great Depression, they had been employed steadily and had earned wages that were a little above average. We know further that most men lost their jobs through no fault of their own. Their experiences on Relief held the clue to their depressed condition. Why should a man continue to look for a job after he has been told day in and day out, "You're too old," "We're hiring only skilled help," "At present we're taking on only women." Why should such a man spend carfare and waste shoe leather? Failure to make one's peace with reality is a sign of emotional unbalance. A too speedy adjustment is also bad. Once a man took himself out of the labor market, he was certainly doomed.

The cases contain additional data on economic drives. Men who save their pennies and borrow what they can from relatives and friends to set themselves up in business are usually assumed to be particularly aggressive. Many are just the opposite. They find difficulty in submitting to the discipline and routine of modern industrial organizations, and they seek escape by setting up their own establishments. More frequently than not, this shift brings them longer working hours and lessened income.

Likewise, our families were conspicuous because of their normal sexual and social behavior. Although we excluded obvious deviants, it is noteworthy that only two men had criminal records. Considering the fact that the majority had been brought up on the borderline of poverty and had suffered severe deprivations during the period of their unemployment, the absence of criminality is important. There is more to crime than poverty.

With few exceptions, their sexual behavior was normal prior to and on Relief. One might think that unemployment would lead to a heightening of the sex drive, but our evidence points in the opposite direction. Loss of income, loss of work, loss of status are sexually enervating, and it was rare for men to seek release in intensified sexual activity.

The history of these families can also be culled for interesting findings about the consumption patterns of the low income group. A weekly income of $30 or $40 leaves little free income after necessary expenditures on food, housing, and clothing. The margins are even narrower when the semimonthly Relief check totals only $27.50. However, variations were found even in expenditures for essentials. For instance, the Irish Catholics spent less on rent than either Protestants or Jews. These Catholic families had lived in the lower Bronx for many years, and had failed to pull up stakes even when they had been able to afford better quarters. During their unemployment, they benefited from low rentals.

Savings in rent, especially those secured by overcrowding, were far from an unmixed blessing. In many families, adolescents of the opposite sex shared the same room, and adolescent girls were frequently obliged to sleep on a couch in the living room, deprived of all privacy. Moreover, children who had outgrown their infancy continued to share their parents' bedroom. One need be no orthodox Freudian to realize that such sleeping arrangements were highly undesirable.

Some families ate better than others. Some women were keen shoppers who kept themselves well-informed about fluctuations in market prices, the advantages of buying unbranded goods, and the locales where one could pick up bargains. Not only were some women good shoppers, but some were good cooks.

Whether a family on Relief would be neatly and warmly clothed depended largely on their reserves at the time when they first made application. Hand-downs from relatives and friends also helped out. Moreover, some women were skilled with the needle and could do wonders with odds and ends.

Striking differences were found in household furnishings. In some families, tables, chairs, and beds looked new; in others, they were in an advanced state of disintegration. The difference usually reflected two conditions: a larger pre-Relief investment in furniture; the age of the children. Despite their pinched circumstances, few mothers thought it advisable to limit their children's freedom in order to protect the furniture.

Our families differed in pre-Relief expenditures in still other regards. Jewish families put money aside for summer vacations; Catholics and Protestants paid less attention to fleeing the city in the hot weather. Much of the surplus income of Catholic families went into parties. Some people saved more than others, but the avid savers were frequently unable to control their actions. They deprived their families of essential services, such as dental care, in order to see their bank balances increase.

Fate also had a hand in determining how these families spent their money. When illness struck, expenditures skyrocketed. Debts took the place of savings. True, New York had elaborate hospital and clinic facilities for the low income group but apparently not enough. Possibly, these people were ignorant of or prejudiced against public medicine. Suspicious of the treatment they would receive in a public hospital or clinic, most families depended upon private practitioners. They were up against it because no layman is really in a position to judge the competence of a medical man. Many families suffered not only from the incompetence but also from the unscrupulousness of private practitioners.

Children absorbed much of the free income of these families. Prior to 1929, few families sought to balance the advantages of having another child against the pleasure of purchasing an automobile or taking a vacation. Having children was normal for these families. After the birth of their second or third child, most Protestants and Jews took steps to limit the number of their offspring. Catholics, seeking to avoid conflict with the church, reared larger families. These people knew from the experience of relatives and neighbors that children could be raised on very little, and they felt secure in bringing them into the world on incomes of $30 to $40 weekly.

After 1929, attitudes changed. Men feared for their jobs. If luck went against them, they would have a hard time providing for themselves, their wives, and their children. They feared to enlarge their families, for they did not want to involve the innocent. Even prior to 1929, but especially thereafter, many in the Private families were hesitant about raising a family.

They fretted about reducing their standards of living, and occasionally these considerations loomed especially important. In the case of a working wife, having a baby would send expenses up while income decreased.

In families with one or two children, the balancing process frequently veered off in a different direction. Would an additional child cramp the health, education, and recreational opportunities of the first-born? This question was raised, in slightly different form, by Relief families, who deliberated about adding to their offspring because they were unable to feed and clothe their present brood adequately.

A serious consequence of the economic insecurity of the last decade has been the fear of people in the low income group to bring children into the world. These people do not think in terms of private schools, summer camps, and college. If they can look forward to a steady income of $30 to $40 weekly, they would have no fear. Today the poor are confronted with these alternatives: to forego having children or to run the risk that poverty will cripple the children they bring into the world. The choice of frustrating the present generation or crippling the next is no real choice. It is a challenge to action.

It was not always easy for families to carry out their plans for limiting the number of their children. Conventional instruction in the techniques of birth control leave much to be desired. Although clinics recommend the vaginal diaphragm, many women are unable or unwilling to use it. Condoms, perhaps the most satisfactory method for many families, present a serious financial drain.

Modern marriage may be grounded in the emotional attraction of the partners, but aside from the evidence suggested by divorce trends, there is reason to question this romantic interpretation. Our cases disclosed many women who, though sexually frigid, tolerated intercourse so long as their husbands brought home the pay check. As soon as their husbands became unemployed they put a stop to sexual relations, or at least rationed them. Modern marriage is still something of a bargain; the woman searches for economic security and the man guarantees himself a sexual partner.

The internal structure of the family revolved around the children, while in externals religion played an important role. Catholics, foreign-born and native, were much more thoroughly indoctrinated than either Protestants or Jews. Ceremonials and confession bound the Catholics to their church. Many people, above all, many women, found comfort and consolation in their religious ties. In New York as in Ireland the priest was held in high esteem and exercised great power.

The Jews, also strongly indoctrinated in childhood, present an interesting contrast to the Catholics. The dietary laws, and Sabbath observance were the crucial aspects of their indoctrination. In Eastern European communities, observance of the religious law was carefully controlled. But this orthodoxy was not easy to transplant. Sabbath observance and the dietary laws placed serious if not insurmountable obstacles in the path of normal economic and social adjustments. An orthodox Jew could accept a position only if he could stay home from work on the Sabbath and on thirteen religious holidays during the year.

On arriving in the United States, the Jews took the law into their own hands and continued to observe what was convenient and to discard the onerous. All except a small minority broke with tradition. Present practices are difficult to categorize. Jews no longer attend the synagogue regularly, but they go to services on High Holy Days; they keep some of the dietary laws in their homes but not outside; their sons, but not their daughters, receive a little religious education. The Catholic who fails to go to mass, confession, and communion is no longer a member of the church. But Jews remain Jews no matter how greatly they deviate from law and precept. The accident of birth, rather than the affirmation of belief, determines their status.

The Protestants represent a less homogeneous group than either Catholics or Jews. Many Protestants have had no association whatever with any religious organization, at least not since childhood or early adolescence. Unlike orthodox Catholics or Jews who broke with tradition, the Protestant group slipped away. Never closely affiliated, they severed their connections without effort.

The second group within the Protestant fold were people who attended services when they found a church or minister to their liking. For them, religion was largely a matter of taste and convenience. Little concerned with their own religious obligations, they nevertheless saw to it that their children attended Sunday school.

The Protestants also had their good church members. Many of these people however appeared to derive more social than religious meaning from their association, and the women were more active than the men. In this respect, Protestants have something in common with Catholics, for in both groups religion made a stronger appeal to the women. The synagogue, however, was the domain of the man, while the Jewish woman dominated her home.

These case studies support the widespread belief that organized religion is much weaker today than it was a generation ago. This holds for each of the three groups, although Catholics have apparently held ranks better than Jews or Protestants. Where the Protestant Church is strong, it serves more as a social than religious center. The Jews have broken with their law and tradition but they are still Jews. They remain a separatist group whose uniqueness is grounded less in religion and tradition, and more in the social, economic, and ideological attitudes of the majority.

The fact that this study was carried out in New York City doubtless exerted an important influence not only on the findings concerning religion but also on the social adjustment of these families. Life in crowded apartment houses, subways, movies, baseball grandstands does not contribute to the maturing of friendships. Most women relied on their neighbors for social contact, but these relations were usually superficial. Thrown back on their own resources, most families were closely tied to relatives. Usually, the bonds were close between parents and children, brothers and sisters, grandparents and grandchildren. There was much sharing of pleasure and anxiety, and people spent a large part of their free time visiting each other.

Not all relatives were on good terms. Many people grew up with a strong dislike, if not a positive hatred, of their brothers and sisters, and once out of the parental home, were quick to break off all contact. Many men and women had no idea of the present circumstances of their closest relatives; in fact, they did not know whether they were still alive. Occasionally these estrangements were precipitated by in-laws. On balance, most families were closely knit but this was not always the case.

One may view with equanimity, perhaps even with approval, the decline of organized religion. One may believe, as does O'Neill, that most families camouflage violent and vicious emotions. These opinions notwithstanding, one is forced to conclude that the trends in the religious and social life of our families were impoverishing, not enriching, them. A progressive atomization of the urban family was taking place. Concern with the standing of the Dodgers or with the love life of Joan Crawford was a poor substitute for the varieties of experience in an orthodox patriarchal family.

The inability of the masses to exercise intelligent political judgment is claimed to be the root of most current ills. The finger is pointed at the political abdication of the German and Italian peoples and their willingness to follow a leader; at the frequent bad judgment of voters and legislators in the democracies. What can be learned from this study about the political maturity of the masses?

Marx, Freud, and even conservative theorists would have us believe that people who suffer serious social and economic reverses will react by political extremism. The facts tell us differently. Neither the Communists nor Father Coughlin gained a single supporter! For the most part, these people continued to vote as they had in the past, which meant that they cast their ballots for Democratic candidates.

Cynics might argue that these unemployed knew not what they did; that they had no real understanding of the issues under debate; that they voted for Mr. Roosevelt because he made them extravagant promises, and they disliked Mr. Hoover because he had a sour visage. It would be silly to claim that these unemployed, with their grammar school education, were able to evaluate the farm parity program, reciprocal trade agreements, deficit spending.

These people had no knowledge of modern economic theory, in fact, they had little or no book knowledge whatever. But what they did have was experience, both personal and vicarious. They had lived through the New Era of Coolidge, Mellon, and Hoover, and they had seen it collapse. They were, in fact, caught in the wreckage. They remembered that, during the early 1930's, the national administration scarcely lifted a finger to alleviate the serious plight in which so many honest citizens found themselves. President Roosevelt impressed them, not because they approved his each and every action, but because they appreciated the wholeheartedness with which he gave himself to the task of social and economic reconstruction.

Although many families had no firsthand knowledge of Europe and others had only dim recollections of "the other side," their appraisal of international developments was no better and no worse than most people's. A few were tricked by their emotions. This was especially true of a minority of Irish Catholics, who were blinded by their insane hatred of the British, and a handful of others enmeshed in the Communist web, who followed blindly the American interpretation of the Kremlin.

The majority were more sensible than sophisticated. When Hitler first came on the scene, their feelings toward the Jews largely determined how they felt about the Nazis. By the time war broke out in 1939 they sensed that Hitler and his Third Reich were a definite menace, but they believed that the British and French could cope with it. When France fell, these people knew that the United States had to help Britain. When the Lend-Lease program was expanded these families realized that our active participation could not long be delayed. They hoped against hope that it could be prevented, but they knew that we were committed to the defeat of Hitler.

The common people can apparently reach sensible conclusions about major political developments. Judgment is not limited to graduate students in the social sciences. If issues are freely discussed in newspapers and on the air, one can trust the mass of the population to respond sensibly on an emotional, almost instinctual level. Book learning is of secondary importance.

If the avenues of communication are controlled and manipulated, there is reason to fear, but it does not follow that these families would believe everything they heard. The men, in particular, were skeptical almost to the point of cynicism about what makes the political wheels go round. Tammany Hall and Reform Administrations had taught them that saints do not go into politics and that vote getting is not a pastime for angels.

Despite their lack of technical training, most men and women appreciated that the New Deal was up against such serious problems that one had to be grateful for small gains. The attitude of these people toward Home Relief and WPA was particularly enlightening. They had much to complain about, but they realized that it was no easy matter to establish and operate an efficient and equitable Relief system.

Further evidence of their balance and discrimination is furnished by their thinking about trade-unionism. Most men had been victimized by union regulations. This was true both of the minority who were members of trade unions and for the majority who were not. Despite their experiences, the majority concluded that in a world of unequal bargaining power, there was nothing for laborers to do but band together. Organization might hurt some, but it would help others. These men went further and distinguished between labor unions and labor leaders. They were well-aware that many leaders exploited their organizations but they felt that poor leadership was no excuse for members to scab.

The key to the basic stability of these people must be found not only in their experiences, but also in their expectations. They were born and brought up in poor homes. They had received little schooling and poverty and war had forced many to leave their native lands. Their start in life exercised a great influence over their aims and ambitions. These people wanted to get ahead—by which they understood a job, $30 or $40 a week, a home, wife, children, a drink on Saturday night, and a movie on Sunday. During the 1910's and 1920's they were able to satisfy these ambitions, and slowly they raised their sights, not so much for themselves as for their children. They were better off than they had been in their youth, and they hoped that their children would have a similar experience.

The Great Depression not only robbed them of their savings and their jobs, but also played havoc with their hopes. Older men, realizing that their chances for re-employment were slim, wrote themselves off. But they went further. With great difficulty they began to revise their expectations for their children. They ascribed their own plight to an unfortunate collapse of the economy, but they were confused and unhappy when they thought about the future of their children. They saw no reason why the United States, rich in natural resources and fortunate in its mechanical genius, why such a country should not provide all its citizens with a healthy and a happy life. They could accept defeat for themselves but they could not countenance it for the United States.

EPILOGUE

THE WAR

When the families on Home Relief and WPA were interviewed in 1940, their future appeared bleak. Clearly, the younger men with good leads to jobs would get off the rolls, but only 20 per cent were in this category. Another group, about 25 per cent, were so severely handicapped for employment by reason of age, lack of skills, poor health, little drive for work, alien status, that nothing short of war or revolution could save them. The remainder, slightly more than 50 per cent, had an uncertain future. Possibly they would be re-employed, but there was nothing on the horizon to make one feel optimistic about their chances.

Almost nothing: war could not be left out of consideration. Many men, especially those interviewed during the second half of 1940, had begun to speculate on how their future might be affected by the war. They realized that the war might cause a vast increase in the demand for labor. Realizing the evil of war, many men felt ashamed even to think how they could gain from its spread.

The defense program expanded rapidly; as the tempo of industrial life quickened throughout the country, the demand for labor increased. However, New York was left behind. Without heavy industry and vulnerable to air attacks, New York received few war contracts. For a time, it looked as if the unemployed would wait in vain. But defense gave way to war, and once again rescue appeared nearer at hand.

To trace the influence of defense and war on the employment status of these men, two surveys were undertaken, one in July, 1941, the second in July, 1942. A few men had returned to private employment by July, 1941, but not many. The second check, in July, 1942, was more revealing. This survey disclosed that only 40 per cent of the original group were still on Home Relief and WPA. In 50 per cent of the cases the men had definitely left the Relief rolls, most of them to work in private industry. The status of the remaining 10 per cent could not be ascertained.

At the completion of our original interviews in January, 1941, we scaled the employment prospects of the entire sample, postulating that "the present rate of industrial expansion will continue." At the time of the second survey, in July, 1942, all but 4 of the 20 men whose chances for re-employment had been rated "highly probable" were back at work in private industry. Of the 31 men who had been rated "highly improbable," 21 were still on Home Relief or WPA. Only 6 had definitely secured work in private industry; the status of the remaining 4 could not be learned. In January, 1941, the chances for re-employment of the majority appeared no better than "Possible." Yet 6 months after the entrance of the United States into the war, 2 out of every 3 "Possibles" had left the Relief rolls.

These figures tell a simple story. They indicate that even a modest improvement in employment conditions enabled many Relief clients to return to private industry and again become self-supporting citizens. Some men overcame what appeared to be insurmountable handicaps in freeing themselves of the need for public charity. This is the final piece of evidence in the long chain which testifies to the resilience, stability, and integrity of the unemployed.

It is a tragic paradox that these unemployed men found their salvation in America's entrance into World War II; that their return to work was made possible only because American industry was called upon to produce an ever-increasing volume of death-dealing instruments; that the unemployed man and his family were rescued from the community of outcasts because of the holocaust which covered the earth.

Yet there is meaning in this paradox and it has a moral, not only for war, but also for peace. Once this country accepted the challenge and actively entered the war, we surprised ourselves and confounded our enemies. Goals were set which brought jeers from the Axis and questions from our Allies. But these goals were met and in many cases exceeded. Overnight millions of men were mustered into an army, equipped with the most modern arms, and trained according to the latest doctrines. Planes rolled off the assembly lines and millions of tons of shipping were floated in the Atlantic and the Pacific. Clearly, there was no challenge too great for this country to meet. The people understood and they did not hesitate. Nothing frightened them.

Money was needed—untold billions; it was found. Manufacturing plants had to be converted; it was done. Traditions had to be disregarded; no voice was raised in protest. Faith gave the country strength.

So it was in war; so it must be in peace. The men who went forth to fight, and if need be to die, did so that the country might live, that their fathers, brothers, and sons could labor to build a more perfect union and a more perfect world. "It is for us, the living, rather, to be dedicated here to the unfinished work which they who fought here have thus far so nobly advanced."

APPENDIX

METHOD

PRIOR to undertaking this study, the Director of Research had investigated the problem of the long-time unemployed in the valleys of South Wales.* Wales knew no work relief, only the dole. Moreover, Wales suggested that there was more to unemployment than lack of work and wages. Tradition could not be overlooked in studying the adjustment of people to crises. In planning this study, two hypotheses were selected for testing: was Work Relief superior to Home Relief; was the adjustment of the unemployed greatly influenced by their racial-religious background?

Available funds made it possible to make an intensive study of about 200 families. The fact that the study was undertaken in New York City implied that there would be a predominance of men with work experience in construction and the service industries rather than in manufacturing. Also typical of New York was a serious housing problem, a large foreign element, better educational opportunities. These differences admitted, the fact remains that New York has much in common with other large cities.

To test whether Work Relief was superior to Home Relief, an equal number of cases was chosen from each category. To test whether unemployment was responsible for changes we observed in families on Relief, a control group was included of families from the same cultural and economic background which had escaped Relief. After the project was under way, a second control group was introduced, composed of families formerly on Relief who had returned to private employment. It was hoped that this group could throw into clearer perspective the factors influencing the re-employability of persons on Relief.

To discover whether racial-religious factors conditioned the ad-

* *Grass on the Slag Heaps—The Story of the Welsh Miners,* by Eli Ginzberg. New York. Harper and Brothers, 1942.

justment of people on Relief, the sample was limited to equal numbers from three groups: Irish Catholics, Jews, and Anglo-Saxon Protestants. The Irish Catholics were either native-born or immigrants; the Protestant group was composed of either native-born Americans or immigrants from English-speaking countries; the Jewish families were either native-born or immigrants from Central or Eastern Europe. No Negroes were included.

A diagram of the sample follows:

	Home Relief	WPA	Closed to Private Employment	Private	Total
Catholic	20	20	10	10	60
Jewish	20	20	10	10	60
Protestant	20	20	10	10	60
Total	60	60	30	30	180

Additional eligibility requirements were established. Only "whole" families were included because it was felt that the effects of unemployment could not be disentangled in cases where death or divorce had struck. To be sure that we did not overlook the possibility of unemployment precipitating divorces, a 5 per cent sampling of 5,000 active cases was undertaken to learn the frequency of separated and divorced persons in the Relief population. This sampling revealed that about 10 per cent of the family units were composed of separated or divorced persons, but in most cases separation or divorce had occurred prior to the man's unemployment.

Originally we had planned to include only whole families of two to five children, where the male head of the household was between 25 and 45, but these requirements proved too stringent. Therefore, no control was placed on the number of children in the family or the minimum age of the man, but 59 years was established as the man's maximum age. It was felt that if age were not to overshadow all other factors in the study of re-employability, men in their sixties had to be excluded. Likewise, men suffering from chronic illness were excluded.

To ensure an adequate test of the role of racial-religious factors in the adjustment of families on Relief, care was taken to keep the categories pure. All cases of intermarriage between Catholics and Protestants or Christians and Jews were excluded; likewise families in which an Irish Catholic was married to a French Catholic.

Although the sample was limited to 180 cases, and all calculations are based on this number, we studied a total of 250 families. Seventy families were excluded because they violated one or another eligibility requirement.

With few exceptions, all interviews took place during 1940, a period during which employment conditions in New York City remained substantially unchanged. The political environment was less stable: some families were interviewed before Hitler advanced in the West; others after; some were seen before President Roosevelt was renominated and re-elected; others after.

Three district offices of the Department of Welfare—one with a predominance of Irish Catholics, the second with a predominance of Jews, and the third with a large number of Anglo-Saxon Protestants—yielded samples, not only of families on Home Relief, but also of those on WPA, and those who had returned to private employment. The neighborhood approach was timesaving, since it greatly reduced the social worker's traveling time.

In the early days of the Work Relief program, men could be assigned to WPA without having their financial need certified by the Home Relief Bureau. By 1940, however, all WPA families had been through one or more certifications, which meant that the district offices of the Department of Welfare had at least a thin file on every WPA worker who had lived or was still living in the neighborhood. From these records we built up our WPA sample, but since we were interested in interviewing families of men currently on WPA, we had the names on our list checked against the current payroll.

The district offices also had "dead" files, which contained sometimes as many as 70,000 folders. Since we wished to visit families previously on Relief who had returned to private employment, we sampled these files and sent letters marked "Do not forward, return to sender." Approximately 8 out of every 9 letters came back, but we knew that the ninth family had not moved.

This procedure excluded from the sample families which had moved. What we knew of the general mobility of this population, before, during, and after Relief, suggested, however, that although the majority had moved, few were living in better neighborhoods or more expensive apartments.

The inactive files of the district offices of the New York State Employment Service gave us our control cases—families of the same socioeconomic background as our Relief sample, except that they had never been in receipt of public assistance. To check on the fact that the family had never been on Relief, the names secured from the State Employment Service were cleared through the Social Service Exchange.

Once again, we had only an old address. Following the same procedure as in the Closed cases, we were able to locate one out of every four families. The smaller loss in this instance is explained by the fact that the inactive files of the State Employment Service did not go back more than 2 years, while those in the Department of Welfare included much older records.

This summarizes the salient points in the construction of the sample, but glosses over the many false starts and the many retreats. Although the government agencies were overburdened with work, they left no stone unturned to assist us.

From the first we were uncertain how to approach these families. The psychiatrist was strongly of the opinion that any bribe, in the form of money or other assistance, would interfere with our basic objective of securing unbiased data. People do not mind giving their pedigrees and answering a few questions when they are to receive something in return. However, we had nothing to offer. We decided, therefore, that the best approach was a forthright and honest statement of what we were about.

However, communication was no easy matter. We knew from the records that many men and women had had little schooling. We felt that "Columbia University" on the letterhead would convey little, and therefore printed stationery to read:

COLUMBIA COMMITTEE

FOR THE

STUDY OF UNEMPLOYMENT IN NEW YORK CITY

All persons who had trade-union, lodge, or church affiliations were acquainted with the word "committee."

The following letter was sent to the woman of the household:

> Dear Mrs. Shea:
>
> One of our social workers is planning to visit you within the next few days in order to talk with you about unemployment. Your kind co-operation will prove a very real help to us in our work.
>
> Sincerely yours,
> Director

This effort proved disastrous. Fortunately, it was sent to only 8 women. When our social worker visited these families, she discovered that 5 women had interpreted the note to mean that a Relief investigator was coming to force them to take a job. Since several women were in poor health, well on in years, with heavy household responsibilities and no skills, the prospect of forced employment was upsetting and they were in a panic by the time our worker arrived.

The letter was immediately recast:

> Dear Mrs. O'Brien:
>
> Because we want to learn how people feel about unemployment, we have been visiting families in your neighborhood and talking with them.
>
> Within the next few days one of our social workers will be in to talk with you about how you think and feel about unemployment. We feel sure that you can help our study and we will very much appreciate your talking with our worker.
>
> Sincerely yours,
> Director

This draft was apparently as good as the former one had been bad. At least there were no serious misinterpretations. Equally important was the limited number of refusals. Actually, only one family on Home Relief and two on WPA balked at co-operating. A few people were uneasy about how we secured their names. Since we were desirous of dissociating ourselves completely from the Relief organizations, we usually tried to deflect the question or gave an evasive answer.

The records in the Home Relief offices not only enabled us to set up a controlled sample, but also contributed greatly to the efficiency of our interviewing. The typical Relief dossier contained much factual material, for every family underwent a thorough investigation before it was accepted. The employment history of the man was carefully reviewed; the financial resources of the family were checked; former employers and relatives were interviewed. If accepted for Relief, the family was visited once a month and the notes on these visits were added to the record. Whenever a worker was assigned to a new case, he would seek to familiarize himself with the background as well as the present circumstances of the family. Since cases were frequently reassigned, the records were full, although repetitious and disorganized. Frequently a file ran to 100 pages or more.

The first task of our social worker, prior to visiting, was to read and abstract this voluminous record. She would then talk to the Relief investigator and to his supervisor. Unfortunately, these interviews proved less rewarding than one might have thought, since administrative exigencies had led to such frequent reassignments of cases that few Relief employees were well-acquainted with the families whom they were currently visiting.

It was recognized from the start that the success of our investigation would depend primarily on the skill with which the home interview was planned and carried out. The appointment to the staff of social workers with psychiatric training was predicated on the belief that they, more than any other group, possessed techniques particularly well-suited for the type of interviewing we planned to undertake. Social workers are trained to elicit information of an emotional nature from people who usually hesitate to talk with strangers about intimate details. However, there was this difference between the interviewing techniques typical of social agencies and our research needs. Clients usually come to the agency office, not once, but many times, and what they have to tell is really a process-interview. For many reasons we had to plan on one, at the most two, interviews with each family.

We were careful, therefore, to outline in great detail all points on which we desired information. Our list included about 200 items. To cover so much during one interview of two to three hours—allowance had to be made for interruptions by children, tradespeople, or neighbors—would be possible only if every step was carefully planned.

Anything as formal as set questions was inadvisable, since the major objective of the interview was to learn what the family really thought and felt about unemployment. A list of questions would have spelled failure from the start. Because it would interfere with the establishment of a relaxed relationship, notetaking also was ruled out. The workers were always on the alert for discrepancies between what was in the Relief record and what the person related during the course of the interview. Upon completing the interview, the social worker would immediately make detailed notes to guide her dictation.

The home interview, usually with the woman, but sometimes with the man and occasionally with both, formed the focus of the research, but office interviews with the men and adolescent children also were important. The three social workers were responsible for all the home visits, but the office interviews, held at a neighborhood health or social center, were conducted by the economist. The psychiatrist saw a few of the men and adolescent children. Just prior to concluding the home visit, the social worker would raise the question of an office interview for the man and prepare the groundwork for the following letter:

> Dear Mr. Shea:
>
> Several days ago our social worker had the opportunity to talk with you and Mrs. Shea about unemployment. What you told her at that time was of great help to us in our study.
>
> You said that you would be willing to come in to talk with me and I should greatly appreciate the opportunity, for I know that by talking with you our study would be much improved.
>
> I could see you at the Mott Haven Health Center, 349 East 140th Street (between Willis and Alexander Avenues), Room 203, any time that you indicate on the enclosed card, on any one of the following days:
>
> Monday, October 7th, between 9 A.M. and 5 P.M.
> Tuesday, October 8th, between 7 P.M. and 10 P.M.
> Wednesday, October 9th, between 9 A.M. and 5 P.M.
>
> I hope that you will be able to come for I know that your ideas will be helpful.
>
> Sincerely yours,
> Director

More than 50 per cent of the men on Home Relief but a much smaller percentage of men on WPA and in private employment came to the office for an interview, although many waited until they had been prodded by one or two follow-up letters. The office interview usually supplemented our information about the man's employment history and it also gave us a different slant on family problems. Not every husband saw things in exactly the same light as his wife.

Most children were too young to be interviewed, but we made efforts to talk with the older children. We succeeded in some cases, but not in many.

Interviewing was not always easy. One antagonistic woman was inveigled into talking to the worker for three hours while both stood at the hallway banister. Mrs. O'Connor responded to the worker's introduction by "turning away from the door saying, 'The hell with this talk on unemployment. My husband is employed for a bloody eight dollars a week. Blast this world we live in.' "

Fortunately, most interviews presented fewer difficulties. The workers were usually made welcome and the women talked freely and at length. However, serious problems presented themselves in preparing the case studies for statistical treatment. The quantitative data offered few obstacles so long as one did not strive after spurious refinements. For instance, it was easy to establish the following intervals in the earnings of families prior to their acceptance on Relief: less than $25 weekly; $25-$40; $41-60; $61 plus. Striving after finer gradations would have led to failure. Emotional data presented a more difficult problem, which we solved by establishing broad classifications—"Attitude toward Roosevelt": Positive, Negative, Ambivalent.

The staff feels that the objective data, especially those dealing with the present circumstances of the families, contain only small margins of error. This feeling of confidence is buttressed by the trust many families showed in our discretion by giving us information which, in the hands of the authorities, would make them vulnerable to severe penalties if not to criminal prosecution. Of course, some families remained on guard throughout the interview and were disinclined to tell the whole truth. For example, Mrs. O'Connell, denied that she had children although the Relief record clearly stated that she was the mother of two sons, both of whom had recently had a brush with the police.

More difficult to evaluate than evasion or misstatement is rationalization. In seeking explanations for their actions, most people give themselves the benefit of every doubt and usually find a good reason for everything. When discussing events that took place 10 and 20 years ago, people have especially wide scope for rationalizing. For the uncertainties introduced by rationalization there is no real control, except a constant awareness on the part of the reader that people are always rationalizing.

TABLES

NOTE

To avoid being swamped by a wealth of unorganized data—a typical experience for investigators working with case materials—we took special care to place our findings in useful categories. To accomplish this end, we constructed twenty basic tables. Separate sets were drawn for each of the subsamples—Home Relief, Work Relief, Closed to Private Employment, and Private—and the entries for Irish Catholic, Jewish, and Protestant families were kept separately.

Hence, the basic data are entered on 240 separate cards: i.e., 60 tables for Home Relief (20 basic tables for each of the three racial-religious groups) and the same for WPA, Closed to Private Employment, and Private. Since there are approximately ten items for each family on each card, 20 cards for each family, 180 families in all, the study contained 40,000 classified items.

The presentation of this material in its entirety could be justified only if other investigators could use the raw data for independent studies. But this is unlikely. We therefore present only a selection, frequently condensed, but sufficient for the critical reader to check our findings.

INDEX OF TABLES

DATE OF FIRST ACCEPTANCE FOR RELIEF

	Before 1934	1934-1938	1939 and 1940
Home Relief (60 cases)	24	29	7
WPA (60 cases)	24	35	1
Closed to Private Employment (30 cases)	11	18	1
Total (150 cases)	59	82	9

STATUS OF FAMILIES SINCE FIRST ACCEPTANCE FOR RELIEF

Home Relief (60 cases) WPA (60 cases)

Home Relief Cases with WPA Experience	27
WPA Cases with More Than Three Months Spell on Home Relief	23
Home Relief and WPA Cases with at Least One Spell of Private Employment After First Acceptance	50
Home Relief and WPA Cases with More Than One Spell of Private Employment After First Acceptance	23
Home Relief Cases Receiving Supplementation From Private Employment at Time of Interview	10
WPA Cases Receiving Supplementation From Home Relief at Time of Interview	13
WPA Cases Receiving Supplementation From Private Employment at Time of Interview	12

DATE OF BIRTH OF MEN

Total Sample

	1880-1884	1885-1889	1890-1894	1895-1899	1900-1904	1905-1909	1910-1914	1915-1919
Home Relief (60 cases)	1	10	6	15	16	6	4	2
WPA (60 cases)	7	9	12	11	5	12	3	1
Total Relief (120 cases)	8	19	18	26	21	18	7	3
Closed to Private Employment (30 cases)	2	3	10	5	8	2	0	0
Private (30 cases)	0	3	7	2	6	5	4	3

CITIZENSHIP
Total Sample

	Native Born		Foreign Born		Citizen		Non-Citizen	
	Men	Women	Men	Women	Men	Women	Men	Women
Home Relief (60 cases)								
Catholic	11	8	9	12	12	9	8	11
Jewish	5	4	15	16	16	12	4	8
Protestant	11	11	9	9	15	14	5	6
Sub-total Home Relief	27	23	33	37	43	35	17	25
WPA (60 cases)								
Catholic	9	10	11	10	20	14	0	6
Jewish	10	7	10	13	20	16	0	4
Protestant	19	18	1	2	20	20	0	0
Sub-total WPA	38	35	22	25	60	50	0	10
Total Relief	65	58	55	62	103	85	17	35
Closed to Private Employment (30 cases)								
Catholic	4	3	6	7	9	8	1	2
Jewish	2	3	8	7	8	6	2	4
Protestant	7	6	3	4	9	7	1	3
Sub-total Closed	13	12	17	18	26	21	4	9
Private (30 cases)								
Catholic	6	6	4	4	9	8	1	2
Jewish	7	9	3	1	10	10	0	0
Protestant	9	6	1	4	9	8	1	2
Sub-total Private	22	21	8	9	28	26	2	4

EXTENT OF UNITED STATES EDUCATION OR EQUIVALENT
Total Sample

	Did Not Graduate from Elementary School		Elementary School Graduates		Some High School Education		High School Graduates		College Education		College Graduates	
	Men	Women	Men	Women	Men	Women	Men	Women	Men	Women	Men	Women
Home Relief (60 cases)	24	33	19	14	12	11	1	1	4	0	0	1
WPA (60 cases)	16	21	17	20	17	9	3	3	5	7	2	0
Total Relief (120 cases)	40	54	36	34	29	20	4	4	9	7	2	1
Closed to Private Employment (30 cases)	11	13	12	9	6	3	0	3	1	1	0	1
Private (30 cases)	4	8	9	4	7	7	4	7	1	2	5	2

AGE AT MARRIAGE OF MEN AND WOMEN
Total Sample

	Below 20	20-23	24-26	27-29	30-32	32+
Men:						
Home Relief (60 cases)	2	17	12	19	3	7
WPA (60 cases)	3	22	10	8	8	9
Closed to Private Employment (30 cases)	0	5	6	6	8	5
Private (30 cases)	3	10	5	6	4	2
Women:						
Home Relief (60 cases)	11	23	15	7	3	1
WPA (60 cases)	17	21	8	2	6	6
Closed to Private Employment (30 cases)	1	14	8	2	1	4
Private (30 cases)	3	14	7	3	1	2

TOTAL NUMBER OF CHILDREN—LIVING AND DEAD
Total Sample

	None	1	2	3	4	5	6	7	8	[illegible]	10	11	12	13
Home Relief (60 cases)														
Catholic		3	7		4	1	3	2						
Jewish		6	3	8	1	2								
Protestant	2	5	7	3	2		1							
Sub-total Home Relief	2	14	17	11	7	3	4	2						
WPA (60 cases)														
Catholic	1	6	6	1	2		1		2					1
Jewish	3	4	7	4	2									
Protestant	4	6	4	1	1	1	1		1				1	
Sub-total WPA	8	16	17	6	5	1	2		3				1	1
Total Relief	10	30	34	17	12	4	6	2	3				1	1
Closed to Private Employment (30 cases)														
Catholic	2	2	2	2	1		1							
Jewish		3	4	1	2									
Protestant	1	6	2	1										
Sub-total Closed	3	11	8	4	3		1							
Private (30 cases)														
Catholic	2	2	3	1		1					1			
Jewish	3	3	3	1										
Protestant	3	6	1											
Sub-total Private	8	11	7	2		1					1			

NUMBER OF CHILDREN IN THE HOUSEHOLD AT THE TIME OF INTERVIEW

Total Sample

	None	1	2	3	4	5	6	7	8	9	10	11
Home Relief (60 cases)												
Catholic	1	3	7	2	1	3	2	1				
Jewish	3	3	4	9		1						
Protestant	3	7	4	3	2		1					
Sub-total Home Relief	7	13	15	14	3	4	3	1				
WPA (60 cases)												
Catholic	3	6	5	1	2	1	1			1		
Jewish	3	4	11	2								
Protestant	6	7	3	1	1		1					1
Sub-total WPA	12	17	19	4	3	1	2			1		1
Total Relief	19	30	34	18	6	5	5	1		1		1
Closed to Private Employment (30 cases)												
Catholic	2	2	2	2	1	1						
Jewish		3	5		2							
Protestant	4	4	2									
Sub-total Closed	6	9	9	2	3	1						
Private (30 cases)												
Catholic	2	2	3	2		1						
Jewish	4	3	3									
Protestant	5	5										
Sub-total Private	11	10	6	2		1						

CHILDREN BORN SINCE FIRST APPLICATION FOR RELIEF
Total Relief (120 cases)

	1	2	3	More Than 3
Catholic (40 families)	12	3	2	5
Jewish (40 families)	11			
Protestant (40 families)	8	3	2	

ECONOMIC CONDITION OF ADULT RELATIVES IN THE UNITED STATES
Total Sample (180 cases)

	Families with Adult Relatives in the U. S.	Families with All Relatives Self-Supporting	Families with Some Relatives Not Self-Supporting	Families with Relatives on Relief
Home Relief (60 cases)	55	13	26	30
WPA (60 cases)	53	17	27	28
Closed to Private Employment (30 cases)	28	8	13	12
Private (30 cases)	28	14	14	0

WOMEN'S WORK HISTORY BEFORE MARRIAGE
Total Sample (180 cases)

	Never Worked	Worked		Factory	Domestic	Office Work	Selling	Other
		Steadily	Intermittently					
Home Relief (60 cases)	10	42	8	17	17	7	1	8
WPA (60 cases)	17	34	9	4	11	9	3	16
Total Relief (120 cases)	27	76	17	21	28	16	4	24
Closed to Private Employment (30 cases)	3	25	2	6	6	5	3	7
Private (30 cases)	4	23	3	2	4	7	4	9

MAJOR OCCUPATION OF MAN PRIOR TO FIRST ACCEPTANCE FOR RELIEF

HOME RELIEF (60 CASES) WPA (60 CASES)

Unskilled Manual:		
Home Relief	20	
WPA	13	
		33
Semi-Skilled Manual:		
Home Relief	25	
WPA	26	
		51
Skilled Manual:		
Home Relief	3	
WPA	4	
		7
Commercial, White Collar, Etc.:		
Home Relief	11	
WPA	13	
		24
Skilled Non-Manual:		
Home Relief	1	
WPA	4	
		5
		120

MAJOR OCCUPATION OF MAN

PRIVATE (30 CASES)

Unskilled Manual	4
Semi-Skilled Manual	9
Skilled Manual	5
Commercial, White Collar, Etc.	10
Skilled Non-Manual	2
	30

LENGTH OF TIME IN PRINCIPAL OCCUPATION

Home Relief and WPA

	Less Than 4 Years	4-8 Years	8 Years +
Home Relief (60 cases)	21	19	20
WPA (60 Cases)	27	11	22
Total (120 cases)	48	30	42

UNIONS

Total Sample

	Union Members		Handicap to Former Occupation	Attitude Toward Unionization			
	Were	Are		+	−	O	?
Home Relief (60 cases)	16	7	16	13	9	7	31
WPA (60 cases)	12	5	13	8	4	7	41
Total Relief (120 cases)	28	12	29	21	13	14	72
Closed to Private Employment (30 cases)	9	9	6	10	3	3	14
Private (30 cases)	12	14		11	4	4	11

LEGEND

+ = Favorable
− = Negative
o = Ambivalent
? = Unknown

MAXIMUM BASIC INCOME AND CAUSE FOR SEVERANCE FROM PRIVATE EMPLOYMENT

Home Relief and WPA

	Maximum Basic Income					Cause for Severance from Private Employment					
	Not Self-Maintaining	Less Than $25	$25-$40	$41-$60	$61+	Lack of Work	Loss of Own Business	Illness	Voluntary	Inefficient	Other
Home Relief (60 cases)	4	7	43	5	1	36	2	11	1	4	6
WPA (60 cases)	2	13	32	11	2	46	4	2	0	4	4
Total (120 cases)	6	20	75	16	3	82	6	13	1	8	10

MAXIMUM INCOME

PRIVATE (30 CASES)

Less Than $25	$25-$40	$41-$60	$61+
3	8	10	9

DEBTS: AMOUNT AND PRINCIPAL CREDITOR

HOME RELIEF AND WPA

	Debts					Principal Creditors	
	None	Under $100	$101-$250	$251-$500	$500+	Trades-people	Friends or Relatives
Home Relief (60 cases)	14	18	15	9	4	21	25
WPA (60 cases)	12	26	12	8	2	33	15
Total (120 cases)	26	44	27	17	6	54	40

HOUSING

Total Sample

	Housing			Housing Inadequacies						Housekeeping			
	Good	Adequate	Poor	Crowded	Poor Light	Poor Ventilation	Condition of Building Poor	No Central Heating	No Toilet in Apartment	Good	Adequate	Poor	Unknown
Home Relief (60 cases)	5	25	30	30	26	21	32	6	2	36	17	6	1
WPA (60 cases)	11	32	17	27	14	13	28	6	1	43	9	6	2
Total Relief (120 cases)	16	57	47	57	40	34	60	12	3	79	26	12	3
Closed to Private Employment (30 cases)	4	17	9	13	10	7	10	2	0	19	7	2	2
Private (30 cases)	12	15	3	5	5	2	6	1	0	23	3	2	2

NEWSPAPERS

Total Sample

	Daily	Inter-mittent-ly	None	Daily News	New York Times	Other Morning Papers	After-noon Papers	Foreign Papers, Etc.
Home Relief (60 cases)	45	15	0	38	19	5	10	22
WPA (60 cases)	43	14	3	43	22	5	13	14
Total Relief	88	29	3	81	41	10	23	36
Closed to Private Employment (30 cases)	22	6	2	21	11	3	14	4
Private (30 cases)	21	9	0	18	15	3	20	8

RELIGION AND BIRTH CONTROL
Total Sample

	Religion								Birth Control							
	Orthodox		Moderate		Reform		Negative Feeling		No		Yes		By Inference		Abstinence, Menopause, Etc.	
	Earlier	Now	Earlier	Now	Earlier	Now	Earlier	Now	Earlier	Now	Earlier	Now	Earlier	Now	Earlier	Now
Home Relief (60 cases)																
Catholic	20	13	0	5	0	1	0	1	18	5	0	8	2	3	0	4
Jewish	19	5	0	11	0	0	1	4	3	1	1	4	16	11	0	4
Protestant	8	7	11	7	1	6	0	0	1	0	9	8	10	5	0	7
Sub-total Home Relief	47	25	11	23	1	7	1	5	22	6	10	20	28	19	0	15
WPA (60 cases)																
Catholic	20	18	0	2	0	0	0	0	17	7	2	6	1	1	0	6
Jewish	19	4	1	11	0	1	0	4	1	0	15	11	4	4	0	5
Protestant	6	4	6	3	8	13	0	0	5	2	5	6	10	4	0	8
Sub Total WPA	45	26	7	16	8	14	0	4	23	9	22	23	15	9	0	19
Total Relief	92	51	18	39	9	21	1	9	45	15	32	43	43	28	0	34
Closed to Private Employment (30 cases)																
Catholic	10	6	0	4	0	0	0	0	4	2	1	1	5	5	0	2
Jewish	9	6	1	4	0	0	0	0	1	0	8	9	0	0	1	1
Protestant	6	5	3	2	1	3	0	0	3	1	2	1	5	4	0	4
Sub-total Closed	25	17	4	10	1	3	0	0	8	3	11	11	10	9	1	7
Private (30 cases)																
Catholic	9	7	1	3	0	0	0	0	7	3	2	3	1	2	0	2
Jewish	7	2	3	2	0	3	0	3	0	0	8	7	2	2	0	1
Protestant	3	1	6	7	1	2	0	0	0	0	7	7	3	3	0	0
Sub-total Private	19	10	10	12	1	5	0	3	7	3	17	17	6	7	0	3

POLITICAL AFFILIATIONS

Total Sample

	Political Affiliations												Attitude Toward Roosevelt				Political Activities			
	Republican		Democrat		Socialist-Labor Party		Communist		In-dependent		Aliens and Unknown						Democratic Club		Workers' Alliance	
	Earlier	Now	Earlier	Now	Earlier	Now	Earlier	Now	Earlier	Now	Earlier	Now	Posi-tive	Neu-tral	Nega-tive	Un-known	Earlier	Now	Earlier	Now
Home Relief (60 cases)	2	3	35	26	0	4	0	0	1	1	22	26	31	18	10	1	7	2	0	5
WPA (60 cases)	3	2	39	37	0	0	0	0	4	4	14	17	40	3	5	12	2	2	2	0
Total Relief (120 cases)	5	5	74	63	0	4	0	0	5	5	36	43	71	21	15	13	9	4	2	5
Closed to Private Employment (30 cases)	5	5	18	20	0	0	0	0	3	3	4	2	20	4	5	1	0	0	0	1
Private (30 cases)	5	6	15	14	0	0	0	0	6	6	4	4	20	3	6	1	2	0	0	0

ATTITUDE TOWARD HOME RELIEF
(60 Home Relief Cases)

Evidence of Resistance to Relief	Complaints					Embarrassment Leading to Secrecy	Use of Surplus Commodities	Own Opinion of Management						Toward Work Relief			
	About Home Relief			About Investigators						Specific Deficiencies				General		With Improved Assignments	
	Procedure	Effect on Individual	Budgeting Income	Specific Investigator	General			Adequate	Inadequate	Amusement and Recreation	Clothing	Food	Rent	Positive	Negative	Positive	Negative
31	33	24	15	13	17	13	50	20	40	10	30	22	15	17	43	17	7

ATTITUDE TOWARD WPA
(60 WPA Cases)

Evidence of Resistance to Application	General Attitude Toward WPA			Complaints			Embarrassment Leading to Secrecy	Own Opinion of Management						Toward Home Relief		
										Special Deficiencies						
	Approve	Disapprove	Ambivalent	Administrative Procedure	Effect on Individual	Income Fluctuations and Inadequacies		Adequate	Inadequate	Amusements and Recreation	Clothing	Food	Rent	Approval	Disapproval	Ambivalent
39	43	14	3	31	18	31	25	30	30	6	28	21	17	9	40	11

ATTITUDE TOWARD FUTURE

Total Sample

	For Themselves			For Their Children		
	Optimistic	Ambivalent	Pessimistic	Optimistic	Ambivalent	Pessimistic
Home Relief (60 cases)	17	18	25	18	33	5
WPA (60 cases)	26	20	14	29	20	2
Total Relief (120) cases	43	38	39	47	53	7
Closed to Private Employment (30 cases)	18	8	4	16	10	1
Private (30 cases)	20	10	0	16	6	1

EVALUATION OF HOME RELIEF RECORD

Total Relief (120 cases)

	Adequacy of Record						Agreement Between Record and Home Visit		
	Factual Accuracy			Feeling Tones					
	+	−	0	+	−	0	+	−	0
Home Relief (60 cases)	45	8	7	4	30	26	32	25	3
WPA (60 cases)	39	11	10	2	27	31	23	10	27
Total Relief	84	19	17	6	57	57	55	35	30

LEGEND

\+ = Great
− = Little
0 = Moderate

INDEX OF CASE NAMES

INDEX

BOOK TWO

CASE STUDIES

CONTENTS

BOOK TWO — CASE STUDIES

INTRODUCTION

THIS is a case book. The collection contains twelve studies: three of families on Home Relief; three of families on WPA; three of families previously on Relief who succeeded in returning to private employment; three of families that had avoided applying for Relief. These twelve studies are representative of a sample of 180 cases.

Publication of these cases has several objectives in view. "What Unemployment Does to People" should be told in the words of the unemployed. Moreover, the publication of a selected number of case studies will enable the critical student to evaluate our research procedures independently. Finally, it is hoped that this case book will fill a gap in the literature of unemployment, which, despite its scope, has few studies of the unemployed.

Every reader will want to know the answers to two questions: How were the case studies obtained? What criteria were used in selecting these twelve cases for publication? Our detailed procedures are recorded in the Appendix to *Book One—Interpretation.* In selecting these twelve cases for publication, three were drawn from each subsample—Home Relief, WPA, Closed to Private Employment, and Private. Every effort was made to select representative cases. This explains the absence of extremes; in the 180 cases one found a few drunkards and a few criminals, but not many. A second principle of selection was coverage. Every man was seen at least once, either at home or in the office, and some men were interviewed twice. Two cases also include interviews with adolescent children.

The home interview, secured by the social worker, is the heart of each case. Because there were three workers on the staff, trained at different schools, with different background and experience, the selection includes cases of each worker.

The careful reader will note inconsistencies in the following cases. There are discrepancies between the government abstract and the home interview, and between statements made by the wife in the home interview and by the husband at the office. But these are minor difficulties. More important is the problem of rationalization.

The inclusion in every case of an abstract of the government record, the entire home interview and office interview has resulted in some repetition. But presenting the data in their fullness has the advantage of preventing the glossing over of uncertainties and contradictions.

These studies should be of interest not only to legislators and administrators, who have been struggling with unemployment for a decade and more, but to other practitioners and students. The economist will be interested in the data relating to income and occupational stratification; the sociologist will find rich materials about different cultural groups living in the same environment; the psychiatrist will be able to trace for himself the emotional responses of a group of disfranchised persons; the social worker will see her clients in broader perspective; even the theologian will find much to interest him.

But these cases are meat not only for the specialist. After all, they tell the story of a group of urban families well-adjusted in years of prosperity, and charges on the state in years of adversity. Who they are, where they came from, where they are going are questions of moment. If awareness is essential for the preservation of our democracy, then the stories of these families have a contribution to make to all citizens interested in social and economic reconstruction.

PART I. HOME RELIEF

Case One

COREY FAMILY

Status Home Relief *Religion* Catholic
Man born 1904 Ireland to U.S.A. 1927 Citizen No
Wife born 1909 Ireland to U.S.A. 1929 Citizen No

Education
Man Graduate, Catholic High School—Ireland
Wife Elementary school—Ireland.

Medical Status
Man Negative.
Wife Very thin, looks undernourished.

Woman's Work History Domestic from age of 14 in Ireland. In U.S.A., department store packer, factory worker until marriage.

Married June, 1930, N.Y.C.

Number of Children in the Home Seven *Ages*—5 months to 8 years.

Basic Occupation Before Relief Billposter.

Average Income before Relief $35 to $40.

Private Employment Terminated March, 1937.

First Accepted for Relief May, 1937.

SUMMARY

Home Relief From May, 1937, *to date.*

ABSTRACT OF HOME RELIEF RECORD

OCT., 1933 *First Application:* (Social Service Exchange—No record.) Man is a billposter, employed by an outdoor advertising company since 1928. Since September, 1932, he has had only two or three days work a week at $5 a day and, during the past three months, only a few days all told. Last week he worked only one day, and the week before only six hours. Friends have helped with food. The couple and their two children live in two furnished rooms at $6 a week. They have moved four times in the last year. The children were described as robust and healthy and, according to the investigator, "home very untidy and ill-kept. Furniture old and battered. Evidence of poverty but no suffering."

Case Rejected because part-time earnings exceeded the deficit that would have permitted Home Relief supplementation.

MAY 12, 1937 *Reapplied.* Billposters have been on strike for the past six weeks and the family has had no income during that time. They are destitute. The woman is pregnant. The family saved $60 for confinement expenses but were forced to use it for food. The investigator described the Coreys as pleasant and willing to co-operate. Their rental at this time was $30. The investigator communicated with the advertising company and learned that Mr. Corey had an excellent record. So far as the company is concerned, they did not recognize the strike and stated that in their opinion Mr. Corey had quit his job and their responsibility was at an end. They said that there was no strike, that the places of those who left had been filled by other employees. The man to whom the investigator spoke made no prediction about re-employment.

The family had bought furniture on the installment plan and now the company was threatening to repossess it. Investigator wrote the furniture company, asking them to wait.

MAY 19, 1937 *Case Accepted.*

JULY 1937 Investigator "explored re-employment possibilities." The local to which Mr. Corey belongs appears to have split with the international union and the international now refuses to do anything about reinstating members of the local.

AUG., 1937 Josephine born at home. Berwind Clinic physician and Henry Street Settlement visiting nurse in attendance.

SEPT., 1937 Man going to employment agencies, looking for work. He asked for WPA employment, but this was denied because he is an alien.

OCT., 1937 Investigator helped the family reach an agreement with the furniture company permitting them to pay $2 or $3 a month out of their Home Relief budget instead of the required $5 a week.

JAN., 1938 Family received court summons about the furniture. Investigator wrote the company asking for leniency.

FEB., 1938 Employees of the furniture company arrived with a marshal's notice and removed all the furniture, with the exception of two mattresses. Mr. Corey was told by a representative of the furniture company that he was unjustified in leaving a $40 a week job to go out on strike. Investigator referred the family to the St. Vincent de Paul Society for furniture.

Investigator called St. Vincent de Paul and asked that the family be given furniture.

Investigator called the Department of Public Welfare housing unit about the possibility of a furnished apartment for the family.

Family moved to a ground-floor apartment, five rooms, rental $30.

APRIL, 1938 Budget revised to deduct Unemployment Insurance Benefits at $15 a week, but the man did not receive them and much hardship resulted while this matter was investigated. The Unemployment Insurance Benefits were to have been received automatically, ten days after the "notice of rights," but this did not happen.

MAY, 1938 Full food allowance was granted, but no rent was given until the matter of Unemployment Insurance Benefits could be clarified.

JUNE, 1938 Man reported that he is receiving Unemployment Insurance Benefits, $15 each check. It was decided that since the family had been deprived of their Home Relief income during recent weeks, the first four checks were not to be deducted from the budget, but were to be used for the rent arrears of $60. The man is to make further application for the four additional checks to which he is entitled.

JAN., 1939 Investigator discovered a new floor lamp in the apartment and questioned the family about it. Investigator knew that such floor lamps were being sold in a "bargain package" by

Edison Company. This "bargain package" included a radio, an electric iron, a toaster and a floor lamp, all for $24.50. The family denied this until the investigator confronted them with proof. She had checked with the Edison Company and learned that Mrs. Corey had made the purchase. Finally Mrs. Corey admitted that she had bought this package, but had sold the radio to a friend for $10. She used $2.50 of this $10 to make the necessary deposit and planned to use the rest of it for the monthly payments of $2 each until the amount is exhausted, after which she will take the payments out of her food budget. Investigator also visited the woman who was said to have bought the radio to check on this statement and found it to be true.

APRIL, 1939 — Man goes out daily looking for work. He goes to markets, etc., any place which might need someone who is strong and able to do manual labor. He stated that he is willing to do anything. He reports at the New York State Employment Service office regularly.

MAY, 1939 — Family took $5 from their food budget to buy a communion outfit for their daughter. Investigator questioned the family closely about the possibility of outside income.

JUNE, 1939 — *Last Entry:* Woman five months pregnant. She hadn't told investigator about it earlier because she "didn't think it was important enough."

The social worker who had abstracted the Home Relief record talked with the investigator and unit supervisor. In the investigator's opinion—he feels he knows the family quite well—the Coreys are a good, simple couple, who worry about their large family but continue to have children because they are deeply religious and feel that they must obey all the dictates of the church. He thinks that there is an excellent marital relationship. He knows that Mr. Corey helps his wife with all the work in the home and that he is more than willing to do anything in the way of a job. He is without skills, other than billposting, and there is little chance of his getting back into this work because the local of which he was a member has been ousted by another local which now has a strong contract with the advertising company. Investigator believes that there will have to be a really widespread upswing in business before an unskilled person such as Mr. Corey could be placed.

He knows that there is real need in this family, believes that they are deserving people, and helps them as much as he can with clothing allowances whenever he has them to give. (This investigator is not the one who made an issue of the purchase of the floor lamp—he considered that episode unfortunate and needlessly painful.) The investigator thinks that it would be good for Mr. Corey to be given a WPA job because the man needs work in order to maintain his self-respect. He thinks that Mr. Corey should be helped to achieve citizenship since this would make him eligible for WPA. In his opinion and that of the supervisor, private agencies should help these people become citizens. In this instance they think that the Catholic Charities should assume that responsibility.

HOME INTERVIEW

Mr. Corey, who was busy washing the floor in the kitchen, said that his wife was at the clinic with the baby. He had all the chairs up on the washtubs and table and was in the midst of his work. When worker explained who she was, he said that he remembered the letter and was sure that his wife would be glad to talk with her. He agreed to worker's suggestion that she come back the next day.

Mr. Corey was again alone and had apparently just finished washing the floor again. The children were in and out of the house during the visit. Mr. Corey said that he was sorry worker had failed to find Mrs. Corey in today after making a special trip to see her and explained that someone had given her the gift of a permanent wave and that she had been gone several hours. He said that she worked very hard and was somewhat run down and he thought it would do her good to get her hair fixed up. He did not know how long it might take and when worker said that it might be several hours before Mrs. Corey returned, he replied that he was surprised that anything should take so long. He was friendly and might have talked freely, but the children were milling about and worker suggested that he seemed busy and that she would come back another time. Mr. Corey agreed to this quite readily, saying that Mrs. Corey was usually in mornings. On the next visit Mrs. Corey and the children were at home.

Home—Five rooms on the ground floor, rear, of an old tenement building in the southernmost part of the lower East Bronx. These blocks south of 138th Street and east of Southern Boulevard are comprised almost entirely of wide streets with factories, garages, etc., and a small number of old buildings. The Coreys live in one of the few tenements in this section. Most of the other dwellings are small frame houses. The Coreys have lived in this apartment for four years. With the exception of the kitchen, which is enormous, the rooms are small and at the time of visit were crowded and somewhat littered, though the floors were clean and the general effect was that of lack of space rather than untidiness. The chairs were again up on the tubs and table in the kitchen and when worker asked had the floor been scrubbed again, saying that Mr. Corey had been in the midst of such an operation on both previous visits, Mrs. Corey explained that they try to keep the chairs off the floor as much as possible because of Josephine, who is very active and climbs about so recklessly that she might harm herself if the chairs were not out of the way. The furniture was simple and rather shabby. Several of the chairs were unsteady.

There are two rooms between the living room and the kitchen. In one of these rooms three girls sleep in one bed and in the other two boys occupy another bed. The twins have a large crib in the parents' bedroom. The twins sleep at opposite ends of this crib, with their feet toward the middle. The apartment, though clean, had a peculiar odor, which, Mrs. Corey explained, comes from the cellar. The floor was warped and seemed damp and Mrs. Corey said that this was the result of the dampness of the cellar, which is flooded every winter. The furnace is on the other side of the building and they get none of its warmth underfoot. Mrs. Corey said that she believes the dampness of the floor is responsible for Mary's illness (the child has rheumatic fever). The family plans to move from this apartment before next winter because they are afraid that the other children might become ill.

BACKGROUND

Man—born in Ireland, October, 1904. He was the second of eight children, with four brothers and three sisters. Mr. Corey attended the Christian Brothers' High School in Ireland and was graduated from that institution. His wife talked about his education with some pride, saying that he went as high as one could go in Ireland and that his relatives and friends consider him an unusually well-educated man. Mr. Corey worked in the stone quarries but was dissatisfied with the work. He saved some money and came to the United States in 1927 to join his older brother, who had emigrated in 1926.

Mr. Corey's father and mother are living in Ireland; his father makes a meager living as a shoemaker. His older brother is the only member of his family in the United States. He was also a billposter and a member of the same union. He was formerly on Home Relief and is now on WPA. He is married and has one child. They have three brothers in Ireland and three sisters in London. Mr. Corey was rather vague about whether or not his siblings were married and about their financial circumstances.

Woman—born in Ireland, April, 1909. She was the second of four children; she had three brothers.

Mrs. Corey says that she had a very hard life as a child in Ireland and bemoans the fact that she had so little education. She completed the equivalent of the seventh grade in parochial school. She stated that she had known her husband as a child because they both lived in the same community. But her father died when she was eleven years old and she and her younger brother were sent to live with an aunt in the country. She did not see Mr. Corey again until she met him in New York. At the age of 14, Mrs. Corey went into service in Ireland as a houseworker. She remembers vividly her experiences as a kitchenmaid at the age of fifteen when she lived in a large house in the country and had to get up every morning at 5:30 in order to get the fires going for the baths. She repeated—"seven days a week at 5:30 in the morning." Gradually she worked up to the position of cook but her clearest memory of the entire experience is that of very hard work.

Mrs. Corey said that she would not go back to Ireland no matter how hard life might become here. There is much more chance for education and a future for the children in this country than in Ireland. She feels that perhaps she made a mistake in coming to the United States, instead of going to England with her brothers, but at any rate, now that she is here, this is her home. She came to the United States and got a job as a wrapper in a large department store at $14 a week. Later she worked in a paper box factory at $16 a week. She also tried doing domestic work but did not like it and gave it up almost immediately. The Coreys were married in June, 1930.

Mrs. Corey's father and mother are both dead. Her mother died in 1919 and her father in 1920. She has no relatives in this country. One brother is dead. The two remaining brothers live in London. Her older brother is married and works as a private chauffeur, earning a small but steady wage. Her younger brother works in an airplane factory and was married recently. He is 23 years old.

BEFORE RELIEF

Upon his arrival in the United States, in 1927, Mr. Corey got employment as a delivery boy in a local branch store of a large grocery chain and remained there until 1928, earning $18 a week. In 1928, through his brother, he got a job with an outdoor advertising company, as a billposter and remained with that company until 1937, when his local union called a strike. He earned $40 a week and the union was striking for a $42 weekly wage. In the course of the strike, a rival local, #2, acted as strikebreakers and took the jobs which Mr. Corey's local, #112, had held. Both these locals were members of the same International Bill-Posters Union, but local #2 was out of favor with the international. There was a court fight and the court finally ruled in the favor of the original local but the company refused to consider taking the men back. According to Mrs. Corey, her husband always worked hard and this is corroborated by the statement of the personnel manager of the company, who had told the Home Relief investigator that Mr. Corey had had an excellent record. Mrs. Corey said that her husband was always a very willing worker and that the men used to tell her that the employer would call Mr. Corey for any of the hard jobs that nobody else wanted to do. According to Mrs. Corey, the family didn't have much money but got along quite well on what they had. She said that she and her husband were very happy together and that they planned for the future and for their children. She told about buying new furniture and how proud they had been of it. She said that Mr. Corey was always a good man, that he never stopped to drink on Friday nights like other men. Sometimes he brought something home to drink, but he was entitled to it because he worked so hard.

FIRST REACTIONS TO UNEMPLOYMENT

Mr. Corey went "everywhere" looking for work. He tried all the big plants, the railroad companies, the American Express, any place where they might need a good, strong, healthy man. He said—and Mrs. Corey repeated it when he left the room—that he used to get up at five in the morning to go to work in the old days and that he got up at the same time to go looking for work after he lost his job. He kept going, tried hard not to become discouraged, but when he was unable to find anything to do, the family was forced to ask for Home Relief. At that time they felt that it was only a question of waiting for the strike to be settled. When they applied for Home Relief their debts totaled about $350: grocer—$50; furniture company—$285. Their friends had helped with food. They were paying $2.15 a week for insurance policies which had not been allowed to lapse.

PRESENT SITUATION

Man—A tall, well-built, powerful-looking man, dressed in old, patched trousers and clean, faded blue shirt. His appearance is typically Irish; he has black hair, blue eyes, good color and fine features. Mr. Corey is a pleasant person, with a ready smile and a mild, quiet manner. He talked with a rich brogue. He seemed rather embarrassed to be talking alone with worker and, while he answered questions readily, volunteered little. He said that he is worried about the fact that he is getting soft and losing his ability to work, that it is very disturbing to find nothing at all to do when he is so willing to do anything.

Woman—A short, very thin, tired-looking young woman, who must once have been quite pretty. Her hair, with its new permanent wave, was disheveled and seemed very much in need of attention. She was wearing an old housedress and a torn sweater, old shoes, no stockings. She greeted worker in a friendly manner, saying that she was sorry not to have been home when the worker called before. She said that a friend, who lived in the house, and for whose little boy her husband had given a transfusion, had presented her with money for a permanent wave and she had been at the beauty parlor on the occasion of the worker's second visit to the home. The permanent wave had cost $1.98 and she was obviously quite proud of it. Worker told her that Mr. Corey had been pleased that she was having a permanent, that he thought her great responsibilities in the home prevented her from getting enough rest or paying enough attention to herself and her appearance. Mrs. Corey smiled and replied that her husband is a very good man and that he worries about her and helps her a great deal.

Mrs. Corey talked freely and seemed to enjoy doing so, but it was difficult to keep the conversation going since the children were in and out of the house throughout the interview distracting their mother's attention by their questions and requests.

PRESENT ADJUSTMENT

When seen alone, Mr. Corey said of his wife that she is a very good woman who has a hard life. He said that together they try to get along as well as they can, they help each other and never quarrel. She knows that it is not his fault that they are having so much trouble. He said that so long as he is unemployed, he spends a great deal of his time making it as easy for her as he can and that he helps her with all the housework. He thinks that all this quarreling and drinking which he knows goes on among the poor people in the neighborhood is bad because it helps no one and just makes life harder for the people themselves. When seen alone, Mrs. Corey said of her husband that he is a wonderful man. He is good to her and to the children. He does all the heavy work in the home, helps with the care of the children and she added that, while she wants nothing more than for him to get a steady job, she doesn't know what she would have done with the twins without his help. Not only does he share all the housework, but he does most of the shopping because the shopping center is quite a distance from their home and, since the bundles are usually quite heavy, they are more than she can manage. He also goes to the surplus commodities depot, which is an even greater distance from their home.

Mrs. Corey also talked about those people who, despite the fact that they are either on Home Relief or employed at very low wages, drink to excess. This is apparently a very real problem in their neighborhood, since there are a number of such families in the apartment building in which the Coreys live. Mrs. Corey thinks it a terrible thing for a man or woman to use for drink the money which would have bought food for their children. It is like taking food from the children's mouths. Mrs. Corey said that she and her husband never quarrel, because they know that each is devoted to the other. She knows that their present trouble is not his fault; he could not have gone against his local and refused to strike since he would probably have been beaten up as a strikebreaker. She knows that there is no one more willing to work than her husband. He still goes job hunting almost daily, and she knows that he is registered in almost every place of business in the neighborhood. She thinks it is getting even harder for him to find work now because his clothing is shabby and there is less chance of his making a good impression on a prospective employer. According to Mrs. Corey, her clothing and that of her husband is shabby because the children need so many things that everything the family can spare from household expenses must be used for them. She added that even by making sacrifices they have been unable to give the children all that they need.

Children:

Margaret—born December, 1931, is a pretty, red-haired child who is rather thin. Her color is poor. She is in the third grade at school.

Mary—born February, 1933, is a thin, pale, obviously delicate child who is suffering from rheumatic fever. She has been out of school for several weeks and the Home Relief doctor has been visiting regularly. She has swollen ankle joints and seems to be in considerable pain. Despite this, it is rather difficult to keep her in bed because she becomes restless and has almost no toys to keep her amused. According to Mrs. Corey, the Home Relief doctor has been kind to the entire family. Whenever he visits he brings the children lollypops and plays with them in so friendly a manner that Michael, who has always been very much afraid of doctors, has begun to like him and look forward to his coming. Mrs. Corey said that the Henry Street nurse has also been kind to the family and is trying to arrange to send Mary to a convalescent home.

Michael—born November, 1934, is small, also rather pale. He seems to be a quiet, shy child.

John—born June, 1936, has red hair and freckles and is an attractive, rather impish child. He was friendly and talkative.

Josephine—born, August, 1937, a small, dark-haired, blue-eyed child, is the most troublesome of the lot. She is aggressive, talkative and seems quite disobedient. Both parents agree that she gives them more trouble than any one of the others or all of them put together. She climbs about on the furniture and it is because of her that the chairs have to be kept off the floor. They had to put a latch on the door, almost at the top of the doorjamb so that she would not be able to reach it by means of chairs and table. She gets at knives, falls off things, and upsets the household generally.

Twins, Patrick and Cathleen—born October, 1939, are plump, attractive babies, who appear to be thriving. They were unusually large at birth, Patrick weighed seven pounds and Cathleen seven pounds, eight ounces, and have been doing well ever since. Someone gave the family a twin carriage and on the occasion of the last visit, the twins were out in this carriage in the sun on the other side of the street. The other youngsters run across the street from time to time to keep an eye on the babies. There is almost no traffic on this block and it seems quite safe.

All but the first two children were born at home with Berwind Clinic physicians and Henry Street nurses in attendance. Mrs. Corey said that it was better that way because, while her husband did not need her to do the work, he did need her there to advise him as to what to do for the children. She got little rest and said that she would have preferred to be delivered in a hospital because that would have meant complete rest in bed for nine whole days with no responsibility. She admitted, however, that she probably would have worried so much about the children that she would not actually have rested. The Henry Street nurse, who assisted at the delivery, has been very good to them. She has obviously taken a personal interest in the family and Mrs. Corey is grateful. Mrs. Corey showed worker a picture of the nurse bathing one of the twins with the mother looking on; this had been taken for New York Fund publicity purposes.

Mrs. Corey said that the Berwind Clinic doctor told her that her heart is weak and she must have no more children unless she wants to die young. He was so emphatic about it that she is afraid he really meant it and she has therefore "practically" made up her mind to have no more children. The Henry Street Settlement nurse referred her to the birth control clinic, but she has not gone as yet. The Coreys have abstained from sexual intercourse since the birth of the twins. As soon as she is stronger she will go to the birth control clinic. Mrs. Corey said that she went through a trying time before the twins were born because in desperation at the thought of having another child, she took something which the druggist recommended. This was a bitter medicine (probably ergot) which had been ineffectual. It made her very sick but did not bring about miscarriage. Throughout her pregnancy she worried all the time about the possibility of having injured the baby by this medication and was very happy to find that the twins were in perfect health at birth. Mrs. Corey said that she was so glad no harm had been done by the medicine and so relieved after feeling guilty for eight months, that she was even happy to find that she had twins instead of a single newborn child.

According to Mrs. Corey, tired and weak as she is, she enjoys the children very much and from her manner, worker was inclined to believe her. The children trooped in and out, ringing the doorbell each time, asking for things, coaxing and teasing, but throughout this her manner remained mild and calm. She answered all their requests as best she could, there was no scolding, she patted them affectionately whenever they came near her to ask for something, and at no time was there any evidence of annoyance with them.

Use of Time: Mr. Corey usually goes job hunting early in the morning. He still goes to the large factories asking for laboring work, to the markets, to the American Express or the railroads, and then comes home and helps his wife with the housework. As stated above, he does all the heavy work, helps with the care of the children, goes shopping, goes for surplus commodities, takes the children out when his wife wants to rest. He generally keeps busy.

Religion: Both Mr. and Mrs. Corey are Catholics, were given religious training in childhood and now attend church regularly. Mrs. Corey says that she does not know whether the priest will accept the doctor's orders about her having no more children because she understands that, even when it is a matter of life or death for the mother, the church still believes that birth control is the same as murder. In discussing what might happen if she should tell the priest in confession that she had practiced birth control, she laughed, blushed and said, "Well, I've done my share already. Seven of them. He can't kick." Her husband is deeply religious but he wants her to do anything that will safeguard her health.

Newspapers: They read the *Daily News* which is given them by one of their neighbors. They are also given books and magazines from time to time. Mrs. Corey says that her husband reads "anything he can get his hands on." He sometimes goes to the public library but that's a long walk and he seldom has time.

Political Affiliations: Both Mr. and Mrs. Corey are aliens. If they were able to vote, Mrs. Corey said that they would probably vote for Roosevelt, because they believe he is a good man and they don't know why the others want to get rid of him.

Management: The Home Relief allowance is $42.55 semimonthly. Rental is $27 a month and Home Relief grants the entire amount in the budget. According to Mrs. Corey, their funds are usually exhausted before the next check arrives and they are forced to borrow a little from one of their friends or neighbors. They would rather do this than buy on credit because running up a bill in the store is much too expensive since the grocer usually adds on more than the fixed price. Mrs. Corey says that she tries to see that the children get plenty of vegetables. She buys seven quarts of milk a day and thinks that the children are fairly well fed though they have none of the extras that are tempting and interesting. She talked with much feeling about the difficult time they had with the company when their furniture was repossessed. She said she was out one day and came back to find only two mattresses left in the whole apartment. They were forced to sleep on the floor on these two mattresses for five nights. Finally they got some furniture from the St. Vincent de Paul Society. She gets discarded clothing from friends and neighbors and makes it over for the children. She says that this is easy because she sews fairly well.

Attitudes:

Toward Relief: Mrs. Corey says that they are grateful for help because otherwise they would have starved. It is very hard to manage; they have not had a clothing allowance in a long time, but Mrs. Corey supposes that the Home Relief funds are low. The investigator understands their trouble, tries to do what he can for them, but he, of course, is limited by rules and regulations and shortage of Home Relief money. She does not believe WPA is any real help when a man has a large family, since it means that the Home Relief Bureau must supplement the WPA wage. Her husband, however, feels that he would like very much to be on WPA because then he would be working and might not get so restless and discouraged. She thinks he's busy enough now; Home Relief would have had to send in a WPA housekeeper after the birth of the twins if her husband had been working on a WPA job.

Toward the Future: Unquestionably Mr. Corey will continue to look for work and his wife added, "who knows—maybe he'll find it." True, he is getting disgusted and discouraged, but he will never stop trying to find a job. At the moment, he has some hope of getting work with a cement company which is opening a branch up at Huntspoint. He tries every place he hears about; most of the firms in the Bronx know him and keep promising him that when things pick up he'll be called. One happy thought, in all this difficulty, is the fact that here in America the children will, at least, get an education and perhaps be fitted for something that will enable them to make a living later on.

Toward Us: Mrs. Corey, as well as her husband, was friendly; she welcomed worker and talked freely. She said that she would be happy to see worker again because she enjoyed talking with her. When worker asked whether she might bring a book or something to keep Mary amused while she must lie in bed, mother said that this would be a great help and Mary, when asked, said that she would like a Mickey Mouse book.

OFFICE INTERVIEW

Impression: Mr. Corey is a large, dark-haired, good-looking Irishman, who looks younger than his thirty-six years. He appears to be in excellent health. His clothes were in poor condition and he did not have a hat. He speaks with a pronounced brogue, so thick that it is difficult to understand him. (He was forced to wait quite a while before the interview began and he made every effort to be unobtrusive during this waiting period.)

Employment History: Mr. Corey was a gardener in Ireland, but he also did other kinds of laboring work. When he arrived in this country, he did unskilled work and then secured a job as a billposter at which he worked steadily for twelve years, earning approximately $40 to $50 a week. Because of intra-union trouble, he lost this job.

Relief: Mr. Corey says that he gets just enough from Relief to make a go of it. The surplus commodities are a real help and the major deficiency is lack of clothing. On the whole he feels that Relief workers are nice people. He said that while on Relief his children have been able to have good medical attention, especially the one child who has rheumatic fever. Since he is not a citizen, Mr. Corey cannot get on WPA, although he says that he would much prefer to do so. He fears that he is getting soft and this will make it even harder to get back into a good, hard, laboring job.

Family: Mr. Corey says that his wife has her hands full caring for their seven children. One of the older children has rheumatic fever and one of the younger ones has just come down with scarlet fever. His brother, who worked for the same firm and lost his job for the same reason as did Mr. Corey, is now on WPA. The rest of his family is in England and this is true also of his wife's family. To the best of his knowledge they are doing well.

Time: Mr. Corey tramps all over town in search of employment, seeking out those spots where he thinks there might be need for a strong, healthy man who is anxious and willing to work. He tries to aid his wife as much as possible in order to make things easier for her.

Politics: Mr. Corey feels very bitter about unions because he holds them responsible for his loss of employment; also because he feels that they have stood in the way of his being re-employed. He emphasized that his old employer was perfectly willing to take back the men who were thrown out during the union trouble, but was unable to do so because of the union. Mr. Corey said that most of the men who lost their jobs at the time of the trouble—there were approximately seventy-five—are still unemployed.

Future: Mr. Corey believes that his best chance for work will come if business improves sufficiently so that all union men secure employment and then employers will be able to take on nonunion men like himself. He said that until recently he had not been very worried, but as his period of unemployment lengthens and all of his efforts are of no avail, he is getting worried.

Case Two

BECKER FAMILY

Status Home Relief *Religion* Jewish

Man born 1888 Russia to U.S.A. 1903 Citizen No

Wife born 1890 Russia to U.S.A. 1898 Citizen No

Education

Man Elementary school—Russia.

Wife None—Russia. Two years of elementary school—Philadelphia.

Medical Status

Man Diabetes. Hernia.

Wife "Nervous stomach."

Woman's Work History Factory worker from the age of 11 until marriage. Went back to work shortly after marriage, when husband became unemployed. Worked for about two years.

Married October, 1914, N.Y.C.

Number of Children in the Home One *Age*—14.

Basic Occupation before Relief Tailor.

Average Income before Relief $25 to $35.

Private Employment Terminated June, 1932. Occasional odd jobs after this date.

First Accepted for Relief February, 1935.

SUMMARY

Home Relief From February, 1935, *to date* with the exception of: *Suspension* for one week in April, 1936, because man was suspected of working.

Private Employment From October, 1936, to October, 1937. Earned $22 to $30 a week. Laid off. Waited three months before reapplying.

ABSTRACT OF HOME RELIEF RECORD

DEC., 1933 — *First Application:* (Social Service Exchange—Free Synagogue, Mental Hygiene—August, 1926; Association for the Aid of Crippled Children—October, 1930; Lebanon Hospital and Hospital for Joint Diseases—October, 1930.) Family living in three rooms at $30 rental since 1932. Prior to this time had lived on the Grand Concourse in the same general neighborhood. Man is a tailor, nonunion, who for ten years, ending in 1929, had had his own cleaning and dyeing shop in the Bronx. Because of poor business he had been forced to sell his shop; amount received—$1,800. This was used to pay his creditors. From 1929 to 1934 Mr. Becker had obtained a few odd jobs but in order to exist the family had been forced to borrow $700 from their insurance company, $1,000 from relatives, and an additional amount from friends (this latter amount not given).

JAN., 1935 — There was some delay in filling application blank because man thought he had a job. Investigator states that the family lives in a nice house, that their home is clean but bare. Mr. and Mrs. Becker quarrel about unemployment. He tells her to go out and try it herself if she thinks he doesn't try to get work. Woman says that she is coming to realize that she must adjust to a lower standard of living, more nearly resembling the one which prevailed when they were first married and had to do without things. She asked, "What is there to live for?" Investigator urged her to keep this attitude from her child and not to take "the joy out of his life." She was assured that this situation was just temporary and that she could look forward to better times.

JAN., 1935 — Man got one day's work with a former employer. He goes about from one old employer to another hoping they will have something for him to do.

FEB., 1935 — *Case Accepted* after many collateral visits and questions about man's store.

MAY, 1935 — Woman obviously takes much pride in her only child, who is bright. This boy was born twelve years after the couple's marriage.

JUNE, 1935 — Man referred to occupational department. He is excited about occupational interview though he knows it is only an interview. States that there is little hope for permanent re-employment in his trade. Says that pressing is so cheap now that tailoring shop owners do not want to hire experienced men. Young boys can do it for a few cents a day.

OCT., 1935 Man is willing to take a laboring job but is not referred because of hernia.

NOV., 1935 Home Relief increasingly bitter and humiliating. Man says that he never expected to be on so long.

DEC. 10, to DEC. 24, 1935 Man secured private employment as a presser. He earned $20 during this time and asked to be allowed to use it for clothing. Decision in this matter not given.

APRIL 16, 1936 *Case Closed* after three not-at-home visits on which occasions notes were left asking the family to remain at home. It was considered likely that Mr. Becker was employed.

APRIL 25, 1936 *Reapplied.* Mrs. Becker stated that her husband is not working, but is continuing to look for work. She said that she had been out of the home when the investigator visited because Charles had whooping cough and had to be taken to the hospital.

APRIL 25, 1936 *Case Reopened.* When the investigator questioned family's continuing to pay a high rental, Mrs. Becker explained that they use part of their food money for this purpose.

JUNE, 1936 Woman has arthritis—is in bed. She complains that they are not able to manage on the Home Relief allowance, that their rent and utility arrears are piling up. She was warned by investigator that failure to meet utility and rent obligations might lead to suspension of Home Relief.

SEPT., 1936 Man keeps looking for work. He manages to earn no more than $2 a week but believes that this is important because it keeps up his skills.

OCT., 1936 Borrowed $30 on insurance policy to pay arrears.

OCT. 9, 1936 Woman reported that man obtained work for which he earned $2.50 the first day. Mrs. Becker stated that her husband expects this to be a fairly permanent job, but asked, when she reported it, that the case closing be deferred for a short time to allow some of the earnings to be used for dental and clothing needs. This was permitted.

OCT. 23, 1936 *Case Closed* to private employment.

JAN., 1938 *Reapplied.* Family still living in the same apartment, the rental for which is now $33. Gave information about earnings 10-36 to 5-37, $22 a week; 6-37 to 9-37, $25 a week; 7-37 to 10-15-37, $30 a week. (There is a discrepancy in these dates, but they are entered here as copied from the Home Relief record.) The family paid back $100 to one of Mrs. Becker's sisters, who is very poor at this time and is in need of help. Mr. Becker is not eligible for Unemployment Insurance Benefits since he was employed by a small businessman who had no other workers.

FEB. 7, 1938 Woman telephoned to say that the family is starving. She was described as hysterical when she said that she had used her last nickel to call the District Office. During the investigation woman was asked why Charles did not eat his lunch at school and she replied that he does not like school food and that she prefers to have him eat at home. When the insurance adjuster checked the Beckers' insurance policies, it was found that no adjustment was possible since almost all of the loan power had already been exhausted. The child had a 25-cent policy which was not adjustable. Family stated that they had fought against reapplying hoping that man would get a job. They are now three months in arrears in their rent.

FEB. 15, 1938 *Case Accepted.* Man has diabetes—no longer attends clinic but watches diet carefully and manages to control his condition. He wears a truss for hernia. He was advised to go to clinic and did so. Morrisania Hospital requested a special diet for him and this was granted. Rental $33—rent allowance $25.50. The arrears are piling up and the utility arrears now are $32.69. Woman states that it is necessary to use the light all the time because the apartment is very dark.

DEC., 1938 Family unwilling to move—state that cheaper quarters are undesirable, as to both apartment and neighborhood. They expect that Mr. Becker will get a job "any day."

APRIL, 1939 Man in hospital for operation on a carbuncle at the base of the spine. Prior to this he had been out on many of the investigator's visits and was suspected of working.

JULY, 1939 Investigator found that family had cashed Charles's policies, obtaining $90 in February and $60 in March. The value of these two policies had been $250 each. Family used $75 of this money to pay premiums on Mr. Becker's policy. The remainder of the money was used for clothing and to pay part of the debt to Mrs. Becker's sister, who is married to Mr. Becker's brother.

NOV., 1939 *Last Entry:* Earned about $9 for several days' work. Investigator suggested that he use this money to obtain citizenship papers.

DEC. 19, 1939 The social worker who had abstracted the Home Relief record spoke with the unit supervisor who stated that due to the recent reallocation of case-loads this family is new to both investigator and supervisor. He thought, however, that the investigator had made one visit, but she is now on vacation and will be back in a week.

DEC. 29, 1939 Worker spoke with investigator and supervisor. The case is new to the investigator but she has made one visit and has seen both parents. Concerning the high rental, she stated that Mr. Becker probably gets a little extra work and uses the income to cover the deficit. There is no way of checking this since there are few pressures that one can put on a client to force him to declare his earnings. She said, with some amusement, that she had seen him on a bus recently and that at that time he had been carrying two coats, the stitching on which indicated that they were being repaired. She said that he looked rather "sheepish" when he saw her and tried to avoid her glance. She has not followed this up. According to investigator, there was no evidence of marital discord at the time of her visit and she stated that the husband and wife seemed to comfort and protect each other. When worker raised the question of insurance, investigator and supervisor explained that it is customary for the Relief Bureau to permit the family to cash small policies in order to maintain premiums on a more important one. Investigator is afraid that the family may get into difficulties about their utility arrears if they allow them to pile up during their stay on Home Relief. It was explained that when the Relief Bureau assumes responsibility for a family, all prior utility bills are written off for the period during which the family receives public assistance. The Relief Bureau is responsible only for current bills and the family must keep these paid up.

HOME INTERVIEW

Home—Three rooms on the ground floor, rear, of a fairly modern apartment building in the residential section just east of the Grand Concourse in the Bronx. The rooms open on a small court and are therefore quite dark and seemed rather cheerless at the time of the visit. The furniture, which seemed minimal, was apparently once good, but is now shabby. The apartment was clean. Mr. and Mrs. Becker occupy the bedroom; Charles has a folding bed in the living room.

BACKGROUND

Man—born in Russia, November, 1888, of Jewish parentage. He was the third of three sons. Completed the equivalent of public school in Russia, where he also learned the tailoring trade. Came to the United States with his family in 1903. He is not a citizen.

Mr. Becker's parents are dead. His two brothers both live in the Bronx and are also tailors. Mr. Becker sees them frequently, is on very friendly terms with them. His eldest brother is married to Mrs. Becker's eldest sister. The eldest brother has a tailoring shop in the Bronx. He is in poor health—has a partial disability, the result of an automobile accident in 1931. The income from his business furnishes only partial support and the remainder is contributed by his two adult children. One of these children is no longer able to contribute her share since her husband recently lost his job. Mr. Becker's other brother is unemployed. He and his wife live with two married daughters and two unmarried sons. The sons are unemployed at the moment. The eldest brother loaned the Beckers $400 during the period from 1932 to their application for Relief in 1934.

Woman—born in Russia, July, 1890, of Jewish parentage. She was the third of five children with three sisters and one brother. Mrs. Becker's father died when she was seven years old and a year later her mother brought the children to the United States with the assistance of relatives who lived in Philadelphia. They came directly to Philadelphia but soon after their arrival found that the relatives had lost interest in them and that they would have to shift for themselves. The two older girls were fifteen and twelve years old, Mrs. Becker was eight and her younger sister four, at the time that their widowed mother brought them to the United States; the youngest child, the brother, had died on the voyage from Europe. The eldest girl worked in a factory and was the family's chief support until her marriage at the age of eighteen. At that time, Mrs. Becker was about eleven and had completed about two and a half years at school. The next older sister, then about fifteen, Mrs. Becker described as so short as to be almost a dwarf, adding that she seemed never to be able either to get or to hold a job. The youngest child was, of course, too young to work and it therefore became Mrs. Becker's responsibility to support the family.

Mrs. Becker described her first job in a jewelry factory at the age of eleven and a half, when, in order to outwit the inspectors, who made periodic visits to the factory, the children were placed in the toilet during the inspector's stay in the factory. With some pride, she stated that she had been a bright, able, willing child and had never had any difficulty in getting or keeping jobs. She remained in the jewelry factory for about a year and then, at the age of thirteen, went out to get herself a better job. She got work as an operator in a bathrobe factory and later, because the busy season for bathrobes was the summer, got additional work for the winter season in a shirtwaist factory. She started at $3 a week and gradually worked herself up to the point where she was making $15 a week, which she considered good wages for a woman.

Mrs. Becker's mother died when Mrs. Becker was nineteen years old. Mrs. Becker talked at length about her very hard life as a child but said that at that time it had not seemed to be so hard. She said that she had been happy and contented to work for her mother, who was sweet and good and appreciated what she did. Her mother used to worry about and cry over her, telling her that it was a shame that other girls should have comfortable homes, where they could rest when they were through working, could afford to take vacations or to spend money on themselves for clothes, etc., while she had to sacrifice herself for her family. Mrs. Becker said that she had not considered it a sacrifice at that time because she had realized her importance to her family and had known that she was the strong, able member of the household.

Mrs. Becker met her husband through her eldest sister, who was married to his brother. She worked until her marriage, in 1914, and again for two years when her husband lost his job somewhat later.

Mrs. Becker's eldest sister is ill at present and Mrs. Becker goes to see her daily. She has had two "nervous breakdowns" and is now seriously depressed. Mrs. Becker thinks that her sister's condition has some connection with the menopause. More recently the sister has had something else to worry about. Her daughter, who is married and has two children, is now having financial troubles because her husband recently lost his job in the circulation department of one of the large morning newspapers. Mrs. Becker's second sister, the one who had been unable to find work when she was younger, is married to a man who is in the junk business. She lives in Troy, New York. When the Beckers first needed help, this sister was able to lend them $600, but now business is poor and Mrs. Becker says that she wishes she could repay the money because she knows her sister needs it. The youngest sister is married, lives in the Bronx and has one son. He is 23 years old and unemployed. Her husband is a window washer, works in the subways, earning $23 a week. Out of her savings she gave the Beckers $100 prior to their application for Relief but during the period of Mr. Becker's employment, in 1937, they repaid the full amount because they knew she needed it more than they.

According to Mrs. Becker, she and her husband are on friendly terms with their own and each other's relatives. They visit back and forth, take a great deal of interest in each other's children and try to help in every possible way.

BEFORE RELIEF

From the time of his arrival in the United States, Mr. Becker worked as a tailor, usually doing cleaning and pressing and repairs. He also did some custom tailoring for private customers. Soon after their marriage, in 1914, Mr. Becker lost his job. Mrs. Becker went back to work. He soon got another job, but Mrs. Becker continued to work for about two years in order to help her husband save enough to start his own business. He did so in 1919. During the first five or six years after this, they had a comfortable income but then there came a sharp drop in cleaning and dyeing prices and their income decreased rapidly. Mrs. Becker stated that in the beginning they had received $1.75 for cleaning a dress and that now dresses can be cleaned for as little as 29 cents. For the last few years he was in business, Mr. Becker earned barely enough to pay his family's living expenses and had many outstanding debts in the shop. In 1929 he was forced to sell his shop. The $1,800 which Mr. Becker obtained by the sale of the equipment was used to pay his creditors.

During the next two years, from 1930 to June, 1932, he had irregular employment as a tailor. He worked for the owners of three cleaning stores; each called him in when there was some extra work which the owner could not handle himself. Mr. Becker averaged between $18 and $25 per week at this work. In the summer of 1932, however, there was no further work for him to do and he was laid off permanently. He managed to find an occasional day's work after this, but had no regular income and was unable to pay his bills. In November, 1933, he rented a machine and set up a tailoring establishment in the basement of an apartment building in the Bronx, but gave this up in January, 1934, because he had been able to make only enough to pay his rent in the shop.

According to Mrs. Becker, during the earlier years of their marriage the family lived comfortably. They lived on the

Grand Concourse and paid $55 a month rent. Her emphasis on the fact that they had lived on the Concourse was evidently intended to show worker that they had been quite "well-off." Mrs. Becker said that during those years she was happy and satisfied; that Mr. Becker was a very good husband; that her sisters liked her husband as much as his brothers liked her. She helped her husband in the shop, brought his meals to him, relieved him during the day so that he could go home to rest. She said that since she did not have a child during the first twelve years of her marriage, she had no desire or need to go away during the summer months because that would mean leaving her husband alone and so far as she was concerned, she was perfectly contented to be in town. She said with a smile that she had worked so hard all her life that to have nothing more to do than to look after a small apartment was a vacation in itself. Besides, she had never been to the country and did not miss it. As she looks back on those years now, she says that it was all too good to last.

When their child was born, after twelve years of marriage, they were ideally happy. He was a lovely boy, her entire family was devoted to him, but from a financial point of view, things were not going so well at the time. They managed, however, to give him everything he needed and she devoted her entire attention to him.

FIRST REACTION TO UNEMPLOYMENT

Mrs. Becker said that their first and strongest feeling was one of shame because in their opinion it was a disgrace for a man who had formerly had his own business to admit defeat and have to go looking for work. Later that feeling became less important because they soon realized that any kind of work was by no means easy to find. Mr. Becker soon discovered that most of the people he knew were having the same financial troubles that he was experiencing. They were forced to let employees go and seldom had enough work for themselves.

In 1932 the Beckers began borrowing on insurance policies and from relatives and friends, thinking that Mr. Becker would soon get another job and be able to pay his debts and once more become self-supporting. Mr. Becker refused to go to the Home Relief Bureau and Mrs. Becker said that she spent many months scolding and nagging before he finally made application. In her opinion, they should have applied long before they did because the long delay only meant that their debts grew larger and they got badly in arrears with rent and utilities. Mrs. Becker said that her husband's only response to her pleading that he go to Home Relief was that he could not stand the shame of asking for charity. And when he was finally persuaded to make application, he put off filling out the application blank for a couple of weeks hoping that he would get a job before he was forced to do so.

When the Becker family applied for Home Relief, they had exhausted $700 borrowed from the insurance company, plus $1,100 which they had borrowed from relatives. They owed two months' rent and a large utility bill.

PRESENT SITUATION

Man—was not seen. He was at home but his wife said that he had a severe cold and was in bed. Mrs. Becker said that her husband has had diabetes for many years but manages to control it by careful dieting. He also has a hernia, for which he wears a truss. Mrs. Becker summed up her description of her husband's physical condition with a statement to the effect that he is in a generally weakened condition; so much so that he is unfit for any work more strenuous than tailoring, since that is chiefly a sedentary occupation. She also said that her husband is much discouraged but still eager for work and that he continues to look for it.

Woman—had been lying down when worker arrived. She explained that she was not feeling well and had therefore gone back to bed after her son left for school. She apologized for her disheveled appearance, but soon appeared to forget about it as she talked. She is a thin, tired-looking woman of medium height, whose hair is gray and whose face is lined. She wore an old bathrobe, which she slipped on when she came to answer the door. She asked whether worker minded her leaving it on; that it was more comfortable on a cold morning than a house dress. She was assured that worker did not mind and that the room did seem rather chilly. Mrs. Becker's lower teeth had been extracted. In some embarrassment, she called worker's attention to this and said that one of the first things she hopes to get when her husband starts working is a set of dentures. Her upper teeth should be removed but she is afraid to have this done since she does not know how long she will have to wait for new ones.

Mrs. Becker spoke English well but occasionally injected a Yiddish phrase, which she thought was more descriptive of a particular point she wished to emphasize. She seemed to worker to be an intelligent person. Despite the fact that she is depressed and disturbed by the circumstances in which the family finds itself, Mrs. Becker displayed a healthy sense of humor and an ability to look at the situation with some objectivity. She said that for the sake of her own sanity she has learned to laugh because it is less painful than crying and one's friends soon tire of tears. Much of this was said in idiomatic Yiddish phrases which are difficult to translate. Several times she stopped herself, when she dwelled too long on the past, and said that women liked to talk and if given a chance would babble on forever.

According to Mrs. Becker, she has not been well since her child was born. She had an extremely difficult labor and her health for some years thereafter was poor. She has never regained her former strength. Mrs. Becker was advised at that time not to have another child. She has what she calls a "nervous stomach" and states that from time to time, when she is upset, she has diarrhea, abdominal cramps, etc. Mrs. Becker thinks that the absence of lower dentures, and the consequent inability to chew food adequately, contribute to this digestive disturbance.

PRESENT ADJUSTMENT

Mrs. Becker says that she feels sorry for her husband. He is a sick man, who is getting older and who has very little to do.

He continues to look for work regularly and sometimes gets a few hours of pressing. The family needs this additional income. He sees their need—she doesn't have to tell him. But when she feels sick and tired, she quarrels with him though she tries to control herself because "he is so far down"—she "should not push him further." She tries hard to remember that things were good before and that it was his hard work that made it possible for her to live comfortably. She believes he is so anxious to support his family that he will always continue to look for work and says that he keeps up his contacts so well that a business improvement will probably mean a job for him. At the moment they are both trying to get along as well as they can, but there are many times when they feel "the water closing over our heads."

Children:

Charles—born February, 1926. Mrs. Becker showed worker a picture of Charles, a tall, well-built boy, who, mother states, is nearly six feet tall. She says that he is a bright, good, mannerly boy and that everybody likes him. He entered Townsend Harris High School this fall and is doing well. At open school week, recently, his teacher told Mrs. Becker that he is a fine chap and that she should be proud of him. Charles takes violin lessons from a cousin, enjoys playing and practices regularly. Mrs. Becker's friends tell her that Charles should have gone to a regular high school where the work would not be so hard as at Townsend Harris and where he would have had time for a job after school. His parents have thought about this, but feel that Charles is bright enough to do the work at Townsend Harris and should not be penalized and sent to a regular high school where it would take him four years to do the work which he will now cover in three. They do not believe that a small after-school job, if he got it, would bring in enough income to make it worth while. They feel that by working hard at Townsend Harris, he will be ready for college much more quickly.

As a small child, Charles was a "poor eater." On the doctor's orders, the bottle was stopped before he was two years old, but even before that time he ate poorly and vomited when forced to eat. His mother fed him until he was in the 1B grade, then he, himself, chose to eat alone and he has been all right since. Mother said that she devoted herself to him when he was an infant and that he is everything to her now. She tried not to spoil him because she felt it would be bad for him when he grew up. She has seen only children who were disgustingly selfish and who got into trouble later on when they tried to get along with other children and with grownups. Charles has many friends. After school and on Saturdays, the house is always full of "nice" boys with whom he plays or studies.

According to his mother, Charles is a sensitive child who understands the family situation. He knows that they are on Home Relief and never asks for things which he realizes they are unable to give him. When she wonders what will happen to them, and begins to cry, he tries to cheer her and encourage her by telling her that things will get better. He knows his father tries hard to find work and is respectful and kind toward him. To demonstrate to his mother that things will improve, he recently showed her a salary scale of college men vs. noncollege men, showing her how much higher the income of college men is and assuring her that he will be able to make a good living later on. Charles plans to go to college and his mother hopes that he will be able to do so.

Use of Time: Mr. Becker goes out every day to visit former employers and friends in the cleaning business. Sometimes he gets a few hours of work. This money is used to help meet the difference between their rather high rental and the Home Relief rent allowance. He is supposed to rest during the day because of his physical condition, but when at home, he usually helps Mrs. Becker with some of the housework. He spends several hours a day reading and listening to news programs or talks on the radio.

Religion: Both Mr. and Mrs. Becker were raised in Orthodox Jewish homes and still observe the dietary laws. They attend synagogue on High Holy Days. The boy attended Hebrew school until he was confirmed at the age of 13. He no longer takes Hebrew lessons.

Newspapers: Charles gets the *Times* at school and brings it home. Both parents read it. Mr. Becker reads the *Forward* (a liberal Yiddish paper) and all three read the *Post* in the evening.

Political Affiliations: Since neither Mr. nor Mrs. Becker is a citizen, they do not vote. Mrs. Becker said that she never had time to think about citizenship and feels that is the reason her husband, too, failed to be naturalized. He hopes to apply for his first papers when he can afford it. While they do not vote, they read a great deal and in most election years, approve of the liberal candidate. They hope that Mr. Roosevelt will run again and be re-elected.

Management: The Home Relief allowance is $29.28 semimonthly. According to Mrs. Becker, she can sum up the question of management very simply—they do not manage on Home Relief. They have been in arrears in rent since the beginning of Relief and do not know when they will be caught up. The Relief rent allowance is $25.50 monthly and they pay as much of the $33 rental as they can each month, but are usually a month or two behind. The landlord came in while worker was in the home. Mrs. Becker gave him $10 and a few minutes later he left, after some bickering, during which he threatened to raise the rent to $36 a month, as he is doing in the other apartments in the building. When he had gone, Mrs. Becker said that he could get it from other tenants, but not from her and she may be forced to move. But since she has lived in the building nine years and the landlord is not so bad a person as he sounds, she is hopeful that she will be allowed to remain. They are sometimes in arrears with utilities, but not nearly so seriously as they were before they came to Relief. Mrs. Becker does most of the laundry, but sends out sheets and other heavy articles. Also during the interview, the milkman came in and his bill was paid. Mrs. Becker laughed and said, "first come, first served," and that when the money is gone, the creditors will just have to go on their way. While worker was in the home, someone rang the bell, and when Mrs. Becker asked who it was, a man said that he had a suit to be pressed for a tenant in the apartment upstairs. Mrs. Becker was somewhat embarrassed by this, but worker ignored it. It would seem that Mr. Becker does some work for tenants in the building. In Mrs. Becker's opinion, it is important to try to keep up one's standards as to dress, home, etc., because if you lose that you lose your self-respect. Mrs. Becker brought out an attractive blue velvet dress which she said her husband had made for her of some fabric which a friend gave him. An uncle recently gave Charles a new suit, which he wears weekends. Mrs. Becker said, proudly, that when "we go out nobody knows we get Relief." The reduction in the standard of living has cut the food budget to a point where Mrs. Becker says her meals are extremely simple but by no means interesting because she must buy so inexpensively.

Attitudes:

Toward Relief: The thought of being on Relief is a shameful one for both of them. Mrs. Becker says that her husband manages to put it out of his mind and she, too, tries not to think about it, because when she does she feels sick. They try not to talk about it because talk doesn't help. They do not get surplus commodities. The thought of going to the depot and standing in line gives her a "nervous stomach." Mrs. Becker is certain that her neighbors do not know she is on Relief and feels that she would die if they found out. She tries to tell herself that if one wants to work and does, and then, for some reason, is unable to continue, that person must be helped, but the thought is still terrible. For most people, Mrs. Becker thinks that WPA is better than Home Relief, since a man would be working for his money, but in her husband's case, he is too sick to profit from it.

Toward the Future: The future is very dark. Mrs. Becker won't let herself think about it. The only hope is that times will pick up and her husband will get work again. If this should happen, all would be well. She has thought of trying to go back to work, herself, but is too weak to do so. She can do her housework because that permits her to rest between tasks, but to hold a job one must be young and strong and be able to work the way she used to work when she was in the factory. Eventually her son will be able to help them, but this is a sad thought because she has never wanted to be the kind of mother who expects a child to support her. She wanted to give him a chance to be a real person with a life of his own. But—and here she shuddered—it is not good to think of these things. She feels it is better to go on from day to day, since such a course, she believes, is less painful. She has trained herself to do so.

Toward Us: Mrs. Becker said that our letter was interesting and that as she read it, she thought the study was a good idea. She talked freely and, at one point during the interview, said that it had been many years since she had talked about these things (her past and family relationships). She stated that she was glad to have been able to help, if worker thought that what she had had to say was of any assistance in the study. She elaborated by saying that our chief thought must be for the younger generation—that it will be their world and that we must try to make it a better one for them. Mrs. Becker was certain that her husband would be interested in coming to the office and that she would be glad to have worker come again at any time.

OFFICE INTERVIEW

Impression: Mr. Becker, aged fifty, looked considerably younger. He was noticeably well-dressed and his clothes appeared to be new. During the course of the interview he remarked, however, that he had bought nothing new in the last ten years. Mr. Becker stutters badly; when his stuttering becomes particularly marked he opens and shuts his eyes, a habit which he seems to be unable to control. Mr. Becker is rather stout; his voice is very soft, and he creates a mild-mannered impression; his health appears to be good.

Employment History: He is a tailor; he first learned the trade in Russia; his father and his entire family were tailors. Mr.

Becker related that he always found the trade to his liking. Upon his arrival in the United States, he got work as a tailor and he became a member of the union. Because of his desire to be his own boss, he eventually established his own business. He said this was rather easy to do for, by investing his own savings and by borrowing a small amount of money, he had sufficient capital to start a cleaning and dyeing establishment. During the prosperous 1920's he estimated his weekly earnings at $50 to $60. The average price for cleaning a suit of clothes was $1.75, but today the price is sometimes as low as 19 cents. He said that this radical drop in price resulted from placing the cleaning and dyeing business on a mass production basis. Because of the general drop in business and because of the big drop in the prices for cleaning and dyeing, Mr. Becker went into bankruptcy about four years ago. Since then he has been able to secure only irregular employment.

Relief: Mr. Becker stated that the Relief allowance was so small as to leave one without sufficient money for rent, clothing, and food. He says that it is frequently necessary for him to go without food in order that his son may have enough to eat. He said that it is sometimes necessary for him to go next door to his neighbor to borrow the 10 cents carfare that his son needs in order to go to high school. During the past years he has been on and off Relief, but he found great difficulty in getting back on the Relief rolls the last time he lost private employment. Since he had exhausted his savings before reapplying, he said that the two months' wait between his application and acceptance was so difficult that he almost went crazy. When he complained about this delay at the Home Relief Office, he was told that next time he should apply before he had used up all his money. He said that the investigators were more or less satisfactory. In discussing free medical facilities, he pointed out that he did not like to use clinics and hospitals because he was nervous when in close contact with sick people and hospital apparatus. He was especially pleased about a coat that the Relief organization had recently given his son. Mr. Becker felt that the surplus commodities were not only poor in quality but were the type of food which Jews don't usually eat, so that they were of little value to his family. He said that despite the heavy rain he had walked to the settlement house for this interview because he had wanted to save the 10 cent carfare. (This is questionable because his clothes were substantially dry despite the heavy rain.) Mr. Becker remarked that 10 cents in these days are like $10 in the old days. Mr. Becker receives an extra food allowance of $2 semimonthly because of a diabetic condition, but most of this money is spent on his son. He does not believe that his diabetic condition is so serious as to interfere with his doing a full day's work.

Family: Mr. Becker remarked that his wife has been sick for a long time and that his chief joy in life is his son. Although Charles is not a brilliant student, he is a good student and a nice boy. Mr. Becker stated that, although he really enjoys a 5-cent cigar, he frequently deprives himself when he remembers that his son can use the money for either candy or entertainment. He said that he has one brother, who is too poor to assist, but that a sister-in-law has aided the family in the past and that even today she continues to pay their insurance premiums. Mr. Becker said that, without desiring to boast, he could say that he used to go out of his way in the old days to do nice things for people, but now people stay away because they know that he is down and out.

Time: Mr. Becker says that he sits around the house a lot and in his opinion there is nothing really worse, both for his nerves and for his wife's nerves. He reads a little, but he said that when one is unemployed one has little desire to do much reading. Formerly he read much more. He attends synagogue. (He misunderstood a remark of the interviewer which he interpreted as a reflection on his religious observance and this led to the only sign of belligerence throughout the interview.) Mr. Becker spends some time visiting tailors in the neighborhood and inquiring whether they have any work for him. He says that there is little point in going downtown since he is no longer a member of the union and nonunion men cannot secure work. He finds it difficult to return to the same tailoring establishments week in and week out to inquire if they have work for him, for he knows that most owners are unable to make a living themselves.

Politics: Mr. Becker feels particularly bitter about unions because they make it so difficult for nonunion people to enter a trade. He pointed out that he had missed several good opportunities for employment because of union regulations. He said that he had once pointed out to the Relief organization that if they would pay the $100 required for membership in the needle trades union it would help to get him off Relief, but the Relief Organization told him it would be impossible to make such a contribution. He has not contacted any of the local political clubs, for he feels that politicians want to "play ball" only with those who are "on the make" and that they have neither time nor interest for down-and-outers. Mr. Becker was resentful about the high income that some workers are able to earn and he feels that steps ought to be taken so that the unemployed can secure an opportunity to share the available work. He believes that the government has made many bad mistakes in matters relating to labor since the new laws are really improving the position of union leaders rather than improving the lot of the working people. He has strong objections to the Workers' Alliance for he believes it to be an organization interested in making trouble. Mr. Becker stated that he always believed in minding his own business.

Future: Mr. Becker definitely hopes to get a job. His major interest in the future is the welfare of his son. Because he is getting on in age and his wife is ill, he is especially glad of the money that his sister-in-law gives him to pay the premiums on his insurance, since this gives him a little protection.

OFFICE INTERVIEW

Charles had been at the university the previous week, but had forgotten the number of the room in which the interview was scheduled. This was his second visit.

Charles is a tall, well-built boy. He was warmly dressed,

wearing a lumber jacket and a sport cap with earmuffs attached. His trousers were well-pressed and his shoes were new.

Charles is completing his second year at Townsend Harris High School, having entered the school through competitive examination. His best subjects are history and English; mathematics and French are difficult for him. He remarked in passing that he finds his schoolwork quite a burden; this, he feels, would not be true if he attended DeWitt Clinton High School where there are so many pupils that the school day is limited to four hours. In discussing whether a coeducational school would be preferable, Charles thought it would make little difference since one could not be distracted if one had much work to do. However, if the school program were light, girls might prove distracting. Charles intends to go to college because Townsend Harris, which is the preparatory high school for City College, affords him a good opportunity to do so. Charles admitted that he had once or twice played with the idea of not going to college but not since entering Townsend Harris. He thinks education is a good thing.

Charles usually gets up at about 6:45 in the morning; his first class begins at 8:30. He finishes school at four in the afternoon, having completed six one-hour periods. He then goes home and idles the time away until dinner. He practices the violin an hour a day and spends approximately two and one-half hours on his homework, although if he were to do his homework thoroughly, he would need another hour. He usually retires at 10:30. Charles estimates his violin expenses for the year—teaching and scores included—at about $60, a price considerably below the average because of his family's special relations to the teacher. He says that he derives much pleasure from playing, though he has no intention whatever of becoming a musician. He has been taking lessons for the last two and one-half years.

Charles says that, when in public school, he thought once or twice about becoming a dentist, but after watching dentists at work he decided otherwise. He also remarked that dentistry would probably not be a wise choice for him since it took many years of preparation. Then there is always the risk that, although there might be money in the family to meet the costs of schooling at an early stage in his course, the money might not be available for him to complete the course and he would therefore be stranded. More recently Charles has thought about becoming a teacher of history. This appeals to him because he does well in history; during the first year he received 89 per cent and although he dropped to 80 per cent at the beginning of this year, he thinks that his marks will rise again. Teaching appeals to him because it is relatively easy work at good pay. He emphasized the fact that he did not want to make a lot of money, nor did he want to work too hard. He is, however, perfectly willing to work hard in the next few years because he hopes, in later years, to derive the benefits from this hard work. Charles emphasized that he was more interested in fun than money by stating that one frequently has to work very hard to make an additional 25 or 50 cents, while if one were willing to forego this additional money one could have a lot of fun. Later in the interview he remarked that he would like to travel and hoped to see the world after finishing college. He thought that he might be able to support himself by writing. When asked whether there might not be a contradiction between traveling around the world and settling down to be a teacher, he said he looked forward to traveling only in the period between the completion of his studies and the beginning of his professional work. He pointed out that there was a vocational guidance counselor in his school and there were lectures about vocational adjustment, but the services of the counselor and the lectures were mostly reserved for seniors.

Charles has had many small jobs during the past years, mostly at the Yankee Stadium, where he is able to earn between 25 and 50 cents by working the turnstiles. This type of work also enables him to see the game without paying. Occasionally he sells programs and that enables him to earn a little more. He explained that he obtained the job by hanging around and being chosen from a group of boys and that, once having got the job, it was easier for him to be chosen a second time. When the next baseball season opens, he hopes to get a better job although he is really not eligible since they are reserved for boys above sixteen years of age and he is only fourteen and one-half. During the past summer, he worked for a tailor and earned approximately $55 for twelve weeks' work. Although the tailor paid him an extra 25 cents on Saturday for washing the windows, he said he would have much preferred not to have made the extra 25 cents and to have avoided working so hard. He admitted that his father's attitude toward work was different, for his father was constantly trying to make more money but Charles explained this by saying that if he had the same responsibilities as had his father, he might be willing to work harder. Charles related that the family was no longer on Relief and, although his father is not earning much, they can get along on it. He said that he had no shame when the family was on Relief, but of course he took steps to hide the fact from his friends. He felt that Home Relief should keep the status of their clients confidential and mentioned the fact that the man who read the gas meter knew which of the tenants were on Relief. He did not approve of WPA, although he thought it better than Home Relief. Charles clearly differentiated the experiences of his own family from those people on Relief whom he defined as "bums"—groups among the Negroes, Italians, and Irish, who had never worked steadily in their lives and who never really wanted to work steadily. He thought it was these people who gave Senator Taft and Mr. Ford the opportunity to say that Relief was wasteful and being given to bums.

A group of boys and girls, under the leadership of a sister of one of his friends, recently formed a Zionist labor group. The group included the son of a prominent Rabbi and several boys whose families were moderately wealthy. Shortly after the club was formed, the sons of the wealthier parents withdrew because they felt that the group was too socialistic and that labor had too much to say in this world and they did not approve of its power. Charles thought that this was a very short-sighted point of view since labor should really have more to say about the control of affairs. Charles is not much interested in girls although he knows a large number of them, nor does he feel that his relationships with them are handicapped by his family's poor economic position.

Charles was confirmed at the age of thirteen, but he does not attend synagogue regularly. He reads constantly and borrows books from his more well-to-do friends. His family frequently visits relatives and friends and Charles believes that his father's unemployment did not disturb these social relations because the economic position of relatives and friends also deteriorated during the last years. He remarked that he was really a "depression baby" since his family met with financial difficulties soon after he was born. Charles frequently commented upon the differences between rich and poor people and concluded that the major difference between them was the type of recreation that the wealthier people could engage in. Charles said that as far as his own family was concerned, they experienced major difficulty when medical services had to be paid for. He cited as a recent example the fact that when he had his teeth cleaned this expenditure made a dent in available funds.

Charles said that when he first came to Townsend Harris he attended a meeting of the American Student Union but he did not like the behavior of the boys. A week or so thereafter, they refused to condemn Russia for its invasion of Finland and he said that that "queered" them with him. He said that he is a liberal but emphasized that that does not mean he is a radical. He recently read Pierre Van Paassen's book and was much disturbed by the role that armament workers played in prolonging the last war and he had assumed, when this war began, that they would play much the same role. Since Chamberlain's withdrawal from office, however, he has been less certain that this war is identical with the last, and he now favors material aid to Great Britain, but does not want to see an expeditionary force sent abroad. Charles said that he was very "mad" at Lewis for his attitude toward Roosevelt, but now he has reached the conclusion that perhaps Lewis was shrewd in realizing that the administration would be forced to pass many laws injurious to labor and Lewis wanted to jump in time. He could not understand, however, why Lewis went so far as to endorse Willkie.

(Charles inquired whether the interviewer had talked with his father, and when told that he had, Charles appeared disturbed. He pointed out that the signature on the letter inviting him to come to the office differed from the signature on his father's invitation. Although an explanation was offered, he remained unsatisfied and somewhat upset.)

Case Three

BARTON FAMILY

Status Home Relief *Religion* Protestant

Man born 1900 N.Y.C.

Wife born 1900 N.Y.C.

Education

Man Completed elementary school.

Wife Completed three years high school.

Medical Status

Man Gastric ulcers

Wife Negative

Woman's Work History Secretarial work, 1918-1924.

Married July, 1922.

Number of Children in the Home Two *Ages*—12 and 15 years.

Basic Occupation Before Relief Taxi driver.

Average Income Before Relief $30 to $50.

Private Employment Terminated April, 1933.

First Accepted for Relief June, 1933.

SUMMARY

Home Relief From June, 1933, to November, 1933. Closed to Private Employment.

Private Employment from November, 1933, to August, 1935. Elevator operator. Employment terminated by illness.

Home Relief from September, 1935, *to date.*

ABSTRACT OF HOME RELIEF RECORD

MAY, 1933 *First Application:* Man has had no steady employment for about three years. For several months prior to April, 1933, he was a taxi driver, but is now blacklisted because an inspector recently reported that he had left his cab for a few hours on one occasion. The income from this source was not sufficient for the needs of the family and they supplemented it by pawning articles of clothing, etc., and borrowing from other sources. Man even pawned his overcoat for $1. They exhausted their savings, borrowed on insurance policies and from a friend. This friend loaned $50 but cannot give further assistance. In 1929 Mr. Barton invested $1,000 in bonds, using $600 from his savings account and $400 inherited from an uncle's estate. With this $1,000 he purchased a junior lien on the Franklin Towers Apartment Hotel. In August, 1930, he received a small dividend, but there has been nothing since, and the bonds are now worthless. At this time the Bartons' only debts are one month's utilities bills and $50 to a friend. The rent is paid to date. The man requested Work Relief, rather than Home Relief.

JUNE, 1933 — *Case Accepted.* Worker planned to refer man for laboring and woman for clerical work.

AUG. 10, 1933 — Man referred for Work Relief.

AUG. 24, 1933 — At the time of the visit the man was in bed and worker deduced from this that he had "evidently driven a cab" the previous night. "Woman stated he seldom earned anything—not enough to amount to a definite weekly income."

SEPT. 1, 1933 — Case reported to Industrial Survey for a taxi clearing. (This department checks lists of employees of all taxi companies in the city to determine whether person in question is on one of these lists.)

SEPT. 28, 1933 — Man reported he expects a job early in October.

OCT., 1933 — Rent paid to date from earnings as taxi driver.

NOV. 16, 1933 — Family reported that Mr. Barton started working during the previous week as relief man (doorman, elevator operator, etc.) in a large apartment building. He will earn $70 a month.

NOV. 27, 1933 — *Case Closed* to Private Employment.

AUG., 1935 — *Reapplied.* Man was unable to go to work during the past week because of bleeding stomach ulcers, for which he is receiving treatment at Presbyterian Medical Center. His job is being held open for a short, indefinite period. The family has a roomer who is paying $4 a week toward the rent.

SEPT. 3, 1935 — Social Service Department of Presbyterian Hospital called to make referral and to urge immediate attention to application. The man will be unable to return to work for a month or two. The family is without resources, rent is one month overdue and there is food in the house for only one more day. Later the investigator spoke with the woman and recorded her impression: "Mrs. Barton appears to be an intelligent, honest person. The family has been co-operative in the past and has asked help only when they were badly in need of it. There appears to be no problem other than the illness of Mr. Barton and consequent unemployment." Later, after a home visit, the investigator stated: "Mrs. Barton seems to be a fine, pleasant, cooperative type. The family seems to be a well-integrated one, the children being extremely well-behaved, courteous, and immaculately dressed." Mrs. Barton reports that her husband's employer will keep his job open for one month. The family had just been able to meet expenses on the man's income, and because of this narrow margin has no savings. The roomer is expecting to leave next week to take a job on which he will live in.

SEPT. 4, 1935 — *Case Accepted.* Relief to be granted for woman and children. Man in hospital.

SEPT. 6, 1935 — Mr. Barton received blood transfusion from his wife's brother. The roomer took care of the children so that the woman could spend as much time with her husband as the hospital permitted. The children and the roomer are very fond of each other. He is temporarily unemployed, but is still able to contribute $4 room rent each week from his savings.

Later: Letter received at District Office from man's employer: "fine man, deserving, apparently no bad habits." There will be a chance of re-employment when he recovers.

SEPT. 18, 1935 — Special diet allowance granted for man at the request of Presbyterian Hospital. He is to return home September 19.

SEPT. 24, 1935 Man described as "tall, slim man of good appearance, like the remaining members of his family. He is a refined, pleasant type." Man feeling better at this time but still very weak.

OCT. 7, 1935 Insurance adjustment made. Family received $65.78 of which $7.63 was allowed for advance premiums, $42.55 for clothing (man needed an overcoat) and $15.50 for one semimonthly food budget. Rent allowance was increased because the roomer had left the home a week earlier.

OCT. 24, 1935 Man reported that the hospital clinic advised against his returning to his old job even when well because his general metabolism, food and rest habits are disturbed by night duty. He requests referral for some kind of clerical work. Investigator reported that the man "was despondent because he liked to work and became restless around the house."

OCT. 28, 1935 Maximum rent allowance of $25 granted. The rental is $28, leaving a deficit of $3. Family has been receiving a rent allowance of $19 and were trying to supplement from the food budget. Change was made on the basis of the health problem presented.

NOV., 1935 Man attending Medical Center Dental Clinic where all of his teeth were removed.

DEC. 6, 1935 Medical Center reported man must not return to work until after January, 1936, when he is due for a follow-up examination at the clinic. He has lost a great deal of weight.

DEC. 11, 1935 Man again requests clerical work, saying he is feeling well and has gained some weight.

JAN. 8, 1936 Man told at clinic that he may now go to work. Clinic reports that Mr. Barton has made an excellent recovery. He has gained almost twenty-five pounds and there is a marked increase in the hemoglobin count, both due to the elimination of worry and aggravation, together with rest. He is not yet, however, fully recovered and the doctor recommends another month's rest; the budget to remain unchanged.

JAN. 17, 1936 Woman reports that Mr. Barton returned to the hospital on January 14, because of another hemorrhage; the cause of this serious relapse is not known at present.

FEB. 19, 1936 Woman reports that man returned from the hospital on February 17.

FEB. 24, 1936 On home visits, investigator found both man and woman very much interested, "but not morbidly so," in the subject of gastric ulcers. The man said he is now being treated as if the etiology lay in mental and emotional factors. The doctor told him that 70 per cent of such cases are, or have been, chauffeurs, and that "inferiority complex is half the disease."

MAR., 1936 Social Service Department of Presbyterian Hospital reports that the recent recurrence of the man's ailment is directly traceable to the emotional upset experienced during an argument with his wife about his unmarried sister. The doctor is of the opinion that the man needs psychiatric help to give him a better understanding of his present difficulties and to assist him in facing his situation without reacting to it in an unfavorable manner. The underlying problem is thought to be deep-rooted, probably dating back to early childhood and his separation from his mother, the subsequent care given him by an aunt and uncle and the establishment later of a strong relationship with his only sister; a relationship which was disturbed when Mr. Barton married. The clinic requests continuation of the present maximum budget until the doctor can say more definitely whether Mr. Barton can be asked to adjust to the environment or whether the latter should be adjusted to meet his needs.

MAY, 1936 Man reports he is feeling much better. He is still attending dental clinic and it will be several months before the work on his mouth is completed.

JULY, 1936 Special diet allowance discontinued.

SEPT., 1936 Special diet allowance resumed.

JAN., 1938 (First home visit since September, 1936, because of three reallocations of case-loads and absence for three months of the investigator who carried the case for the longest period, from December, 1936 to April, 1937.) Family has been meeting a $4 rent deficit from the food budget during this time. Mr. Barton is still attending clinic, reporting every three months for follow-up examinations. He feels he is employable for light outdoor work and has been trying for several months to find a position as doorman or elevator operator, but without success. Such jobs are hard to find, especially since his membership in the Apartment House Workers' Union lapsed in 1937. He plans to get in touch with the union to see what arrangements he can make that will permit him to work if he finds a job.

FEB., 1938 Because of his health, man refused laborer's job, offered by the Occupational Division.

JUNE, 1938 (First record of visit since January, 1938.) The family has made no effort to find a roomer since Mr. Barton needs a room of his own because he is restless and has so many sleepless nights. Special diet allowance is still in force.

AUG. 2, 1938 Man looks very ill. He is paying $3.57 for medication semimonthly. This is a tonic which has brought about an increase in appetite, so that Mr. Barton is now able to eat all kinds of food. The doctor says he is much improved but must continue to report for follow-up examinations and must continue with the medication. The family is finding it much harder to manage on the Home Relief allowance because of Mr. Barton's increased appetite, and because the cost of the medicine that is bringing this about also comes from the food budget. The doctor told him to attempt to do no heavy work and to remain outdoors, getting as much sun and fresh air as possible. He is therefore spending his days in the park. His wife brings his lunches to him so that he need not climb the five flights of stairs more than once a day.

AUG. 22, 1938 Special diet allowance discontinued.

OCT., 1938 Special diet allowance resumed at the request of the clinic.

FEB., 1939 Family's rent deficit, now $1.50, still being met from food budget.

MAR., 1939 Man looks weak and ill; not making any effort to find employment because he feels too sick to work.

MAY, 1939 — Man still unable to work.

AUG., 1939 — *Last Entry* (case abstracted April, 1940). Man registered at the bureau for the physically handicapped since he is unable to do any but the lightest sort of work. Mrs. Barton says she is able and willing to work.

MAY, 1940 — The social worker who had abstracted the Home Relief record talked with the Home Relief investigator. The case was only recently allocated to her and has not yet been read or visited. She could, therefore, add nothing to the information already in the record.

HOME INTERVIEW

Home—Six rooms on the fifth floor of an old apartment building in the Washington Heights section of Manhattan. The street is wide and clean; there is much traffic, including a bus route—and there are retail shops on the ground floors of most of the buildings. The building and apartment are in good physical condition. The home is well and attractively furnished and was clean at the time of the visit. Because the apartment is on the top floor, the rooms are bright and well-ventilated. Rental is $28.

Each of the children has a bedroom, and the parents also have separate rooms. Mr. Barton sleeps poorly and therefore has a room of his own so as not to disturb the other members of the family.

BACKGROUND

Man—born in New York City, March, 1900. His father and mother were born in the United States. He was the second of two children; he has an older sister. His parents died when he was an infant and he was reared by a paternal aunt and uncle, now dead. Mr. Barton completed grammar school. His sister was reared by other relatives but there was a bond of affection between them which became stronger as they grew older. They made their home together for a few years prior to his marriage and the sister has always resented his wife because this home was broken. The sister is self-supporting.

Woman—born in New York City, January, 1900. She was also the younger of two children; the older child was a brother. Mrs. Barton completed three years of high school. She learned stenography, and after leaving school found employment with the Telephone Company laboratory, in their department of specifications. Her job was a responsible one and she liked it. She got along well with her employers, who were very considerate. She says that she was happy in her work. Her salary was $25 a week. Mrs. Barton said that it would have made her unhappy to leave her job had the reason not been that she had been anxious to have a child and was pregnant. Mrs. Barton was married in 1922, but did not leave her job until 1924.

Mrs. Barton's parents are dead. Their family had never been a close one and for years Mrs. Barton knew nothing about her brother. When her husband needed a transfusion, mutual friends got in touch with her brother who donated the blood and then went away again. He also was a taxi driver, but Mrs. Barton believes he is now on Home Relief. He has six children. Beyond the donation of blood, they have never assisted each other in any way.

BEFORE RELIEF

After his graduation from grammar school, Mr. Barton went to work but this early work history is not given. His chief occupation was that of chauffeur and he was a taxi driver for many years. Prior to his marriage Mr. Barton drove a taxi and contributed his income from this occupation to the home that he maintained with his sister.

The Bartons were "very well off" from the time of their marriage in 1922 until about 1930. The first child was born about three years after their marriage and Mrs. Barton kept her job until her pregnancy. Mr. Barton's work as a taxi driver furnished such a good income that he almost never bothered to work a full week. Their combined income ranged from $75 to $100 a week. They had a comfortable savings account, bought good furniture, and had a "lovely home." They never had to worry about the cost of Mrs. Barton's confinements nor about emergencies which might arise. When his wife stopped work, Mr. Barton was able to maintain the family's income standard by working a few more hours a week. Mrs. Barton took the children to the farm of a friend in Pennsylvania each summer and her husband joined them for week ends.

In 1928 income began to drop off, and the Bartons had to retrench a little, but Mr. Barton worked longer hours and was able to keep their income at a comfortable level. In 1929 things looked a little worse, and they invested most of their remaining savings ($1,000) in bonds to ensure a little supplementary income. This proved to be a foolish venture and within two years the bonds were worthless. From 1930 to 1933 it was all they could do to manage. Mr. Barton worked as a private chauffeur for about six months in 1930, at $35 a week, but his employer was forced to let him go because he could no longer afford to keep him on. He also drove a truck for a few months at the end of 1932 but the company went out of business. The Bartons pawned all the jewelry they owned, borrowed on their insurance and from friends, and Mr. Barton "worried as hard as he worked." Mrs. Barton believes that beyond a doubt the strain of this period was responsible for her husband's later acute illness.

FIRST REACTIONS TO UNEMPLOYMENT

Mrs. Barton could not say that there were any specific reactions because unemployment approached slowly, and for some time before it actually arrived they were aware that it would come sooner or later. They did everything possible to delay it, hoping constantly that things would pick up. Mrs. Barton said that her greatest distress was her husband's illness, because even at that time, though they did not know what was the matter, he already had ulcers. Food did not agree with him and he suffered intense stomach pain, which they thought was "acute indigestion" but which she now knows was caused by worry. It was she who insisted that they apply for Relief because she could see what the strain was doing, not only to her husband, but to the entire family. At that time, 1933, they considered themselves fortunate because they were on Relief for only three months and then Mr. Barton found work. They were very happy when this happened because, even though the income was small, it was steady and sufficient to live on, and they were independent again. But this joy was short-lived, and when real long-time unemployment arrived, it came at a time when Mr. Barton was so acutely ill that he was not expected to live. Her concern about him was so great that Mrs. Barton did not even stop to think of unemployment. All she knew was that her husband must get well. She applied for Relief again, this time without any sense of shame or embarrassment, knowing that she must spare her husband even a moment's worry about how the family would manage. She did not care if he never worked again, if they lived on Relief the rest of their lives, just so he got well.

PRESENT SITUATION

Man—Not seen. According to his wife, Mr. Barton is almost entirely recovered.
Woman—Mrs. Barton is very attractive, looks much younger than forty. She speaks well, is interested in current events and has read much about them.

PRESENT ADJUSTMENT

Mrs. Barton seems a happy person. She explained that the past years have imposed a great strain on her, but that her husband's recovery has made it all worth while. When he was ill and nervous, he was inclined to be irritable with the children and she had to be a buffer between them. It has been hard to keep up her husband's pride and position as head of the household during this long period of dependence. She has tried to maintain a careful balance between the danger of hurting his pride by not consulting him about decisions she could make herself and the danger of hindering his recovery by making him worry about decisions on which she really needed his help. It was necessary to consider each word carefully before speaking it, to avoid upsetting him. Mrs. Barton firmly believes that the doctor was right in blaming the illness on "emotional factors," and, with this in mind, she did all she could to protect him and aid his recovery. She is well and strong and would have been willing to go to work herself but did not dare to do this for fear of the effect on her husband. She was afraid of what it would do to him to have her go out to work and leave him at home to be the "housemaid." Now that her husband is so much better, the strain is greatly reduced and she is quite content.

Mr. Barton may have to get some kind of retraining unless he can find work without it in a field other than taxi driving. Mrs. Barton does not believe, however, that this will be necessary; she is certain that her husband will easily get work that is not too heavy in some branch of building service and maintenance. His former employer and fellow employees have remained interested and will undoubtedly help him in finding work. This former employer has promised him the first opening in his building. The only problem is health—with that solved, re-employment will follow.

According to Mrs. Barton, the family bond is strong and the members enjoy each other. She says that they are anxious to be independent again, but that they have had no sense of shame about this period of dependence that has given her husband his chance for health again. The children understand the family's financial limitations and accept them as well as children can be expected to do because they know they are based on their father's illness.

Children:

Barbara—born February, 1925, is in the sixth term at Washington High School. Her mother is worried about her. She has no particular vocational interests and in another year will be through school and at home with nothing to do. She is a restless child and is now, at fifteen, beginning to question adult authority. Mrs. Barton understands that this is not unnatural at Barbara's age but is worried about the dangers it presents to the family's happiness. Barbara is also quick-tempered and impulsive. Her mother fears that she will become restless and irritable without the regulating routine of school and knows that Mr. Barton's response will be to criticize and attempt to control, with the result that he and his daughter will quarrel. Her mother realizes that Barbara will need more freedom and less questioning about her activities and is not likely to get either of these from her father, not because he does not recognize and want to give them, but because he often loses sight of the children's needs in his worry about his own illness. These problems may be avoided if Barbara can find something to do, even though she earns little in doing it, but they are stumbling blocks which the family may have to face in the coming year.

At present the parents have to exert little control. While Barbara is not much interested in school, she does attempt to do well so long as she has to go. Her time is occupied with school, homework, and keeping herself well-groomed. Because she must be at school early she seldom stays up late during the week. While at home she is busy with preparations for school, and since her father approves of this activity, there is little friction. She has an active social life through the church and a social club which she joined when she began to lose interest in Girl Reserve and Girl Scout activities. Much of the family's recreation is related to her activities in connection with this group. She is interested in boys and has "dates." Her family approves of this so long as the boys she goes with seem "nice," call for her at the house, and bring her home at a reasonable hour. Recently some of the men who gather in front of the drugstore downstairs have begun to talk with her father about the fact that she is growing up and that the time has come when she will have to be watched more carefully. Mr. Barton now worries about her, and arguments sometimes crop up. They have not been serious to date, but Mrs. Barton fears that Barbara will resent it as she grows older and that, unless her father stops worrying and scolding, the arguments will become more serious.

Kenneth—born November, 1928, entered junior high school this fall. He has recently become interested in chemistry experiments and "just about drives us all out of the house" with some of his results. He is a "steady" boy, a good student, interested in science of all kinds. He belongs to the Boy Scouts and is a happy, active boy.

Use of Time: Mr. Barton has had to spend much of his time resting, as prescribed by the doctor. Both Mr. and Mrs. Barton like to read and they use their library cards a great deal. There is much joint recreation in the form of picnics in the park. The children are permitted to invite their friends. This activity has become so popular that the family never goes on a picnic without at least one more family from the building. Sometimes three or four other families pack their lunches and spend the whole day in the park. Books, balls and bats, cards, and whatever else may be desired are taken along. Often meals are cooked there, and these special treats are popular. The adults occasionally spend an evening away from home, visiting with friends so that one of the children can have a party of young people, unhampered by the presence of "old" people. The adults try to attend all the activities of the children to which parents are invited and encourage them in their clubs and sports activities.

Religion: The family is Episcopalian. Neither Mr. nor Mrs. Barton is particularly regular in attendance at services, going only occasionally, but the children attend regularly. All participate to a large extent in the social activities.

Newspapers: No special preference.

Political Affiliations: The Bartons do not belong to any political club or organization. They favor the Democratic party but are independent voters and always choose a candidate whom they consider good regardless of party. Mrs. Barton says she thinks they usually say they are Democrats to prevent arguments because the entire neighborhood seems to belong to that party.

They think Roosevelt has been a fine president. They do not encourage talk about the European war in their home because they have a wide variety of friends—German, Italian, Jewish, English, etc.—all of whom get along well together, go on the same outings, and they do not want any of these relationships spoiled by war talk. They also want to avoid development of racial prejudice in the children, if at all possible.

Management: The semimonthly Home Relief allowance is $31.50 of which $14 goes for rent. The rental is $28 and Home Relief rent allowance is $25.50. They meet the deficit from food allowance. Mrs. Barton says that, while it is not easy to manage on this amount, it can be done. The family has sufficient food and manages to entertain friends occasionally. The Relief has been good about providing clothing. Medication has been the hardest thing to manage because the tonic recommended by the doctor is a patent medicine and cannot be prescribed; therefore, no allowance can be made for it by Home Relief.

Attitudes:

Toward Relief: Mrs. Barton said that she feels only gratitude toward Home Relief. She has found the investigators understanding, sympathetic, and helpful. The allowance has been sufficient to keep the family comfortable, if without luxuries, and the medical care and clothing allowances have been generous.

Toward the Future: Mrs. Barton was optimistic. Her husband is regaining his health; will soon be able to go back to work. While they might anticipate some trouble with Barbara in the future, they will find a way to meet it, as they have other problems, if and when it happens.

Toward Us: Mrs. Barton was much interested in the project asked what kind of things we were trying to determine and whether we felt we were getting any significant information, what response most of the people made, and the source of our interest in the family. She thought her husband would be equally interested and willing to come in for an office interview.

OFFICE INTERVIEW

Impression: Mr. Barton, although wearing a sport shirt, was neatly dressed. He is a good-looking man; he has a good set of false teeth. He was thoroughly tanned and looked healthy. He is soft-spoken and appears to be in the early forties.

Employment History: Mr. Barton says that he started work when he graduated from public school because when he was young that was the usual thing to do; only rich children went to high school. He was brought up by an uncle and aunt. His first job was with a silver company, where he earned $7 a week. After only a short time with the company, he was forced to leave because his uncle thought the $7 wasn't enough. He found a job with an importing concern, where he remained for several years. At the end of each year he received a raise of $2 per week and in addition got a "nice" bonus. When he had been there three years, his uncle again pushed him to ask for an additional raise. Mr. Barton asked for the raise at a time when the concern was making little money. Although the boss liked him, he could not give him this raise. His uncle then forced him to leave. Mr. Barton says that this was the great mistake of his life, for it was the only real chance he ever had. Shortly after he left, the owner died and left the business to his employees and in his will provided that the people in the ranks were to move up step by step. Mr. Barton says that he has kept sufficient contact with the people in this concern to know that those who were there in his day have done very well. He consoles himself now with the fact that if he had dared to defy his uncle, he would have been "cuffed around." Mr. Barton then got a job as a handyman in an apartment house at $18 a week. Shortly thereafter he wanted to marry and looked around for a way to increase his income. He took advantage of the Yellow Cab Company's school to teach drivers. Mr. Barton said that in the early days of the taxicab business it was necessary to train drivers. At the completion of this course, he became a taxi driver; he earned as much as $70 a week in the "good days." Mr. Barton said that taxi driving is hard on the nerves since there is always a chance of an accident and he stated that he had one or two very "close shaves." (After one of these he had to stop driving for a week and after the second near-accident, he was unable to touch the car for twenty minutes.) Mr. Barton said that when business started to drop off he not only had to work very hard in order to earn a little, but he also had to put up with the complaints of the boss, which he hated to listen to. In the early thirties it was impossible, Mr. Barton said, to make a living in the taxi business. He therefore secured a job as elevator man and general assistant. He was forced to give up this job because of an attack of bleeding ulcers. He got his job back but then had new attacks and his employer finally let him go. His gastric ulcers have been very serious and he is just now "coming out of the woods."

Relief: Mr. Barton says that he is able to earn a few dollars a week by helping an undertaker in the neighborhood, but he hides this fact from Relief. In order to make these few dollars he says it is necessary for him to hang around a candy store near his house, waiting for the undertaker to telephone him. Because he hates to lose these few dollars, he does not usually go looking for work anywhere else in town. Recently Mr. Barton said he had a bad experience: he was taking charge of the undertaker's shop when the bell rang and his former investigator came in. When she recognized him, he tried to tell her that he does not do this often and therefore asked her not to report it. He was, however, badly frightened by this experience and has been worried ever since because he does not know whether she will report him. He thinks that she will not do so because she is a very nice person.

Although his two children are old enough to understand about the family being on Relief, he does not talk to them about it. Mr. Barton says he got good attention when he was at the Medical Center. He does recall, however, that when he was in bed the "professor" was taking a group of students through the ward and discussing the causes of ulcers. Mr. Barton heard him say that the major cause of ulcers was a lack of responsibility in the man. Mr. Barton says that this made him mad because he knew "better than anybody else in the world" that this could not be true. Mr. Barton also told of the fact that one of the specialists at Medical Center reached the conclusion that 70 per cent of the patients suffering from ulcers were cab drivers. He said that the surplus commodities that he receives from Relief are good and he has no complaint to make about Relief in general. He does not like people who go around complaining all day. According to Mr. Barton, he would prefer to be on WPA because he would then have the feeling that he was earning money. Although he does not spend much time looking for jobs, he did try to get one with the American Can Company, because he thought, from reading the papers, that they might be hiring men. He not only went to their downtown office, but also to Newark, but has had no luck as yet. Mr. Barton says that he was registered at the Handicapped Division of the New York State Employment Service and that they recently offered him a job, seven days work per week of which three days would be spent moving heavy ashcans around and four days running an elevator. The pay was $62 per month. It makes Mr. Barton angry that a state agency should offer a job that is against the state labor laws. When he realized that the Handicapped Division showed so little sense as to offer him a job moving ashcans around when he still had bleeding ulcers, he changed his registration from the Handicapped Division to the uptown office of the State Employment Service. He says that he would like to be retrained; however, he has never discussed this problem with his Relief investigator.

Family: Mr. Barton says that he knows that his wife is shielding him and he realizes that she does this because of his gastric ulcers which, according to the doctors, get worse if he worries. Mr. Barton says that the family has little opportunity for recreation except when they go to the park and take their lunch along. He says that he is anxious to give his children those things which he did not have as a child. His daughter and son are, in his opinion, rather difficult. His daughter, who used to get good marks in school, is now having difficulty with her studies. His son, in fighting with other boys, cannot "stick up for himself," and it seems to him that his children give up easily. This disturbs Mr. Barton. Both children belong to social organizations—his daughter was a Girl Scout for many years—and both children belong to clubs at the present time.

Time: Mr. Barton spends most of his time "hanging around" the candy store, waiting for a telephone call to report to work at the undertaker's establishment. He says that occasionally he suggests things to the undertaker about how to improve the shop and the yard, etc., and this gives him an opportunity to earn a few extra dollars by working on these improvements. Mr. Barton says he also spends a lot of time in the sun, trying to get his health back and that formerly he used to spend many hours at the Medical Center waiting for treatment.

Politics: Because most apartment buildings have become unionized, Mr. Barton thinks that it will be difficult for him to get his old job back. He has, however, kept up his contacts with the two houses where he used to work. Some time ago he had a job waiting for him and wanted to get his union card brought up to date, but the union wanted $24 in back dues, which is the cost for one year. He says that he was finally able to convince the union to accept $10 for a paid-up book, but he had so much excitement convincing the union to do this that he had an ulcer attack that night and therefore lost the job. Despite his own difficulties with the union, he thinks unions are a good thing because they have increased the wages of handymen from approximately $70 per month to $92 per month. He says that he has no doubt that there is much graft in the union and he has begun to notice that certain unemployed men get jobs while others just hang around. He has tried to find out how to bribe a delegate but has not had much luck in making contacts.

Future: Mr. Barton feels that he is getting stronger every day and that he ought to be able, if conditions improve considerably, to get a job which he will be able to handle.

OFFICE INTERVIEW

(Barbara arrived with her mother, who waited in an adjoining room during the interview).

Barbara is a tall, fairly attractive girl of fifteen, who was extremely reticent, shy, and obviously embarrassed, especially at the beginning of the interview. Despite the fact that the office was much overheated, she could not be persuaded to take off her coat and throughout the interview she sat bolt upright in her chair. (Her unwillingness to take off her coat was probably not due to the fact that her dress was shabby; the rest of her clothing was in good repair and immaculate.) She answered all questions simply and directly but in the briefest possible terms; volunteered no comments and made no inquiries of any kind. She impressed one as a fairly typical adolescent preoccupied with her own personal problems.

So far as the Relief situation is concerned, Barbara feels that this has caused the family few hardships; they are on Relief only because of her father's illness and as soon as he is better, there is no question but that he will be re-employed. This explanation, which apparently is accepted by the entire family, serves to remove much of the stigma of their Relief status. One had the feeling that much of her reserve was an attempt to protect her father and to avoid giving the impression that their difficulties grew out of any defect in him. She emphasized a number of times how ill he had been and that now that he is better again, they will soon be on their own.

Barbara has felt no privations in the things which she enjoys doing because most of the activities she likes are free. Most important among these are her activities at the swimming pool. She gets up early to take advantage of the swimming privileges before the beginning of classes and is in the pool every free moment. She enjoys all forms of athletics and is expert in many of them. Walking to and from school is pleasant and helps her keep in condition. Around her swimming and the activities of the club to which she belongs she has developed quite an active social life. She says she is interested in boys but "only as friends."

Barbara had no comments to make on the question of Relief, the budget, and similar matters, repeating always that she had nothing to do with these things and that her parents take care of them. She has no curiosity about them. Barbara has read little; has little interest in current events, and her schoolwork in general is something that she tolerates as a necessary evil.

She thinks life will be smoother when her father is back at work. She is restless and irritable and at times this results in clashes with him. However, these do not seem to be of any great moment to her and her only concern about them is that they might upset him and make him sick.

It was impossible to interest her in a discussion of politics or religion or evoke any comment on her attitudes toward the social setup. She would simply reply "I don't know" or smile and say nothing. She was not curious about us and said that she had no questions to ask. When asked what she wanted to do in life, she said that she has not decided as yet, but would probably get a job; she has no idea as to what or how, etc. Her only real interest is in athletics but she can see no way to exploit this in terms of a job. She sews well but "hates it," and has refused to take further training in this direction.

In the midst of the interview she suddenly said, "I must go now," and left without any explanation.

PART II. WPA

Case Four

MAHONEY FAMILY

Status WPA *Religion* Catholic

Man born 1883 Ireland to U.S.A. 1921 Citizen 1935

Wife born 1884 Ireland to U.S.A. 1921 Citizen No

Education

Man Equivalent of elementary school—Ireland

Wife Equivalent of elementary school—Ireland

Medical Status

Man Negative.

Wife Symptoms connected with menopause.

Woman's Work History Domestic worker prior to marriage.

Married April, 1925, N.Y.C.

Number of Children in the Home One *Age*—12 years.

Basic Occupation before Relief Cement mason. Carpenter's helper.

Average Income before Relief $30 to $40 weekly.

Private Employment Terminated August, 1933.

First Accepted for Relief November, 1933.

SUMMARY

Home Relief November, 1933, to October, 1934. Closed to WPA

WPA *October, 1934, to date* with the exception of:

Home Relief for three weeks in September, 1939, following WPA layoff because of "18-month ruling."

Reinstated on *WPA, October, 1939.*

Few reclassifications or shifts while on WPA—*Cement mason, $82.80 month.*

ABSTRACT OF HOME RELIEF RECORD

NOV. 21, 1933 — *First Application:* Mr Mahoney has had no regular employment since 1930. Since that time the family has managed on odd jobs, irregular employment, savings and loans including $100 from man's sister. He last worked three weeks in August, 1933, at $30 a week. Rent is four months in arrears; gas and electricity two months in arrears. There are no other debts. The family is living with the woman's sister and paying half of the $45 monthly rent and half of the gas and light bills. The sister's family is now on Relief. The Mahoneys had surrendered two insurance policies on the children for $42.63. Two policies on the man are still in force. Mr. Mahoney has his first citizenship papers.

NOV., 1933 — *Case Accepted.*

APRIL, 1934 — The man requests work of any kind. He considers himself a skilled laborer and cement finisher.

OCT. 9, 1934 — The man reported that he had been placed on CWA at $61.40 a month.

OCT. 11, 1934 — *Case Closed to Work Relief.*

SEPT. 20, 1939 — *Reapplied.* The man was dismissed from WPA on August 31st in accordance with the 18-month ruling. He had worked as a cement mason, earning first $85 and later $82 a month. The family now have an apartment of their own, paying $30 a month rent. Since the Relief rent allowance is only $25.50, the family planned to economize in some other way in order to make up the deficit of $4.50. The rent at this time is paid to October 1st. They have no savings. The family had managed, however, to pay up all their debts while on WPA. There is sufficient cash on hand for food to the end of the month, pending acceptance.

SEPT. 21, 1939 — *Case Accepted.*

OCT., 1939 — *Case Closed to WPA.* The man was assigned to WPA as cement finisher at $82.80 a month. Relief to the amount of $23.97 had been granted to carry the family to October 10th and it was figured that they could manage from that time until the first WPA check arrived.

WPA RATING SCHEDULE

There were three ratings for Mr. Mahoney and all three were for the job of cement mason:

	December, 1938	*June, 1939*	*December, 1939*
Quantity of Work	Excellent	Good	Good
Quality of Work	Good	Good	Good
Personal Characteristics	Good	Good	Good
Ability to Understand New Ideas and Instructions	Good	Good	Good
Knowledge of Job	Good	Good	Good
Overall Rating	Good	Good	Good

The review rating agreed with the original in all instances.

HOME INTERVIEW

Home—Three rooms on the first floor, rear, of an apartment building in the Washington Heights section of Manhattan. The building is one of a row of similar houses on a residential street, east of Broadway. They are all fairly modern and in good condition. The apartment was well-lighted and well-ventilated, adequately furnished, and attractive. It was immaculate at the time of the visit. The rental is $30 a month. Mr. and Mrs. Mahoney said that while on Relief they had looked for a cheaper apartment but could find nothing at a cheaper rental which could be compared with this one.

Cecilia sleeps on a studio couch in the living room and the parents occupy the bedroom.

BACKGROUND

Man—Born in Ireland, May, 1883. He was the eldest of three children. Mr. Mahoney completed grammar school in Ireland. His parents owned a small farm. At an early age Mr. Mahoney realized that there was little opportunity for making an adequate living on a small farm, and as soon as he completed his basic schooling, left home to go to a near-by city, where he found employment doing odd jobs in construction. After some years of this work, he learned the trade of cement mason. He came to the United States in 1921 because he had heard that there was more opportunity to "make good money" here. His sister joined him later. There has continued to be a good relationship between Mr. Mahoney and his sister, who lent him money while he was trying to avoid application for Relief. The whereabouts of his parents and the other sibling is not known.

Woman—Born in Ireland, November, 1884. She was the younger of two children, both girls. Mrs. Mahoney completed grammar school in Ireland. Her work history prior to emigration is not given. She came to the United States with her sister in 1921. Until her marriage, in 1925, she worked intermittently as a domestic; she has done no work out of the home since her marriage. Following Cecilia's birth in 1928, Mrs. Mahoney suffered an acute gynecological condition and two years later was operated on. The operation made it impossible for her to have children. There had been a miscarriage prior to her pregnancy with Cecilia.

The whereabouts of Mrs. Mahoney's parents is not known. Her sister tried to help the Mahoneys by sharing an apartment and expenses, to assist them in their effort to keep off Relief. This sister is now on Relief.

BEFORE LOSS OF PRIVATE EMPLOYMENT

From the time of his arrival in the United States, in 1921, until 1930 Mr. Mahoney worked either as a cement mason, or as a laborer and carpenter's helper. During those years, his lowest wages were $30 a week, while on occasion he earned as high as $50 and $60 a week. From 1930 to 1932 he was able to get only odd jobs. Then, from September of 1932 to August of 1933, he had irregular work as a laborer for a firm of landscapers and gardeners. He earned $30 a week at this job. During the twenties Mr. Mahoney worked for a number of different contractors but was always fairly certain of employment with either of two construction companies, where his record was good. From 1927 to 1930 he had a period of steady employment as a laborer and carpenter's helper on the Long Island subway. This ended when his work on the subway was completed.

Mr. Mahoney's income was never really "steady" because his work was largely seasonal. There was also the fact that he was hired by contractors for a specific job and that as each was completed, it became necessary for Mr. Mahoney to find another. The Mahoneys say that they had no trouble managing, however, because the pay was good and periods of unemployment between jobs relatively short. Mr. Mahoney had always liked his work, his wife had liked taking care of her home and was able to manage economically so that the salary was usually enough to carry them over slack seasons. While they managed to meet expenses, this seasonal income did not allow them to have large savings. They had insurance on Mr. Mahoney and considered this a form of saving. When work fell off in 1930, they found it convenient to share a large apartment with relatives, paying half the expenses. This was cheaper than it would have been to maintain their own small apartment and they were able to have much better living conditions for the same money.

FIRST REACTIONS TO UNEMPLOYMENT

Since they were used to Mr. Mahoney's being out of work for a few weeks following the completion of each job, they had no particular reaction to his layoff by the construction company in 1930, when he had finished working on the Long Island subway. The only difference that they noted until 1933 was that there were longer periods out of work and shorter periods on the job. Mr. Mahoney continued to earn a basic wage of about $30 a week but the work was irregular for those three years. Not until Mr. Mahoney was unable to get even small odd jobs between August and November, 1933, did they realize that he was really unemployed. By that time they had exhausted all their resources and had to apply for Relief.

PRESENT SITUATION

Man—A short, heavy, nice-looking man, whose age is indicated by his white hair, rather than his general appearance. His face looks much younger than his 57 years and he gives the appearance of a strong, active man in good health.

Woman—Mrs. Mahoney is a frail, slender woman who looks much older than her husband. She explained that her health was affected by childbearing so late in life; she was forty-four when Cecilia was born. During the last few years she has suffered from symptoms related to the menopause and has felt weak. She says that it has aged her considerably. She was feeling slightly better at the time of the visit and felt that she had weathered the worst of it.

PRESENT ADJUSTMENT

Mr. Mahoney is working as a cement mason on WPA, earning $82 a month. While he would prefer to be in private industry, he feels that WPA is better than Home Relief in that he is able, in this way, to keep up his skills and not get "soft." He feels that one of the worst things that can happen to a man is to lose his skills and get "soft" because then there is little chance for re-employment. He says that he continues to look for work with private contractors and has made application at a number of offices, which should benefit by the new defense program. He has also placed his application at the Navy Yard.

The family feels that their present situation is relatively comfortable. Work in private industry and increased income would, of course, be welcome, but under the circumstances they do not complain. They feel that they are getting along much better than most families on Relief. They hope that things will improve and in the meantime manage to keep out of debt.

Children:

Cecilia—Born November, 1928, is in the third grade of public school. Her parents say that she has always been "slow" in school. To some degree this is due to minor illnesses which have interfered with her attendance. Lately her health has been much better and they hope that she will get along better. They say that she is a sociable child and has quite a wide circle of friends. She does not care much for reading and plays outside rather actively most of the time. She says that she likes school, but does not study hard.

Use of Leisure Time:

On Home Relief: The family's longest period on Home Relief was eleven months, during which Mr. Mahoney spent much of his time looking for work. He went around to all the contractors for whom he had previously worked and found a great many of them out of business. Those that were managing to get along at all were not employing much help because most of their jobs were small. He continued to go out regularly, however, spending whole days at a time. He would go to one office to learn that there was nothing there but that another company across town might have something. He would follow up that lead and out of that he would get not a job, but another lead, and so on and so on. After a while the cost of doing this every day became much too high because taking so much carfare out of the Relief allowance left little for food and other necessities. Mr. Mahoney then began walking instead of riding, looking for work in the neighborhood. He was able to find an occasional repair job. His earnings from such odd jobs gave him the money with which to make another tour of the various contractors in hopes of finding something a little better.

On WPA: Mr. Mahoney says he now has less leisure to look for employment. He continues, however, to do so whenever he has any leads. If he hears that a new building is going up, that a contractor has been hired to do a job, or that some industry in which he might work as laborer is opening up, he makes application as soon as he has a free moment. These were not so frequent because of bad days. Today, for instance, even though it is raining, he had to report on the job early in the morning, spending carfare and using the best job-hunting hours for traveling; he had to do this to avoid a black mark on his record. It also means that he will have to make up time on another day which would ordinarily be a day off, and on which he might have looked for work.

Religion: The Mahoneys are Catholics. They go regularly to confession and to mass.

Newspapers: The family takes no newspaper regularly but likes the *Daily News* rather well.

Political Affiliations: The Mahoneys belong to no political party. Mr. Mahoney was naturalized in 1935; his wife is not a citizen. They have never belonged to the Workers' Alliance. They like Roosevelt and what he has done and feel that he has the interest of the people at heart. They wonder, however, how much he can do in the future with the rich people so much against him. They are not sure, at this time, whether it would be wise to keep him in a third term or elect a new man who might have the support of business. They do not feel that WPA is the answer to the unemployment problem. The only answer, as they see it, is co-operation with industry and the opening up of private employment. If they feel that some other man can work more effectively to this end, they will vote for him.

Management:

On Home Relief: The Mahoneys say that they do not even like to think about the trouble they had managing on Home Relief. There was a large rental deficit; they tried to find a place at a lower rental but failed to do so and had to use food money for rent. This meant that they did not have enough to eat. There was no allowance for carfare, and their diet suffered. They believe that lack of proper food was one of the reasons for their child's poor health.

On WPA: WPA provides a better income but it is still rather hard to manage. They do, however, have enough to eat and are able to pay their rent. It is not so easy to buy clothing or to replace household linen on this income. They feel that they manage fairly well. Mrs. Mahoney explained that she has always been a good manager, and has had to plan for periods of unemployment in the past by economizing while her husband was employed. She believes, therefore, that she finds it easier to manage on $82 a month than would the average woman.

Attitudes:

Toward Home Relief and WPA: The Mahoneys believe that Home Relief is necessary and that it is administered as well as possible. They did not like it for themselves, however, because they did not like the feeling of living on charity. They realize that WPA is a kind of Relief, but since Mr. Mahoney gives some return for the Relief given them he is able to keep up his self-respect. They think that there are many flaws in the way Home Relief and WPA are handled, some of which probably come out of lack of funds, others out of the dishonesty of the people applying for help, and still others which are the result of poor planning by people in authority. WPA seems to the family the better of the two, from the standpoint both of higher income and of work. Not only does WPA give a man a chance to work and keep from growing "soft" and a chance to keep his self-respect by giving some return for Relief granted, but there is also the feeling that the money received is one's own and can be spent according to one's need, and not according to a budget worked out by someone who is concerned only with budget classifications and not with family needs.

Toward the Future: On the whole, the family is optimistic about the future. Mrs. Mahoney's health is improving. In spite of Mr. Mahoney's age, he believes that there will be some opportunity for him in regular industry should business improve. He thinks his chances for employment are good because of his wide contacts from past work experience.

Toward Us: The worker felt that Mr. and Mrs. Mahoney had only a vague conception of the purpose of the study. They were pleasant but it was difficult to obtain information from them. Both said that they were willing to help as much as they could, but seemed to feel that much of the information requested was not relevant to the study. Mr. Mahoney said that he would be quite willing to come in for an office interview.

OFFICE INTERVIEW

Impression: Gray-haired man with ruddy cheeks and pleasant expression, who appears to be in his late fifties; poorly dressed. Although Mr. Mahoney was willing and pleasant during the interview, he did not talk readily; he was especially reticent about personal matters. He said that he had come to the office because he was glad to help.

Employment History: Mr. Mahoney, a Catholic, was born in Northern Ireland, where he learned the cement mason's trade. He emigrated to the United States because his future wife wanted to return to this country, where she had held a job before returning to Ireland on a visit. During the 1920's Mr. Mahoney was employed on subway construction and his earnings approximated $35 a week. He said that, although this wage was considerably below that earned by men on general construction, work on subway construction had the great advantage of being steady and Mr. Mahoney said that his yearly earnings were pretty good. According to Mr. Mahoney, he never had any dealings with unions; where he worked, he said, no man would even mention the word "union" for fear of losing his job. Mr. Mahoney said it was easy to get jobs in the twenties and that working conditions were good. Work became more irregular in 1930, but Mr. Mahoney was able to hang on until the end of 1933, when he was forced to seek public assistance. When first unemployed, Mr. Mahoney said that he used to go looking for jobs every day and frequently spent up to $2 for carfare, but he soon came to realize that since there were scarcely any jobs to be found, it was not sensible to keep on spending $2 a day in search of work.

Relief: As soon as Mr. Mahoney came on Home Relief, he made a strong plea to the worker to put him on Work Relief. He thinks that the Home Relief allowance was much too small, while he finds his earnings on WPA satisfactory. He enjoys his work on WPA. He thinks that the quality of work that he does on WPA is about the same as that in private industry.

He says that it is not right for people to say so many nasty things about WPA. Mr. Mahoney finds only two things wrong with WPA: he thinks it would be a good idea if WPA paid the carfare of men going to and from work, and he thought it was very important for WPA to see to it that when there is a spell of bad weather as in the winter months, the men receive their wages and be permitted to make up lost time when good weather comes. It is very difficult for his family to manage when he is able to earn only half his ordinary wages. The only way that the family gets along at such times is by borrowing from friends. Mr. Mahoney said that he has not bought a new suit in the last six years.

Family: Mr. Mahoney talked little about his family, but his face brightened when he talked about his daughter. He said that he does not go to the movies often because he likes to give the necessary 10 cents to his daughter so that she can be in the swing of things and go to the movies with her friends. Mr. Mahoney says that there is one big difference between the 1920's and today and that is that in the twenties he never had to count his pennies and always had money in his pocket, while today he has to keep careful account of every cent. When asked whether he had ever taken a vacation in the twenties he replied, "Oh, no, I was working all the time."

Politics: Mr. Mahoney has never had any connection with unions. He thinks that President Roosevelt is a good president. Mr. Mahoney feels uneasy about the war, but he does not know what is going to happen and thinks there is no use worrying until it does happen. He was asked whether he had tried to get help from his church before he came to Relief and he said, "Oh, no, it would have been silly even to ask, because there is no chance of getting any help."

Future: Mr. Mahoney does not make any real effort to get off WPA any more because he has lost his contacts with his old contractors and he knows that many of them have gone out of business. He realizes also that he is pretty old and he knows that old men are not being hired. His only real worry at the moment is that there might be a long wait between one work assignment and another. There are rumors going around that when the job on which he is now working is finished, it will be a long time before the men are reassigned.

Case Five

BERGER FAMILY

Status WPA Home Relief Supplementation *Religion* Jewish

Man born 1893 Poland to U.S.A. 1913 Citizen 1934

Wife born 1895 Poland to U.S.A. 1920 Citizen 1939

Education

Man Very little formal education. Attended Hebrew school Poland.

Wife No formal education.

Medical Status

Man Negative.

Wife Negative.

Woman's Work History Never worked outside of home.

Married 1912, Poland.

Number of Children in the Home Two *Ages*—14 and 17 years.

Basic Occupation before Relief Grocery clerk. Previously small businessman.

Average Income before Relief $20 to $30 weekly.

Private Employment Terminated October, 1936.

First Accepted for Relief November, 1936.

SUMMARY

Home Relief From November 2, 1936, to November 23, 1936. Closed to WPA.

WPA November, 1936, *to date* with the exception of:

Home Relief for two weeks in August, 1939, following WPA layoff because of 18-month ruling.

Reinstated on *WPA September, 1939.*

Applied for and received *Home Relief Supplementation of WPA* wages *March, 1940, to date.* Earlier applications rejected.

Few reclassifications or shifts while on WPA—was a laborer; at present—*watchman, $52.80 a month.*

ABSTRACT OF HOME RELIEF RECORD

OCT., 1936 *First Application:* (Social Service Exchange—No record.) Family is living in four rooms at a rental of $28 and has lived here since 1934. Their rent is paid to October 31st. The man was a grocery clerk from 1929 to October, 1936, when he was laid off because the owner's brother-in-law was in need of a job. Mr. Berger earned $20 a week and on this the family managed fairly well. Their rent had been $25 a month until last year, when it was raised to $28. Mr. and Mrs. Berger are said to have been panic-stricken at the thought of public assistance. They are especially concerned about their rent, which they have always paid in advance. The man stated that they had always managed adequately, but had not been able to save any money because of their low income. Therefore, they had no resources and it was necessary for them to come to Home Relief only two weeks after Mr. Berger lost his job. The man said that he is "too proud to stay on Home Relief long."

NOV. 2, 1936 Investigator visited Mr. Berger's former employer, the grocer, who said that Mr. Berger is a "most honest, diligent, conscientious worker" and that he was sorry to let him go. He said that his wife's brother was unemployed and that she had prevailed upon him to give this brother the job.

NOV. 2, 1936 *Case Accepted.*

NOV. 17, 1936 *Man assigned to WPA* as a laborer at $60.50 monthly.

NOV. 23, 1936 *Case Closed to WPA.*

NOV. 9, 1937 *Applied for Home Relief supplementation.* There is an estimated budget deficit of $4.05 semimonthly. Family is still living in the same apartment; their rental is now $31. It was raised recently and it is for this reason that Mr. Berger is asking for help. He says that he applied for supplementary assistance at Borough Hall, when first assigned to WPA, and was told that a family with only two children was not eligible for supplementation. The investigator questioned the family's management to date. Both Mr. and Mrs. Berger said that they managed somehow by doing without meat, fruit, etc., by purchasing no new clothing, and by saving in every possible way. Mrs. Berger cried as she talked about their difficulties. She explained that she watches every penny; that her husband takes his lunch with him and that her boy walks to school because they do not have the carfare to give him.

NOV. 16, 1937 Investigator visited the grocer to whom the Bergers owe a debt of $25. The grocer says that he extended credit to them because they are the type of family who try their best. He knows that they would not apply for assistance unless their need was great.

DEC., 1937 *Case Rejected* "because it does not seem possible for this family to have managed without some other kind of assistance."

JAN. 4, 1938 *Reapplied for Supplementation:* Mr. Berger says that the last time he applied for supplementation he was ashamed to say that he had borrowed money in order to manage. He says that he borrowed from a friend, $10 or $15 at a time as he needed it for rent, and then paid it back when he got his check. He now owes two friends $15 each. He pays a little on these debts and then borrows again when the need for rent or utility bills becomes acute. Mrs. Berger showed investigator the contents of the kitchen cupboard. There seemed to be little more than potatoes. Mr. Berger showed investigator his old, torn coat. Investigator reports that "during the interview, Mr. and Mrs. Berger were not resentful at any time. Mr. Berger was resigned to the interview and slightly disgusted." He did not see the reason for such an intensive investigation. "Investigator still not able to understand the family's ability to manage on about $5 a week for food." The woman was told to keep a daily record of food expenses for the next few days. Man says that he has talked with other men on the job who have families the size of his. They are two or three months in arrears with their rent. He says that he could not stand this; that he has to feel that his rent is paid no matter what else happens.

JAN. 25, 1938 — Mr. Berger presented a diet list kept by his wife. The family seems to have been living on a diet which excludes milk, meat, or fish. They use potatoes, evaporated milk, canned fish, etc., as indicated by the list for a week.

FEB. 8, 1938 — Man at the District Office. Still no decision by Home Relief. According to investigator, "visitor stated that the list of foods composed by his wife seemed to create some doubt in our minds of the ability of the family to manage over a period of a year on such a diet without there being some apparent decline in health." The decision on the case is left up to the nutritionist. Man states that the family's need is great; that otherwise he would not have applied. He says that the $3 increase in rent brought about the present emergency. He says that they also hope to be able to get some clothing if they are accepted for supplementation.

FEB. 15, 1938 — The nutritionist stated that in her opinion "the family could not have lived on this budget for any length of time without seriously impairing their health."

FEB. 15, 1938 — *Case Rejected.* "It seems apparent that the family has not explained management freely."

AUG. 16, 1939 — *Reapplied for Full Home Relief.* Man was dismissed from WPA, August 10, 1939, because of the 18 month ruling. Questioned again about how the family has been able to manage, they replied they have managed somehow so far. Their rent was increased to $33. They have a roomer who pays $10 a month and Isaac, who was graduated from high school this June, received $3.80 a month from NYA while at school. Mrs. Berger is unable to say how much she needs for living expenses, repeating what she has frequently said in the past, that she managed with what she had on hand. The home is described as crowded, with a boy and girl sleeping in the living room so that the roomer may have a room of his own. Man is anxious for work. Goes to stores and markets but is unable to obtain work. He says that he wants to return to WPA rather than stay on Home Relief.

AUG. 31, 1939 — *Case Accepted.*

SEPT. 12, 1939 — *Reassigned to WPA* as a laborer at $52.80.

SEPT. 14, 1939 — *Case Closed to WPA.*

FEB., 1940 — *Reapplied for Home Relief Supplementation.* When asked why they had not applied sooner they said Isaac had received $15 a month from NYA while at City College, which he entered last fall, and that he had given it all to his mother to use for the household expenses. She gave him carfare and he took his lunches from home so that he used little of the $15 himself. He was dropped from the NYA rolls this semester because his average fell below C.

The rent was raised two months ago and is now $34. They were able to make ends meet until this month with the help of the $10 from the roomer and Isaac's $15 income. Their rent is paid to date but they still owe $15 to the grocer. He has been lenient because they pay something regularly, but recently they have failed to keep the bill down and were told that the grocer must have something on account before extending further credit.

MAR., 1940 — *Case Accepted for Home Relief supplementation.*

MAY, 1940 — *Last Entry*—Clothing check for $5 granted.

HOME INTERVIEW

Home—Four rooms on the ground floor of an old tenement building on a residential street in the upper East Bronx. There are a few old buildings, several new ones and a number of private houses on this quiet, rather pleasant street. The rooms are small, two of them—the living room and the parents' bedroom—face the street; the other two, the kitchen and the room in which the lodger sleeps, are on a court. The apartment was clean and in good condition. The furniture was shabby, but showed excellent care and all the scarves, slipcovers, etc., were clean and adequately mended. The rental as stated in the Relief record is $34, of which $10 is paid by the roomer. Mrs. Berger stated that he is a pleasant, old man, who receives a pension and pays his rent regularly. He occupies the room alone and gives no one any trouble. According to Mrs. Berger, he goes out during the day, spends the evening in his room and seems satisfied with the care she gives to his room; they in turn are satisfied because he is so quiet and gives so little trouble.

According to Mrs. Berger, the rental is high but she likes the neighborhood and the street, says that her children have many friends here and thinks it a pleasant place to raise children in contrast to the crowded blocks in the lower Bronx. The Bergers have lived here six years, The parents occupy the bedroom and both the children sleep in the living room on a studio couch which opens into twin beds.

BACKGROUND

Man—Born in Poland, April, 1893, of Jewish parentage. He was the third of six children. Mr. Berger said that he had little education in Poland because when he was of school age few poor children, and certainly few Jews attended school. He had some religious training in a Hebrew school and learned to read and write Yiddish but had no formal schooling other than this.

Mr. Berger's father was a butcher in a small town in Poland and was able to do little for his children. Several of Mr. Berger's brothers and sisters left Poland as soon as they were able to go elsewhere and make a living. So far as Mr. Berger knows, three remained in Poland and he has heard nothing from them since the present war began. Mr. and Mrs. Berger were married in Poland in 1912, when Mr. Berger was 19 and his wife 17. A year later he came to the United States in order to avoid military service. He hoped to get a job, save some money, and send for his wife. But the outbreak of the World War made it impossible for Mrs. Berger to leave Poland, so she remained at home, living with her mother until 1920 when she came to the United States to join her husband.

Both Mr. Berger's parents are now dead. He has heard from only two of his immediate relatives, both of them younger than he. One is a brother who was a shoemaker and whom he has not seen in twenty-four years. He heard from this brother recently and gathered from his letters that the brother had come to Cuba to await admission to the United States under the Polish quota and while there had met a girl whose home is in Minneapolis. He married this girl, and, having married an American citizen, was able to enter the country without waiting for the quota; he now lives in Minneapolis. Mr. Berger has a sister in Argentina, but has not heard from her in years. There are no relatives in New York City.

Woman—Born in Poland, March, 1895, she was the eldest of four children, all girls. Her father, who was a tailor, died in 1902, when Mrs. Berger was 7 years old. Her mother was forced to go out to work in order to support her children and Mrs. Berger looked after her younger sisters. She, too, had no formal schooling in Poland, but did manage to learn to read Yiddish. According to Mrs. Berger, it was customary for girls to marry very young; she was married at the age of 17. In 1913 her first child was born, at about the time her husband left Poland to come to the United States in order to escape military service. Mrs. Berger stayed on with her mother and sisters. Mrs. Berger says that she has heard nothing from her three sisters and does not know whether or not they are alive.

Mrs. Berger never worked out of the home, either before or after her marriage.

BEFORE LOSS OF PRIVATE EMPLOYMENT

When Mr. Berger arrived in New York City he had no intention of taking up the trade he had learned and practiced in Europe. In Poland he had been a shoemaker, but said, with considerable feeling, that he had always hated it and had no desire to be a shoemaker in this country. Not only is there no living in it; it is very unpleasant work. He had been apprenticed in Europe and had had no choice of a trade there but felt that he could decide for himself in the New World. He started work here as a "customer peddler," but after a few years found out that it was difficult to make a living let alone save enough to bring his wife to this country. Mr. Berger communicated with a friend who lived in Charleston, South

Carolina, telling him about his difficulties. He said that he had gone to Hebrew school in Poland with this friend and had been close to him when they were boys so he felt able to call on him for assistance. His friend told him to come to Charleston; that he would see what he could do for him. Mr. Berger worked for the friend for several years as a clothing salesman. During this time he was able to save enough money to send for his wife, who arrived in 1920. In 1925 Mr. Berger opened a shoe and clothing store and ran this business for a period of two years. At the end of this time he sold out because business was dropping off. He then bought a restaurant which he ran for two years, from 1927 to 1929 but which he sold because he saw he could no longer make a living from it. He said that both places of business were in the poorer section of Charleston and that most of his customers were Negroes. According to Mr. Berger, as times grew worse and the Negroes had less money to spend, it became impossible to make a living dealing with them.

Both Mr. and Mrs. Berger said with real feeling that they had loved Charleston—that it was a beautiful city and that the life there was good because it was so quiet. New York to their mind is too hectic and large. They came back here only because they thought that if there were jobs to be found anywhere, New York City would be the place to find them. Soon after the family's arrival in New York, Mr. Berger got a job in a grocery store, July, 1929, and worked there until October, 1936, when he was laid off because the brother of the owner's wife needed a job. The Bergers talked at length about the fact that life in Charleston was much easier and pleasanter than it is here; that Negro help is easy to obtain and that the Negroes are willing to do housework for $1.50 a week. Mrs. Berger said that she supposed this was enough wages for them since they live very cheaply. The Bergers both feel that a small community is much better for children and believe that both Isaac and Mildred had a happy childhood there. Mildred was only three years old when they left Charleston and therefore did not have as much of it as Isaac. They said that because of their fondness for a quiet, small town or city, they selected the street on which they now live since it is not like the usual New York street; it even "has trees." According to Mrs. Berger, she and her husband have known each other from childhood and have always been fond of each other. She said that their life together has been happy. They have also found much pleasure in their children. After losing their first child during the war in Poland and then their second in Charleston, they concentrated their love and attention on the two remaining children and before 1929 were able to give them everything they needed.

FIRST REACTIONS TO UNEMPLOYMENT

The Bergers were frightened and panic-stricken at the thought of applying for charity. They had to come to Home Relief almost at once because on $20 a week they had been unable to accumulate savings to fall back on. They had no relatives in New York City who might have been asked to help. Mrs. Berger said that her husband had hoped for a job when he came to the Relief Bureau.

ADJUSTMENT TO HOME RELIEF

The Bergers were on full Home Relief twice—for three weeks after the first acceptance, November, 1936, and for two weeks following the 18 months WPA layoff, August, 1939. They have been receiving supplementary Home Relief since March, 1940 (see Relief History for account of rejections by Home Relief while the family was existing on subsubsistence diet). They expressed little resentment about their earlier rejection by Home Relief. Mrs. Berger said that the investigator had not been understanding or sympathetic but that their present investigator is pleasant and kind.

PRESENT SITUATION

Man—A short, slender, black-haired man, who looks much younger than his age, which is 47. He was quiet, talked little, seemed rather shy. Mr. Berger is conversant with current events, has apparently thought deeply about the difficulties which face an untrained, middle-aged man, and is quite discouraged. He said that he feels he is neither educated, intelligent, nor aggressive enough to make a go of things. He appeared to rely on his wife to carry on most of the conversation. Mr. Berger speaks fairly well but with a marked accent. Several times he used Yiddish to make his meaning clear, explaining that he was unable to do so in English.

Woman—A tall, well-built, rather attractive woman who also appears to be younger than her stated age, 45. She was alert, interested, and friendly. She had less difficulty than her husband in making herself understood in English, though she, too, occasionally used Yiddish phrases. Mrs. Berger carried most of the discussion, frequently glancing at her husband to bring him into the conversation. She looked to him for corroboration and he gave it by nodding and smiling.

PRESENT ADJUSTMENT

Despite the financial difficulties and rather bleak future, Mrs. Berger says that her family is a happy one. She elaborated on this at great length. As stated above, she and her husband married young because they were in love. They have remained fond of each other and derive great happiness from their relationship. She talked about her experiences in Europe during the war and said that nothing in America could ever compare with that. She described graphically the circumstances surrounding her eldest child's death in Poland at the age of three. She said that he had had scarlet fever but that there had been no money for doctors and that even the doctors knew so little they would have been unable to save the child had she called them in. She said that a great many children died of scarlet fever at about the same time. According to Mrs. Berger, anyone who has lived in a foreign country should be grateful indeed to be in the United States and an American citizen. She said that people born in America do not appreciate their good luck. No matter how difficult life is, or how poor one is, one is a free individual in America. (Prominently displayed on the living room wall is a banner with the inscription, "God Bless

America.") She went on to say that we have a President who wants to help the poor and that even though Congress makes it hard for him, he does his best; Jews are not persecuted here; children can be educated. With considerable feeling she repeated several times that America is the most wonderful country in the world and to this her husband agreed with great emphasis.

Their second child also died at about the age of three. This child was born in Charleston and was given the benefit of good medical attention, but the doctors were unable to save the child, who died of poliomyelitis. Mrs. Berger said worker could understand that having lost their first two children they lavished all their affection on the two who remained and said she was proud to say that these children have repaid them for their devotion. Both parents agree that their children are good, responsible, understanding, and considerate and that they present none of the difficulties of which one hears other parents complain. Mrs. Berger does not believe that loving your child and giving it a great deal of affection and attention will spoil it. She believes rather that a child who has had much love and security in the family is able to take whatever hard knocks life presents. Mrs. Berger believes that their present good relationship with their children is helped by the fact that the children have never heard their parents quarreling or being disagreeable to each other and have always understood that their parents want nothing more than their children's happiness. She discussed further her belief that since the children had a happy childhood they were therefore better able to take adversity than they would have been had they had nothing but deprivation. Both parents said that their children have always known the extent of the family's resources and for that reason are never insistent about the things they need if money is not available.

Mrs. Berger emphasized the fact that if one is happy and secure in the home one can stand anything because one has one's family and their love. Her husband, who was less articulate than Mrs. Berger, agreed with everything she said. Mrs. Berger said that she disapproved of nagging women because they succeeded in doing nothing but antagonizing their husbands. She asked how can children respect their father if the mother doesn't. She knows her husband has always tried to make a living and that now he continues to try to get work. He goes about in the neighborhood and if he has carfare goes downtown, but since he has no trade and no education, there is little that he can do. He said that he is willing to do anything and is able to learn if only given a chance. When he got the job in the grocery store, he knew nothing about the work but learned quickly and did a satisfactory job. He was quite willing to do laboring work on WPA and did it for a while but he is now a watchman because his supervisors thought that he did not look strong enough for laboring. He said that in his opinion the only people who can do laboring work easily are Negroes and Italians, who are accustomed to such work.

Children:

Jacob—born in Poland, in 1913. Died in Poland, 1915, of scarlet fever.

Charles—born 1921 in Charleston, South Carolina, died there in 1924 of poliomyelitis.

Isaac—born January, 1923, in Charleston, South Carolina, attends City College. Isaac was dropped from the NYA rolls because his average fell below C last semester. He is anxious to go to work and is registered at the New York State Employment Service, but since he will not be eighteen until January, 1941, is not yet eligible for placement. His parents said that he would prefer working during the day and going to college at night, because then he would feel that he was contributing to the family income. The parents agreed that Isaac is very bright and could do much better work than he is now doing if he were not so worried about the family's troubles. He has registered for a number of training courses for defense work but is too young for these and must wait until January.

Isaac answered the door when worker visited in the morning. He said that his mother was not at home and suggested that worker come back in the afternoon. Isaac is a short, slender, dark-haired boy, very good-looking, with a pleasant manner and an agreeable speaking voice.

Mildred—born April, 1926, in Charleston, South Carolina, is completing junior high school this term and will go on to high school. She was seen as she passed the door while worker was talking with her brother at the time of the morning visit. She is a pretty, dark-haired child, attractively dressed.

Mrs. Berger said that Mildred does not eat lunch at school because she is ashamed to do so. It is well-known in the neighborhood that children who eat lunch in school do so because their families are on Relief, and in this neighborhood, where Relief is not so common as it is in adjoining sections of the Bronx, such children are looked down on by their classmates. Mildred has many nice friends who do not know that the family is on Relief. The mother said that she understands her child's feelings about this and, since Mildred is willing to walk ten blocks to come home for lunch, the mother raises no objection. On rainy days the mother gives her her lunch to take along. Mrs. Berger said that some of the girls at school pay 30 cents for their lunches in the school cafeteria, but Mildred understands that her mother could not possibly afford to give her 30 cents a day, nor even 20 cents, since 20 cents pays for two home-made lunches.

As stated above, both children are good and a great source of satisfaction to their parents. Mrs. Berger said that they make no complaints about the crowded condition of the home, the fact that they must share a room, and do without a great many things. She says that when she worries about their financial troubles Isaac tells her to keep up her courage, that things will be better later on and that they must all try to make the best of the situation.

The Bergers practice birth control because they believe that their financial situation is such that they have no right to bring children into the world. Mrs. Berger said that had she remained in Poland she would probably have gone on having children since Europeans didn't know "any better," especially those in poor circumstances.

Use of Leisure Time: Mr. Berger goes looking for work whenever he has free time. He does not have a week off as do other laborers, but works steadily. Watchmen shift from one time period to another, working either from four P.M. to midnight, or from midnight to eight A.M., and also on Saturdays and Sundays. The Bergers cannot afford any recreation for which they must pay but sometimes go out for a walk. They do not go to the movies unless they get passes. Mrs. Berger said that through some friends in the neighborhood they manage to get movie passes for two people several times a week and Mrs. Berger takes either her son or her daughter or lets one of them take a friend.

Religion: Both Mr. and Mrs. Berger were reared in Orthodox Jewish homes. They observe the dietary laws, but cannot afford to go to synagogue on Holy Days since the tickets are too expensive. Mrs. Berger mentioned that Isaac is deeply religious, much more so than his father. She thinks that such orthodox behavior in an "American boy" is not entirely normal, but does not attempt to discourage his deep interest in religious matters.

Newspapers: The *Forward*, a liberal Yiddish daily, which is read regularly by Mr. and Mrs. Berger; the *Times* and *Post*, which the children read when they can afford to buy them. Mrs. Berger said that the radio is their chief source of pleasure and recreation. It brings the world into the home and they can keep in touch with everything that is going on. They listen to the news regularly, but sometimes, Mrs. Berger says, the news about the war gets so painful she has to turn it off because she can't stand it. The children like the quiz programs and so do their parents, although the parents cannot always understand the questions. They like comedy programs and some music.

Political Affiliations: Mr. Berger votes Democratic, but does not belong to any club. Mr. Berger was naturalized in 1934; Mrs. Berger became a citizen in 1939 and said that she is anxious to vote in the coming election since this will be her first chance. She said that poor people are usually Democrats; the Republican party is for the rich. According to both Mr.

and Mrs. Berger, Roosevelt is a wonderful man. Willkie is young, inexperienced, a businessman, and definitely not the person we need at this time. Mr. Berger said that he wishes he could speak well enough to be able to go out electioneering for Roosevelt. They believe that the fear of dictatorship is stupid because if a man is not a dictator at heart, another term in office will not make him one. Mr. Berger said that he is amused by the political arguments on the WPA project; he thinks it foolish for men who are being supported by government money to say they want to vote for Willkie who is much against the kind of work relief which is supporting them and their families. He said with some amusement that his foreman, the other day, came to work with a Willkie button on, but that the supervisor made him take it off. WPA supervisors discourage all political talk on the projects.

In Mr. Berger's opinion the Workers' Alliance is a Communist organization and he has no use for it. He does not want anybody to fight his battles for him. He tells the truth in his dealings with government institutions and if that does no good there is no point in seeking help from other organizations. He thinks the Communists are either foolish or bad. Their reasoning is so mixed up that sometimes he wonders how they themselves can follow it. First they urged everyone to fight for Spain so that she could defeat Germany and now because Germany and Russia have signed a pact, England becomes as bad as Germany and we should therefore not help her. Their idea seems to be that Germany should conquer the world and that then Russia will step in and take over; but he is afraid that they will be fooled, because if Germany is powerful enough to conquer the world, she can conquer Russia as well. The Communists are against conscription, possibly because they want the men to remain untrained so that they can be slaughtered more easily if war comes. He said that their anxiety to divide the money of the rich among the poor is contrary to human nature. Why should Ford, or duPont, or Morgan give him their money? They, especially Ford, were smart enough to make their money and are entitled to it. He is uneducated, not aggressive enough to make a fortune and can't expect to have a fortune given him. People are different and he does not believe it is all just luck. He is happy that his son is having the opportunity for an education such as he never had, and hopes he'll learn something useful.

The question of refugees is one about which the Bergers have apparently thought a great deal. They know that there are German Jewish refugees in this country who are working for less money than Americans, but have no great feeling of resentment about it. Mrs. Berger said that she knows that Klein's and Ohrbach's both have taken on a great many refugees and are paying them less than the employees who were fired to make room for them. She believes that the refugees have a right to work as well as the others. Just because we came here first does not mean that we have more right to a job than those who came only a few months ago. According to Mrs. Berger, most of the people who came to the United States during the last forty or fifty years have been refugees from one country or another. The Bergers feel strongly that we should help children escape from the war areas and should send money to help those who are suffering. The only strong feeling displayed on the refugee question was about German Jews who never "learn from experience." Mrs. Berger said that she does not think they ought to be so grateful that they would be willing to kiss the "hem of my gown," but she did think that they should have learned their lesson, that they are Jews and not Germans, as they still maintain. She said they still feel superior to the Russian Jews who have spent their money to help them.

Management: Mrs. Berger said that she has always been able to manage on whatever the income happened to be at the moment. Under the present circumstances they have to exercise extreme care and watch "every penny." She said that she shops on Bathgate Avenue because everything in the markets there is very cheap. She uses the Home Relief surplus commodity book and is careful of her budgeting. The most important item on her budget is rent. Both Mr. and Mrs. Berger expressed considerable feeling on this point. They said that having a roof over their heads is the most important thing in their lives and they therefore pay their rent first, then their utilities, and then worry about food. They have great fear of a dispossess, which is the most disgraceful thing they can think of. They are proud of their landlord's good opinion of them, and of the fact that the grocer on Bathgate Avenue with whom they deal trusts them whenever it becomes necessary. Mrs. Berger explained how it is possible to feed a family of four on the budget or on even less than the budget, as they were forced to do earlier on Work Relief when they were not able to obtain supplementary Home Relief. Each item that she buys is at least 2 or 3 cents cheaper on Bathgate Avenue than it is in her neighborhood. She said, for instance, that in the immediate neighborhood 10 cents would only buy an ordinary loaf of bread which would not feed the family for the day, while on Bathgate Avenue for ten cents she can get a loaf twice the ordinary size, which takes care of all the family's bread needs for a day and a half. While milk in the neighborhood is eleven cents a quart, on Bathgate Avenue it is nine. She can get meat for as low as 15 cents a pound, and sometimes buys chicken for 10 cents a pound if she shops at the right time, just before the markets close for the day, when all perishables are being sold at less than cost. She does not think that the children have suffered by this kind of diet since she tries her best to give them a certain amount of fruit and meat. She cannot always afford to buy oranges, but manages to find a substitute. It is relatively simple to manage on the present income, but during the period when they were refused supplementary assistance for Home Relief, the children frequently went hungry. Mrs. Berger said that she would make a potato soup, thicken it and reheat it and that was all the family had to eat for several days on end.

The budget is $39.65 semimonthly and from this, the WPA income of $28.60 and $5 from the roomer are deducted, leaving $6.05, which is the semi-monthly Home Relief allowance. The greatest problem at present is clothing. While they get useful dresses and underclothing from WPA commodities, it is most important now that both children have winter coats, and Mrs.

Berger said that she is worrying about this. They both feel that supplementary assistance is a great help because not only do they get the actual cash allowance but the extra services as well. The surplus food depot has been giving them a dozen eggs a week and this is all that Mrs. Berger needs for cooking during the week. The medical assistance which they can have if they need it and the fact that they get clothing allotments have been helpful. Mrs. Berger does all her own work.

Attitudes:

Toward Home Relief: They are very much ashamed of receiving Home Relief assistance and are certain that no one knows about it. They have no relatives in New York City and their friends have not been informed. They believe there is no need to "advertise it to the world." They have clean, well-cared-for clothing and they look well when they go out.

Toward WPA: In the opinion of both Mr. and Mrs. Berger, WPA is much better than Home Relief. They would have liked WPA wages to be high enough so that they would not have needed to ask for supplementary assistance, but under the circumstances it is necessary. Mr. Berger said that WPA is a wonderful thing in that it has given him a chance to work and not to feel that he is receiving charity. It is, however, actually a form of Relief in that it is a kind of "made work." Despite this fact, Mr. Berger thinks that WPA can be very proud of all the fine work it has done. He said that if he were younger and had education and skill, he could probably have gotten off Work Relief, but under the circumstances he is glad of the opportunity to stay on.

Future: Both Mr. and Mrs. Berger feel that there is no future for them to look forward to, but have high hopes for a better future for their children. Mr. Berger said that his only chance for a job may come when the draft takes a large number of men away from their work in New York City and leaves openings in some of the unskilled trades for middle-aged men like him.

Toward Us: Both Mr. and Mrs. Berger were friendly, approved of the study, and said that they were glad to be able to help. Mr. Berger was rather embarrassed about the thought of coming down to the office for an interview, saying that he doesn't speak well, but his wife said that she would persuade him to come.

OFFICE INTERVIEW

Impression: Mr. Berger came in about twenty minutes late. He was dressed in a sweater and a pair of flannel trousers, but he was neatly groomed and appeared to be younger than his 47 years. Although he has been in the United States since 1913, he speaks with a pronounced accent and several times during the course of the interview used Yiddish idioms.

Employment History: Mr. Berger's father was a butcher and his older brothers were trained as butchers, but he was apprenticed to a shoemaker and, although he learned the trade, Mr. Berger said he always disliked it. He fled Poland in 1913, one year after his marriage and four weeks after the birth of his first child, because the government was trying to force him into military service. He said that many other men from his and neighboring towns ran away at the same time. When he arrived in the United States, he got in touch with a fellow townsman who had settled in Charleston, South Carolina and went there to join him. After working in Charleston for some time, Mr. Berger opened a shoe store; this was pleasant because he had two Negro employees, who did all the work. At the end of the World War, his wife came to the United States (his child had died in Europe), and when she joined him in Charleston, Mr. Berger changed his business on her advice, from shoes to dry goods. But he did not make a go of his new business. He then opened a restaurant, largely because Mrs. Berger was a good cook. During the war she had supported herself in Warsaw, working as a cook. But the restaurant venture also failed. Mr. Berger says that he likes to think about Charleston and life in the South although he can never figure out why several persons he knew there were able to make a lot of money while he was not able to do so. He thinks that luck can explain the fact that he did not make money while others did. When his restaurant failed, in 1929, the family moved to New York and Mr. Berger got a job as a grocery clerk in a store in Harlem. He said that he often worked 80 hours a week, but earned only about $23. The work was hard because he frequently had to carry 100-pound sacks of sugar up five flights of stairs to customers who were in the bootlegging business. He said that bootleggers always lived "five flights up." In 1936 he lost this job because the building in which the store was located was condemned and his boss went out of business.

Relief: When Mr. Berger lost his job, he went to Home Relief almost immediately and after a short stay on Home Relief was put on WPA, where he has been ever since, except for a short layoff following the "18 months dismissal." Mr. Berger thinks that WPA is pretty good except that the wages are too small for a family to live on. This is why he needs supplementation from Home Relief. Fortunately he has a roomer who pays $10 a month, which is a real help. Mr. Berger said that he had a hard time getting supplementation from Home Relief because his investigator, a Jew, was "tough" and refused to give the family supplementation because he did not believe that the Bergers could live as well as they did on only $6 or $7 a week, which they said was all they spent on food. Although Mr. Berger applied for supplementation several times, he did not get it until his son, a student at City College, who had been receiving $15 a month from NYA, lost this assistance because his marks fell below the minimum requirements. Mr. Berger felt that the investigator was mean to him, but he said, "After all, I couldn't go and shoot him, could I?" Mr. Berger thought that the investigator was hard on him because he wanted to make a good record for himself. He said that for a long time he had not known he could get supplementation since he only had two children, and he smiled and said, "Go make more children these days." He says that the family is much better off with the supplementation because Home Relief gives his wife and daughter dresses, and there is also extra food from surplus commodities, besides other services. Mr. Berger said that the worst thing at the moment is that there is no money to fix his wife's teeth, which need fixing badly but would cost $75. Mr. Berger says that they are now able to manage on the money they are getting; his wife is a good housewife and makes the most of what they get. He pointed out that by walking a few extra blocks one can get a loaf of bread for 5 cents which costs 10 cents in the neighborhood store. His wife buys kosher food, and when I suggested that kosher meat was more expensive than other meat, he said that that was true, but if one did not insist upon first cut of lamb chops and was satisfied with the second, one could get these pretty cheaply at the market. Mr. Berger is proud of the way in which his wife runs the household. He said that the grocer extends credit if they run short before payday; they pay their debts when Mr. Berger's check arrives. He thinks that WPA is doing many good and useful things, like building roads, playgrounds, and parks and he feels that the men on WPA are happy about the work they are doing. Mr. Berger feels, however, that these men are poorly fed and have poor clothes. He says that this is especially hard on the poor devils who have to work in the sewers. He said that his supervisor never makes him do that. At present Mr. Berger is a night watchman and his boss treats him well. Most of the men on the project are Negroes and Italians; there are only a few Jews. Mr. Berger said that few men are now getting off WPA and into private employment, but he thinks that when the draft starts to work, most of the younger men will be taken off WPA. Mr. Berger emphasized that his wife will have nothing to do with Relief and always insists that he go to the office, the surplus commodity depot, etc.

Family: Mr. Berger said that Mrs. Berger is the center of the household and is largely responsible for the way things go. He is proud of her ability.

The Bergers lost their first child in Poland and another child died of a spinal disease when they lived in Charleston. Mr. Berger told how smart their doctor in Charleston had been, for he prophesied that the child, who was injured at birth, would die at the age of three and Mr. Berger said that sure enough this happened. Mr. Berger has two living children, one a student at City College, who is specializing in accountancy and would like to get a job but is unable to find one, and a younger child, a girl, who is in junior high school. Mr. Berger said that his boy had tried to get work during the summer but had been offered jobs that paid only $2 to $4 a week and had refused them. Mr. Berger says that the boy is unusual because he has never played with other boys on the street. He is also religious and observes all the ceremonials. He goes to synagogue every Saturday and Mr. Berger thinks he gets much pleasure from his religion. How the boy came to be so religious is not clear to Mr. Berger, for the boy is much more observant than either Mr. Berger or his wife. Mr. Berger pointed out that when his son visits friends, he never eats any food in their homes because he believes that the food may not have been prepared according to ritual. His daughter, on the other hand, has many friends and gets along with them easily. Mr. Berger is somewhat worried about his being drafted for the war, but he shows no concern about the possibility of his son's being drafted. He said that he has many relatives in Palestine, Argentina, and in the western part of the United States, but that one really has relatives in America only when one "has a dollar in his pocket. If you have the dollar you have relatives; if you don't have the dollar, you don't have relatives." Mr. Berger was disturbed as he recalled the fact that his mother and sister were living in Poland when the Nazis moved in. Since then his mother has died, and he thinks that she probably was killed by the Germans because she had been in good health before the war started. He has not heard a word from his sister. He says he always goes to the synagogue on the High Holy Days and this year, because he must say prayers for the dead, he goes to the synagogue regularly. Occasionally he goes to the movies but never on week ends because he said there is no sense in spending 30 or 40 cents when one can get in for a dime. His wife also goes on weekday afternoons. When the weather is nice they often sit in the park. Mr. Berger mentioned that if his first child had not died in Poland, he would probably have been a grandfather by now, at the young age of 47, and this would have pleased him. He said that even now he would like to have more children, but his wife thinks that it is silly to have more children when one cannot take care of the children one already has.

Politics: Mr. Berger likes the United States very much and says that things are much better here than in Europe. He always remembers this when he thinks about his bad experiences with Relief. He is frightened about the United States coming closer to war but, on the other hand, he said that one cannot allow Hitler to win. He is much upset about Hitler's treatment of the Jews. He hates the Communists and says that he has nothing to do with them, and has never had anything to do with them. If he had his way and was in power, he would put them on a boat and ship them straight to Russia. He said that we are lucky to have Roosevelt as President, Lehman as Governor and La Guardia as Mayor. Mr. Berger feels that England would not have been able to hold her own so far had she not received help from the United States, but he thinks the United States could do a lot more.

Future: Mr. Berger thinks that the draft will take young men out of industry and that there ought to be a big increase in business because of governmental spending. This might give him a chance to get back into private employment. He says that he still looks for a private job but that his chances are not good because he is not a union man and the unions have most of the jobs tied up. Although he never did laboring before getting on WPA, he does not object to WPA, but rather likes it. He said that his health is now better than when he first went on WPA.

Case Six

GUNTHER FAMILY

Status WPA *Religion* Protestant
Man born 1884 N.Y.C.
Wife born 1887 New Jersey.

Education
Man High school graduate; 2 years business school.
Wife Completed elementary school.

Medical Status
Man "Nervous."
Wife Hypertension, arthritis, asthma.

Woman's Work History Woman says—never worked. Home Relief record states—jewel setter in watch factory prior to marriage.

Married 1929, N.Y.C.

Number of Children in the home None

Basic Occupation before Relief Bookkeeper—sales manager.

Average Income before Relief $35 to $45 weekly.

Private Employment Terminated December, 1934.

First Accepted for Relief September, 1935.

SUMMARY

Home Relief—September, 1935, to October, 1935, when case closed to *WPA. Reopened* almost immediately because man said he was not strong enough to do laboring.

Home Relief—October, 1935, to August, 1939—again closed to *WPA. Reopened* a month later—for same reason.

Home Relief—September, 1939, to October, 1939, when case was closed to:

WPA—From *October, 1939, to date*—as junior clerk—$52.50 per month.

ABSTRACT OF HOME RELIEF RECORD

AUG., 1935 — *First Application:* For twenty years Mr. Gunther was a buyer and sales representative for a paint company which had been founded by his father. This business was taken over by its creditors in December, 1934. From that time to the present, the family has lived on $380 received through adjustment of insurance policies, on withdrawals from their savings account, and on money borrowed from friends. At this time they owe $175 to friends and are three months in arrears in rent, which amounts to $135. The Gunthers are described by the worker as "fine-looking people."

SEPT., 1935 — *Accepted for Home Relief.*

OCT. 16, 1935 — *Mr. Gunther assigned to WPA as a laborer at $50.50.*

OCT. 23, 1935 — *Case Closed to WPA.*

OCT. 23, 1935 — *Case Reopened.* Mr. Gunther was unable to do the job to which he was assigned. Investigator says she believes that he was willing to work but unable to do a laborer's job; and adds, as her impression, that "Mr. Gunther is accustomed to high standards of living, taking all pleasures of life and spending everything he earned." Mr. Gunther says that his sister has told him that he would have been able to save had he married sooner. Before marriage he was in the habit of spending all he earned and after he was married saving was not possible because his income from the business was dropping off.

JAN., 1936 — The family was forced to move after receiving a dispossess. They are unable to pay their back rent. They moved into a furnished room at $6 a week and stored their furniture. Mr. Gunther is still confident of securing work although he is discouraged by the fact that he was unable to secure a janitor's job for which he made application.

JULY, 1937 — The record indicates that Mr. Gunther attempted to find work but was unsuccessful. On this date investigator questioned Mr. Gunther regarding possible attendance at Adult Education classes "to prepare himself for some future work." The investigator stated she "asked him very frankly if he were content to remain on Home Relief." Mr. Gunther assured the investigator he is not content to stay on Home Relief, but that he has been unable to find a job. He was informed by the investigator that, in view of the fact that his health seems to be good, he must give some satisfactory explanation of his efforts to look for employment, or the matter would be taken up with the administration at the District Office. On the investigator's advice, Mrs. Gunther is attending Knickerbocker Clinic for treatment of asthma and a cardiac condition.

OCT., 1938 — Mr. Gunther was classified by the occupational department as "wholesale paint salesman, obviously unfit for manual labor."

DEC., 1938 — Mrs. Gunther states that the family is using the surplus food commodities which they find helpful in supplementing the Home Relief allowance. In addition to this, Mrs. Gunther's sister frequently assists with food.

FEB., 1939 — Mr. Gunther states he is attempting to locate work and showed the worker copies of five letters sent in response to newspaper "ads."

APRIL, 1939 — Mrs. Gunther was confined to Knickerbocker Hospital for observation for high blood pressure and neuritis.

JUNE 1, 1939 — The family moved to an unfurnished room in an elevator apartment, rental $20 a month. It was necessary to secure an elevator apartment because of Mrs. Gunther's illness.

JUNE 5, 1939 — A new investigator questioned Mr. Gunther regarding his efforts to obtain employment and stated that in the four years the family had been known to Relief, Mr. Gunther had not reported having earned any money at either odd jobs or occasional work. In response to this Mr. Gunther stated that he feels his age, 55, is against him. He stated he had made frequent efforts to locate paint-selling jobs but all these jobs were on a commission basis. He had tried selling paint before applying for Relief, but expenses were so high that he could not make a living by doing this. He had attempted to secure drawing accounts from companies but was unsuccessful; he was not able even to supply his own carfare. The investigator suggested that Mr. Gunther try to secure a loan from a friend, $2 or $3 a week, with the goal of establishing himself with a firm; that he might in this way eventually bring in enough business to warrant a small drawing account. Mr. Gunther replied that he had thought of many possibilities for securing employment but that none had materialized. He stated further that he is not well, has had three operations in the past few years for hemorrhoids at St. Luke's Hospital. This condition prohibits much walking. Mr. Gunther said that his parents had exhausted their savings in the fall of 1938 and were forced to apply for Old-Age Assistance. His sister is helping them until this assistance is granted.

AUG. 14, 1939 — Report received from Home Relief physicians that Mr. Gunther previously refused a WPA laborer's job, claiming ill-health. The report stated that Mr. Gunther is employable and is able to do a laboring job. At present Mr. Gunther is attending Fordham Hospital Clinic. The diagnosis is hemorrhoids.

AUG. 24, 1939 — Mr. Gunther was informed he must accept a referral for a laborer's job or Relief will be discontinued.

AUG. 31, 1939 — *Case Closed to WPA.*

SEPT. 15, 1939 — *Reapplied.* Mr. Gunther showed his dismissal as of September 7, 1939, reason—"physically unable to work." On August 31, 1939, he became ill on the job and the foreman sent him to the WPA doctor. In view of conflicting medical statements, the investigator said it would be necessary to secure further statements from WPA examining physician.

SEPT. 19, 1939 — Mr. Gunther reported that the family is to be locked out of their room for nonpayment of rent. Investigator's telephone inquiry of the WPA examining physician brought the reply that information cannot be given over the phone. The case supervisor decided that if Mr. Gunther indicates his willingness to accept reassignment to WPA in any available category the case will be accepted for reinvestigation.

SEPT. 25, 1939 — *Case Accepted* as an emergency, pending Mr. Gunther's reinstatement on WPA.

OCT. 10, 1939 *Mr. Gunther assigned to WPA as junior clerk at $57.20 a month.*

OCT. 14, 1939 *Case Closed to WPA.*

HOME INTERVIEW

Home—Two rooms on the fourth floor of a well-constructed walk-up apartment building in a residential neighborhood. The building is attractive and well-kept. The rooms are small but pleasant and nicely furnished with pieces which Mrs. Gunther says were borrowed from a friend. The apartment consists of a living room and bedroom and private bath. A kitchenette unit is screened off at one end of the living room. The family has been living here since December, 1939. The rent is $35 a month.

BACKGROUND

Man—Born in New York, June, 1884, of German parentage. He was the second of four children, with two brothers and one sister. Mr. Gunther was graduated from high school and then completed two years of business school training. He was a bookkeeper in his father's paint company at the time of the loss of this business in 1934.

For about fifty years Mr. Gunther's father operated a successful paint business. He employed his sons until the depression caused a decline in the business. The father died three weeks ago. His mother was taken to Welfare Island last week; she was committed by Mr. Gunther's sister. According to Mrs. Gunther, her mother-in-law is now 82 years old and practically blind. Mrs. Gunther regrets that she and her husband are unable to care for her. She condemns Mr. Gunther's sister for having had the "old lady" placed in an institution, saying that the least the sister could do would be to try to make her mother's last years comfortable and happy. According to Mrs. Gunther, her husband's family is "cold" and unsympathetic, but she hastened to add that Mr. Gunther is not at all like his family in this respect.

In addition to the sister already mentioned, there is a brother who lives in New York City. His wife, a telephone operator, returned to work when the Gunther firm was dissolved and her husband became unemployed. Mr. Gunther's other brother is dead.

Woman—Born in New Jersey, July, 1887, she was the third of three children, with a sister and a brother. Mrs. Gunther completed public school. She says that she has never worked. (There is a discrepancy between Mrs. Gunther's statement and the Home Relief record, which says that Mrs. Gunther worked in a watch factory in New Jersey as a jewel setter but had to give this up when her vision became impaired. The Home Relief states that she then came to New York City and secured work as a collector for a downtown nursery. She presumably gave up her job when she married in 1929.)

Mrs. Gunther's father was a carpenter. She says that they were always poor but were able to get along. Her parents died some years ago. Her brother also is dead. Her sister, a widow, lives in Jersey City. She is supported by a daughter. Mrs. Gunther lived with this sister for several years prior to her marriage in 1929. (Mrs. Gunther made no mention of an earlier marriage but the Home Relief record stated that Mrs. Gunther was first married in 1903.)

BEFORE LOSS OF PRIVATE EMPLOYMENT

Mr. Gunther worked for his father from 1901 to 1922, starting at $3 and later earning $40 a week. In 1922 he became restless and felt that he wanted to travel. He left his father's store, went to California and remained there about two years, working as a bookkeeper for a chemical company in Los Angeles. He then returned to his father's business and remained there until 1934. His average earnings were $40 a week; at the chemical company in Los Angeles he had earned $45.

According to Mrs. Gunther, she and her husband were comfortable financially until he lost private employment. They had many friends and were in the habit of entertaining a great deal. Although it was not large they had always had a bank account, and carried insurance. They enjoyed their home and always preferred staying home to going out to the theater, etc.

FIRST REACTIONS TO UNEMPLOYMENT

Mr. and Mrs. Gunther were greatly disturbed by Mr. Gun ther's loss of work. It was especially difficult, Mr. Gunther said, in view of the sense of security the whole Gunther family had felt because of their long-established business. His father realized some money from the sale of the store and equipment but the sons received nothing. Mr. Gunther tried desperately to secure work. They sold insurance policies, exhausted a small bank account and received a little help from Mrs. Gunther's sister. When Mr. Gunther had exhausted every possibility for work and they no longer had resources they were forced to apply for Relief. At the time of their first application they owed three months' rent and several hundred dollars which they had borrowed from friends and relatives. They have never been able to repay the borrowed money.

ADJUSTMENT ON HOME RELIEF

Mrs. Gunther said she cried a great deal when they were forced to apply for Relief. The time they spent on Home Relief was very trying. They were without insurance policies except for 10-cent ones which they felt were not much good and which they were forced to drop later. Mr. Gunther begged to be assigned to WPA as a clerk but they were on Home Relief for five years before the assignment came through and then he only got it by nagging the investigator. Mrs. Gunther says "you have to have connections" to get on WPA. Mr. Gunther was even asked by a Home Relief investigator if he knew a "New Dealer" who would get him the job. Home Relief investigators were constantly bothering them, asking questions or checking and rechecking. Mrs. Gunther states that Home Relief investigators never trusted them. They were often discourteous and she dreaded having them come to the house. She added, however, that she finally got used to it. She said she also got used to the furnished room which they were forced to take and was even able to laugh at the varied experiences they have had in furnished rooms. According to Mrs. Gunther, the fact that her friends are not "fair weather" friends but real ones made it easier to go on Home Relief than it might have been. The fact that they had to accept Relief and Mr. Gunther was unemployed made no difference to their friends. Mrs. Gunther states she could write a book about her Home Relief experiences and her experiences living in furnished rooms. She says she is able to laugh about it now because she knows there was nothing else for them to do.

PRESENT SITUATION

Man—Not seen. Mrs. Gunther describes her husband as tall and good-looking, a man who makes an excellent appearance. She says that he is very intelligent. According to Mrs. Gunther, her husband is not well; he has been extremely nervous ever since he lost his job and is still sensitive about it. She tries to get him to go to clinic but he refuses to do so.

Woman—An attractive, gray-haired woman of medium stature. She says that she is not well and is supposed to attend the Jewish Memorial Hospital, where she is to be treated for arthritis and high blood pressure. She was recently transferred from the Knickerbocker Hospital to the Jewish Memorial because she is out of the Knickerbocker Hospital district. She found, however, that at the Jewish Memorial Hospital she would have to pay 50 cents a visit and $1 weekly for the treatments for her arthritis. She told them that she was unable to pay so much and was referred to Morrisania, a city hospital, which, she says, is too far away for her to attend.

PRESENT ADJUSTMENT

Mrs. Gunther speaks well of Mr. Gunther and there seems to be a happy relationship. She says he is "smart as a whip" and she feels it is too bad for him to be tied to a WPA clerical job. He has worked himself up to a job as supervisor and attends WPA classes on Wednesday evenings to improve his position, but has not received any advance in pay. Mrs. Gunther said again that this is due to politics and that one must have connections to get along, even on WPA. Mr. Gunther is now getting older and his chances for private employment are not hopeful, despite the fact that his wife is sure he can still do good work. Mr. Gunther resents the fact that on WPA one is not chosen for his ability to do a job. In discussing Mr. Gunther's ability, his wife said that he listens to all the radio quizzes and knows all the answers. She has suggested many times that he try to take part in radio quizzes and laughingly added that if she went with him she and not he might be called and that that would be fatal.

There is evidence of disagreement between Mrs. Gunther and her husband's relatives. She commented several times that her husband's relatives are cold and thoughtless and would not do anything to help others even if they were starving. She cannot understand how Mr. Gunther can be so thoughtful when he comes from such a cold, calculating family. She claims that his parents were just as bad as his brother and sister.

Children:

None—After mentioning the fact that one child died some years ago, Mrs. Gunther changed the subject quickly. It was not learned whether this child was born of her first or her second marriage.

Use of Leisure Time:

On Home Relief: Mr. Gunther looked for work constantly. Mrs. Gunther, in discussing this, showed letters her husband had written and stated that the usual response to his letters of application, sent in reply to newspaper employment ads, have been literature advertising products and requesting money. He has become discouraged but continues to answer ads in the hope that eventually something will turn up. The family was unable to continue any form of recreation while on Home Relief. They did, however, keep up friendships and the radio has afforded them much pleasure. Both of them have always liked the radio; they listen to quiz programs and to some of the stories.

On WPA: Mr. Gunther continues to look for work and continues to answer ads but with no results. They have no money for recreation but occasionally go to the movies if they can find a good one near by. They do not like to go to the movies "just to be going to a show." Mrs. Gunther proudly showed worker a beautifully crocheted bedspread, which she stated she made while on Home Relief and finished recently. She said she cannot stand being idle and puts every spare nickel into the purchase of material for her bedspread. She said it kept her busy and helped her not to think too much about her troubles. Now that she has finished the bedspread, she will have to think up something else to do.

Religion: The Gunthers are Protestant. Mr. Gunther was formerly a Lutheran; Mrs. Gunther a Methodist. Both attended church when they were children, but do not go now. Mrs. Gunther, half in earnest and half jokingly, stated she has been tempted to accompany a friend to the Christian Science Church. She thinks it might be helpful. She has suffered for a long time with arthritis and other ailments and the friend says Christian Science will cure her. Mrs. Gunther believes, however, that one must have implicit faith in order to become a member of that church and fears she would be too skeptical. However, she may try it.

Newspapers: The Gunthers read the *Daily News* regularly and the *Times* on Sunday. Mr. Gunther is fond of reading and always reads papers thoroughly. He also likes detective stories.

Political Affiliations: Mrs. Gunther thinks her husband is a Democrat, but she knows he does not belong to any club. They both voted for Roosevelt in the last election but do not want to see him run again. He has not been too successful. Mrs. Gunther thinks Mr. Willkie might introduce new ideas that would be helpful. The family has never been interested in the Workers' Alliance. Mrs. Gunther said that she believes members of the Workers' Alliance get more than others because of their constant rebellion, but the Gunthers have never been interested in joining. Mr. Gunther has never been affiliated with any union.

Mrs. Gunther believes the United States has enough to do to take care of its own people without bringing refugees into the country. She thinks it is quite unfair for only the wealthy children of England to be brought to this country; all children deserve the same treatment. But if she had children who were in danger, she would keep them with her. It would be better for them all to die together than for the children to go to a strange country or people.

Management:

On Home Relief: It was impossible for the family to manage on Home Relief and Mrs. Gunther's sister helped them frequently. The surplus food commodities were helpful but they were unable to use the large amounts of flour and cornmeal which were provided them. The clothing was not at all useful. Mrs. Gunther laughingly told of various articles she had received which were too small or too large and which could not be exchanged. She criticized the government for allowing the department to give away things regardless of size, stating that there was a great deal of waste because of this. She says she has become used to wearing secondhand clothing now and doesn't believe that she has a thing that is really her own, with the exception of shoes, which she cannot secure from anyone else.

On WPA: Management on WPA is difficult. Mr. Gunther is earning $52.50 now. Out of this they pay $35 a month rent. They should move to the first floor because Mrs. Gunther has been told not to climb stairs, but they have been unable to find a suitable apartment within their means. Mrs. Gunther told of her discouragement when she returned from the Jewish Memorial Hospital the other day. She said she was so discouraged she just sat down and cried. The whole thing seemed so hopeless. Illness, unemployment, transfer from one hospital to another, etc.

In addition to the rent, they must have food and clothing and Mr. Gunther must have carfare. Mrs. Gunther packs a lunch for him to take to work so that they can avoid a cash outlay. Mrs. Gunther believes that if WPA were abolished, private industry would be forced to absorb the unemployed. She and Mr. Gunther think that WPA should never have been established. She had much to say about the "niggers," "wops," the "sheeneys" who get all the jobs; adding that a good honest American is out of luck.

Attitudes:

Toward the Future: Mr. Gunther is hopeful that he will secure work in private industry but his wife is not so optimistic despite the fact that she knows Mr. Gunther could do the work if he had the opportunity. She says he has courage and ability, but is getting old and an older man doesn't have much chance of getting private employment.

Toward Us: Mrs. Gunther thinks the study might be helpful. She knows Mr. Gunther will be glad to discuss the study with the director and suggests that this week would be best since he now works from 6:30 A.M. to 2:30 in the afternoon and his schedule will change in September.

OFFICE INTERVIEW

(Mr. Gunther came to the office with a friend, who works on the same WPA project, and during the course of the interview, Mr. Gunther turned to this friend to ask him to confirm the more extreme criticisms.)

Impression: A tall, well-dressed man, who appears to be in the early fifties. During the course of the interview he mentioned that he suffers badly from hemorrhoids. He also related that in the old days, when he was on the road selling, he did a lot of drinking.

Employment History: For twelve years Mr. Gunther was eastern sales manager for a chemical company and his territory stretched from Richmond to Toronto. He earned about $100 a week, but said that he has nothing to show for it. However, he had a good time while it lasted. In 1927 he entered his father's business, a well-established paint store. He undertook to keep the business going after the death of a younger brother, who had formerly been the manager. With the beginning of the depression, in 1929, conditions became difficult and by 1934 it was no longer possible to keep the creditors off. Mr. Gunther believes, however, that if his father had been willing to make certain readjustments—specifically, if he had been willing to dismiss an employee who was taking too much of the current receipts for living expenses, the creditors might have played along. He later admitted that this "somebody" was his brother. According to Mr. Gunther, he had exactly 80 cents in his pocket when the paint business folded up. His father, however, had been able to rescue a little money from the bankruptcy and was able to hold on to most of it until his wife became ill. Then the money was spent for doctors and hospital bills. Mr. Gunther says that he was lucky in being able to build up a nice business selling coal to friends and acquaintances, but just when it was starting to net him a good return, the coal company took his customers away from him.

Relief: This left him with nothing to do and a friend advised him to seek Relief. He did so but he had great difficulty in obtaining assistance. Mr. Gunther said that he was given "the run-around" by Home Relief. The investigators said that his brother-in-law should take care of him and then they said that his father should take care of him, but after much arguing, he succeeded in getting on Home Relief. He was on Home Relief only a short while before he was told that he would have to report to WPA and accept a laborer's job. Although Mr. Gunther told the Relief investigator that he was physically unfit to do hard labor, they refused to believe him and threatened to cut him off Relief if he did not report. He was sent to Orchard Beach on a laboring job and when he told the foreman there that he suffered from cardiac asthma, the foreman refused to let him work and sent him to the WPA doctor who agreed with him that he was unfit for laboring work. After getting off WPA he had great difficulty in getting back on Home Relief but he finally succeeded. He was on Home Relief only a short time before he was reassigned to a laboring job on WPA. He then had to go through the whole trouble all over again of explaining that he had a cardiac condition which made it impossible for him to do laboring. Mr. Gunther said that it is not clear to him why he was repeatedly reassigned to laboring jobs when his inability to do this type of work was clearly marked on the record. According to Mr. Gunther, Relief investigators are bad and the only good treatment that he ever got was from a Negress. He said that friends had "tipped him off that if he joined the Workers' Alliance he would receive better treatment, but Mr. Gunther said: "That is one thing, after all, they can't get me to do. They can't buy my lousy little vote. I wouldn't have anything to do with those people." Mr. Gunther was again reassigned to WPA as a laborer, but was given a clerk's job, which he now holds. He receives $52.50 a month, but says that his work is really of a supervisory nature for he has twenty people under him and he should really receive $82.50. The fact that he is doing work that deserves a higher rate of pay annoys Mr. Gunther and he thinks that unless he is reclassified shortly, he will give up his supervisory job and just become an ordinary clerk. He says that he has not done so as yet because he has passed the supervisor's test and hopes that the reclassification may come through shortly. Mr. Gunther says that he passed several supervisors' tests, one as a painters' supervisor and another in a different field. He resents the fact that some of these tests are unfair to people who have been out of school for a long while because they ask many questions that only a recent graduate would know. Nor would knowing the answers be proof that one could do the job well.

Mr. Gunther is at present working on card indexing the United States census of 1880 and thinks that this is a "silly" job. Prior to this work on the 1880 census, the project completed indexing the 1920 census. Mr. Gunther thinks that the card indexes might be of some use to the Social Security Board in connection with Old-Age Assistance, but says that he is not sure of this and that neither he nor anyone else on the project knows what they are doing or why. Mr. Gunther thinks that the level of efficiency on the project is "rotten"; he says that the government is lucky if it gets 2 cents' worth of work out of every $5 that it pays for labor. Mr. Gunther is also bitter about the impossibility of improving one's status on WPA unless one has political pull. Moreover, Mr. Gunther is "sore" about the fact that WPA does such a bad job matching skills and men, especially because there are many jobs on WPA that would fit a man's skills, which cannot be obtained without political pull. Mr. Gunther also resents his project because, he says, the work is really "women's work" and that no "real man" should do clerical work.

Mr. Gunther says that when he had to deal with WPA headquarters he was given the "run-around." There is no doubt in Mr. Gunther's mind that WPA is a "racket" and has retarded the industrial recovery of the United States. He says that the project upon which he is working is known as "Alcatraz." However, there are many people on this project who have made a good adjustment to WPA; by "good," Mr. Gunther means they are no longer interested in getting off WPA and are quite satisfied with their work and their wages. He says such an attitude is incomprehensible to him because unless there is other income in the family, or unless one is a single man, it is impossible to be satisfied with $52.50 a month.

Mr. Gunther says that he and his wife could never live on this amount were it not for the fact that one of his wife's friends, who comes to New York every week end, stays with them, pays something toward the rent, and buys much of the food. Mr. Gunther said that if he could only get a $15 a week job in private employment, he would throw his hat "so high in the air that it would never come down." He says that he has tried to keep up all of his contacts and always answers ads on Sundays. During the last few months he had two interviews for jobs in private industry and in each instance the interview went along well until the employer asked what he was doing at the time; when he said that he was on WPA the employer lost interest. He now realizes that honesty is dangerous and he has no intention of telling the truth next time. He thinks that he is going to have difficulty in getting a job because he is over fifty years of age, but he hopes that he will finally land something.

Family: Mr. Gunther's father died recently and Mr. Gunther had with him a clipping from the New York *Times* which told of the important paint business that Mr. Gunther, Sr. had owned. His mother was recently taken to Welfare Island, where, he says, she is receiving excellent medical attention. She is blind and also has a severe hip dislocation, the result of an accident several years ago. He estimates that his father spent approximately $8,000 for medical fees and services in connection with his mother's illness. Before her removal to Welfare Island, his mother had been receiving Old-Age Assistance. A sister's husband had supplemented this assistance by paying the mother's rent. This brother-in-law is employed in a large railroad ticket office and Mr. Gunther hopes that he will be able to get a lead to a job through him.

Mr. Gunther talked a little about his brother, whom he considers the "bad member of the family." It is this brother upon whom Mr. Gunther blames the failure of the business, for he thinks that he drained the business of most of its cash. He says he knows this must be true because his brother has not worked in the last six years, so "he must have put a pretty penny away somewhere." His brother's wife has, however, been working these past years. Mr. Gunther said that he probably made a mistake in not draining the firm himself, as his brother did, but added that at least nobody is able to point a finger at him now and say, "See, he went and took money." Mr. Gunther mentioned that he has been married about ten or eleven years, but this was the only statement he made about his wife.

Politics: Early in the interview Mr. Gunther said that he is a Republican, that he has always been one, and that the Republican party is the best party. Later he said that he had played politics with Tammany and had even held a position on a local board, but when a post became vacant to which he thought he was entitled, and which he did not get, he broke with Tammany. Mr. Gunther says that he will never go back. Mr. Gunther is bitter about refugees and cited the example of a friend of his wife's, who after holding a job with a large department store for eighteen years was laid off and replaced by a refugee. He says that the refugees crowd the sidewalks of Washington Heights from 155th Street to 181st Street and he feels that there are so many of them around that they will probably grab any new jobs that will come along if business conditions improve. Mr. Gunther says that he has never had connections with any church and that he really isn't interested in religion. Concerning the war, he expressed little interest, but added that if the war continues, younger men may be drained off for the draft in which case there may be a better chance for him to get a job. *Future:* Mr. Gunther realizes that his age is a handicap in getting a job in private industry, but he says that he plans to keep on trying and that he still has a few connections which might prove useful.

PART III.
CLOSED TO PRIVATE EMPLOYMENT

Case Seven

CLANCY FAMILY

Status Closed to Private Employment *Religion* Catholic
Man born 1894 Ireland to U.S.A. 1920 Citizen No
Wife born 1900 Ireland to U.S.A. 1923 Citizen No

Education
Man Elementary school—Ireland
Wife Elementary school—Ireland

Medical Status
Man Negative
Wife Negative

Woman's Work History Saleswoman—department store, 1923-1924. Maid—Columbia University, short time, 1935.

Married—July, 1924.

Number of Children in the Home Two. *Ages*—14 and 15 years.

Basic Occupation before Relief Painter.

Average Income before Relief $30 to $40 weekly. Seasonal.

Private Employment Terminated December, 1930. Ten weeks work in the summer of 1932.

First Accepted for Relief January, 1933.

SUMMARY

Home Relief *From January, 1933, to May, 1940,* family received Relief between jobs in private industry.

CWA for five months early in 1934 as a painter. $9.20 a day.

Private Employment Case was closed eight times during those seven years when man found work as a painter. During each job family paid debts, built up small home savings, and put off reapplication until all resources were exhausted.

Present Job Painter. Usually works for contractors but has also done some contracting for small jobs. Is building up small contracting business. Averages $30-$40 weekly.

ABSTRACT OF HOME RELIEF RECORD

DEC., 1932 — *First Application:* The man is a painter who has been been unemployed for about eighteen months, with the exception of about ten weeks, when he worked for Columbia University, in June and July, 1932. At this last job he made about $30 a week. The family has exhausted $400 in savings and has borrowed from friends. Nine insurance policies, some of them five years old, have lapsed. At the time of application, the family owes two months rent and utilities, has no cash on hand and no resources.

JAN. 4, 1933 — The man at the District Office. He was given an *emergency food ticket* for $4, pending investigation.

JAN. 6, 1933 — Home Visit by investigator. "Type of family—Irish American, noncitizen, never applied for citizenship papers, but will do so when in position to do so. Laborer, painter, nonunion." The family showed the records for thirteen insurance policies, on which the last payments were made in December, 1931. At the time of the visit the family owed $108 for three months' rent; $60 to one friend, $30 to another; a month's utilities. At this time they said that their original bank account had amounted to $580.

JAN. 11, 1933 — *Case Accepted.* $10.50 for food; $25 for rent were given for one month. "Morale needs careful watching. Mrs. Clancy discouraged over present conditions."

JUNE, 1933 — *Case Closed to Private Employment.* (Interim entries all dealt with delivery of vouchers.)

NOV. 24, 1933 — *Reapplied.* The man was employed at Columbia University from July 1st to October 1st, as a painter at $38.50 a week. Since the termination of this job, the family had managed on $65 home savings. This was used for rent, food, moving expenses and clothing, and the family has no further resources. They are no longer in debt, however, having paid their debts while the man was working.

NOV. 29, 1933 — *Emergency food and coal ticket* issued to the family. They were entirely without food or fuel and unable to wait for the completion of the investigation.

DEC., 1933 — Mrs. Clancy said she and her husband had helped her relatives, who were in desperate need of assistance. They were nonresidents, recently moved from New Jersey and not eligible for Relief. Mr. Clancy worked off his first month's rent in their new house by painting his own apartment. Rent of $25 is due on January 1st. The family is living in a five-room, cold-water flat with three bedrooms.

JAN., 1934 — According to the investigator, "There is a very pleasant atmosphere in the home, which is shown by interest displayed toward their children."

FEB. 8, 1934 — The man is expecting work at Columbia University again in the near future.

FEB. 22, 1934 — The man was disappointed by his lack of success in getting work on snow removal.

MAY 3, 1934 — The woman reported that her husband began working as a painter on CWA, April 24th. He is to earn $9.20 a day; his first pay will be received on May 11th.

MAY 14, 1934 — *Case Closed to Work Relief.*

NOV. 19, 1934 — *Reapplied.* The man was discharged from Work Relief on July 19th. He found employment at Columbia University almost immediately and worked there three months, earning $38.50 for 5½ days a week. The family moved to a four-room steam-heated apartment at $26 a month rent.

NOV. 27, 1934 — According to the investigator, "The man is of slender build, cowed-looking"; woman "of small stature, fair-complexioned, portrays good health." The family paid $10 for a tonsillectomy for John at St. Francis Hospital three weeks ago. They borrowed $25 from a friend in July. They now owe $3.60 for utilities.

DEC. 26, 1934 — Visited woman's relatives, who are being supported by Catholic Charities.

Family reported that they are getting into debt. They borrowed $25 from friends, owe their grocer $12; $26 rent; $1.60 on utilities. The man is expecting employment from Columbia University in the summer. If Home Relief does not help soon, the family will have to go to Catholic Charities.

DEC. 31, 1934 — *Case Accepted.*

FEB., 1935 — *Case Closed to Private Employment.*

NOV. 4, 1935 — *Reapplied.* The man worked six weeks at Columbia University at $38.50 a week. The major portion of the work was recently given over to a contractor and the extra men were dismissed. Since that time Mr. Clancy worked very irregularly, earning $5 a day. He has had no work in five weeks. The family moved to a cold-water flat at $23 a month. They have saved no money, but have managed to keep their bills paid. The November rent is now due.

NOV. 29, 1935 — *Case Accepted.*

DEC., 1935 — The man very angry because the family has received no rent money. (At that time rent was not being given on cases accepted after November 1, 1935 except on dispossess or eviction notices.) He said that he has no money for moving expenses and does not know what he will do if he is dispossessed.

JAN., 1936 — $16 for rent issued because the landlord is threatening to dispossess the family. The man is much upset, says he has visions of the children in institutions and his wife and himself walking the street.

FEB. 10, 1936 — *Case Closed.* The man has a job in private industry at which he expects to earn about $20 a week.

FEB. 11, 1936 — *Family reapplied for emergency aid.* Man has not worked in three days, but is expecting to be called very soon. He has been unable to obtain credit in local stores; he was given an *emergency order for food and coal.*

FEB. 18, 1936 — The man in District Office with a note from his employer indicating that he can expect no more work at present. The man had earned $32, paid $23 on rent and used the rest for food.

FEB. 20, 1936 — *Relief reinstated.*

MAR., 1936 — The man reported employment at $5 a day.

APR., 1936 — *Case Closed to Private Employment.*

NOV., 1936 — *Reapplied.* The man has had no work since November 1st. He earned $20 to $22 a week from April to August and worked two weeks at Columbia University at $38.50, but was laid off because of a strike. He was unemployed three weeks, then had intermittent work for a short time.

DEC., 1936 — *Case Accepted.*

MAR. 10, 1937 — The woman reported that man goes out daily looking for work. The woman is pregnant, is expecting the baby in July. Her mother died in July, 1936. The $60 insurance received did not cover the cost of the funeral and the children had to contribute. The family has a rent deficit of $4 a month, which is usually met by odd jobs for the landlord, or by money taken from the food allowance. The family is finding it difficult to manage on the Home Relief budget. The man's union dues are three months in arrears; utilities one month in arrears; $10 was borrowed from friends recently.

MAR. 15, 1937 — Special diet for woman's pregnancy included in budget.

APR., 1937 — The children do not take lunch at school because they are ashamed to do so.

MAY 6, 1937 — The woman reported that her husband began work yesterday on a private job. He will earn $36 a week. The name and address of the employer were withheld because of his tendency to "take advantage" of people on Relief. The union was not told of this job because the wages are below the union level.

MAY 13, 1937 — *Case Closed.*

NOV. 16, 1937 — *Reapplied.* The man has been out of work since October 31st. Prior to that date he had worked irregularly, averaging $24 a week. His actual earnings had varied from $12 to $30 a week. The employer has had no work for him in the past two weeks. Tenants are refusing to pay rent increases and landlords are therefore refusing to redecorate. The man has not gone to the union as yet because his dues are in arrears from July. Because of these arrears in dues, the union will not give him work until he has picketed for five or six days. The man said that the record of his last work is not on the union books, because it was a nonunion job. The union does not mind a man's doing such work, if he cannot find work with a union firm. Rent was paid to November 30th and the family managed on the home savings of $25. They had saved no more than this because they had bought clothing which the family needed badly. (Family had tried unsuccessfully to get clothing while on Home Relief.)

NOV. 19, 1937 — The man again stated that the union does not know of his non-union employment. When his family is in need, he will work on any job, even nonunion. Too many union painters are unemployed now. The man is hoping to get work soon from a lead which a friend gave him.

NOV. 26, 1937 — *Case Accepted.*

JAN., 1938 — Man asked for WPA. The job he was expecting did not materialize.

FEB., 1938 — The woman asked for WPA housekeeping job, but was rejected because she is not a citizen.

MAY, 1938 — *Case Closed.* The man is employed at $7 a day and will receive his first pay on May 21st.

FEB. 21, 1939 — *Reapplied.* The man had a contract to paint a Catholic church in the East Bronx. The contract had been for $3,400, out of which he had to pay for labor and materials. He hired four men, paying them $9 a day, with no social security, rather than $7 to $8 with social security; this arrangement was made by agreement with the men. The job lasted from June to

October, 1938. Mr. Clancy paid himself at the same wage rate as the other men. He estimated labor costs at $2,400, materials at $900, miscellaneous at $30. At the end of this job Mr. Clancy had home savings of about $160. They paid $72 for three months' rent, $19 on insurance, $5.40 for utilities, and the remaining $55 for food for three months. They were told by the investigator that they could not have managed on so little for food. The man said he was not sure how much the woman had saved, perhaps more than $160.

FEB. 24, 1939 Man's ledger showed that the family had received $302.41 from the contract, plus $100 home savings on which to manage; of that $15 a week, or $240 in all, was spent for food, bringing the major expenditure to $379.73. The rest was spent on carfare, Christmas expenses, etc. The man was urged to try to manage without Relief until he could find work again. He was vehement in his refusal, although sure of work in a month or two. He said that he has no money on hand, no source of loans, even if he wanted to go into debt.

MAR. 2, 1939 The man has been dropped from the union rolls because of nonpayment of dues. It will cost $15 for reinstatement, because of failure to pay dues for the past three months. He told the worker that this is the best evidence of need, for if it had been possible, he would have paid this, since loss of membership means that one more avenue of work is closed to him now. (Although names of employers were given by the man, Home Relief did not seem to realize that one was Mrs. Clancy's brother.) The man had worked during May, 1938, for about $37.50 a week.

MAR. 6, 1939 *Case Accepted.*

MAY, 1939 Neither man nor woman seems much concerned about the large rental arrears. The man said that he will pay it when he finds work. He thinks the Home Relief allowance much too small for decent living.

JUNE 7, 1939 *Relief Suspended.* The man had refused to give the name of his prospective employer, for whom he hopes to begin work about June 12th, because he believes premature inquiry by Home Relief would jeopardize his chances for employment.

JUNE 16, 1939 — The Irish-American League requested that the suspension of Relief be lifted since the job Mr. Clancy had hoped for did not materialize. The family managed by borrowing from the woman's relatives, who were on Relief themselves and could ill afford to help her.

JUNE 19, 1939 — The woman reported that the man had started working that morning and asked that Relief be continued until the first pay check.

JUNE 23, 1939 — *Case Closed without giving the Relief requested* because the investigator could not get hold of the employer to verify the date of employment.

1940

JAN. 5, 1940 — *Reapplied.* The man had worked until November 15th at Medical Center, earning $38.50 a week. The family had $140 home savings at the time he lost his job. They paid rent for December and January and the rest went for food.

JAN. 11, 1940 — The man admitted that he is in the United States illegally and that this had been his reason for rejecting suggestions of Work Relief rather than Home Relief during periods of unemployment. Prior to coming to the United States, he had been a seaman in the British Navy and a member of the Seaman's Union. In 1922 he and his brother jumped ship at Port Arthur; the brother later returned to England. This is also the reason for Mr. Clancy's not having applied for citizenship earlier. He says that there is now a new law, making it possible for him to apply and that both he and his wife have applied for first papers.

JAN. 15, 1940 — The woman reported that she pawned her ring in order to buy food. The Home Relief record on the woman's family showed three siblings whom she had not reported.

JAN. 23, 1940 — At first the woman denied having any relatives, but finally admitted it, saying that she did not want the whole world to know she had to apply for Relief. These relatives, whom she had omitted, are self-maintaining but not in a position to give assistance to the family.

JAN. 24, 1940 — *Case Accepted.*

MAY, 1940 *Case Closed to Private Employment.* (In the interim period several anonymous complaints were received about the employment of both the man and the woman. These were definitely proved groundless.)

HOME INTERVIEW

Home—A five room railroad flat on the second floor of a rather drab, walk-up building in a semicommercial, semiresidential neighborhood. The street is one of the major crosstown arteries in the Bronx, with a trolley line and much commercial traffic. This is one of the poorest sections of the city. The apartment was adequately furnished, but most of the pieces were obviously quite old. The building has central heating; the rent is $35. The parents share a bedroom, while the boy and girl each has a room.

Man:

Description: Mr. Clancy came in during the course of the interview. He is tall and angular in appearance, but not too thin. His white hair and lined face make him look older than 46. He was, however, youthful in his enthusiasm and sense of humor, and in his companionship with and attitude toward his children. He seemed interested in current affairs and discussed them thoughtfully. Mr. Clancy is in good health.

Background: Born in Ireland, December, 1894. He was the third of six children. His father was a soldier in the British Army. Mr. Clancy attended National School until he was 14 years old.

Work History: For several years after leaving school, Mr. Clancy worked at various odd jobs, among them truck driving and coal mining in Wales. He finally became a painter's helper and in 1920, when he thought he knew enough about the trade, came to the United States where there seemed to be greater opportunity to "get ahead." He managed for a couple of years on seasonal jobs, but when he married, in 1924, went to work for a real estate company since this offered out of season work in apartment painting. He remained with this company for six years, until December, 1930, when he was laid off because work was so slack. He had been a union member in good standing for some years and through this source had been able to find extra jobs independent of the company for which he worked. His income averaged about $42 a week.

Interim Period: Mr. Clancy had only about 10 weeks' work during the next 18 months. This was a temporary job at Columbia University, in the summer of 1932, and paid about $30 a week. He had worked for the university in former years. Family managed on about $600 they had saved and the income from this seasonal work. They were anxious to remain independent. Both Mr. and Mrs. Clancy tried to find work, were willing to do anything. They borrowed about $100 from friends, borrowed what they could on insurance and permitted policies to lapse. Their landlord was patient but when the rent bill mounted to more than $100, they were finally forced to apply for Relief.

Relief History: The Clancy family first applied for Relief on December 22, 1932, and on January 4, 1933, were given an emergency food ticket before the investigation was completed because of the desperate circumstances which had resulted from their delay in application. They continued on Relief intermittently up to May 14, 1940. During each successive year, from 1933 to 1940, Mr. Clancy found one or more temporary seasonal jobs; enabling the family to manage independently for about six months of each year. Mr. Clancy had only about three months of Work Relief, in 1934, on CWA, as a painter, at $9.20 a day. The jobs which Mr. Clancy obtained were with various contractors; some were jobs which he contracted for himself. He enjoyed the contracting jobs and hopes to be able to build up his own business.

Present Job: Mr. Clancy had just finished a job on the day of the visit. He worked at union wages for a contractor for whom he has often worked in the past. He has been offered another job but has not definitely accepted it because he has another job lead for the immediate future. He said that the "family council" will decide tonight which he should take. They have learned one thing in the past few years, when times have been so bad, and that is that the man who seems to be anxious to work is often exploited, is offered less money for more hours of work. The Clancys have learned to save; they realize that the loss of a few days here and there is not important so long as Mr. Clancy can keep up his self-respect and not hire himself out for wages that he knows are less than his work is worth. While Mr. Clancy's jobs have been short, there have been few long periods of unemployment and he has made fair wages. He is also slowly building his own contracting business, working on small jobs in areas too poor to employ union labor at union wages. Mr. Clancy has good friends in the union who know what he is trying to do, and since he makes no effort to take away union work, no pressure is being put on him; he hopes to be able to build this business up to union standards

Attitude toward Present Job and Future Prospects: At this time Mr. Clancy is quite confident about his future prospects. Business in general is picking up, rents will rise, more painting and decorating will be done. Mr. Clancy has enough contacts so that between working for other contractors and on his own, he will have little unemployment and his income will probably rise to the level of the twenties. By accumulating a large number of small jobs he can get expert union labor and do the job quickly. He now averages $30 to $35 a week, including periods of unemployment, and $35 to $40 excluding them. They are saving as much as possible in order to give Mr. Clancy some reserve with which to run his own business.

Woman:

Description: A tiny, dark-haired, blue-eyed person, dainty and neat in appearance, although her rough hands and broken nails indicated hard work. She was gay and witty, seemingly absorbed in her family and their plans.

Background: Born in Ireland, April, 1900. She was the fourth of seven children, with three brothers and three sisters. She completed elementary school at 14 and after that remained at home, helping her mother with the housework. Her entire family came to the United States in 1923, because they believed that there were better possibilities for employment in this country. They settled in New Jersey. Mrs. Clancy's father died in 1926, at which time the family had already become scattered.

Mrs. Clancy came to New York City in 1923 and found work as a salesclerk in a large department store. She quit work after her marriage in July, 1924, and did not work again until the summer of 1935, when she found a job as maid in one of the dormitories at Columbia University. She kept this job only a short time because she did not get along well with the chief housekeeper. Mrs. Clancy criticized the university's personnel practices severely. Wages were low and assignments heavy. It was practically impossible to do the number of rooms assigned as carefully as expected within the hours the women were supposed to work. Many worked overtime without pay, saying nothing, because they needed the work so badly. Mrs. Clancy thinks this exploitation of the unemployed is probably widespread. Any income at all becomes so important that people put up with almost any conditions in order to keep a job. Mrs. Clancy did not do so because she found her earnings too low to meet other costs of her employment. For example, she had to send out her laundry, had less time to shop carefully and spent long hours making the cheapest foods fit to eat. Catherine had been well-trained in domestic duties, but she was just a child at that time, with responsibility for good schoolwork, so not too much could be expected of her. The Clancys decided that mother contributed more when at home than the value of her cash earnings at work, so she did not look for other work after that experience. She said she likes homemaking, and believes it a full-time job for a woman. She does not mind having to stretch dollars as far as possible, provided there are enough to stretch; she compared her ability to save from her husband's present income with her ability to manage on Home Relief. She showed worker a pan of biscuits she had made from a new recipe; they had come out beautifully and she is planning to surprise the family tonight. The Clancys cannot afford pastries, even homemade, because of the high cost of dairy products. Into these biscuits, however, Mrs. Clancy had put a little sugar, butter, and an egg, making them more cake-like, and with applesauce they will make a tasty dessert, yet cost less than apple cake or apple pie, and at the same time will be more substantial and filling.

Children: Both children came in during the interview and took an active part in the discussion, showing much liberal thinking in their attitudes and conversation. Both are tall, handsome, well-built, intelligent young people.

John—Born June, 1925, had been rather delicate as a child, subject to colds and sore throats. Following a tonsillectomy in 1934, he became much stronger, and is now a healthy, active boy. He is considered an exceptional student and at 15 is in the sixth term of high school. He has made consistent A grades in his science courses and has done well in all other subjects. The Clancys are much concerned about John's vocational choice. His school is urging that he apply for a university scholarship and follow one of his interests—architecture or law. His father feels he should learn a trade because the professional fields are already overcrowded. However, if the boy has special talents, they do not want to prevent him from making the most of them. The Clancys are fully aware of the fact that they could not afford to meet all the boy's college expenses. If he can get a scholarship or scholarship loan, and work during his spare time, the family will help as much as possible. John, himself, is uncertain. The only openings he might expect to find in law or architecture would be in a minor capacity in some large firm. He does not expect "to stand at the top," but is doubtful of any security in such placement, especially when he looks back upon his father's experience in working for others. He could go in with his father, learn the trade, help build up the business, and later take over from his father when the latter is ready to retire. He plans to go ahead on his work for the scholarship and hopes that a compromise can be worked out. He might, for instance, put in his summer vacations with his father and in the end have both a trade and a profession between which to choose according to the demands of the labor market.

Catherine—born October, 1926, has always been a healthy, sturdy child. She is in the second term of high school, plans to take a business course during the next three years and then to go to business college. She remarked, laughing, that she has not ruled out marriage as a good career, and is learning from her mother the skills necessary for success in that field. She and the family believe, however, that a woman should have vocational training which might come in handy in spite of, or even because of, marriage. Too many young men's salaries are too low to meet the demands of marriage and a family. This does not seem right, and they believe that more adequate wages for men is a better solution than employment of wives, but the latter solution is better than none. Mr. Clancy and his daughter discussed this at some length; he thinks that the willingness of women to work is to some extent the reason why men's wages and employment chances remain low. John and his mother thought few women want to stay at work if it is unnecessary financially, but that those who do should have as much right to make that choice as does a man. Mr. Clancy finally said that the latter is true, that if democracy is to work, choices should not be limited to one group. He does think, however, that perhaps homemaking has not been made as pleasant a choice as the freedom of work in industry. Too many women just become household drudges, receiving neither cash wages nor recognition for their important contribution to the welfare of a family.

The Clancy family is governed by a "council" in which each parent carries a full vote and each child a half vote. At 18 a child's vote will equal that of a parent. Since the children are vitally concerned in everything that happens, the parents think it only wise and fair that they should participate in planning. If saving for father's business means sacrifice, children should know why the sacrifice is necessary and help decide what should be sacrificed—richer foods, recreation, clothing, etc. Plans for all members are worked out in this way, and each considers it useful and constructive. Not only do the family discuss their own affairs together, but social, political, and international affairs as well.

Relatives: Mr. Clancy's older brother is a head porter at General Electric in London. He is married and has two children. A younger brother, unmarried, has been head groom for a racing stable but is now engaged in some aspect of home defense in England. It is with this brother that Mr. Clancy worked his way to the United States as a seaman, jumping ship at Port Arthur, in 1920. The brother later returned to England. A married sister also lives in London. Her husband has been employed throughout the depression, but Mr. Clancy does not know him or just what kind of work he does. They have three children.

Mrs. Clancy's mother was almost eighty at the time of her death. She was supported by her children. Members of Mrs. Clancy's family have been on Home Relief and have received assistance from the Catholic Charities. An unmarried sister is unemployed; she had formerly kept house for the mother, and now keeps house for a single brother. The latter is a laborer who has worked only intermittently during the past 10 years. Another brother is married and has three children. He is unemployable because of ill-health and receives a veteran's pension. (He came to the United States some ten years before the rest of the family, became a citizen and served overseas in the United States Army.) A younger brother left home when Mrs. Clancy's family had to apply for Relief, and has not been heard from since. Mrs. Clancy said he was "proud and selfish," and that he probably managed to take care of himself. Two married sisters live in New Jersey; their families remained independent throughout the depression. During periods of extreme need the Clancys borrowed small amounts from relatives who could afford to help.

Religion: The Clancys are devout Roman Catholics. The children attended parochial schools until the completion of the elementary grades. The parents explained that in addition to the religious education children received at parochial school, they had more individual attention than in public school.

Birth Control: The Clancys said little about birth control other than that they believed the size of a family to be a matter for individuals to decide. Later, after Mr. Clancy went out, his wife discussed this a little more freely. She believes there is a great difference between the use of contraceptives and abortion, that is, between prevention of life and getting rid of life, and she can see no sin in the former. The Clancys would like more children, but when their daughter was old enough so that they might have had another, business was already too shaky to "add another mouth." Mrs. Clancy became pregnant in November, 1936, but had a miscarriage in June, 1937. The doctor said that malnutrition and worry had been responsible for this. Mrs. Clancy does not believe she will have another child now. Things are so uncertain; they have the needs of the two growing children to consider. She plans to wait a few years to see whether conditions improve, but realizes that at the end of these years, however few, she and her husband will be too old. Mrs. Clancy thinks that a child has little chance for free development with old parents. Either he is spoiled or the parents are too set in their ways to see his problems from the point of view of the younger generation.

Newspapers: The Clancys read the *Daily News* because, in spite of the fact that it is a tabloid, it holds interest for all members of the family and reports the news about as accurately as any other paper. They liked its editorial policies during the recent election campaign.

Political Affiliations: Mr. and Mrs. Clancy are both aliens and therefore cannot vote. Both have taken out first papers, however, and intend to get final papers as soon as possible. Both are much interested in the political situation and pleased with the results of the election. Mr. Clancy discussed the inevitability of change and said that he sees the entire economic process now in transition and thinks it will probably become more democratic in spite of the activity of totalitarian states. He believes that we are actually at war without the formality of a declaration, that the total victory of either side is impossible, and that return to the status quo of the years from 1928 to 1933 or from 1920 to 1928 is equally impossible. He does not believe that the outcome of the last election was terribly important, for no party can stop the progress of this country socially and economically. He evidenced some anti-Semitism, expressing the belief that the Jews control most of the money and industry in the world and that they stepped up production methods before the world was prepared to make the necessary adjustments which might have saved human values in the process. He cited the opening of industrial plants in Ireland, drawing in country youth, paying them more per month than they could have earned in a year on farms, but also stepping up costs so that these apparently large salaries were really too small for decent living. He spoke of the demoralization which then occurred when men were displaced by machinery. Both children interrupted to remind him that Jews alone aren't guilty of all this, that in them are found the entire range of characteristics found in any race or group of human beings. The family then discussed the failure of the Irish to "stick together." One hesitates to hire another for fear the new one will supersede the first. They are jealous of each other and belligerent when together. They can never work together for common ends because they cannot agree. The family believes this is one of the reasons democracy can never work perfectly, i.e., the human characteristics of greed and jealousy crop out, not only in the masses but in the elected leadership. But the social legislation of the past few years and that which is to come will carry us further toward the goal of real democracy. The family is anti-Hitler, but not totally pro-Ally. They believe that the Allies had played a large part in setting the present "conflagration" and hate to think the United States "might get burned" putting it out. They do not want our young men losing their lives for something we had little to do with, but are agreed that if this sacrifice is necessary to prevent the spread of totalitarianism, it must be made.

Family approved of all possible aid to refugees.

Mr. Clancy has never belonged to any political club. Some men tried to start a neighborhood social club some years ago and politics had been much discussed, but the club did not last long. Mr. Clancy originally belonged to the Painter's and Decorator's Union. The family's only use of a pressure group was in the summer of 1939 when Relief was suspended without adequate reason. They were unable to get a hearing and were in great difficulty: a dispossess notice pending, no money for food, let alone rent or moving expenses. Through pressure from the Irish-American League, the matter was cleared up.

Family Adjustment and Attitudes:

Before Relief: Family has been happy, always, but knew the least pressure and the highest hopes before Relief. Income was always seasonal, but seasons were long, income good. Mrs. Clancy was a good manager and in addition to making seasonal earnings last throughout the year, set aside savings for emergencies, vacations, etc. They had good food, adequate clothing, and above all, a sense of security they have never achieved since. The parents had planned that, if they so desired, the children should have the educational opportunities which the parents had missed.

On Relief: On Relief the family lost their confidence, security and much of their pride. (John added "and frequently our temper.") The parents laughed and said that they had frequent "run-ins" with investigators because of the latter's suspicious attitudes and the investigation of relatives. They were usually sorry about these incidents because when they "cooled off" they realized that these people were working people like themselves, performing a job under orders "and according to specifications." The family suffered a great deal on Relief. There was a constant rent deficit, usually met from the food budget, which meant not quite enough to eat for a man who was "tramping the streets looking for work" and for two active, growing children. They did not realize how much Mrs. Clancy had been denying herself until she lost "the baby," because she was not strong enough to carry it to full term. After that the children "swallowed their pride" and accepted the free school lunches which they had previously refused.

At Present: The Clancys are still pressed by financial problems, but really only because they are making choices. All are interested in gathering a cash reserve for Mr. Clancy's business and are proud to deny themselves now for future gains.

Future: The Clancys believe they are going on to happy times such as they knew before the depression. The children are coming to the point where they want to be independent and to follow their own interests, and Mr. Clancy is confident he can build up enough to take care of his wife and himself, and perhaps "leave a little to our grandchildren some day."

Attitude toward Us: The children seemed more interested in the study than their parents. Mr. Clancy was pleasant, but said he did not think such studies at all effective. He later expressed some appreciation of the possible importance of a university group's recognition of need for planning in a time of "inevitable change." A university can touch and influence so many different groups but Mr. Clancy is afraid the influence is not great. The children think that social planning is important and should be based on careful, scientific study of the weaknesses and strengths of the existing order. Their father continued to insist that there is no "status quo," that things are constantly shifting, and today's findings are invalidated by tomorrow's changes. Mrs. Clancy expressed surprise that such a group should be interested and sympathetic with problems of the masses and hoped our results would be more effective than her husband predicted. Mr. Clancy will not come to the office. He has said everything he has to say and can see little sense in repeating it. He is not sure of his free time, since much of it is used to make further contacts for work or to rest after a heavy job.

Case Eight

WALLACH FAMILY

Status Closed to Private Employment *Religion* Jewish

Man born 1893 England to U.S.A. 1920 Citizen Yes

Wife born 1901 Poland to U.S.A. 1916 Citizen No

Education

Man Completed elementary school—England.

Wife Six years elementary school—Poland. Night school—U.S.A.

Medical Status

Man Cardiac condition

Wife Gynecological condition

Woman's Work History Shipping clerk, novelty company—until marriage.

Married 1925, N.Y.C.

Number of Children in the Home One. *Age*—14 years

Basic Occupation before Relief Tailor

Average Income before Relief $40 to $50 weekly.

Full-Time Private Employment Terminated 1931. Followed by eight months of unemployment.

Irregular Private Employment From 1932 to application for Relief. Income insufficient to support family.

First Accepted for Relief March, 1936.

SUMMARY

Home Relief Supplementation of Private Employment—March, 1936, to April, 1937. Case closed when man began working full time.

Present Status—Tailor, working for same employer since 1932. Average income about $25 to $30 weekly.

ABSTRACT OF HOME RELIEF RECORD

FEB. 18, 1936 — *First Application.* Referred by the National Council of Jewish Women. The man has been earning from $3 to $5 a week as a tailor at a cleaning and dyeing shop, since Christmas, 1935. They owe two months' rent, totaling $64, two months' utilities—$7.51, and a grocery bill of $23. Although they have lived in this apartment for ten years and the landlord is patient, they cannot remain here indefinitely without paying rent. The man had at one time earned $30 a week, working full time for his present employers, but work became so slack that they could use him only part time. If work should pick up his hours of employment will be increased. The family formerly carried $6,000 insurance. They had borrowed the full loan value of the insurance, and were finally forced to drop the policies. Their savings have been exhausted supplementing low income for the last four or five years. In terms of the man's income during good years, these savings were small, because so much of their money had to be expended on medical care for the woman, who had needed several operations, and for the boy, who had always been slight and needed special foods.

FEB. 25, 1936 — *Home Visit.* The woman said she has suffered from a gynecological condition since the birth of her son. She is still being treated by the family doctor, who is now giving his services gratis. The boy is 25 pounds underweight. The man is hopeful that work will pick up in the spring and that he will be taken on full time. He is in need of glasses.

MAR., 1936 — *Case Accepted* after verification of debts, earnings, employment.

APR., 1936 — The woman is suffering from symptoms connected with the menopause. She has trouble with her eyes and is unable to see clearly in the morning. The man is in good health but handicapped in his search for full-time employment by lack of teeth.

AUG., 1936 — The woman is planning to fast two days during the Jewish Holy Days as a sacrifice so that her husband may find full-time work.

JAN., 1937 The boy has been ill for six weeks and the woman is very much upset. The investigator made some effort to cheer her and made arrangements for payment of the medical bills through the District Office.

MAR., 1937 Man certified as "cardiac—unemployable" by the Occupational Division.

APR., 1937 Woman reported the man began full-time employment on April 22nd.

HOME INTERVIEW

Home—Three rooms on the second floor of a brick walk-up building in a crowded residential neighborhood in the upper East Bronx. The street is lined with apartment buildings, some of them with retail shops on the ground-floor level. The building is in fair condition and well-cared-for; the apartment fairly light and well ventilated. The bedroom and kitchen are small, but the living room, where Edward sleeps on a studio couch, is quite large. Except for the studio couch, the furniture is of heavy walnut, which seemed to be of good quality. It has obviously been well-cared-for; Mrs. Wallach said that it is fifteen years old. Efforts have been made to brighten the rooms with attractive curtains and pillows. Mrs. Wallach showed worker some of her crocheted table scarves, saying that she cannot afford good coverings and prefers these to cheap cotton scarves. She said she is much attached to this apartment in which she has lived since her marriage. She and her husband furnished it with great care and pride. They bought a heavy dining suite, because at that time it was the fashion to entertain at dinner, and they considered a dining room even more important than a living room. When they first moved in, the rental was $55. It has been reduced, a few dollars at a time, until it is now $34. The landlord is raising the rent in other apartments, but has assured the family that theirs will not be raised. He is, by this time, practically one of the family, and willing to do almost anything for them in order to keep them in the apartment. When work was slow, he accepted their rent a few dollars at a time, yet continued to keep the apartment well-decorated and to add any improvements for which Mrs. Wallach might ask. Despite these things and her attachment to the home, however, Mrs. Wallach said she has often wanted to move and probably would if things worked out all right for her husband. Edward needs a room of his own and she now wants a living room. She laughed as she explained that a woman who is closely confined to her home needs a change of scenery now and then. She added, hesitantly, that her friends have all moved to a newer, more modern part of the Bronx, and while her cooking can still compete with theirs, her home cannot.

Man:

Description: Mr. Wallach was not seen. Mrs. Wallach said her husband is rather small and slight, and younger looking for his years than she. His most delightful characteristic, she thinks, is his clipped, precise English speech which has not been affected by his twenty years in the United States. According to his wife, he is alert and intelligent; he reads widely and can converse on almost any subject that might arise.

Background: Born in London, October, 1893, of Jewish parentage. Mrs. Wallach was not certain about his ordinal position but believes he is the sixth of the eight living children. She thinks that three others are dead. Mrs. Wallach believes that the family was comfortable and that the children were all well-educated. She believes that Mr. Wallach had at least the equivalent of an American high school education.

Work History: After completing his schooling, Mr. Wallach became a tailor. His wife thinks that he learned this trade through other members of his family, several of whom are expert tailors. After considerable training and experience, he came to the United States to join his sister, who was married to a tailor. He and his brother-in-law opened a business of their own, but in 1926 their venture failed. Mr. Wallach then found work with the Ritz Cleaners and Dyers, where he remained for a year, leaving in 1927 to become the manager of a branch of a large chain of cleaning establishments. This was an excellent position until 1931, when because of poor business several branches, his among them, were discontinued. He was out of work, except for occasional odd jobs, for eight or nine months. In August, 1932, he got work as a tailor with the Paris Cleaners and Dyers and has remained there to date, although the work has been irregular. For the past four or five years he has done piecework, his income ranging from $3 to $30 a week.

Interim Period: It was interesting to note that Mrs. Wallach made no voluntary mention of her Relief experience, and that when asked directly whether the income had ever dropped so far that they had had to ask for assistance, replied that they had been spared the necessity of having to ask for Relief, but had had to accept assistance from relatives during periods of stress. She said that during Mr. Wallach's first period of unemployment their savings (comfortable but smaller than they might have been had not so much money been spent in earlier years on medical care for Edward and herself) helped out. The loan value of their insurance had been exhausted for living expenses and to pay for an operation which she had to have just a few days after her husband lost his job. Since the Relief record shows no resources in 1936, and Mrs. Wallach said that her husband's work was irregular from about 1934, it is reasonable to suppose that the family had been unable to build up adequate resources again and so had had to apply for Relief as soon as the earnings dropped below the level on which the family could manage.

Relief History: The record indicates that the family applied for supplementation of the man's irregular earnings on February 18, 1936, and was accepted on March 2, 1936. There were periods between the latter date and the closing date, April 23, 1937, when the man earned nothing for several weeks at a time, but for the most part he earned a few dollars a week and Relief was supplementary. The family seemed to make no demands for special services, but during the child's illness, some of the medical expense was borne by the District Office. The case was closed on April 23, 1937, because Mr. Wallach's income rose sufficiently to support the family.

Present Job: Mr. Wallach is still employed at his regular trade and by the same employer for whom he worked prior to Relief; and the only change is in relation to time and salary. Although not a union member (he has never belonged to any union in the United States) he receives union wages; but since he is employed on a piecework basis, seldom makes more than $30 a week, and frequently much less. It is difficult to plan and manage on an irregular income which probably does not average $25 a week; Mr. Wallach has therefore been most anxious to get more regular work.

Attitude Toward Present Job and Future Prospects: Mr. Wallach is happy to be working at all, and has hoped during the past few years that things will pick up so that he may have full-time employment. He has never liked repair work as much as making new clothing. He is, therefore, much elated about an interview he had recently with a Fifth Avenue clothing house where he was told that his qualifications were what they wanted and that he might expect to be called after the first of next month, if business continues to be good. His salary will be full union scale, and he will have to join the union. He does not foresee any difficulty with the union because he has a number of influential friends who will be glad to speak for him. Because of such friends and interested relatives, Mr. Wallach has never doubted that his future will be secure. He is certain that they can help him get a job and that he can keep it through his own efforts, because he likes his work and knows he is expert in his own line. He does not, of course, expect them to perform miracles and create an opening where there is none. But the present prospective job is the break that they have been waiting for, and they are confident that things are about to change for the better.

Woman:

Description: A slight, short, lively person, attractive because of the vividness and mobility of facial expression. She looked her age, and said she thought the intensity with which she has met all the experiences of her life is responsible for the lines in her face. She added that she has not been well since the birth of her son, has had a number of gynecological operations and was now in the beginning of menopause. She thinks that the greatest single factor in her aging so rapidly was her son's recent serious illness.

Background: Born in Lemberg, Poland, March, 1901, of Jewish parentage. She was the fifth of nine children (two of whom had died before she was born). She came to the United States in 1916. She had had six years of schooling in Poland and wanted to attend school in the United States, but could not afford to do so. She contented herself with attending night school long enough to learn to read and write English.

During the first five years after her arrival in the United States, she was able to find only odd jobs at a few dollars a week. In 1921 she got work in the shipping department of a novelty company, where she remained until her marriage in 1925. She spoke of this period as one which had given her great satisfaction. Before she left Poland, her mother, who never expected to see her again (but later came here to join her and her sisters), had told her that there were two rules by which she must live: first, be honest, never lie, steal, or even think dishonestly; second, keep clean "underneath," both physically and spiritually. If she were too neglectful to follow either of these rules, other people might not always know, but she would. As a result, she would lack self-respect and, lacking self-respect, she could never command the respect of others. Mrs. Wallach believes her mother was right; that she was proved right by Mrs. Wallach's own work experience. She was advanced rapidly, was permitted to go to the safe without supervision, and unlike those of the other employees, her bundles were never checked when she went out. At the time of her marriage, her salary had reached $25 a week and her employers offered to raise it if she would remain there. They attended her wedding, have kept in touch with her, and are now interested in her son. She has made many purchases there, paying wholesale prices; they sent her son a check for $25 on his last birthday, which was more than the amount of her purchases within any one depression year. Mrs. Wallach said she has always made friends easily and has found that one keeps them by being thoughtful and considerate; a card or telephone call on birthdays, anniversaries, and Holy Days is a good investment in friendship and she is trying to teach her son the value of this consideration for others.

Children:

Edward—born September, 1926, is an only child. Mrs. Wallach nearly died during the delivery; he was not a big baby but Mrs. Wallach was unusually small in pelvic structure. She was badly injured and the doctor advised against her having another child. She wanted another, however, and in 1929 became pregnant again. She had a miscarriage at four months, brought on by her attempts to lift her mother, who, just before her death, fainted several times. She has grieved over the loss of this child, because the doctor had said it was probably a little girl, and Mrs. Wallach would have liked a daughter. Following this miscarriage it became impossible for her ever to have another child because of the damage to her organs. Since both Mr. and Mrs. Wallach love children, Edward became the center of their lives. He is a brilliant boy and despite frequent absence from school because of illness, has always made exceptionally good grades. At 14, he is in his third year in high school, a favorite with his teachers, and considered to have an excellent chance for a university scholarship. He is interested in electrical engineering.

While presenting no feeding problems from the standpoint of food fads, Edward has had to have special foods because so many kinds of food disagree with him and because no matter how much he eats he is underweight. He has had frequent and severe colds. In 1937 he had pneumonia and for ten days his chances for recovery were considered poor. During that time his temperature remained at 105.5. He was too ill to move and nurses and consultants were called in by the family doctor. The only doctor willing to concede Edward a chance for life was the "young" doctor, the family physician's son. He sat by the bed night and day, permitting no one else to touch the child, bathing him to reduce the fever, feeding him, giving him hypodermics. He called his father, and the specialists who were brought in, "old-fashioned and afraid to take responsibility." The boy, who seemed conscious much of the time, despite the fever, was sure he was going to die because there were so many people around, and said he did not want to die because it was "too cold out." Mrs. Wallach's response to this was to become hysterical and her screams further frightened the boy. The "young" doctor did not let the others send her away, however, but gave her so much to do she had no time for another attack. She was a serious problem to them, however, because she could neither eat nor sleep and did not urinate for "eight days." It was during this time that she found out how many friends the boy and his family had. A Catholic priest came to the house to see if he could do anything, as did the minister of a near-by Protestant church. Children with whom Edward had played were found in the churches crying and praying for his recovery and seemed so distressed that the priests offered to see what they could do. The principal and teachers came from the school, and later, when Edward was convalescing and worried about his progress in school, the principal came again to assure him that he would be promoted. Neighbors whom Mrs. Wallach had never met before, both from her own building and from other apartment houses in the vicinity, asked about him. The landlord was found praying for Edward in the trunk room, and although the family owed him $105 (three months' rent) at that time, he insisted on their accepting a check for $100 in case they should need it. Money was left in the home anonymously so that the boy might lack for nothing. The child's recovery was greeted with great joy from many sources.

Mrs. Wallach said she and her husband have always been aware of the danger of spoiling Edward, an only child and not too strong. Both feel that he could not have been badly spoiled and still have made and kept so many good friends. He has been much affected by financial insecurity in the family, trying to hide his clothing and even his school needs when he sees how difficult it is for his parents to manage on their meager income. This has been unnecessary because relatives have always been ready to see that he does not suffer, and his parents ready to ask help of relatives for him even when they would not ask it for themselves. Edward was seen by the worker as he was leaving for school. He is very tall and thin. Had his face been mature, he might have looked 18 or 19 because of his height and large bony structure, but he weighs only about 125 pounds. He is quite handsome, was well-poised and pleasant in his manner, which seemed more adult than that of most 14-year-olds. He is interested in music and is planning to study an instrument, probably the violin, as soon as the family's financial difficulties are cleared up.

Relatives:

Man—Mrs. Wallach said that her husband's immediate family is in England. They maintained regular correspondence with them until the war began, after which communication became difficult. Mr. Wallach's family were comfortable financially when last heard from. Two of his brothers are expert tailors. The last word from them indicated that all were engaged in defense activities of one sort or another. Mr. and Mrs. Wallach had arranged to take his favorite brother's two sons, 2½ and 7 years old, for the duration of the war, but they have not heard from the relatives since the attack on a refugee ship in which many children were lost. They are worried that the children might have been on that ship, but believe they would long since have received word had that been so. The only relative Mr. Wallach has in this country is an uncle, a wealthy man, who has recently begun to show some interest in Edward, sending him $50 on his last birthday and mentioning the possibility of the boy's visiting him at his home in New Jersey.

Woman—Mrs. Wallach's three sisters, who are in this country, have a joint business—bakery and cafeteria—and support their father. The business suffered some losses during the depression years, but is picking up again. Her other relatives are in that part of Poland which is now under Russian rule.

The family feels that they are relatively safe. The sisters had just made arrangements to bring three nephews to the United States when the war broke out and their plans were ruined. They had hoped to get the entire family together in this country, could not afford to bring all members at once, so had planned to do it gradually, beginning with the younger members, who had more chance for employment. These plans have been abandoned for the duration of the war. Mrs. Wallach's family is a very close one, they have always helped one another; her sisters helped the Wallachs as much as possible during difficult times, although all have heavy family responsibilities. They have large families, all the boys are brilliant, and some sacrifices are necessary in order to send those who are old enough to college. Two boys of 19 and 20 have already finished their work for bachelor degrees; one is in his third year at college, at the age of eighteen.

Religion: The Wallachs are Orthodox Jews who observe the dietary laws and attend synagogue. Mrs. Wallach said that she believes firmly in religion and is certain that her son's life was spared through the mercy of God in answer to prayers and faith.

Birth Control: Mrs. Wallach said that she knew little about birth control because she has not needed it. She does think it a good thing to plan a family and to have no more children than one can provide for adequately.

Newspapers: The family reads the *News, Times* and *Post.* Mr. Wallach considers an evening incomplete which does not include a careful reading of the newspapers. According to his wife, he reads widely, in addition to newspapers, and is considered a generally well-informed person. They listen to most of the regular commentators on the radio, as well as any other talks and discussions on politics, medicine, consumers' problems, child guidance, etc. There is much that Mrs. Wallach doesn't understand in these talks, and her husband goes over them carefully with her, teaching and explaining. He is patient with her, and eager for her to learn all that she can about subjects of current interest. She is glad of his help, since now she never finds herself at a loss, no matter what subject is being discussed. They have a wide circle of friends from many fields of work with diversified interests. Much of their social activity involves animated discussion of one or another current event. Occasionally they play cards or go to a movie.

Political Affiliations: Mr. Wallach is a citizen and a stanch Roosevelt supporter. Mrs. Wallach lost her citizenship by marriage to an alien, and did not realize it until the 1936 election. She immediately went to take out her first papers, but ran into some difficulty because she could not remember which boat she came on, and earlier records were not easily located. She expects her final papers soon, and regrets only that they will not come in time for her to cast her vote for Roosevelt. She said that the whole family loves the United States as its fatherland, and related with amusement how her father, the first day he was in New York, before he could speak any English, disappeared for several hours. The sisters became concerned, feared he was lost, and were in great confusion as to whether to get in touch with the police or not, when he turned up in the midst of the excitement and drew from his pocket the evidence of his application for citizenship. They scolded him for not waiting until they had got him decent American clothing, but he said this was more important. He was so proud the day he got his second papers that the family had to give him a big party. Mrs. Wallach said that her feeling for Roosevelt is beyond her feeling for a good leader, it is really love. She listens, as does her husband, to all his radio addresses, and both are resentful of any interruption when so occupied. She reported remarking frequently that she would like once in her life to get close enough to him to ask God's blessing upon him for what he has done for the people of the land. She explained that she has nothing against Willkie, does not know if he would make a good President or a bad one, only that he could not begin to be the President that Roosevelt has been.

The Wallachs have some pro-British leaning because of relatives in England, but recognizing the source of this feeling, say that they would like England to win the war, would like the

United States to give what help is possible, but would not want the United States to become actually involved in warfare abroad unless it became necessary in order to forestall war on these shores. They are quite in sympathy with giving all possible help to refugees.

Family Adjustment and Attitudes: Mrs. Wallach said she first met her husband at a party to which she had been taken by a very handsome man with whom she considered herself violently in love. Mr. Wallach, seeing her across the room sought an introduction and refused to leave her side all that evening. He insisted upon seeing her home despite her protests that she must go with her escort. He was insistent about a date the following evening, but she said she might not be free, because she had a tentative date with the man she cared so much for, and told Mr. Wallach to telephone after 7 P.M. When she came home from work, before 6 P.M., her sister said the new man was waiting for her in the parlor. After her first irritation, her sense of humor saved the situation and she went out with him. Before the evening was over, she found herself experiencing a sense of respect for him and a warm liking that she had never felt for the other man. Once she realized that it was only the other man's handsome appearance she had admired, her romance with the "new" man swept easily on to marriage. Her sisters liked her husband, had not liked or trusted the other man, and therefore helped this romance along. She feels that the only change from courtship to marriage was in the growing depth of love and sense of security they had in each other. According to Mrs. Wallach, she has thanked God many times that her husband courted her so strenuously that he swept aside her infatuation for the other man. Their son has added much to their feeling for each other, each seeing some of the other in the boy as well as the child himself. Mrs. Wallach says they are a warm, loving, demonstrative family. Her husband has been an excellent provider and she believes herself a good wife and mother. They are sensitive to each other's moods and emotional needs and neither is excessively demanding of the other. This relationship has been too deep to be affected by either good luck or bad. Mr. Wallach was worried when he could not provide for her as well as he wished, but she took great pains to let him understand she did not hold him responsible because there was no work for him to do. Even now he spends too much of what should be his recreation and rest time working at home on clothing for individuals who come to him; just to fill out the slender pay check. She is sure he does this, not because they cannot manage the necessities on what he earns, but because he wants her to have a few of the extras that the money brings. She will be glad when he gets work that pays adequately for his working hours and leaves his evenings free for rest and recreation.

Attitudes toward Us: Mrs. Wallach was much interested in the study and had a fair understanding of its purpose. She thought her husband would be interested and might come in for an office interview, if we wrote him. She was cordial and pleasant and invited us to stop in again if we were anywhere in the neighborhood.

OFFICE INTERVIEW

(Note: Mr. Wallach stated that he would be at the office at 9 P.M., but when I arrived at 8:40 P.M. he was already there, accompanied by his wife and sister-in-law. The two ladies waited in an adjoining office while the interview took place.)

Impression: Mr. Wallach seemed to be about 50 years old. He speaks fluently but has a limited vocabulary. Although he was born in England, he frequently mispronounces simple words in a manner typical of people to whom English is not a native language. Throughout the interview he constantly repeated the expression "to be perfectly frank with you." His clothing was in fair condition. He says that he has not bought any new clothes during the last two years, but that when last he was "in the money" he outfitted himself with "good stuff." Mr. Wallach's teeth are in noticeably poor condition. He remarked that he didn't mind having his teeth pulled, but objected very much to having the "needle" stuck into his gums.

Employment History: Mr. Wallach was born in London and spent most of his childhood in Hull. After completing grammar school, he entered his brother-in-law's tailoring shop as an apprentice. After a few years of tailoring, the union in which he was interested began to expand and he accepted a full-time trade-union position. Shortly after he became secretary of the union, membership grew from 300 to 3,000. Mr. Wallach related with considerable pride the extent of his power and influence, especially during the last war, when he had the authority to decide who was to go to the front and who was to remain at home. He said that he himself volunteered but was not permitted to leave for the front until 1916. After the Armistice, he returned to his trade-union job, but shortly thereafter his mother's sister, long resident in the United States, came to England for a visit. She told Mr. Wallach that a man of his capacity would doubtless be a great success in the United States and encouraged him to emigrate. Since she was wealthy, he assumed that her judgment was good. He arrived in the United States in 1920 and went to New Brunswick, where his aunt lived, but "the town was too small to hold me." Mr. Wallach then went to Montreal, where he also had relatives, and from Montreal to Toronto, where he worked as a tailor for a year or so. He then came to New York, but soon thereafter left for Utica, where he also had relatives. He worked in Utica until his employer went out of business. A brother-in-law, who had formerly lived in Montreal, had moved to Newark, New Jersey; when his employer's business failed, Mr. Wallach went to Newark where he and his brother-in-law went into business as partners in a cleaning and dyeing establishment. According to Mr. Wallach, he had thought that his brother-in-law knew this business well and he was therefore willing to put up the additional capital needed to get going. But he soon discovered that his brother-in-law knew little about the business and was, in fact, a poor businessman and it was not long before the venture failed. He says that his wife was really happy when the business failed because it was possible for them to leave Newark and come to New York. She preferred New York because her family lived there; Mr. Wallach said "she was a constant plague" to him while they lived in Newark because she did not like the town. After coming to New York, he got work in the men's clothing industry, first with one firm and then another and finally with a large manufacturer. He said that at the height of the boom he earned approximately $75 a week plus 5 per cent commission, which brought his earnings to $125 a week. About 1930, the firm removed its business to London, England, and offered Mr. Wallach a chance to go along, but Mrs. Wallach would not hear of it and Mr. Wallach says he could not blame her since all of her relatives were in this country.

Mr. Wallach then found it difficult to get work because business had begun to decline and he was forced to use his savings for living expenses. He says that he was totally unemployed for about nine months in 1931-1932 and that he was forced to cash about $9,000 worth of insurance policies. In 1932 Mr. Wallach managed to find some work again and since then things have been a little better. At present he is the manager of a small cleaning and dyeing shop in the North Bronx. He earns about $1,600 a year and says this is, of course, "no money at all" in comparison with what he used to earn. Several years ago Mr. Wallach had a chance to get a good job in the men's garment industry through friends, but he said he was unable to do so because he could not "crack the union." At the present moment he again has prospects of getting a job with a firm in the ladies' garment industry, a job that would give him employment for 46 to 50 weeks of the year. Mr. Wallach says that such jobs are ordinarily given only to relatives or friends of the top union bosses. Mr. Wallach feels that the worst part of working in the garment industry is the fact that it is so seasonal and that the few jobs that are not seasonal are reserved for the union bosses or their relatives. During the past years Mr. Wallach has been able to add to his income by doing a little tailoring at home. He says that he is a highly skilled worker on both men's and women's clothes although in recent years he has lost some of his speed.

Relief History: (Mr. Wallach never admitted, during the

course of the interview that he had been on Relief.) Mr. Wallach thinks that President Roosevelt has done an excellent job in trying to take care of the poor and that WPA was a good idea. In discussing the WPA clothing project, however, Mr. Wallach said that although he didn't know much about it, what he had seen of the work was not good. He thought the poor work could be blamed on inferior materials and on the fact that the people in charge of the project did not know much about the work, and added that after all this was to be expected. Mr. Wallach says he is pleased "to throw bouquets" at Mayor La Guardia for having given Home Relief to people without letting the public know who was on Relief.

Family: Although he used to earn a lot of money, Mr. Wallach says that most of his savings went to pay medical bills for his son and wife. The boy has been sickly since birth and several years ago developed a streptococcus pneumonia from which they thought he would never recover. Since birth the boy has had trouble with his skin and Mr. Wallach relates that he has taken him to every skin specialist in New York and that each visit cost him $25. In discussing his wife, Mr. Wallach said that he had "quite a lot of trouble" with her because of illness, but fortunately she is more or less "fixed up" now. She had a difficult delivery and had to be operated on shortly thereafter; she has had two more operations in recent years.

Mr. Wallach talked at length about his son, who is now 14 years old and precocious. Last summer they made all necessary preparations for sending him to camp and Mr. Wallach even went along with him and remained there overnight. The next morning, however, the boy flatly refused to stay and insisted upon going home. Mr. Wallach was not sure why the boy refused to stay but thinks it had something to do with the condition of the lavatory in the bunk, for he says that the boy insisted upon going home after using the lavatory. Mr. Wallach went on to say that the boy reacts to every kind of odor and that if his food has any odor whatever, he will not touch it. According to Mr. Wallach, the boy keeps himself very clean.

Mr. Wallach says that the boy is much interested in sports.

"Just like I am. I was a great amateur athlete before I broke my knee cap. I was able to run 100 yards in 10 seconds flat and came out fourth in the Sheffield handicap." According to Mr. Wallach, the boy knows the averages and records of most athletes. Because of his fragile health, however, the boy does not participate much in organized games.

Mr. Wallach says that he is not particularly interested in Jewish problems. Although he is not anti-Zionistic, he says that he is not sure that the Jews, even if they got Palestine, would be able to hold it since they once had it but lost it. He knows all the Hebrew prayers because he attended Hebrew school from the age of 5 to 14, and remembered all that was taught him. He is a member of a synagogue and fasts on the Day of Atonement, but he says he fasts because it doesn't cause him any trouble. According to Mr. Wallach, people who do not believe in something are little better than animals and he made sure that his son got a religious education. He says that the boy has never missed saying his morning prayers since his confirmation at the age of 13 and that his wife observes the dietary laws strictly.

Many of Mr. Wallach's relatives are in England and he says that he corresponded with them regularly until five or six months ago and had even made plans to bring a young cousin to this country, but when several boats carrying child refugees were sunk, these plans were changed. Although Mr. Wallach twice remarked that he has not heard from his relatives for the last six months, he did not show any real concern about this fact.

Politics: Mr. Wallach talked in the most glowing terms about President Roosevelt, who, he believes will rank as one of the greatest men in the history of the United States, equal to Lincoln. He says that no man has done as much for the poor as has Mr. Roosevelt; nobody has understood the true course of world events as has Mr. Roosevelt; nobody has been as courageous in forcing home his point of view to the public. Mr. Wallach also admired Lloyd George, who, he said, could get things done. He thought that Mayor La Guardia and Churchill were also to be admired. According to Mr. Wallach, the British are largely responsible for much of the present trouble for if the British had helped the Socialist government when it was in power in Germany things would have been different. He thinks the fall of France was largely the work of fascist fifth columnists in that country. He admitted that the Communists in France were also an untrustworthy group. In talking about Stalin, he said he would not trust him although he thought that Russia could not afford to play ball with Germany much longer. Mr. Wallach is much in favor of the President's policy of aiding Britain without sending men abroad. He thinks there is no question but that there will be no peace until Hitler is destroyed.

In discussing his experiences in British and American trade-unions, Mr. Wallach says that the most striking difference is the low level of leadership in this country, especially in matters of honesty. He said, of course, he does not mean people like Hillman, Dubinsky and Heywood Broun, but by and large, he did think that there was much racketeering among American trade-union leaders. In contrast, he pointed to the head of his own union in England, who, although he had been offered a job by Asquith during the last war at a salary three times that which he was receiving from the union, flatly refused to accept it. This leader said that he would be willing to co-operate with the government but would never take office until Labor was in power. Mr. Wallach thinks that by and large unions are good and he believes that conditions in the dyeing and cleaning industry are particularly bad because there is no union.

Future: Mr. Wallach feels pretty good about the future. He is especially happy that his wife and son are now in fairly good health. He thinks that the war will bring about an improvement in the living conditions of the mass of the laboring population, because there will be much new social legislation. Mr. Wallach believes that there will be an increased demand for skilled tailors in the near future and he has several specific openings in view. So far as his son's future is concerned, he does not think it will be a good idea to push the boy into medicine, although the boy is an excellent student, because he does not have enough money to pay for a medical education and because he knows a lot of doctors who do not make a living. He thinks that law is an even worse field. He is glad that his son is considering engineering as a vocation because that seems sensible these days.

Case Nine

CALDWELL FAMILY

Status Closed to Private Employment *Religion* Protestant
Man born 1893 Ireland to U.S.A. 1911 Citizen Yes
Wife born 1898 Scotland to U.S.A. 1912 Citizen Yes

Education
Man Completed elementary school—Ireland.
Wife Completed elementary school—Scotland.

Medical Status
Man Negative.
Wife Negative.

Woman's Work History Never worked outside of home.

Married January, 1921, N.Y.C.

Number of Children in the Home Two *Ages*—14 and 15 years.

Basic Occupation before Relief Salesman-driver, baking company.

Average Income before Relief $25 to $35 weekly.

Private Employment Terminated October, 1935. Because of strike.

First Accepted for Relief December, 1935.

SUMMARY

Home Relief Supplementation of strike benefits December 17, 1935, to February, 1936. Case Closed to Private Employment.

Present Status—Salesman-driver, baking company. Returned to former job at end of strike, January, 1936. Works on commission—averages $30 to $40 weekly.

ABSTRACT OF HOME RELIEF RECORD

DEC. 3, 1935 — *First Application:* Mr. Caldwell is unemployed because of a strike at the large baking company at which he is employed. The family is in a serious financial predicament because of the children. Mr. Caldwell's brother John, who lives in the Bronx, has assisted temporarily but cannot continue to do so. Mr. Caldwell is receiving $6 a week from the local union. There are four more checks due.

DEC. 12, 1935 — The family lives in a modestly furnished apartment; rental is $35 a month. Mr. Caldwell has worked as driver and salesman for the bakery for 22 years, ever since his arrival in this country. His average earnings have been $28 a week except from 1931 to 1934, when they were $22 a week. Mrs. Caldwell has not worked since her marriage. The family had a small account at the Dollar Savings Bank and one at the Central Savings Bank. These savings were exhausted by expenses connected with the death of a child about three years ago. Mr. Caldwell received a veteran's bonus of $800 three and one-half years prior to their application for assistance.

Mr. Caldwell is a member of the Bakery and Confectionary Workers' Union. The union is striking for "recognition and a living wage." Mr. Caldwell is eligible for strike benefits for 10 weeks at $6 a week.

Their debts at this time are $40 to Mr. Caldwell's brother John and $35 to a friend. They are two months in arrears with rent and owe $4.93 for gas and electricity.

Mrs. Caldwell's mother is seriously ill with "some sort of nervous disorder." Her father is a building foreman whose earnings are small. He is supporting an unemployed brother. Mrs. Caldwell's sister is married; her husband is a carpenter on WPA.

Mr. Caldwell has only one brother, John, from whom he has been estranged for two years; despite this, John has assisted as much as possible.

DEC. 17, 1935 — Investigation at the bakery revealed the fact that there is a collectible bond of $160 but that withdrawal of this eliminated any possibility of re-employment. No information was available regarding the duration of the strike.

The family's circumstances were investigated through the friend from whom they borrowed money. Since the friend is also on strike, there is no possibility of further assistance. Mrs. Caldwell's mother was not visited because of the family's request that she not be disturbed in view of her nervous condition.

DEC. 17, 1935 — *Accepted for Home Relief supplementation of strike benefits.*

JAN., 1936 — Mrs. Caldwell reported that Mr. Caldwell returned to work following the settlement of the strike. He is earning $28 a week.

FEB., 1936 — *Case Closed to Private Industry.*

JUNE, 1939 — WPA assignment slip for Mrs. Caldwell's father filed with Mrs. Caldwell's record since her father was "nonrelief status."

HOME INTERVIEW

Home—Four rooms on the fifth floor of a modern walk-up apartment building in upper Manhattan. The building is well-constructed and in good repair and is located in a residential neighborhood between Broadway and Amsterdam Avenue. The apartment is adequately, although not elaborately furnished and showed evidence of good housekeeping. The parents sleep in one bedroom, the two boys in another.

Man:

Description: Tall, slender, with dark-brown hair and angular features. He was very friendly. Mr. Caldwell seemed to worker to be an intelligent person. He is apparently in good health. He was not in the room during the first part of the interview but answered questions from the kitchen when asked by Mrs. Caldwell. He finally came into the combination living-dining room, where the interview was held and during the remainder of the interview entered into the discussion quite freely.

Background: Born in the North of Ireland, in November, 1893. He was the fourth of eight children, with three brothers and four sisters. He completed the elementary grades. Mr. Caldwell's father was a farmer. Mr. Caldwell was an apprentice for three years in a dry goods store in Ireland. The total apprenticeship agreed upon was five years but he says he was adventuresome and stopped at the end of three years. In 1911, when he was 17 years of age he came to the United States.

Work History: According to the Home Relief record, Mr. Caldwell has been employed by a large bakery ever since he came to this country. Mr. Caldwell states he was employed by the I.R.T. as a conductor during his first five years in this country, earning $25 a week. From 1915 to 1917 he was a driver and salesman for the bakery, earning $28 a week. From May, 1917, to July, 1919, he was in the United States Army, and served overseas. He returned to his job at the bakery following his discharge from the army. He and Mrs. Caldwell went to Ireland on a visit in 1925 but stayed only a few months since Mrs. Caldwell would not consent to remaining there. Mr. Caldwell would have stayed on in Ireland if Mrs. Caldwell had agreed to do so. Upon returning to this country Mr. Caldwell returned to work at the bakery. The only unemployment Mr. Caldwell has experienced was during a 7-week strike in 1934. Mr. Caldwell states he had never been greatly interested in unions but was forced to join in 1934 and shortly afterwards a strike was called since at this time the company was taken over by a new management and there was an attempt to replace old employees. The union called a strike and forced the company to reinstate discharged employees. Mr. Caldwell has found the union helpful in maintaining standards.

At the time of the strike Mr. Caldwell was able to borrow a small amount of money from his brother and from friends. They would have been able to manage during the strike period if they had not incurred heavy expenses three weeks prior to this, due to the death of their eldest boy. (The Home Relief record states that the child died three years prior to the application date.)

Following settlement of the strike, Mr. Caldwell returned to work and has been working steadily ever since.

Interim Period: During the strike Mr. Caldwell borrowed

from his brother and from a friend and had a total debt of several hundred dollars. He also cashed some insurance policies. Their small savings were used and bank accounts closed. Their eldest boy was ill the entire summer preceding the strike and was under medical care. This medical expense together with burial expenses made it necessary for them to request assistance. Mr. Caldwell was out of work two and one-half months.

Relief History: The Caldwells were extremely embarrassed at having to request assistance. They never thought anything like that would be necessary. However, they had exhausted their resources and could borrow no longer. The boys were young and it was necessary to apply for assistance for their sakes since there was not enough money for food. Relief assistance was little but it helped. The family appreciated the help received but were discouraged over the necessity for investigation through friends and Mr. Caldwell's employer. The investigator tried to force them to move because Home Relief could not meet the family's rent. They were just about to apply for further insurance adjustment when Mr. Caldwell returned to work. Mrs. Caldwell said it was a relief not to have to look for another apartment or give up their insurance.

Mr. Caldwell would have been referred to WPA during their stay on Relief had he not been required to picket.

Present Job: Mr. Caldwell is averaging $36 to $40 a week as commission salesman and driver for the baking company. His earnings are better in winter than in the summer months, since he serves wealthy families and schools. Many of the families are out of the city during the summer and schools are closed. Governor Lehman is one of his customers. Mr. Caldwell works harder in summer because he is sent to Long Island, where the routes are longer and there are fewer customers. Mr. Caldwell has noticed a falling off in business within the past year; he thinks the reason for this is that there are so many reducing fads and women are eating less bread and pastries. This has definitely affected the bakery business.

Mr. Caldwell is proud of his work record and, although he discussed some discouraging features, seems fairly secure in his present job. He stated that the union does not control working hours for commission salesmen, which means the salesmen are required to work overtime and can be called upon 24 hours a day. Mr. Caldwell works about 12 to 14 hours a day. He starts on his route at four in the morning, reports to the office at 2 P.M. to make out reports and check customers' lists and tries to be finished by 4 P.M. In the summer they are given one week's vacation with pay and are forced to take three weeks at their own expense. (Mr. Caldwell is on a week's vacation at present.) The four weeks are split up and spread over the summer months. Mr. Caldwell averages about $10 a week less in the summer than in the winter. The family finds it more difficult to manage on his summer earnings.

Attitude toward Present Job and Future Prospects: Mr. Caldwell, as previously stated, is proud of his work record. While his job has disadvantages, he accepts them philosophically and states there is nothing he can do but like it. He does not seem too discouraged over the decline in sales of bakery products as previously discussed, and seems fairly secure in his job.

Woman:

Description: Mrs. Caldwell is short, stockily built, with gray-brown hair. She seems intelligent. She was more reserved than Mr. Caldwell but became very friendly during the interview. She is in good health.

Background: Born in Scotland, July, 1898. She was the youngest of five children, with three brothers and one sister. She had an elementary school education in Scotland and then came to this country with her family when she was 14 years old. Mrs. Caldwell prefers the United States to Scotland and states that once a person has lived in the United States she is sure he would not live elsewhere.

Mrs. Caldwell has never been employed. She and Mr. Caldwell were married in New York City in 1921.

Children:

Douglas—born January, 1925, in New York City. He is tall, of medium coloring, and described by Mrs. Caldwell as quiet and reserved. He is in junior high school. Mrs. Caldwell states Douglas does not like school much but gets along fairly well. He is in good health. Douglas was in bed at the time of the visit although it was after eleven in the morning. He came in before the interview was over but had little to say. Mrs. Caldwell says the children were not affected by their former Relief status since they were too young. She also says that since Mr. Caldwell returned to work in a very short time, the children were probably not even aware that he had not been working. Douglas is active in church clubs and derives much pleasure from being with his friends there. His Sunday-school teacher took the boys camping at his camp near Asbury Park, New Jersey, several weeks this summer. They enjoyed it very much.

Thomas—born December, 1926, in New York City. Thomas is tall, slender, and blond. He is more outgoing than Douglas and when he came in during the interview, joined the conversation with apparent ease. He is also in junior high school. He is in good health. He is also active in the Sunday-school group and enjoyed his camping trip this summer. He is a member of the Boy Scouts but expressed little interest stating he does not care for the routine. At present he is working as a delivery boy for a neighborhood tailor and earns $2 a week.

Relatives:

Man—Mr. Caldwell's parents are dead. He has two brothers in Ireland who had been operating a farm. They are now in the army. One brother, John, is in New York City and works for the I.R.T. According to the Home Relief record and Mrs. Caldwell's attitude while discussing relatives (Mr. Caldwell was not in the room at the time), the brothers have little to do with each other. There is no information from relatives now in Ireland. Earlier letters came through opened and "scratched" so they did not continue correspondence. Mr. Caldwell's sisters are married and also living in Ireland.

Woman—Mrs. Caldwell's mother died three years ago. Her father was formerly a carpenter foreman, but never earned much money. He is unable to work much now and is being supported by her brother, with whom he lives. Another brother and one sister live in Scotland. They are both married and have families. Mrs. Caldwell knows little about them. A sister, living in New York City, is married; her husband is on WPA. Mrs. Caldwell expressed little emotion in discussing relatives in Scotland and Ireland. In discussing her father's employment, she gave the impression that they had difficulty in managing in Scotland and came to this country because of better opportunities for employment.

Religion: The Caldwells are members of the Presbyterian Church. Mrs. Caldwell was formerly a member of the Scotch Presbyterian Church in Scotland and Mr. Caldwell of the Presbyterian Church in North Ireland. (The Home Relief record states that the family belongs to the Seventh-Day Adventist Church.)

The family attend church regularly. Mrs. Caldwell is a member of the Mothers' Club and the children belong to church-school clubs. Mrs. Caldwell believes religion is necessary to wholesome living, and they have found associations with their friends at church helpful.

Birth Control: There was little discussion regarding birth control. Mrs. Caldwell discussed the policy of the Catholic Church in forcing people to have large families but not assisting them in caring for their children. She does not believe this is right and states she does not understand how people can be so blind as to be controlled by the church in this manner.

Newspapers: The family reads the *Journal, News,* and *Times* alternately. They listen to outstanding radio programs and news reports.

Political Affiliations: No clubs. The family voted for Roosevelt before and will do so again. Mr. Caldwell believes Roosevelt has done and will continue to do a good job. He believes that the country should stand united during this present crisis. He knows little about Willkie and does not know whether or not he would be a good President. Theoretically, he thinks the Republicans might be the outstanding party at this time because they have money, but he believes Roosevelt will be the best President. Mr. Caldwell believes thoroughly in the Conscription Bill and hopes it will pass immediately. He believes it should include ages 18 to 45, not 21 to 35. He will gladly give his boys for their country's service just as soon as they are old enough. He believes training is good for all young men and will not necessarily make them "warlike" as some people think. Preparedness is necessary for this country and training programs are essential. He states the British will not give up this war. He knows them too well. They will fight to the last man since they prefer death to subjugation. He believes that this is true of Americans too. He discussed the Irish attitude toward England, stating that it is a religious problem. North Ireland, which is chiefly Protestant, will stand united in support of England. In South Ireland, the people are largely Catholic and are opposed to English rule on the basis of religion.

Mr. Caldwell does not oppose refugee assistance. He says after all we were all refugees at one time. He dislikes communism intensely.

Mr. Caldwell is a member of the Bakery and Confectionary Workers' Union, Local #56, and while he was not interested at first, now believes that the union is helpful.

Family Adjustments and Attitudes:

Before Relief: The family was always able to manage adequately on Mr. Caldwell's earnings up to the time of the strike in 1935. They had enough money for food, rent, recreation, etc., as well as a small savings account and insurance.

On Relief: During the one and one-half months on Home Relief they had a difficult time. All their resources were exhausted and they had to live on a smaller food budget. There was no recreation, Mrs. Caldwell stated that the time on Home Relief was so short and they had so much difficulty prior to it, they were not interested in recreation in any case. The boys were too young to notice any difference. While the Caldwells were ashamed they knew there was nothing else to do and also knew that Mr. Caldwell would be returning to work soon. This made it more bearable.

At Present: They have never been able to reach the standard of living they had prior to 1934. They had many debts and it took a long time to pay them off. They lost their bank account and have never been able to reopen one. They were fortunate in being able to keep their insurance which would have been lost had they remained on Home Relief any longer; the investigator had informed them that they would have to submit it for adjustment. They are able to afford little recreation, but Mr. Caldwell states that he prefers his home and radio, and these are free. He listens to the radio constantly when he is at home. He does not like movies. He occasionally attends church groups but enjoys his home better. Mrs. Caldwell likes movies and goes frequently. They are not on close terms with other tenants in the building since they find neighbors easier to get along with if they are not too intimate. However, they do have friends at the church.

Future: The Caldwells do not seem concerned about the future. Although Mr. Caldwell discusses difficulties on his job he does not appear dissatisfied and seems secure in his relationship with the company. The family seems content and fairly well-adjusted.

Attitude toward Us: There was a great deal of resistance toward the study and the worker. On one visit, July 15th, Mrs. Caldwell met worker at the door and made an appointment for July 18th saying that that day would be more convenient. On July 18th she said she was busy and was planning to leave on vacation; she suggested an appointment the week of August 5th. August 5th a visit was made and Mrs. Caldwell informed worker she would not be able to talk then since it was too early in the morning and the boys were still in bed. She suggested a return visit in the afternoon, but was not at home when the visit was made.

On August 28th Mrs. Caldwell was rather distant at first but became more friendly and was fairly free in discussion during most of the interview. It was probably because of Mr. Caldwell's presence that Mrs. Caldwell admitted worker. Mr. Caldwell was friendly and apparently quite willing to discuss his situation. He believes the study might be helpful and is willing to come to the office for an interview.

OFFICE INTERVIEW

Appearance: Mr. Caldwell is more than six feet tall, slender, and of youthful appearance. He was very well-groomed. He was extremely pleasant and friendly throughout the interview. Soon after he arrived Mr. Caldwell asked the interviewer to please use simple words because he had had little education and really didn't know very much about economics. The purpose of the study was explained to him in simple terms and he became quite relaxed and comfortable.

Mr. Caldwell stated that as a youngster of 16 in the old country, Ireland, he was a drunkard and used to go on protracted "sprees." He said, however, that after coming to the United States he was little interested in drink, although he does take a drink for social purposes and occasionally gets pretty drunk at large social gatherings. He also commented on the fact that he has rather strange working habits, in that he always arrives at the same point on his route at the same moment every day, and the cooks and housekeepers remark that they never have to look at their watches; when his wagon appears, they tell time by it. He said also that if he is delayed by as little as ten minutes on his route he drives "like hell" to make it up, though there is no point whatever in this behavior.

Employment History: Mr. Caldwell comes from the North of Ireland where his father had a prosperous farm. Mr. Caldwell was apprenticed to the drapery trade where he had completed three years of the required five, when he decided to come to the United States. He said that his family tried hard to keep him in the home country; they used both threats and promises, but to no avail. Mr. Caldwell had an elder brother who sat for competitive examinations for a bank job in Canada, but who because of illness and age was finally unable to accept the post;

he migrated to the United States, just before Mr. Caldwell came here. He was on friendly terms with two other young men of the town in which he was apprenticed, and all three made plans to leave together. They first hoped to get subsidized passage to Australia, but his father got wind of this plan in time to stop it. His first job in New York was in a chain grocery store, where he worked 17 to 18 hours a day and earned $9 per week. Shortly thereafter he got work as a ticket taker for the Boston and Westchester Railroad. He was well-liked and was promoted, but one night went out drinking with the "cops" and was later picked up by an inspector who forced him to leave because of intoxication on the job. He then found work for a short time with the I.R.T.; after he left that job he went to work for the bakery where he has been employed for many years. In fact, he stated that he has been with that bakery ever since. But much later in the interview he mentioned the fact that in about 1929, he took the last of his savings, bought a taxicab for $2,000 and ran it for two years. He found, however, that it was a "cutthroat racket," and very hard work, so much so that when he had a chance to go back with the bakery he did so. He smiled rather sheepishly when he mentioned the failure of this venture. He said that between 1921 and 1929 he had been a foreman at the bakery, but that toward the end of the twenties, one of the owners had persuaded him to take over the job of night manager for a Bronx neighborhood with the promise that he would sooner or later become day manager. He discovered, after accepting the job, that one of his major responsibilities was to report to headquarters on the misdeeds of the staff during the night. He found this not to his liking and gave it up. He says that before his marriage he had managed to accumulate about $7,000. He gave a small part of this, about $1,500, to his brother who wanted to leave the I.R.T. and establish himself as a farmer upstate. This brother found the task of becoming a farmer more than he could manage and the farm finally had to be liquidated at a substantial loss. Mr. Caldwell then arranged to look after his brother, whose health had suffered from the strain. Mr. and Mrs. Caldwell got him back on his feet and also helped him secure re-employment with the I.R.T. Mr. Caldwell invested the rest of the money in stocks during the twenties, first in the bakery, then in the French Building, and finally in City Service. He said that the stocks are now good for decorating the walls, but little else. In 1935 there was some change in management at the bakery and the new executive, after looking over the payroll, came to the conclusion that there was too much dead weight on the books, and decided to get rid of most of the older men. There had been attempts to unionize the men long before this. The attempts had not succeeded and Mr. Caldwell said he, himself, had been quite cool to the idea. Now, however, it was easy to get almost 100 per cent participation, and the men went out on strike. Those men who had previously paid their 75 cents in dues were now granted $6 a week by the union for a 10-week strike benefit. Mr. Caldwell said that he might have been able to manage on this had it not been that the recent death of a child had exhausted all his reserves; he was therefore forced to ask for Relief. When the strike was settled he got his job back, and then became rather active in the union; he is now on the executive board of the local and is also shop foreman. He has a good route, that is, in the East Seventies, between Fifth and Park Avenues, but says that the bakery business has not been the same since 1930. He receives one week's vacation with pay in the summer and must take an additional three weeks without pay. The firm offers the men the opportunity of having a route in the Rockaways during the summer, but the men find that by and large this is not satisfactory since it means establishing two homes. His working hours are from about 4:30 A.M. to approximately 2 P.M.; this does not mean ten hours of steady work, since one has time off for meals and rest. He also pointed out that the job has one thing in its favor, a man is not bossed by a supervisor.

Relief: Mr. Caldwell had a short and simple experience with Home Relief. He made application in 1935 because he was out on strike and had used up the last of his savings when his youngest child died. He did not tell Relief about his stocks since he believed them to be practically worthless. Relief was nice to him and gave him what he asked quickly and without difficulty. The amount of Relief he obtained was inadequate. The investigator suggested that he go on WPA, but he pointed out that he must report for picket duty; that since he was trying to get his job back in private industry, he must take part in the necessary union activities. The investigator sympathized with this point of view and did not force him to go on WPA. He informed Relief two days before the strike was concluded that it was about to be ended and that he would no longer need assistance. They answered this with a letter thanking him kindly for being so co-operative.

Family: One of the most important episodes in Mr. Caldwell's life was the death of his eldest son, in the early twenties; he ascribes this to neglect by the doctor who failed to diagnose the illness as pneumonia. He says that although he is really a quiet man, had he met that doctor on the street at that time he would probably have killed him. He also lost his youngest son in the 1930's, just before coming to Relief. This boy developed leukemia following measles. Mr. Caldwell says that he had a bad experience with the public hospitals at that time; even when he was giving blood transfusions to his own son, he had to pay $10 every time he did so. The child had four transfusions. He was shocked at having received such bad treatment at the Presbyterian Hospital, for he, himself, is a Presbyterian. He said that his wife is a placid woman, and added that even if the "building came down on her head" she wouldn't get very excited.

Mr. Caldwell's immediate and most serious problem is concerned with his eldest son, who, although a quiet and nice boy, is a confirmed school truant. Mr. Caldwell is haunted by the fear that the school authorities will sooner or later demand that the boy be placed in a reformatory. Mr. Caldwell said that on one occasion when the boy was only 12, Mr. Caldwell had been so angered by his truancy that he had beaten him until he "drew blood." His son had not uttered a sound during the beating, and for months thereafter Mr. Caldwell felt so guilty about the beating that he frequently wanted to jump his route and come home. He remarked that the boy really resembled him in many ways, for he is extremely tall and also very quiet. He recalled that in his own youth he would often go up to the school door, and just as he was about to open it, would turn and run away to the fields to spend the day. Mrs. Caldwell has taken the boy to what Caldwell believes to be a child guidance clinic, where the doctors warned her to "go very easy" on the youngster, and not to try to force him, because he is pretty high-strung. The boy wants to join the navy and Mr. Caldwell says that he would be happy to have him go, but it seems that the school regulations demand that he stay at school for another two years. According to Mr. Caldwell, his younger son is much more active and playful than his brother. He differs too in his strong desire to have money of his own and at present is delivering clothes for a tailor who pays him $2 a week. Mr. Caldwell remarked in passing that the boys are always cheering for Joe Louis, because they go to schools where there are large numbers of Negroes, and the white boys believe that if Joe Louis should lose the Negroes would beat the "stuffing" out of the white boys.

Mr. Caldwell's sons have taken communion and participate fairly actively in the church. Mrs. Caldwell belongs to a sewing circle at the church. Mr. Caldwell says that he, however, has never been much interested in the church, although he became a more active member last year, at least from the point of view of contributions. He says that since he is forced to get up at 3:30 almost every morning he likes the idea of staying in bed on Sundays. After the death of the first boy, while Mrs. Caldwell was pregnant with the second, they took a trip home to North Ireland. At that time his father again made a strong effort to have Mr. Caldwell stay at home, and offered to establish him on a chicken farm. Mr. Caldwell said that he would gladly have done this, but that his wife would not hear of it. She is a native of Dundee, but came to this country at an early age and has become completely acclimated to the United States. He believes that she feared to remain in North Ireland because she would have had responsibilities and duties greater than she has in New York, and that she did not want to assume them. He says that his family's standards have not changed much during recent years. Last year they took a bungalow for a week on the Jersey coast, but it was so dirty and unsightly that they will never do it again. He remarked that he himself seldom goes out, because when he comes home and gets out of his work clothes he is glad to sit down and relax. His wife, however, goes out often. He remarked that the social worker had had trouble getting into the home because his wife was afraid to talk with her since she knew so little about economics. He told his wife, however, that it was silly not to ask "the girl" in, since she could just tell her what she knew, and admit when she didn't. He said that it was the social worker's good luck to make the last call, and the successful one, when he was at home, because this facilitated the interview.

Politics: Mr. Caldwell says that he thinks WPA has done a lot of good things for the city, although there is no doubt that the men on the projects do not "strain themselves." His opinions about unions have changed. When they first tried to unionize the bakery, he would have none of it and was not interested until he became frightened by the threatened dismissal of the older men. Since the strike, he has participated actively in the union. He thinks that by and large it is a good thing. The dues have gone up from 75 cents to $2.25 a month, but now the dues include illness and death benefits. Mr. Caldwell benefited by the allowance for illness when he was sick for two weeks recently. Asked whether there was any trouble in his union, such as there was with Scalise and other racketeers in the Building Service Employees' Union, he responded with an emphatic no. The men in his union are much preoccupied with the small differences among themselves. In a specific case there was an extra week's work which became available while most of the men were out on their forced three weeks' vacation, and the manager asked whether this week's work could be given to one of them. Mr. Caldwell, a shop steward, warned the manager that it would probably create considerable friction and that it would be much safer to bring in somebody from the outside. The work, however, was given to one of the men, who was a "crybaby," and the rest of the men have been "hounding" him ever since.

Mr. Caldwell says that he has always registered Republican, but he has always voted independently. He has been in favor of Roosevelt, and he will vote for him again, because Roosevelt has done more for the common man than anybody else. Mr. Caldwell enlisted in the last war three days after the United States entered and put in 19 months of service abroad. He said that in his opinion the United States ought to declare war now, not because England needs man power at the moment, but because of the moral effect it would have on Germany and Italy. He remarked that freedom of speech and freedom of conscience are just as typical of England as they are of the United States and that these are the really important bonds. He is particularly bitter toward Father Coughlin for stirring up religious hatred and animosity toward the Jews. He said that, although he is in favor of allowing people to speak their minds, he felt that Father Coughlin went too far. He is particularly resentful of the fact that the Catholic Church seems to be playing such a reactionary role. He said that he was brought up not to hate anyone because of differences in opinion and beliefs, and he has always followed the principle. The only organization to which he has ever belonged is the Masonic Order.

PART IV. PRIVATE EMPLOYMENT

Case Ten

O'LEARY FAMILY

Status Private Employment *Religion* Catholic

Man	born 1910	Ireland	to U.S.A.	1929	Citizen	1935
Wife	born 1912	Ireland	to U.S.A.	1930	Citizen	No

Education

Man Graduate Christian Brothers High School—Ireland.

Wife Completed elementary school—Ireland.

Medical Status

Man Negative.

Wife Negative.

Woman's Work History Domestic—prior to marriage.

Married November, 1936, New York City.

Number of Children in the Home Two. *Ages*—2 and 3 years.

MAN'S RECENT WORK HISTORY

Milk Company	—Truck driver, 1930-1932. Laid off.
Intermittent Employment assisting a carpenter	—Six months in 1932.
Milk Company	—Platform worker 1932 to November, 1938. Laid off.
Construction Company	—Compressed-air worker. November, 1938—December, 1939. $50 week. Job completed.
Milk Company	—*Platform worker. December, 1939, to date. $33.50 week.*

New York State Employment Service Record

"Good type worker." From December, 1938 to November, 1939 compressed-air worker, iron man, placing sections in rings, tightening bolts, miner's helper, assistant driller.

HOME INTERVIEW

Home—Four rooms on the third floor of an old, but well-kept apartment building on Cauldwell Avenue, opposite Lebanon Hospital. (The street is residential at this point. The elevated runs by at the corner, on Westchester Avenue, and the house in which the O'Learys live is three houses from the corner.) The apartment was clean, the furniture, while apparently inexpensive, was attractive, the rooms were fully furnished and well-cared-for, although the beds were not made at the time of the visit. The two boys have their own bedroom, which, like that of the parents, opens off the living room. The boys each have a crib in their small bedroom.

The rental is $36. The O'Learys have lived here two years. They moved here because their three-room apartment was too small for them after their second child was born. Mrs. O'Leary said that their original apartment on Townsend Avenue had been a beautiful one, that they had had three rooms and the rental had been higher than for their present four-room apartment.

Man:

Description: Tall, slender, neatly dressed, freshly shaven. He has reddish hair and a pleasant smile. He talked with a decided brogue. Mr. O'Leary seemed an intelligent person and talked co-operatively. He was pleasant but a little shy, much more so than his wife, who was an outgoing, friendly individual.

Background: Born in Ireland, January, 1910. He was the fourth of five children, with an older brother and three sisters. The New York State Employment Service record states that Mr. O'Leary completed seven years of grammar school, but Mr. O'Leary says that he was graduated from the Christian Brothers High School in Ireland.

Work History: After Mr. O'Leary completed school, he spent some time helping his father, who was a carpenter. He learned enough to make him a fairly skilled carpenter, but he did not like the work. He liked machines and picked up enough information and skill so that he could do all sorts of mechanical work on automobiles. He worked as a private chauffeur, doing all the repairs on the car, until he left Ireland to come to the United States. He came here in 1929, the only one of his immediate family to do so. An aunt, who worked as a domestic for a wealthy family in this city, wrote him that the family needed a second chauffeur and that he could have the job if he would come to the United States. He said that he had always wanted to see what this country looked like and jumped at the chance to come over. However, at about the time he arrived here, the family for whom he was supposed to work went south and his aunt, who remained in New York, would not allow him to go there. She suggested that instead of going south, where she was afraid he might get into trouble without her around to look after him, he stay with her until the family returned home. At about this time, however, the Wall Street crash occurred and when the family did return to New York, they said that they had suffered such financial reverses that they would not be able to take on a second chauffeur.

Mr. O'Leary got work at a Chrevolet sales company as mechanic and helper and remained there for about six months. He had known that this was to be only a temporary job and had therefore looked about for something else to do. When he was laid off, he started work with a large milk company, driving one of their large trailer trucks. This was in 1930; he did this work until 1932, when, he explained, the company stopped using cans and put on the milk trucks, which had refrigerated vacuum tanks. They needed fewer men and Mr. O'Leary was one of those laid off. He was unemployed for six months. During this time, while he had no regular work, he was able to earn enough to support himself by helping a friend who was a carpenter. This friend was employed by a contractor, doing installations and repairs, etc., on bars in saloons. When the work was more than he could handle alone, he asked Mr. O'Leary to help him. At the end of the 6-month period, that is, in 1932, Mr. O'Leary was again taken on by the company, this time as a platform man. He has remained with the firm to the present time, with the exception of a period of about a year, when he was a compressed-air worker.

Mr. O'Leary explained that the work at the milk company is seasonal and that several of the platform men are laid off every winter, usually in December, when the slow season begins. The period of unemployment is usually about a month or six weeks, during which time Mr. O'Leary always managed by using savings and getting a few odd jobs to do. In December, 1938, when he was laid off, he managed to get work as a compressed-air worker and joined the Compressed-Air Workers' Union. He was laid off in November, 1939, when the job ended. He had earned $50 a week during this time. While the wages are higher, Mr. O'Leary believes that this work is much less secure than his job at the milk company and was therefore glad to get back with it again.

Mr. O'Leary is a member of the Milk Workers' Union, Local #584 of the American Federation of Labor. He said this is a subsidiary of the Teamsters' Union. The union began in 1936 and in 1937 was a large, active organization. Mr. O'Leary is a charter member and feels strongly about the importance of unions. He says that this is one of the few good unions because all the members play a part in decisions; it is not run by "higher-ups" who have no real interest in the workers. His wages are $33.50 a week and the union dues $2 a month. They get two weeks' vacation with pay and on their own decision, as members of the union, agreed to take one additional week without pay because in this way they are able to keep many more men working at least part time. These vacations begin early in the year and run through until the winter. In this way many of the men who do not have steady work are able to get part time work relieving those on vacation. The layoff in the slow season comes in December, because at this point all the vacations are finished and the staff is too large for the amount of work to be done. Mr. O'Leary said that another good feature of his union is the fact that people are not required to pay up back dues. They are carried along during a period of unemployment, and start paying their dues only when they begin to work.

Mr. O'Leary works at the Fulton Street Branch, which requires about 1½ hours traveling from his home. He has been shifted about so much, however, that there is no point in trying to move near any one branch. His hours are from 10 P.M. to early morning, after the milkmen have left on their routes.

Attitude toward Present Job and Future Prospects: Mr. O'Leary believes that he is going to lose his job with the layoff which will come next month. The fact that the milk companies have shifted from milk bottles to milk containers has been responsible for the loss of many jobs in large milk companies. Formerly, when everyone used milk bottles, the platform men had a great deal to do. They had to prepare the bottles prior to their delivery, receive them from the milkmen who brought them back from their route, and prepare them again. Since milk containers have come into use, this work has been eliminated and many branches of the company have been closed down for this reason. Five branches in metropolitan New York have closed during the past year. The branch where Mr. O'Leary is now working is not at the moment in danger of closing, but one of the largest branches in the city, on Neck Road, in Brooklyn, is to be closed shortly, a development which places his job in jeopardy. There are twelve platform men at the Neck Road branch, all of whom have seniority. The one who has been with the company the shortest time came on the staff in 1926. According to the policy, with both the company and the union, these men will be placed in existing branches and if anyone is to be laid off, it will be someone who does not have seniority. Mr. O'Leary believes that this is only right, but is afraid that the layoff this December will be permanent for him. Because of this fact he is making plans to find another job. If it were the usual layoff of only a month, he would be able to manage, but under the present circumstances, even if they take him back this year, next year will perhaps mean the end of his employment with the milk company and it is therefore necessary for him to make other connections. With the general upswing in business, he believes he can get something else to do and plans to go about looking for this something else as soon as he is laid off. (See Family Adjustments and Attitudes for his plan.)

There is no chance for advancement with the company. Formerly it was possible for men to move up to supervisory jobs, but no rank-and-file member of the union can be in a supervisory position. If they are promoted, which is rare, they must leave the union. Such promotion is unusual because in recent years many college graduates have been glad to get minor supervisory jobs and, according to Mr. O'Leary, the firm prefers college graduates to an ordinary uneducated man.

Woman:

Description: A pretty, slender young woman, her hair attractively arranged, wearing a pretty house dress. She talked well with no trace of brogue and when worker commented on this, said she knew no reason for it, except perhaps that her mother always spoke excellent English. She said that she comes from County Kerry and there is no other reason why she should speak with less of a brogue than anyone else from that region, but she has noticed this fact herself. She said that in listening to her friends talk, she has frequently been amazed to hear their thick brogues. Mrs. O'Leary seems to be an intelligent person; a gay, friendly young woman, who has a real sense of humor.

Background: Born in Ireland in 1912. She was fifth of six children, with two sisters and three brothers. Her father, a farmer, died when she was 4 years old and her youngest brother only 2. Her mother raised the children and took care of the farm; all the children continued at school until they had completed the eighth grade, with the exception of the youngest brother, whose education went beyond that point. Mrs. O'Leary worked as a domestic until she was 18, at which time, 1930, she came to the United States to join an older brother and two sisters, who were already in this country. One sister, who works as a domestic in Connecticut, had a job waiting for her in Hartford. Mrs. O'Leary said that she went right to this job from the boat. This lasted for two years and was very easy. She was a housekeeper for a young couple; the man was an art dealer. They had no children, traveled a great deal, and Mrs. O'Leary had little to do in this large house except take care of herself. She earned $22 a week. She described the art collection which this man had in his home and was much amused as she talked about the delicacy of the furniture and about the fact that one could not sit on the chairs, which were things of beauty and not to be used. The couple went abroad to live and gave up their home, thereby terminating her employment. She then worked for three years for a family that lived on Park Avenue and had a staff of servants. She was the cook. She said that the work was harder, but that she liked it. In 1935 she had saved what she thought was a large sum of money and went home on a visit. She stayed there three months and then came back. She worked another year as a domestic for a family on Park Avenue and then married in 1936. She has done no work since.

Children:

Joseph—born January, 1938.

Michael—born December, 1938.

They are both tall, well-built, good-looking youngsters with red hair and fine complexions. They were friendly, cheerful, active youngsters, who kept busy without being a disturbing influence during the interview.

Relatives:

Man—Mr. O'Leary's parents are living in Ireland, where his father works as a carpenter. His eldest brother was killed during the "trouble." He has two married sisters, both of whom live on the outskirts of Dublin, and one unmarried sister, who works in the post office in Dublin. He hears from his family as often as possible under the present circumstances. He understands from their letters that things are hard over there but that they are getting along quite well.

Woman—Her father is dead, her mother lives in Dublin with her two brothers. One brother has been lame for years as the result of an accident and is unable to work. The youngest brother supports this brother and the mother. This youngest brother teaches in Dublin. He is a graduate of Dublin University and has done graduate work at Trinity University. According to Mrs. O'Leary, he is a wonderful boy, brilliant and good. She said that he and a sister, who died in 1936, were the only ones in the family with brains. Mrs. O'Leary said that she had recognized the fact that her younger brother was worth making sacrifices for and had therefore helped him through school. In her opinion, it was worth it. Her other sister lives in the neighborhood, is married and has three children. Her husband is a trackman with the New York Central Railroad. The brother who is in this country is a chauffeur in Hartford, Connecticut.

Religion: Both Mr. and Mrs. O'Leary are observant Catholics and attend church regularly.

Birth Control: Mr. and Mrs. O'Leary practice birth control because they believe that their two children, both so young, are all that they can manage to take care of at the moment. Mrs. O'Leary says that it would be wonderful to have more children because she loves them and does not find them at all troublesome, but the question of feeding and clothing them is of vast importance. If her husband gets a good, steady job, they will unquestionably have more children. Mrs. O'Leary said that, while it is true that some people have conflicts about the religious question involved, this has disturbed neither her nor her husband. She goes to confession and finds that the priest does not raise any objection, other than the wish that she perhaps change her mind. She receives absolution and, according to Mrs. O'Leary, the question of birth control has not interfered with her regular church attendance. According to Mrs. O'Leary religion is important for personal well-being but only in so far as it gives solace and support, not when it makes life harder than it already is. She does not believe it necessary to obey all the rules and regulations in order to be a truly religious and good person.

Newspapers: The *Journal,* the *News,* and the Irish papers from time to time.

Political Affiliations: Mr. O'Leary is a citizen. He says that he got his citizenship papers as soon as possible, that is, in 1935. Mrs. O'Leary is an alien, but has applied for her second papers. Mr. O'Leary said that he voted for Roosevelt and his wife said she wished that she had been able to vote at that time because she would have liked to cast her vote for him. They believe that he is a real friend of the people. They feel that he knows everyone and is interested in everyone's welfare, while Mr. Willkie is only a businessman. Mr. O'Leary said that as a union member and a worker he knows that a businessman is not interested in the welfare of the workers. Their one strong political antipathy is Mr. LaGuardia because of his agitation to bring about the use of containers in place of milk bottles. This, Mrs. O'Leary explained, is a purely personal dislike because it has affected their lives.

In discussing the war, both Mr. and Mrs. O'Leary said that they were strongly anti-British because of their background, but that they believe we will have to help Britain for our own sakes. Mr. O'Leary said that he thinks the Irish will eventually come around and see that this is a new Germany which one cannot trust. He thinks that they will prefer England to Hitler when it comes to a showdown. In discussing the "trouble" in which his brother was killed, Mr. O'Leary said that, while he was young at the time, he knew enough of what was going on to realize that there was more bitterness within Ireland between the factions than against Britain. He believes that eventually they will come to see that their choice lies between the destruction of the British Empire and helping before it is too late. They both believe that the refugees should be helped as much as possible, whether here or abroad. As stated before, Mr. O'Leary is strongly pro-union.

Family Adjustments and Attitudes: Mrs. O'Leary said that she never knew there was a depression until she was married because she had worked in wealthy homes, had had no period of unemployment, no contact whatsoever with people who were unemployed or suffering financial loss. Though things have been difficult since they were married, they have managed. Mrs. O'Leary said that, though times are hard, if you have good spirits and have enough sense of humor to enjoy life you'll get through. She says that her husband is a good, hard-working, responsible individual whose family is of prime importance. When they were first married, they used their savings for nice furniture and had a "lovely" home. When they had to, they moved to cheaper quarters. They do not like it but it really doesn't matter much so long as you are happy with your family.

The O'Learys manage to pay their bills, give the children what they need, and also manage to have fun. They think movies, etc., are unimportant. What is important is that they have friends and relatives and that there is much social activity which costs next to nothing. For instance, when worker arrived, Mrs. O'Leary said that they had just got up, though it was quite late in the morning. She said that they had had company until 3 A.M., just having fun and talking and that this is their idea of entertainment.

The children, according to both Mr. and Mrs. O'Leary, are wonderful and no trouble whatever. As worker watched Mrs. O'Leary's attitude toward them, she could see that they really were no trouble to their mother because in their playing and running about they are allowed a great deal of freedom and since there are few restrictions they seldom disobey. Both parents played with them whenever the children asked and when the mother suggested that they go into their room for a few minutes and play with their toys, the children did so quite readily. Mrs. O'Leary said that she takes the children everywhere with her. They travel with her on buses, subways, and are afraid of nothing. She laughed as she said that they are so funny that people always stop to play with them and she believes that that is why they are so friendly and at ease with strangers. She does not find it difficult taking two such young children about with her and said that she could easily take care of a couple more if she did not have to worry about paying bills.

There was some discussion of Relief and Mrs. O'Leary said that this would be a last resort, that the very application for Relief breaks people's morale. Both said that they had never thought of Relief for themselves, that they would put that off until the very last moment, believing that their families would help them over any really trying period.

Mr. O'Leary is planning, as soon as he is laid off by the milk company, to go to Hartford, where Mrs. O'Leary's brother works. This brother has let them know that the streetcars are soon to be replaced by buses and he is quite sure that he can get Mr. O'Leary a job as a driver. They have also heard about the fact that the airplane and munitions plants in Connecticut are working overtime and Mr. O'Leary thinks that with his mechanical skill he will have no difficulty in getting work. He plans to go to Connecticut as soon as he is laid off. An important factor in planning for the future is the fact that they will have Unemployment Insurance Benefits for a while. Mr. O'Leary said that this will be only half of their usual income, but it will enable his wife and children to get along fairly well while he is establishing himself in Connecticut. Worker mentioned the fact that she had heard that Bridgeport factories were taking on people and Mr. O'Leary said that he had friends there. He will also plan to stop in Bridgeport. He said that he has good mechanical skill and knows that he can do anything in that line with a minimum of retraining. He was able to do compressed-air work without any difficulty. They have no real fear of the future. Mr. O'Leary says that he will get a job, get settled, and then send for his wife and children.

Attitude toward Us: Very friendly. Mrs. O'Leary talked for a while and then asked about the study, saying, "Now I've told you the story of my life, how can we help you?" This was explained and she said she was glad to be of help. Her husband, too, thought that the study was interesting and worth while and said that he was pleased to contribute by talking about his experiences. He said that he would try to come to the office for an interview, but was not at all certain that he could do this because he is tired during the day and usually sleeps the better part of the morning and afternoon. And since he will probably be laid off soon and is going out of town, there is little likelihood that he will be able to come in. Both Mr. and Mrs. O'Leary urged worker to come again, saying that she had obviously enjoyed playing with the children so much that she ought to come again and spend some time with them.

Case Eleven

KATZ FAMILY

Status Private Employment *Religion* Jewish
Man born 1898 Russia to U.S.A. 1911 Citizen Yes
Wife born 1900 N.Y.C.

Education
Man Graduated—City College; completed law course—admitted to the bar.
Wife Graduated—Central Needle Trades High School.

Medical Status
Man Negative.
Wife Negative.

Woman's Work History Dress designer—Brother's factory, 1917-1930.

Married 1935, N.Y.C.

Number of Children in the Home One. *Age*—4 years.

RECENT WORK HISTORY

Plumber—Steady work in season for a number of contractors. Some part-time work out of season, $2 per hour—$60 per week in season. (Worked as chemist in early 1920's. Left this to open plumbing contracting business, which he lost in 1931. Learned the plumbing trade while working his way through college.)

New York State Employment Service Record

"Plumber's Union, Local #1; journeyman plumber, 22 years in the trade, as of 1939. Reads blueprints and makes estimates."

HOME INTERVIEW

Home—Three rooms on the third floor of an apartment building on the Grand Concourse in the upper Bronx. The family has lived here two years; the rental is $40. This block of buildings is older than most of the Concourse. It is not near any business district or major crosstown street. The building in which the Katz family lives is on a corner and the apartment looks out on the side street, which is a quiet, one-way street, with little traffic. The children play there in apparent safety. The home was simply but well-furnished and in good taste. It was clean and attractive.

The son occupies the bedroom, while the parents sleep on a studio couch in the living room. Mrs. Katz said that they made these sleeping arrangements because they wanted the boy to be able to sleep comfortably and quietly in the evening, when they had company. Even when there is no company, they think that their child should have some privacy and since they stay up much later than he they chose the living room for their sleeping quarters.

Man:

Description: Not seen. According to Mrs. Katz, her husband is a fine-looking man, in good physical condition, intelligent and good.

Background: Born in Russia, in 1898, of Jewish parentage. He was the eldest of six children with two brothers and three sisters. He attended school in Russia, until 1911, when his father brought him to the United States. According to his wife, Mr. Katz was graduated from high school in 1915. In his last year in high school, Mr. Katz worked during vacations and in the afternoons and evenings, in order to support himself. Mr. Katz entered college, but when he was 18, that is in 1916, it became necessary for him to go to work full time because his father suffered a stroke. Prior to that his father had been able to save enough to bring the rest of the family over from Russia. Because of his father's illness it became necessary for Mr. Katz to support them. Mrs. Katz said that, impossible as it seems, her husband was graduated from college with a chemistry major in 1920. He completed the four-year course in five years, the last three years in evening session, while working full time during the day as a plumber.

Work History: When Mr. Katz was graduated from college in 1920 he went to work as a chemist, remaining at this work until 1925, earning about $30 a week. In 1925, when business, especially in the building trades, was good, he decided that he could earn more money in business for himself and therefore gave up his job. He was a plumbing contractor from 1925 to 1931 and so far as Mrs. Katz knows, had a very good income until after 1929. In 1931, when there was an almost complete cessation of building operations, Mr. Katz lost his business. From 1931 to 1936 he had only part-time work as a plumber. He was unable to get anything to do in the chemical line. In addition to his part-time work as a plumber during these five years, Mr. Katz attended law school, was graduated and passed the bar examinations. He was able to maintain himself fairly well and received some help from his relatives for tuition, etc. In 1936, when he was admitted to the bar, he found that he was unable to do anything in the field of law because he had no finances. He could not afford to begin as a law clerk, since by this time he had already been married a year and had responsibilities toward his family. He was able to earn enough in his part-time work to support himself and his wife and in 1936, when his child was born, was able to get full-time employment. The two employers mentioned in the New York State Employment Service record are: J. L. Murphy and Company, from June, 1937, to June 20, 1939, as a journeyman plumber at $2 an hour; William Levy, Inc., July, 1939, to September 8, 1939, at the same rate of pay.

According to Mrs. Katz, her husband's chief periods of employment are during the spring, summer, and fall; he is unemployed most of the winter. He sometimes gets a few days' work, but it is during this time that they must draw most heavily on their savings. Mr. Katz had a good summer this year, but is on strike at the moment. Mr. Katz is a member of the Plumbers' Union, Local #1.

Attitudes toward Present Job and Future Prospects: According to his wife, Mr. Katz knows his work well, has a good reputation in the trade, and is well-liked. He can do some of the more skillful tasks of the plumbing trade and can work directly with the architects because he has technical knowledge of blueprints, etc. She said that of course he would prefer one of the two professions in which he was trained, but is afraid that he would be unable to make a living. He has no reserve funds to finance a period of waiting around. Mrs. Katz says her husband has no feeling about the dignity of one job as compared with another and would be content to remain in his present trade were it not so seasonal. He is always certain of getting full-time employment during the busy season, but all the money which they are able to save is usually nearly exhausted each winter. During the winter he receives Unemployment Insurance Benefits of $15 a week and this helps in that it pays the rent and other incidental expenses, so that they need not exhaust their savings. Mr. Katz is on several civil service lists, but these are so long and replacements so infrequent that Mrs. Katz is afraid that he will never be placed. He has told his wife that his age is against him since he can no longer take civil service examinations now that he is 42 years old. There is also the problem that even though he is on a list, he may not be accepted when his turn comes since he is over the 40-year mark.

Woman:

Description: A short, well-built, gray-haired woman. She is good-looking and has a charming smile. She is obviously intelligent, seemed to worker to be very much at ease and well-poised, but said that she is a very nervous person as a result of her experiences during an earlier marriage. She spoke very well, and when worker asked whether she too is a college graduate, said, with some pride, that while she only graduated from high school, most people think she has had a college education, because her grammar and diction are so good. Mrs. Katz added that she has always been eager to learn, reads a great deal, and discusses things with her husband.

Mrs. Katz was wearing an attractive cotton dress and was sewing on a new silk dress. When worker commented on her skill, she said that she has always made all her own clothes.

Background: Born in New York City, in 1900, of Jewish parentage. She was the second of four children and the only girl. Mrs. Katz was graduated from the Central Needle Trades High School downtown. In 1917, when she finished her high school course in dress designing, she went to work for her older brother, who had a dress factory. She worked for him as a dress designer until 1930, five years following her first marriage. At about this time her brother died and the business was liquidated. Not long after this, she was separated from her first husband and went home to her family. She was divorced from her husband in 1933. While separated from him and prior to her marriage to her present husband, Mrs. Katz worked in a factory. She talked a little about her first husband, but the subject was obviously painful to her and she seemed to prefer not to go into details. She indicated that it was an unpleasant marriage, because of the fact that her husband was impotent and sterile. She said that her husband had many personality problems related to this condition; whether cause or effect, she could not say. According to Mrs. Katz, she had always wanted a child and this, of course, was denied her. She was anxious for a more normal life and after some years of much unhappiness, finally left her husband. Mrs. Katz had known her present husband since childhood and when she left her first husband, she and Mr. Katz saw a great deal of each other and soon fell in love. They were married as soon as he was able to support her, despite the fact that she had been quite willing to marry him earlier. She did, however, respect his desire to be responsible for her support. They were married in 1936.

Children:

Robert—born 1937.

Relatives:

Man—Mr. Katz's parents are dead. His two younger brothers and three sisters are all self-supporting but in rather poor circumstances. They are, apparently, friendly with the family, because, according to Mrs. Katz, they remember that their older brother was very good to them and helped support them when they were younger. One brother and one sister are unmarried and the sister keeps house for the brother.

Woman—Mrs. Katz's father is dead and her mother is living with her youngest brother and keeping house for him. The older brother, who had been very kind to Mrs. Katz, is dead. The next brother teaches economics in a downtown high school. He was graduated from City College and also has a law degree. Mrs. Katz said that when she was working prior to her first marriage, she had helped this brother through school, contributing as much of her wages as she could. She said that she has never felt that she wanted any recompense for this, but he has always appreciated her help and there is a strong bond between them. The youngest brother did not have any interest in school and when he completed high school went to work for the Metropolitan Life Insurance Company, where he is still employed as an office worker. Mrs. Katz said that she and her husband and child visit her mother weekly and that they are in constant touch with one another.

According to Mrs. Katz, her husband's relatives helped him during his period of underemployment in the depression years and her relatives helped her when she needed money for a divorce. She says that they know they can always call on her and that if she is able she will help them.

Religion: Both Mr. and Mrs. Katz were reared in Orthodox Jewish homes on the lower East Side, but Mrs. Katz said that neither has any religious feelings. They both questioned the validity of religious belief when they were still quite young and do not understand how people can find satisfaction in it. It is therefore disconcerting for them now to find that they have become very conscious of their religion and race since anti-Semitism has spread. Mrs. Katz says that she worries about it for her child, because it is even worse to bear if one has no conviction about it. She does not know how either she or her husband can give their child any positive feeling about religion since they have so little faith in it; they think that those who have faith can stand persecution better in the knowledge that they are suffering for a cause.

Birth Control: They were both anxious to have a child and Robert was born within a year after their marriage. Since that time they have practiced birth control because they do not feel that they can afford another child. If there is the definite upswing in business which has been forecast and if her husband's income improves, they will plan to have another child soon because Mrs. Katz is now 40 and must have the child soon if she is to have it at all.

Newspapers: The *Times* and the *Post* regularly and sometimes *PM*. Mrs. Katz enjoys the radio though she seldom turns on anything but music, except for regular news periods and commentators. She thinks the radio serials during the day are silly.

Political Affiliations: Both Mr. and Mrs. Katz are independent voters and this year will vote for Roosevelt. Mrs. Katz says that the spectacle of the Republican campaign is nauseating. True, Roosevelt has faults, but despite the mistakes he has made, he is sincere and it is especially important that labor vote for his re-election; if they do not vote for him, they deserve everything that might happen to them under a reactionary Republican administration. Mrs. Katz believes that the United States should help Britain for its own sake; it would be difficult for anyone, who knows anything about Britain and her imperialistic policy, to be pro-British and want to help for her sake. She thinks that the isolationist group brings to light many strange bedfellows. She mentioned Lindbergh, Ford, Johnson, the Communists and the Fascists. Mrs. Katz believes that conscription is necessary.

So far as refugees are concerned, she feels that they should be helped with all the resources at America's command. She feels that as many children as the United States can accommodate should be brought over away from the struggle in Europe. She thinks, however, that the beginning of the British children's drive was most unfair. She mentioned that most of the children who were brought over from Britain seemed to have been the rich and the royal children, while all the thousands of poor British children were left to their fate. In Mrs. Katz's opinion, the Communist party held some promise of a better world some years ago, but in more recent years has proven to be something in which no honest person can believe.

Family Adjustment and Attitudes: Since their marriage in 1935, Mr. and Mrs. Katz have been happy together, and have managed fairly well financially. Mr. Katz earns $2 an hour when he works and during the season averages $60 a week, plus some overtime when he is very busy. During this time Mrs. Katz says he receives all the money to which he is entitled, but during the slow season, when he manages to get work, there is a kickback of nearly half of what he earns. When he earns $60 a week or more, they never use all of it for living expenses. They always save because they know that in the winter they must use their savings. The Unemployment Insurance Benefits, $15 a week, are of great assistance during these times. They use their savings to pay their rent regularly and the $15 a week takes care of their food and other incidentals. Mrs. Katz says that they frequently wish that it would come more promptly, but it is good to know that they can get it at all. At no time since their marriage has Mr. Katz had difficulty getting work during the season, but the certainty of hard times in the winter is always present, even when the pay envelope is bulging. According to Mrs. Katz, a trade is good because it gives the man a sense of a job well done and the knowledge that business needs him, but the construction trade has never been able to spread its work over an entire year. Mrs. Katz said that, if either she or her husband were extravagant by nature or had desire for things better than they could afford, it would be extremely difficult for them to manage but, as it is, there has never been a time when they had no resources. She is certain, too, that should anything serious happen to them, she could rely on her family for help.

Mrs. Katz says that she admires her husband and respects him for taking the law course during the worst of the depression, when work was slow and he had time. She said that, instead of moping, he added to his knowledge, which in her opinion is a healthy approach to life. While he was taking the law course, he knew that he would not have much chance to use it professionally, but realized that increased knowledge would make him a better person. Mrs. Katz said that even a good mind gets rusty when not used and the plumbing trade certainly does not exercise the brain cells. She admires his personal dignity, which does not feel that an honest trade is beneath him. According to Mrs. Katz, what her husband does during the day in his work satisfies him and when he is at home with her in the evening it makes little difference whether he comes from a plumbing job or from a law office. They read good books, try to keep up with current events, listen to music, and do their best to improve their knowledge of the world in which they live.

Mrs. Katz talked about the trying times she had in her first marriage and about the nervousness which resulted from it. She said that she is feeling much better now and thinks it is because she has a normal happy marriage. She said that she is now living with the man she loves, a man who is devoted to her and their child. The child is the object of much affection and concern on the part of the parents. She has read a great deal about child care and has tried to avoid the mistakes parents sometimes make with an only child. She said, for instance, that she has forced herself to let him go out and play with other children without her. She watches from the window and is worried constantly about what might be happening to him, but does not let him see this concern. She said that she managed to avoid feeding problems, which she understands are prevalent among only children. Somewhat apologetically she said that she thinks Robert is a beautiful, bright, wonderful child and that they are crazy about him, but that they try not to let him see how much.

Both her relatives and those of her husband are friendly with the family and there is much visiting back and forth. Also, as stated above, they visit her mother every Saturday. They have a large circle of friends who visit frequently. They go out little at night because of their child, but their friends come to visit them, and week ends, when her husband is free, they go visiting.

According to Mrs. Katz, her husband is assured of steady work in season and they are pleased to realize that the upswing in business will give him more work. It is unquestionably true that new housing is needed and that something will have to be done about it. So far as their child is concerned, they will give him a good education and then hope that circumstances will permit him to use it.

Toward Us: Mrs. Katz was interested, willing to co-operate, and said that she thought the study was a good idea. She talked about her personal problems in her first marriage and said that she was surprised to find herself saying such things because she has never talked to anyone, either relative or friend, in this way. She said that perhaps it was the fact that worker is not a part of her immediate environment which permitted her to do so. She thought that we had come to her home because she had written to Columbia for some literature on child care and that her name had been obtained in that way. She was told that names were selected at random. She said that her husband might be interested in coming to the office and that she would talk with him about it.

OFFICE INTERVIEW

Impression: Short, stocky man in the early forties, very well-dressed; he had a new hat and a new overcoat. His speech was softer than his physique would have led one to expect. He spoke well. He is obviously an intelligent individual. The interview was long, lasting nearly three hours. Mr. Katz remarked that in recent years when applying for new jobs he has found that employers look at him and, because of the gray hair at his temples, start calling him "pop." He considers himself an excellent workman and at one point in the interview said that he is the only Jew who has ever worked for a large Brooklyn utility company. He obviously takes pride in the fact that he is able to break down racial barriers by virtue of his great skill as a workman.

Employment History: After Mr. Katz completed elementary

school, his first job was that of office boy. He remained at this job only a short time and he was then apprenticed in the plumbing trade. It appears that he saved up enough money during the latter part of the World War and the early twenties to enable him to stop working in order to take courses at Cooper Union and Brooklyn Polytechnical Institute. Though the information was not definite, it appears that he first attended Cooper Union in the evening session. He studied chemistry, came to the attention of the instructor because of his good work, and was soon offered several jobs as assistant chemist. He earned between $25 and $50 a week and received the higher figure at the completion of his course at Brooklyn Polytechnical Institute. For a time Mr. Katz worked for a well-known industrial chemist. Without going into details, he explained that because of personnel difficulties he lost that job. He looked around for another at that time and was offered one at $35 a week in a powder factory, manufacturing gunpowder. He said that he realized at that time that his ability in chemistry was not so great that he would ever set the world on fire and he was confronted with an alternative opportunity of earning $65 a week as a plumber. He took the plumber's job and very shortly worked himself up to a position of copartnership with the plumbing contractor; he then earned $75 a week plus commissions. This was in 1925 and 1926. Before the end of the boom, he says he was worth, on paper, approximately $50,000. In expanding his business, he began to have dealings with the brother of one of the large real estate men in New York City. They formed a partnership and Mr. Katz says that he not only invested all his own funds but also persuaded several people with capital to invest therein. His partner, however, turned out to be an unscrupulous person and when Mr. Katz found this out he remained in the firm only long enough to get his creditors out safely and then found himself without a penny to his name. During these years in business he kept his union privileges by paying $2 a year, but when his real estate venture collapsed in the early thirties, his ability to re-enter the union as a laborer was purely a formal privilege since there was no work going on at that time except odds and ends that one was able to pick up on repair jobs but for which the union was of little aid.

Period of Unemployment: Between 1931 and 1935, finding time heavy on his hands, Mr. Katz decided that he would like to attend law school in order not to get into a rut. Mr. Katz said he didn't want to remain idle with no work for either his hands or his mind. He chose the Brooklyn Law School and made arrangements to attend evening classes; the dean allowed him to pay installments on his tuition as rapidly as his finances permitted. He received considerable financial assistance from his family, but there were periods when he was without any tuition money and under constant threat of dismissal from the school. He then explained to the dean that he was not, after all, a youngster and that he could be relied upon. He received his degree in 1935 and passed the bar examinations, although he realized, toward the end of his studies, and surely when he had completed them, that there was no possibility of a successful legal career for a man of his age and rather limited connections. Mr. Katz's most serious period of unemployment occurred in 1931 to 1933, but it appears that even then he was able to pick up at least a few dollars a week from repair jobs. As business improved a little after Mr. Roosevelt's first election, Mr. Katz found an increasing number of jobs, so that by the time he had completed his law course in 1935 he was supporting himself adequately as a plumber. He states that, although the basic union wage rate for plumbing was $1.50 an hour at this time, he had worked for as little as 90 cents and he said that there were many other plumbers in the trade who had worked for considerably less than that. Mr. Katz discussed the union's attempt to keep wage rates up and the general effect of this practice. Most of the men who managed to secure employment did so only by cutting union rates, sometimes without the knowledge of the union and sometimes with the consent of the business agent. He said that the formal maintenance of the wage scale worked most adversely on some of the large contracting companies who did not want to do business by bribing agents and by maneuvering around union scales. These companies therefore closed down completely during the periods of severe depression and made no attempt to keep things going by cutting wages. The fact that these strong, rather decent companies were thrown out of business or at least closed down for the period of depression meant that smaller contractors had a chance to get along. It is Mr. Katz's belief that from the point of view of the union and of the men there really would have been little increase in the total demand for the plumbing even if wages had been cut radically. He said that repair work looms rather large in plumbing and need not be undertaken unless an emergency arises; when there is no emergency, repair work can be postponed indefinitely.

Mr. Katz brought along his report from the Unemployment Insurance Division which showed that his annual earnings had been as follows: 1936—$2,000; 1937—$2,800; 1938—$2,800; 1939—$2,600; he estimates that his earnings for 1940 will be approximately $2,600. The basic rate of pay has been raised by the union to $2 an hour, but Mr. Katz explained that he is now receiving a bonus on his present job of $3 a day. Instead of six hours at $2 an hour, which would equal $12 a day, he is receiving $15 a day. At this moment there is a jurisdictional fight on between the plumbers' union and one of the construction unions and work has been suspended, but the contractor is paying Mr. Katz his $65 a week because he is afraid that Mr. Katz, who is highly skilled, might obtain a job elsewhere and that at the end of the strike the contractor will find himself without his best workman. It does not seem that the strike will last long since it is a city contract and there seems to be every prospect that the city will interfere at the end of a few more days. Mr. Katz is very well-informed about the reasons that underlie this particular jurisdictional strike; he explained that one of the larger internationals that belongs to the American Federation of Labor, and has voting strength superior to that of his own union, had established a local a few years ago, whose rights were constantly increased until it now assumes the right to encroach upon the domain of the plumbers. The plumbers are outvoted in the councils of the American Federation of

Labor, and there is little that they can do except by intensified local fighting. As Mr. Katz talked about his work, he did not seem to be boasting; the evidence he gave led the interviewer to conclude that Mr. Katz is a highly skilled plumber and that he possesses not only the technical plumbing skills but also the capacity to plan and to use judgment and that these factors combine to make him a most desirable employee.

Family: Mr. Katz was married in 1926. He says that his first wife was a "good-looker." She divorced him at the time of his financial reverses but he says that he has never had any strong feeling of animosity toward her for her actions. He was simply unable to support her adequately at that time. He remarried, but did not mention the fact that his present wife had also been married before. Mr. Katz says that she is a "nervous woman," who worries a lot about their child and about herself. Recently she decided that her son needed glasses and took him to a Bronx doctor, who prescribed glasses. When the boy complained about wearing them, he was taken to a prominent specialist, who re-examined him and said that the glasses were not at all necessary. Mr. Katz said that he had had to pay $30 to establish the fact that the boy did not need glasses. He realized that his wife's "nervousness" was responsible for the expenditure. A little while ago, Mrs. Katz decided that she was having trouble with her heart, a fact which Mr. Katz explained was partly due to the fact that her mother and sister both died of rheumatic cardiac conditions. Mrs. Katz went to a physician in the Bronx, who examined her, charged her $5 and told her that she was all right. She was not satisfied by the diagnosis and later went to see a well-known heart specialist. Mr. Katz accompanied his wife to the doctor's office; the doctor examined Mrs. Katz carefully and then called Mr. Katz in to tell him what he had learned. The doctor said that the physical findings were completely negative, but explained to Mr. Katz that this did not mean that his wife was in good mental health, far from it. He said that his own impressions were that Mrs. Katz, who is now turning 40, is probably missing the amount of attention she formerly received from men. The doctor then went on to suggest to Mr. Katz that he pay as much attention to her as possible in order to allay the anxieties that were connected with increasing age. Mr. Katz said that this corroborated his own impressions and that he believes the doctor was perfectly correct. He told the doctor that he will do all he can in this regard, but that he had to point out that he could not guarantee that "the baker and the grocer and the butcher would act likewise." He said that his wife had had a "nervous breakdown" last summer and the summer before while she was in the country with their son. It is hard for him to isolate the cause for the nervous upset; he feels that it might have something to do with sex, but he does not, of course, want to suggest that his wife is unfaithful to him. He then went on to say that his wife really suffers from having too much time on her hands. They have only one child. Mrs. Katz has a cleaning woman come in to do the heavy work in the home, and on holidays they take their meals out. Mrs. Katz had tried some organizational work, such as activities on behalf of the Loyalists during the Spanish war, but Mr. Katz believes that women are really unfit for that type of work because they are so hotheaded and unpolitical. He went on to explain how his wife and another woman went to Woolworth's and tried to get the manager to contribute $2 worth of supplies for the Loyalist cause. It appears that the managers of Woolworth stores have the right to contribute up to $2 for certain charities. The manager told them that he would be very glad to do so for any local charities, but did not see his way clear to do so for Spain. His wife and the other woman then became highly abusive and it almost became necessary to call the police to have them put out. It was Mr. Katz's feeling that the manager was perfectly reasonable and that if the women were unable to make enough of a case on behalf of Spain and if the manager offered to contribute to any other of their charities of more local significance, he saw no reason for their getting so hotheaded. But, he said, "that's women."

Mr. Katz had little to say about his son. In general he seemed to prefer not to talk about family matters; he obviously thought they had little place in this interview. One could not, however, avoid the inferences that Mr. Katz had rather cool feelings toward his wife and also feelings of great superiority. He complained bitterly that she is unable to read or concentrate on anything at all serious, and a popular novel is as much as she can handle. He obviously considers himself her intellectual superior by a wide margin; in fact, there was a sort of a generally negative attitude toward the intelligence and emotional stability of women.

While discussing the future, Mr. Katz said that of course he feels relatively secure because of his great skill in the trade and many good connections, but, on the other hand, he occasionally gets a little "chilly" when he thinks about his responsibility for his wife and child. Things were noticeably different in the early thirties. These responsibilities are really great when one wants to do things for children. Mr. Katz has two brothers, one works for Saks' and one for another large concern; they have been employed steadily for many years and are earning good wages. They helped him during the depression. Aside from that, there was little conversation about collateral relatives. Mr. Katz says that at present he spends about $50 a week, although he could do very well on as little as $35 and still have all the necessities. He believes it is a general tendency to spend money when one has it and that is why his family spends as much as $50 a week now.

Union: Mr. Katz talked at length about his union and other unions. He realizes that, on the one hand, the unions are really doing good work both for their own members and in a certain sense for the labor movement as a whole. On the other hand, Mr. Katz says that he is honest enough and smart enough to see the abuse of power within the union and the many practices which are really detrimental to the public at large. He pointed out in passing that it is interesting to note that the delegates once defeated in a union are unable to win their way back. He thinks that one of the important determinants as to who becomes a union leader is the amount of drinking a man can do, the amount of toughness that he can convey, and the rate at which he can talk. In short, he thinks that the very worst characteristics are influential when leadership selection is involved. He said that in his plumbers' union Communists are in the minority and are thoroughly disliked both for their tactics and for their general attitudes. He admitted, however, that one of the Communists is really a good organizational man, is bright, and works hard for the best interests of the union. He explained that in the plumbing trade, sending men on jobs is now almost completely under the control of the union; the rotation system is substantially honest because the first five men on the list are the committee to consider all requests for new employees and as one is sent out, the next person on the list moves up and becomes a member of the committee. He thinks that the number of abuses in this area is limited. He pointed out, however, that occasionally a request for just one day or two days' work comes in from a given employer and that, if this happens in midwinter, the men are frequently reluctant to go out on the job. His attitude, however, is different because he feels that it is always possible to make connections on a short job which will stand one in good stead later. His theory was substantiated recently; the good job which he now has in Brooklyn really grew out of his willingness to accept a day's work in midwinter, when conditions were rather unpleasant and the place of work damp and cold. His employer was so impressed that when he had an opening he specifically asked the union for Mr. Katz.

According to Mr. Katz, the plumbing contracting business in Brooklyn is exclusively in the hands of Jews; they do a fairly large amount of work, both construction and repair. He said that of course he understands the reason why they indulge in some shady practices; they have to cut corners or else they would be forced into bankruptcy just as has happened with many others. The membership of the plumbers' union is comprised of many nationalities, while, according to Mr. Katz, the steamfitters' union, for instance, does not have a single Jewish member. Mr. Katz pointed out that, although the plumbers' hourly wage had risen from a basic $1.50 to $2 per hour, this does not mean that the cost of the work done per job is higher now than in previous years. He says that an ordinary residential plumbing job in Brooklyn which formerly cost $360 can be done today for $260, even with better materials, for one is able to buy better materials at the same price and labor is speeded up through better planning. He says there is a noticeable difference between the amount of time wasted by plumbers in previous years and the much greater efficiency in the planning and working habits of plumbers today. And that means that the cost of the job has been reduced even though wages have gone up. Mr. Katz views this as a net gain for the banks, who, so far as he can see, are the people who make money out of building. Mr. Katz told of his experiences with a Brooklyn utility company for which he worked for many months; he remarked that they were exceedingly nice to him, keeping him on in the winter, when they really had no work to justify the wages they paid him. He said, however, that he knew perfectly well, from what he observed then, that the utilities were undoubtedly "rooking" the public badly. They made a practice of selling tools to their workmen and entering it in their books at a price five times higher than that which they originally paid for the tools. He also found that the payroll contained names of many people who had never been inside the building but happened to be relatives of influential employees. Mr. Katz said that he became quite friendly with many of the white-collar employees there, and found them favorably inclined toward their bosses, and surprisingly anti-union in their general orientation. He then said that he was even more surprised by the fact that those people who work for the city, especially at slightly higher grades of work, were particularly jealous about the hourly wage rates of union labor, because they were stupid enough to compare their own hourly wage rates with those of union labor and were amazed to see that men working with "their hands" were better paid than men working with "their heads." He said that as far as his own union is concerned, the men are a rather mediocre lot, who are politically ignorant and whose interests seem to lie in drinking or loafing on their time off. He obviously feels quite superior to them. Mr. Katz had little to say that was favorable about vocational training in New York City; he has had occasion to observe this at first hand since he was delegated by the union to act as an examiner of applicants for admission. He says that the level of instruction is exceedingly poor and that obviously politics determine school appointments.

Mr. Katz expressed amazement at the backwardness of this country in the matter of standardization of parts in the plumbing trade. He said that if one or two specific concerns were to go out of business, or if anything should happen to their stock, it would literally be impossible to do most of the repair work that is now going on since these concerns alone have the parts which would fit the large apparatus already installed. He thinks that we are very much behind the times and that every effort should now be made, especially because of the defense program, to bring about a much higher degree of standardization of products.

It is Mr. Katz's impression that there is an ample supply of skilled labor available for the defense program but he does not think that it will be brought into employment quickly. He thinks that there is much anti-union bias in the charges that are being made about the great shortages of skilled labor. So far as his own trade is concerned, he has no doubt that there is a substantial backlog of skilled men. Mr. Katz estimates that his contributions to the union will amount to approximately $36 for the year plus special assessments which will bring it to about $50. In the old days the union had a system of insurance for death benefits and injuries, but officials absconded with the money and specific assessments are now used to take care of death and special injuries. The union usually tries to collect an amount sufficient to enable an injured man to start a small retail business so that he can remain self-supporting. Mr. Katz has much admiration for the electrical union, largely because of the fact that they have brought about a high degree of regularization in the apportionment of work. They have a system of rotational work which means that men can earn up to a certain basic figure, approximately $2,600 per year, and no more. A less favorable aspect of the electrical union, however, is the marked restriction of output stipulated by the union. The union states that the maximum number of outlets that may be installed in one day is twenty-one. He added that the members go further than this and that a good union man seldom installs more than fifteen. Mr. Katz estimates that the output could literally be doubled without any deterioration in the quality of the work. He knows that in former years an electrician could easily install as many as sixty outlets in a day.

Unemployment Insurance Benefits: According to Mr. Katz, the present regulations governing the Unemployment Insurance Bureau leave much to be desired, for if a man gets an odd day's work in midwinter he may actually lose income by accepting it, since the waiting period is counted from the last day of work. If Mr. Katz received $12 for a day's work, it might mean that he would lose his benefits for an entire week; the benefits are $15 per week. Therefore working for a single day would actually mean a loss of $3. He said that he once did that because an employer whom he liked asked him to do a job and he was disinclined to refuse. He said that, of course, he could have lied when he was asked by the Unemployment Insurance Bureau when he last worked, but he was afraid to do that since he is a member of the bar and such a statement would have been perjury. He said, however, that next time he will either not accept the single day's work or he will lie about it. He also objects to the regulations which govern the time period against which one is able to draw Unemployment Insurance. As he explained it, this period terminates as of the end of March of any given year. One can count against that all of the work done in the previous year, which means that if one becomes unemployed in May, all of the time a man worked between January of the previous year and March 31st of the present year is disregarded. This long period makes serious inroads into one's financial reserves.

Politics: Mr. Katz was distinctly pro-British and pro-Roosevelt. In fact, there was no doubt in his mind as to what the United States should do in the present crisis. He believes that this country should continue to give Britain all necessary assistance.

Case Twelve

PARSONS FAMILY

Status Private Employment *Religion* Protestant
Man born 1904 U.S.A.
Wife born 1910 England to U.S.A. 1920 Citizen Yes

Education
Man Three years high school.
Wife Graduated high school.

Medical Status
Man Negative.
Wife Negative.

Woman's Work History Office and library work from 1928 to date.

Married 1931.

Number of Children in the Home One *Age*—6 years.

RECENT WORK HISTORY

Floor Worker—Employed by one company, 1930 to date. Seasonal trade, $1.85 an hour. Now averaging $30 a week. Laid off for several months in 1938 and 1939.

Wife—Steadily employed before and since marriage, except for one year, 1934-1935, when daughter was born. Present salary $30 a week.

New York State Employment Service Record

"Floor scraping. Used Universal Speedomatic machine. Member Carpenters' and Joiners' Union, Local #1663. Received Unemployment Insurance Benefits.

HOME INTERVIEW

Home—Four rooms on the first floor of a modern apartment building on Post Avenue in the Inwood section of Manhattan.

Post Avenue at this point is a pleasant, wide, residential street. The apartment contains four large rooms, all of them simply and attractively furnished. The rooms were clean. In the hallway and living room there were large bookcases filled with books. Worker noticed a number of Literary Guild and Book-of-the-Month Club volumes as well as numerous others. On the table were Hemingway's *For Whom the Bell Tolls* and Bayles' *Dictators in Lockstep.* There were a number of current magazines on the coffee table.

The Parsons family has lived in this apartment for five years. Mrs. Parsons explained that they moved to this four-room apartment soon after Barbara was born because they needed the extra bedroom. Barbara has a room of her own; the parents occupy the other bedroom. The rental is $55.

Man:

Description: A tall, slender, rather good-looking man who seemed much younger than his age, which is 36. He seemed to be an intelligent person. He is in good health. Mr. Parsons talked when questions were directed at him, but seemed rather shy and retiring and allowed his wife to speak for him much of the time.

Background: Born in Rochester, New York, August, 1904. He was the younger of two boys. His family has lived in Rochester for many generations. Mr. Parsons said that "if you go back far enough you will probably find an Englishman, but we have been Americans for generations." His father is an undertaker who has been in the undertaking business in Rochester for many years. The father wanted his elder son and later Mr. Parsons to complete school and join him in the business; both brothers refused. Mr. Parsons completed three years of high school and then, feeling that he did not want any further education, planned to go to work. This was in 1921.

Work History: Mr. Parsons was able to find nothing but odd jobs, such as office boy, shipping clerk, etc., for the first two years after leaving school. In 1923 he went to Albany, where his father had a friend who was secretary to the Mayor. This man helped him get an office job, but Mr. Parsons did not like the work. He talked with this man, who suggested that he go to New York where the chances for learning a trade and getting work were greater. He came to New York City that year, to live with an aunt. In talking with his aunt and with some of the friends he made in New York City, he came to the conclusion that he ought to take up an apprenticeship in a trade. In 1924 he apprenticed himself to learn the floor-working trade. During this time he lived with his aunt. He supported himself by earning small sums of money while still apprenticed and also used some savings which he had brought with him to New York. In 1926 his apprenticeship was completed and he received a union card. He got work without any difficulty. He is a member of the Carpenters' and Joiners' Union. From 1926 to 1930 his income averaged about $60 a week, but dropped off sharply at the beginning of 1930.

In 1930 he obtained employment with a flooring company, which, he explained, is one of the largest in the city. He believed that there was more chance for steady work with such a company since they had a number of well-established contracts with large apartment houses, real estate companies, etc. Mr. Parsons was married in 1931. Until March, 1938, things went fairly well. Mr. Parsons earned $1.50 an hour and in season could make $60 a week plus overtime, so that some weeks he was earning $70 or $80. But in the slow season he had only two or three days of work a week. He says that he is well-liked by his employer and that he is given as much off-season work as possible. He seldom averaged more than $30 a week, however, during these seven years and frequently the average was less than that. In the Spring of 1938 building was down to an all-time low, there was little moving or apartment redecorating, and most of the staff was laid off in March. They were taken back in May of 1938 for the moving season. Mr. Parsons remained at work with the company until December of 1939, at the end of the moving season, when he was again laid off. He began work again in March of this year and has been steadily employed ever since. Things are picking up, Mr. Parsons thinks, and his average earnings this year have been somewhat higher than in the thirties. He had a lot of overtime work during the moving season this year and is more cheerful about his prospects. He came home early today because when he reported for work he found that there was little to do; he plans to go in tomorrow. He reports for work daily, or is told to wait for a call if there is something to be done near where he lives. He gets about three days' work a week now since the season has slowed down. He receives $1.85 an hour.

Attitudes toward Present Job and Future Prospects: Mr. Parsons likes his work and the company which employs him. If there is any upswing in the trade they feel it and he is secure with them. He enjoys all parts of the work and considers it highly skilled, requiring a variety of skills. He said that a good floorworker can do anything from building a floor, double-flooring, insulating, to scraping and polishing, which are the finishing touches. He has no thought of changing his trade and he believes that now that we are out of the depression he will do well. He also hopes, since he has been with the company so long, that there will be some chance for promotion.

Woman:

Description: A tall, slender young woman with blond hair neatly arranged. She was neatly dressed, wore no make-up, looked attractive and pleasant. She seemed quite intelligent, has considerably more poise than her husband, and seemed to enjoy the intellectual aspects of the discussion. Her health is good.

Background: Born in Devonshire, England, in 1910. She was the youngest of four children with one brother and two sisters. Her father was a railroad employee. He was in the British Army throughout the four years of the first World War, and when it ended returned home crippled from wounds received in action. He went back to work for the railroad, this time as an inspector, but shortly thereafter was killed by a train. The family moved to London, since they had relatives there. The mother worked and tried to take care of the children. They had some money from the father's insurance policy and a lump sum received from the railroad; in consultation with relatives, it was decided that the mother would have a better chance to raise her children and get the most out of the money she had if she brought her family to the United States. She had a sister here. They felt that it was important for the children to receive as good an education as possible and that this was not so feasible in England as in the United States. Therefore, the mother brought all the children with her in 1920, when Mrs. Parsons was 10 years old. Mrs. Parsons' mother worked and took care of her children until they became old enough to go to work and contribute to the household expenses.

Mrs. Parsons was graduated from high school, where she took a bookkeeping course. She also took extra English courses because she hoped to go to college despite the fact that she knew there was little chance for it. College proved to be impossible and she had to go to work at the end of her high school course. Mrs. Parsons said that she never had any trouble getting jobs and always got her jobs through good agencies. She said that she was frequently sorry for the girls she met at the agency offices; some of them had tried for months and had failed to get work. She has had her present job for three years. She earns $30 a week and loves her work. She said that she would not leave it even if she were financially secure because it is fascinating. She also said that she has the best employer in the world. She works for a large national magazine, where she is in charge of the biography department in the "morgue." She has two assistants. She said that her experience as a page in the Public Library, while she was going to high school, stood her in good stead on this job. According to Mrs. Parsons, the magazine has one of the biggest and best-organized morgues in the city and they are called upon all the time to furnish material for authors, scholars, for research and fiction, and have been told frequently that they give excellent service. Mrs. Parsons said that she has never denied the fact that she is married because she believes that, while many employers disapprove of hiring married women, they also understand that sometimes a woman may have to work because her husband's income is too small to support the family adequately. She believes that it is wrong to deny the fact that one is married.

Mrs. Parsons, in talking about getting her job, said that at the time she applied, she was not asked about a college education and wondered about this omission. She said that two weeks after she started working her employer came to her and asked what college she had been graduated from. She said that she thought "Well, here I go" but could not lie about it because she knew that it would catch up with her sooner or later and so she told the truth. Her employer merely expressed surprise that she was so capable without having had any college training and there was never any question of her staying on. Mrs. Parsons was married in 1931, has worked steadily before and since, except for the year 1934 to 1935, when her child was born.

Children:

Barbara—born, 1934. A tall, slender, blond youngster, with her hair neatly combed and wearing an attractive dress. She talked with worker while her lunch was being prepared, showed considerable poise, talked well about school, her teacher, her friends, etc.

Relatives:

Man—Mr. Parsons' parents are living in Rochester, where his father is still engaged in the undertaking business. His brother lives in Albany. They see each other occasionally, correspond rather irregularly. As far as Mr. Parsons knows, his brother is an office worker, earning a small salary.

Woman—As stated above, Mrs. Parsons' father is dead; her mother lives in the neighborhood. Mrs. Parsons' brother is married and one of her sisters also is married. The other sister is employed and lives at home with her mother. All contribute to the mother's living expenses and visit frequently. Mrs. Parsons said that her mother is a wonderful woman, who made every sacrifice for her children and who has made no demands on them. It is therefore a pleasure and a privilege to do what they can for her. According to Mrs. Parsons, her brother and sisters got work as soon as they were of age, and while they met with hard times during the depression, it was never necessary for any of them to ask for public assistance. They have always carried on as independent citizens.

Religion: Both Mr. and Mrs. Parsons are Episcopalian. They attend church fairly regularly and enjoy the many social activities connected with the church. They have less time, however, than many of their friends for such activities since they both work. Mrs. Parsons reminisced about her early church experiences in England, said that she liked the Episcopalian church because it does not preach a harsh religion.

She remembers during the war, when she was a small child, the minister cautioning the children against hatred of the German prisoners who were quartered near their home. She remembers the church as being very important in her childhood and a pleasant experience. Their daughter attends Sunday school.

Birth Control: Mr. and Mrs. Parsons practice birth control because they feel they cannot afford more than one child at this time. They would like to have more children, but must wait until things pick up enough so that they will be able to save a sufficiently large amount to take care of any possible emergencies. They believe that children must be given a good education and that their childhood and adolescence must be made comfortable and easy so that they will grow up to be happy, useful men and women.

Newspapers: The *Times* and the *Telegram* regularly. There were a number of magazines—*Time, Life, American Magazine, Harper's*—plus, as already mentioned, many new books. The Parsons listen to the news on the radio, the commentators, quiz programs, and concerts.

Political Affiliations: Both Mr. and Mrs. Parsons are Republicans. Mr. Parsons' family has been Republican for generations. But for the most part they do not think the party, as it exists today, is too good. They voted for Willkie, not as a Republican, because they said he had always been a Democrat, but as a man. Mrs. Parsons said that they believed Roosevelt responsible for the class hatred which exists and had hoped that Willkie would unite the divergent groups in this country. Roosevelt did some good earlier in his career. His intentions have always been good but his ability has not been equal to the intentions. Mrs. Parsons said that he has made too many enemies unnecessarily and that he was taken in by the wrong pressure groups. They agreed with his foreign policy and felt that Willkie would have carried it out in the same way, or perhaps better, since he would have had a more united country behind him. Now they believe that we should support Mr. Roosevelt since he is the newly elected President of the United States. Mrs. Parsons thinks the fact that businessmen are clamping down for the duration of Mr. Roosevelt's term in office makes them as bad as Nazis and Communists because they are doing an un-American thing in spreading disunity.

Mrs. Parsons talked about the new Hemingway book and the fact that it had shown her a side of the Spanish Civil War which she had never understood. Mr. Parsons pointed out that the *Times* had carried an unfavorable review which he had not understood because he did not believe the premise on which the review was based. Mrs. Parsons said that she thinks we are actually in the war now, except in name and that that will come soon. She thinks the same result would have occurred if Mr. Willkie had been elected. Mrs. Parsons says that she is English but they both feel for our own sake, that is, for America's sake, that we must go in one day soon because Hitler has got to be stopped. She thinks that the Atlantic Ocean means nothing to him and that he will find a way to attack America if he is successful in Europe. She mentioned a new book about dictators. She said that this book presented Hitler in a different light and made the whole situation more frightening. She used to think that it was just he who was to blame and that if anything happened to him the whole movement would stop, but now she realizes that he is only one of a group and really, so far as she can see, not the worst of the group. She talked about Von Ribbentrop, Goebbels, Goering, and the other members of the inner circle. She thinks that they are much more scoundrelly than he and that he is actually more fanatic than scoundrel. She believes that the world is not big enough for that group and a free America. Mrs. Parsons told of letters received from her mother's relatives in Ipswich and of the problems which they are meeting in wartime England.

In Mrs. Parsons' opinion, we should help all refugees; she believes that they should be brought to this country. She believes that we will get along even if we bring over some refugees and give them a chance to exist. She thinks that such an influx of new people will stimulate American ingenuity to create more work.

Family Adjustment and Attitudes: Mr. and Mrs. Parsons knew one another for several years before their marriage. Mr. Parsons' work was so irregular until 1930, when he became affiliated with a large, substantial company, that they did not feel they could get married. However, in 1931, after his status in the company was pretty well-established, they felt secure enough to venture marriage. There was never any question about her continuing work. Mrs. Parsons said that if she could earn enough to pay for part-time help, she saw no reason why she should stop working. They both had standards of living which, while not extravagant, were decent and required more than Mr. Parsons could earn alone. Mrs. Parsons said that in their case, her income did not mean a jump from "comfort" to "luxury" but rather from "not quite enough" to "comfort." Besides, she likes to work. They agreed on this before marriage because, while the husband would have preferred to support his wife completely, it would have meant a lowering of standards and his wife's becoming a household drudge if they had tried to live on his earnings during the depression years. Neither wanted this and both, Mrs. Parsons said, were sufficiently intelligent and objective about this to arrive at a compromise. Mrs. Parsons said that she felt it would have spoiled their love and their life together to have had to cut down and do without any of the niceties of life. Besides, she wanted to continue to assist her mother and she could not expect her husband to do this in addition to supporting her. She would have accepted it gladly had it not meant financial strain for him.

Mrs. Parsons talked at length about the question of employment for married women and said that she has strong objections to their working if they have no financial need for doing so. She realizes that people work for something and that a woman's job and income frequently make things much easier at home, but she does not think that women should be allowed to work if their income is such that they need do without only the more extravagant luxuries.

The birth of their child in 1934 was planned. They had enough money saved to take care of any emergencies that might have arisen, Mrs. Parsons stopped working for about a year and everything went off as they had planned. She said that she was glad they had the child when they did because never since then were things any better financially than they were at that time. Barbara is a great joy to them; she is a bright, alert child, who fills and completes their lives. They would like more children because they do not believe in a one-child family, but feel that they cannot afford to have another now.

They are managing well at this time. They budget their income so that the earnings of the busy season are stretched over the slow season. Mrs. Parsons uses part of her earnings to pay a young woman to look after the home and Barbara while she is at work. This woman is a friend who has had a period of bad luck and is pleased to have this work. Mrs. Parsons believes that this is a good arrangement because not only does she help her friend, but is also more secure knowing that the person who is looking after the home and the child is someone she can trust. Mrs. Parsons said that the only time her work isn't completely satisfying is when Barbara is not well. She says that it is difficult to go to work in the morning, knowing that the child has a temperature, etc. Mrs. Parsons works five days a week and usually has Saturday and Sunday off, except every third month, when she works weekends and is off Tuesday and Wednesday.

Mr. Parsons was quiet and rather shy. He had little to say and allowed his wife to carry on most of the conversation, nodding his head in agreement with what she said. Sometimes she turned to him for comment, but usually after he remained silent for a while, she continued the conversation alone. Mr. Parsons had little to say about unions except that his is an American Federation of Labor union and is as good as unions can be these days, but that he objects to the racketeering and leaders who care little for the members. Mrs. Parsons said that the C.I.O. is much worse and that she disapproves strongly of its Communist aspects. She talked about John L. Lewis and said that, if she were Willkie, she would have been ashamed to have had his endorsement. Mrs. Parsons refused to join the Guild which has a contract in her office. She doesn't like the leadership and thinks that it is Communist-controlled. She believes in the theory of trade-unionism but not in the kind of union leadership which she sees practiced today.

During the periods of unemployment Mr. Parsons received Unemployment Insurance Benefits of $15 a week. Mrs. Parsons said that this was little better than nothing, just a pittance which would not pay any one of their expenses, such as rent or food. If she had not been working, they would have had to exhaust all their savings, but as it is they made only small inroads into their reserves. Mrs. Parsons believes that Home Relief is bad and talked about its effect on the individuals who receive it. She mentioned the fact that in some agencies she had visited she had talked with girls whose families were on Relief and who told her that their fathers were completely licked by their periods of unemployment. The Parsons believe, too, that WPA is bad for people since it gives them poor work habits. They believe that even if a man is not an inefficient worker to begin with, he gets that way from being on WPA. Mr. Parsons said that his place of employment is very near 70 Columbus Avenue, which is the WPA headquarters and that he sees the men running in and out all day long asking for things, like children running to teacher. He says that they hang around in the luncheonettes and restaurants in the neighborhood, play the pinball machines and cry about the fact that they do not have jobs.

Mrs. Parsons indicated that they are getting along as well as can be expected and that her husband has great desire to work and support his family. He is a devoted person and one on whom she can rely. There was little actual discussion of personalities. Mrs. Parsons' manner throughout was one of intellectual interest in the study, but she was quite restrained and displayed a certain dignity which did not permit of discussion of personal adjustment.

Mrs. Parsons plans to continue to work; she said that she finds her job stimulating and remunerative. Now that things have picked up they hope there will be a period of steady employment for Mr. Parsons. They seem to have no insecurity about the continuance of their independence and indicated that at no time had they actually felt that they might have to ask for help. They are piling up their savings account and keeping up rather large insurance policies. They hope that they will be able to give their daughter a good education, and Mrs. Parsons said that she certainly wants to see her go to college. She has always regretted not having done so herself.

Toward Us: They were both much interested. Mrs. Parsons was, perhaps, more interested than her husband. She approved of the study, said that she was glad to help, and showed considerable enthusiasm. She wished us luck and urged us to come again. Mr. Parsons said that he was not much on talking and would rather not come down to the office for an interview, if we did not mind.